MODERN BRIBERY LAW

The Bribery Act 2010 is the most significant reform of UK bribery law in a century. This critical analysis offers an explanation of the Act, makes comparisons with similar legislation in other jurisdictions and provides a critical commentary, from both a UK and a US perspective, on the collapse of the distinction between public and private sector bribery. Drawing on their academic and practical experience, the contributors also analyse the prospects for enforcement and the difficulties facing lawyers seeking asset recovery following the laundering of the proceeds of bribery. Broader international perspectives are provided via comparisons with the law in Hong Kong, the United States and Italy, together with broader analysis of the application of the law in relation to EU anti-corruption initiatives, international development and the arms trade.

JEREMY HORDER is Edmund-Davies Professor of Criminal Law at King's College London. He was a Law Commissioner for England and Wales from 2005 to 2010.

PETER ALLDRIDGE is Drapers' Professor of Law at Queen Mary, University of London.

MODERN BRIBERY LAW

Comparative Perspectives

Edited by

JEREMY HORDER

and

PETER ALLDRIDGE

CAMBRIDGE
UNIVERSITY PRESS

CAMBRIDGE
UNIVERSITY PRESS

Shaftesbury Road, Cambridge CB2 8EA, United Kingdom

One Liberty Plaza, 20th Floor, New York, NY 10006, USA

477 Williamstown Road, Port Melbourne, VIC 3207, Australia

314–321, 3rd Floor, Plot 3, Splendor Forum, Jasola District Centre, New Delhi – 110025, India

103 Penang Road, #05–06/07, Visioncrest Commercial, Singapore 238467

Cambridge University Press is part of Cambridge University Press & Assessment, a department of the University of Cambridge.

We share the University's mission to contribute to society through the pursuit of education, learning and research at the highest international levels of excellence.

www.cambridge.org
Information on this title: www.cambridge.org/9781107018730

First published 2013

A catalogue record for this publication is available from the British Library

Library of Congress Cataloging-in-Publication data
Modern bribery law : comparative perspectives/edited by Jeremy Horder and Peter Alldridge.
pages cm
Includes bibliographical references and index.
ISBN 978-1-107-01873-0
1. Bribery–Great Britain.
I. Horder, Jeremy, editor of compilation. II. Alldridge, Peter, editor of compilation.
KD8045.M63 2013
345.41′02323–dc23
2012040138

ISBN 978-1-107-01873-0 Hardback

CONTENTS

CONTRIBUTORS

PETER ALLDRIDGE is Drapers' Professor of Law at Queen Mary, University of London.

INDIRA CARR is Professor of Law at the University of Surrey, and Visiting Professor at University College London.

TIM DANIEL is a Partner at Edwards Wildman Palmer UK LLP.

DAVID C. DONALD is Professor of Law and Director of the Centre for Financial Regulation and Economic Development at the Chinese University of Hong Kong.

STUART P. GREEN is Distinguished Professor of Law at Rutgers Law School, Newark.

ROBERTO GUERRINI is a Professor of Law and Head of Department at the University of Siena.

DARIO GUIDI is a Research Fellow at the University of Siena.

JEREMY HORDER was a Law Commissioner for England and Wales, from 2005 to 2010. He is currently Edmund-Davies Professor of Criminal Law at the Dickson Poon School of Law, King's College London.

JAMES MATON is a Partner at Edwards Wildman Palmer UK LLP.

VALSAMIS MITSILEGAS is Professor of European Criminal Law, Director of the Criminal Justice Centre, and Head of the Department of Law at Queen Mary, University of London.

CHARLIE MONTEITH is Counsel in the global White Collar group at White & Case LLP. Prior to joining White & Case, he was Head of Legal and Operational Assurance at the UK Serious Fraud Office.

BOB SULLIVAN is Emeritus Professor of Law at University College London.

SIMON N. M. YOUNG is Professor and Director, Centre for Comparative and Public Law, Faculty of Law, University of Hong Kong.

TABLE OF CASES

Canada

Canadian Dredge & Dock Ltd v. *The Queen* (1985) 19 CCC (3d) 1 (SCC) 148

Hong Kong

Attorney General v. *Hui Kin-Hong* [1995] 1 HKCLR 227 78
Ng Ka Ling v. *Director of Immigration* (1999) 2 HKCFAR 4 282
Ching Kwok Yin v. *HKSAR* (2000) 3 HKCFAR 387 276
Secretary for Justice v. *Lam Tat Ming* (2000) 3 HKCFAR 168 284
Wong Pui Sham v. *HKSAR* (2000) 3 HKCFAR 449 277, 278
Yu Chee Yin v. *Commissioner of ICAC* [2001] 2 HKC 91 (CFI), [2001] 4 HKC 532 (CFI) 279
HKSAR v. *Lee Ming Tee* (2003) 6 HKCFAR 336 275
HKSAR v. *Lau Wai Tim*, unreported, CACC 152/2003, 4 March 2004 (CA) 275
Sin Kam Wah v. *HKSAR* (2005) 8 HKCFAR 192 269
HKSAR v. *Chan Kau Tai* [2006] 1 HKLRD 400 (CA) 275
Koo Sze Yiu v. *Chief Executive of HKSAR* (2006) 9 HKCFAR 441 270
Leung Kwok Hung v. *Chief Executive of HKSAR* [2006] HKEC 239 (CFI), aff'd [2006] HKEC 816 (CA) 270
HKSAR v. *Lee Wing Kan* [2007] 3 HKC 368, 67 (CA) 274
Lee Wing Kan v. *HKSAR* FAMC 28/2007, 18 September 2007, CFAAC 274
Z v. *HKSAR* (2007) 10 HKCFAR 183 289
P v. *Commissioner of ICAC* (2007) 10 HKCFAR 293 285
HKSAR v. *Ng Po On* (2008) 11 HKCFAR 91 285, 286
Peter Gerardus van Weerdenburg v. *HKSAR*, unreported, FACC 9/2010, 27 July 2011 (CFA) 284
HKSAR v. *Egan* (2010) 13 HKCFAR 314 276
HKSAR v. *Ying Jim Ming Jimmy*, unreported, HCMA432/2009, 6 May 2010 (CFI) 275
HKSAR v. *Tse Tat Fung*, unreported, CACC 167/2008, 13 May 2010 (CA) 284
HKSAR v. *Shum Chiu* [2011] 2 HKLRD 746 (CA) 273
HKSAR v. *Wong Hung Ki* [2011] 1 HKLRD 183 (CA), FACC 9/2010, 27 July 2011 (CFA) 273, 275
Vivien Fan v. *HKSAR*, unreported, FACC 6/2010, 15 July 2011 (CFA) 277

Italy

Switzerland

United Kingdom

United States

EU cases

TABLE OF STATUTES AND INTERNATIONAL INSTRUMENTS

France

Italy

Hong Kong

Saudi Arabia

United Kingdom

United States

EU legislation

International instruments

Introduction

This collection of essays from scholars around the world seeks to set the law of bribery in its proper contexts, an especially important task following the enactment of the UK's Bribery Act 2010 ('the 2010 Act'). In their separate ways, most of the contributors seek to shift the primary focus away from what has hitherto been a perfectly understandable preoccupation with the implications of the coming into force of the 2010 Act for UK businesses. The preoccupation has been with questions such as: will it still be acceptable to take an important client to see a sports game?; is it lawful to give a present to spouses or partners at corporate functions (or to invite them to such functions at all[1])?; what can a multinational firm do to ensure that it has adequate systems in place to prevent bribery when the way it does business varies so greatly across the globe?; what should a firm do when asked for an 'administration fee' by a hospital overseas in order to ensure that its employees receive treatment if they fall sick? These are all questions of great importance in practice, although they are not new. They have always been difficult questions to answer – sometimes legally, sometimes morally, and sometimes both. The 2010 Act has widely been understood to invite reconsideration of a long-standing willingness on the part of investigators and prosecutors to treat such situations as inappropriate for investigation, or even for guidance on prosecutions.[2] In that respect, though, little is likely to change, even though it is widely accepted that, for example, the impact of sustaining a culture of 'small' bribes on the ethics and politics of vulnerable states is ultimately a

[1] As far as inviting foreign public officials to such events is concerned, the OECD has expressed the view that such behaviour is 'high risk', namely, likely to be corrupting: see OECD, *United Kingdom: Phase 3 Report on Implementing the OECD Anti-Bribery Convention in the United Kingdom* (Paris: OECD, March 2012).

[2] The OECD clearly still detects a residual unwillingness in UK public authorities to subject such matters to serious scrutiny: see OECD, *Phase 3 Report.*

damaging one.[3] In 2010, the pervasive requirement for such bribes to be paid in Afghanistan for any kind of public service meant that Afghans – many of whom already live far from comfortable lives – were said to be paying US$2.5 billion (a quarter of the country's GDP) in bribes.[4] The changing role of the prosecutor in bribery cases is a subject central to the final section of these essays.

What, then, do these essays more broadly bring into focus? To answer this question, we must consider what makes bribery an unusual or even unique crime.

In important respects, a critical analysis of bribery will share many of the important concerns that preoccupy scholars and practitioners who think and write about crimes more commonly featured on the criminal lawyer's menu. As in the case of fraud, for example, there is a proper focus on one or more of the concepts employed to define the offence ('breach of an expectation', say, in the case of bribery; 'dishonesty', perhaps, in the case of fraud), and on the overlap between the offence in question and other offences in English law (such as misconduct in a public office, an offence now on the Law Commission's reform agenda). There is also interest in the policy underlying the way in which statutory provisions have been fashioned to take the place of older legislation or the common law, in the defences available (if any), and in the territorial scope of the new policy and law. Even on this familiar territory, though, key issues must be addressed that are far from those commonly encountered in an analysis of serious criminal offences. A disputed theme running through the chapters in Part I, for example, is the issue of whether, and to what extent, bribery law should have an application beyond that of attempts to corrupt 'public officials'. Many jurisdictions focus mainly – and some solely – on the public sector, however defined, and public sector bribery is usually understood to be both different and in some sense more serious than bribery in the private sector. By contrast, the 2010 Act draws no distinction between private and public sectors. It concentrates instead on the nature of the function someone was performing when offered, when accepting, or when asking

[3] TRACE International, *The High Cost of Small Bribes* (London: TRACE, 2003). The policy of the Serious Fraud Office is not to prosecute for small bribes (such as 'facilitation payments'), if a company has a commitment to eliminate such payments over time. The OECD has questioned the efficacy of such policy, in the absence of guidance on what it means, in concrete terms, for a company to be seen to deliver on its commitment: see OECD, *Phase 3 Report*.

[4] www.spiegel.de/international/world/0,1518,672828,00.html.

for an advantage of some kind. Loosely speaking, the issue is, did that function – whether arising in the public or the private sector – involve some commitment to impartiality, to a relationship of trust, or to acting in good faith, such that it would be improper to accept or ask for the advantage given that the person in question was performing such a function? In a way, this kind of radical approach makes bribery more like other criminal offences, the vast majority of which do not draw distinctions between those acting in a public or private sector capacity. In taking this approach, though, the question is whether something of moral significance – in terms of 'labelling' – is lost if public sector wrongdoing (supposing that such a notion can be adequately defined, in a world where public and private sector provision is increasingly merged) is not singled out for separate treatment, as under the law that the 2010 Act replaced? A final issue relates to the moral significance of the bribe. Is the bribe evidence of corruption (which might, with appropriate controls, be furnished in other ways), or is it an essential element of the corruption, so that performing equivalent acts absent the bribe is not corrupt at all? English law has never had crimes of nepotism, gratuitous but corrupt doing of favours or the asynchronous exchange of favours. The modern emphasis upon the single large international contract can distract attention from these common and insidious types of corruption.

One of the underlying themes of this book is the way in which an appraisal of bribery law requires scholars and practitioners to embrace a new set of law and policy issues, to revise their assumptions about the criminal process, and to concern themselves much more than is commonly the case in seeking to understand the substantive law with the available punitive and non-punitive sanctions and remedies (although specialists on corporate liability have had to come to terms with these issues for many years).[5]

For example, while it has been possible for many years to punish public officials for committing crimes overseas, as if those crimes had been committed within the jurisdiction,[6] the singling out of bribery of a foreign public official as a specific offence in the 2010 Act, whatever the status – public or private – of the accused, adds a new dimension to bribery as an offence. It is an unusual example of a criminal statute treating the public interest in the integrity of officialdom in a *different*

[5] Although, of course, the mandatory life sentence for murder continues to over-shadow analysis of the scope of that crime.

[6] See the Criminal Jurisdiction Act 1802, s. 1.

jurisdiction as a matter of concern so serious as to justify criminalisation of those connected to *this* jurisdiction who seek to undermine that integrity. This brings out an important difference between the ways in which the creation of a criminal law can be justified. Some writers have taken a distinctly 'inward-looking' view of that justification. For example, C. K. Allen wrote that behaviour is criminalised because, 'it consists in wrongdoing which *directly* and in serious degree threatens the security or well-being of society';[7] but, although it may do in some circumstances, bribery of a foreign public official committed overseas by a UK company is in principle unlikely to pose that kind of threat. Perhaps more promisingly, Antony Duff has recently argued that criminal wrongs are public wrongs because, 'they are the proper concern of all citizens in virtue of their shared membership of the polity. The sanctions [the criminal law] imposes on offenders ... express the polity's condemnation of the offender's conduct as wrong'.[8] While there are problems with it (which cannot be gone into here), this looks, at first glance, to be a more promising line of argument in this context. Any sophisticated set of moral principles in accordance with which condemnatory judgments about citizens *qua* citizens are made includes 'outward-looking' principles. These are principles to which citizens should adhere when outside – or when dealing with those outside – their 'polity'. So, for example, sexual abuse by UK citizens of non-UK children overseas is just as much within the condemnatory legal scope of the polity (on Duff's view), as the occurrence of such abuse within the United Kingdom.[9] However, the criminalisation of bribery of foreign public officials may expose a tension in Duff's thesis.

Unlike the commission of sexual offences against children overseas, which is an offence only if the conduct in question would also be an offence in England and Wales,[10] the discrete offence of bribery of a foreign public official is a non-dependent offence in its own right. It does not depend on the conduct in question also being an offence covered by the law applicable in a domestic context; and properly so. For there would be just as sound a reason – preventing harm in

[7] C. K. Allen, *Legal Duties and Other Essays in Jurisprudence* (Oxford: Clarendon Press, 1931), pp. 233–4 (added emphasis).

[8] R. A. Duff, 'Perversions and Subversions of the Criminal Law', in R. A. Duff, L. Farmer, S. E. Marshall, M. Renzo and V. Tadros (eds), *The Boundaries of the Criminal Law* (Oxford: Hart, 2010), pp. 88–9.

[9] Sexual Offences Act 2003, s. 72.

[10] Sexual Offences Act 2003, s. 72(1)(b).

foreign states[11] – to condemn as criminal bribery committed through improperly influencing public officials overseas,[12] even if, for whatever reason, similar conduct in relation to a domestic official was not criminalised, but treated merely as a civil wrong. Thus understood, criminalising bribery of foreign public officials would have something in common with, say, making it a crime for UK companies to bury toxic waste in overseas lands or seabeds, whether or not the latter is also an offence in the United Kingdom.[13] The justification for criminalisation in such instances does not turn, in a way that it does in many other cases, on whether the conduct in question is also a crime in the home jurisdiction. Why does this point raise an issue in relation to Duff's thesis?

It is perfectly plausible to suppose that UK citizens do not view bribery of foreign public officials, especially when such bribery is an accepted custom and practice in the foreign jurisdiction in question, as a matter, to use Duff's words, for, 'the polity's condemnation of the offender's conduct as wrong'. Yet it could still be right to criminalise such bribery on the grounds that, in his words, it is, 'the proper concern of all citizens in virtue of their shared membership of the polity'. Criminal law theorists have yet to come to terms with an emerging, cross-cutting European and global set of moral norms that play an indispensable part in the criminalisation agenda for all states opting into transnational governance systems based on a subset of these norms. In some – perhaps many – instances, ordinary members of the 'polity', whom the governments opting-in represent, are indifferent or even hostile to compliance with those norms (and *a fortiori* resentful of the use of the criminal law to secure compliance). So, the legitimacy of a government's decision to criminalise breaches of the norms depends on the legitimacy of a legislature's claim to exercise a right to decide for itself (even in the face of an indifferent or hostile public) what a society's commitments are to be 'in virtue of shared membership of the polity', and hence to incorporate international norms into the range of issues said to be, in Duff's words, 'the proper

[11] On the nature of remote harm in bribery cases, see J. Horder, 'Bribery as a Form of Criminal Wrongdoing', *Law Quarterly Review*, 127 (2010), 37–54.

[12] 2010 Act, s. 6.

[13] For the sake of argument, suppose that the unauthorised burying of toxic waste is a matter for civil recovery in the United Kingdom, but that this approach would be ineffective in relation to such conduct when engaged in overseas, and so the criminal offence is confined in its application to conduct overseas.

concern of all citizens'. The 'outward-facing' character of key elements of bribery law is addressed in Part II of this volume.

Seeking a rationale for bribery offences in general, and in particular for the territorial scope of the offence is, however, only one side of the coin. The history of the last thirty-five years of the law of bribery in the United Kingdom indicates something about the role of human agency and human mistakes in legal historiography. None of the developments outlined in the book would have occurred, however, had 'events' not conspired to bring bribery to the top of the political agenda. Had it not been for Lockheed and the other matters that gave rise to the Foreign Corrupt Practices Act (FCPA) 1977, and had it not been for the adoption by the OECD of the principles in the FCPA in the Paris Convention, the Bribery Act 2010 would not have happened. Had it not been for the attacks on the United States in September 2001, the UK Government would not have put in place the stop-gap provisions in sections 108–110 of the Anti-terrorism, Crime and Security Act 2001, and the reform would have turned out very differently. Had the 2003 Draft Bill not been written so as to retain the principal–agent nexus in the offence from the previous legislation, and had it had provisions that dealt better with the issues of parliamentary privilege that arose, then the 2003 Draft Bill might have been taken forward and become law in 2004. Had the 2009 Draft Bill not been introduced into Parliament by means of the Draft Bill procedure (which, by that stage was an unnecessary delay) it would have become the 2009 Act. Although it generated a great deal of concern at the time, it is by no means clear that the legislation was speeded up by the furore over the decision to end the Al-Yamamah enquiry. The UK Government was late in complying with its obligations, but more by inadvertence than any conscious desire to prevaricate.

In short, the interest in bribery law that has arisen in the United Kingdom and elsewhere over recent years has been a consequence not only of the reappraisal of the rationale of the offence, but also of political and economic pressures, usually of an international nature, arising in one way or another from the influence of globalisation on markets. Of these types of pressure, two are most noteworthy. First, there is that exerted as a consequence of investment by relatively wealthy nations in international development. The underpinning idea had always been one of enlightened self-interest. Investment overseas would create economies that would be better able to trade with the investor nations. The old theory, stemming from some American economists in the 1960s, was that if bribery was what was necessary to engage in any economic activity with a given jurisdiction, then so be it. This has now been displaced by the rather obvious consideration that if large amounts of the money, paid in taxes in wealthy nations and designated for aid, are in fact to be spent on 'white elephant' projects (building dams where there is no river, unnecessarily sophisticated air traffic control systems or whatever else), or are to furnish retirement income for deposed despots, then the objective is not being achieved. This line of pressure will differentiate the public from the private sector. The further argument is frequently made that corruption (broadly understood, so as to include, but not to be restricted to, bribery) operates as a disincentive to inward investment in developing economies. The evidence on this is at best equivocal, but if the claim is correct, then this is a further reason for giving greater attention to enhanced enforcement between jurisdictions.

Secondly, there is the more general fair competition consideration that if international companies are competing for business in a jurisdiction whose own domestic system is unable to deal adequately with bribery, then controls should be imposed where they *can* be effective. This is the basis of the OECD Convention. Thirdly, there are some supra- and intranational organisations that assert jurisdiction over the sources of the money they administer. The European Union is one such.

It is no real surprise that the first, and at the time of writing, the only, prosecution to have been brought under the 2010 Act was for a quotidian piece of local government corruption – a clerk at a Magistrates' Court fixing speeding tickets for money. Nor is it a surprise that the behaviour in question came to public notice, not because of diligent and well-resourced policing, but because of a newspaper 'sting'.[14] Nonetheless, there have been successful prosecutions under the previous law for offences that would now be charged under section 6 of the 2010 Act,[15] even against corporations.[16]

[14] *R.* v. *Munir Patel*, unreported, 18 November 2011, available at: www.judiciary.gov.uk/Resources/JCO/Documents/Judgments/munir-patel-sentencing-remarks.pdf.

[15] *R.* v. *Tumukunde & Tobiasen*, unreported, 2008, available at: www.business.timesonline.co.uk/tol/business/law/article4832416.ece; *R.* v. *Dougall* [2011] 1 Cr App R (S) 37; *R.* v. *Messent* [2011] EWCA Crim 644.

[16] *R.* v. *Mabey & Johnson Ltd* [2011] UKSC 9; *R.* v. *Innospec Ltd* [2010] EW Misc 7.

The chapters in Part III deal with the question of enforcement. It was, until the late 1990s, unusual for there to be more than a dozen bribery prosecutions per annum in the United Kingdom, and until 2008 there had been none for bribery of officials abroad. There were few investigations, and alternative charges (conspiracy to defraud) were available and frequently easier to prove. There were no special incentives, financial or reputational, either to investigate or to prosecute. The instantiation of the OECD Convention changed all this, because it requires not only 'paper' compliance, but also that the sanctions be 'effective'. Site visits deal with the signatory nations' prosecution record and the United Kingdom had been subject to increasingly pointed criticism in respect of its investigation and prosecution record. The repeated visits and the reports have directed attention to the enforcement record in respect of this specific offence and the effect of this publicity has been to spur action.

Following the 2011 site visit to the United Kingdom, a Report was published in 2012.[17] While it was nothing like that which arose from the highly condemnatory 2008 site visit, significant concerns were still expressed. In particular, the OECD commented adversely upon the increased use of civil recovery, because of the dangers to transparency of the sorts of agreement that can be reached, and the visit took place at a time of uncertainty as to the future of the Serious Fraud Office and its directorship.

The international efforts to suppress bribery, of which the OECD Convention is currently the most important, put in issue the relationship between criminal justice enforcement and other means of dealing with wrongdoers. The trend in recent years in many areas has been to approach crimes like bribery from a standpoint rather different from the traditional one of *ex post facto* investigation by the police, prosecution by prosecutors and punishment by courts. As with many areas of financial crime, prosecution is no longer regarded as the only plausible enforcement mechanism, and policing no longer the only means of securing compliance. In the last twenty years financial services regulation has been imposed under the aegis of the (soon to be abolished) Financial Services Authority. Leverage has also been put in place by enlisting corporates to police, and, if appropriate, to report themselves. These kinds of development invoke regulation and corporate

[17] OECD, *Phase 3 Report*.

governance, including training and internal systems, as the alternatives or supplements to the stark use of the criminal sanction. They are to be welcomed. In this sense, the Bribery Act 2010 is only a part of the huge shift in the approach to bribery law that has taken place over the past twenty years. The importance of bribery and controls upon it, from many quarters, can only increase.

In the production of this book we have benefited enormously from the assistance of Aleksandra Jordanoska.

Unless otherwise indicated, we have tried to ensure that statements of law are correct as at 1 July 2012.

Jeremy Horder and Peter Alldridge

PART I

Bribery law: between public wrongdoing and private advantage-taking

1

Reformulating bribery: a legal critique of the Bribery Act 2010

BOB SULLIVAN

Introduction

The Bribery Act 2010[1] is an important step forward for the United Kingdom[2] in terms of the legal response to corruption that takes the form of offering or taking bribes. An effective codification of the law of bribery has been achieved. The new substantive law of bribery in its entirety comprises just four offences. There are the two core offences of bribing another person[3] and being bribed.[4] Additionally, there is an offence of bribing a foreign public official;[5] and an offence, confined to 'commercial organisations', of failing to prevent bribery.[6] All previous statutory and common law offences relating to bribery are abolished.[7] Aside from the bribing a foreign public official offence, there are no longer any differences in legal terms between proscribing bribery in the private sector or in the public sector. In particular, there are no presumptions of corrupt conduct in the case of public officials.[8] For of all four offences, the burden of proof for all elements of the offence lies with the prosecution.

So, a new start, following a long and difficult gestation.[9] For the two core offences of bribing and being bribed, there seems no radical

1 Chapter 23. 2 The Act applies to England, Scotland, Northern Ireland and Wales.
3 Section 1. 4 Section 2. 5 Section 6. 6 Section 7.
7 Schedule 2. The principal statutes repealed are the Prevention of Corruption Act 1889, the Prevention of Corruption Act 1906 and the Prevention of Corruption Act 1916. Also abolished is the common law offence of offering undue rewards to public officials.
8 As was the case under the Prevention of Corruption Act 1916, s. 2.
9 In brief summary, the reform process was initiated by the publication of Law Commission, 'Legislating the Criminal Code: Corruption', Law Com. CP No. 145, 1997, followed by a final report, then another consultation paper, another final report, various interventions by the Home Office, the Ministry of Justice, several parliamentary select committee reports, and parliamentary debates along the way. The Act finally received the Royal Assent in April 2010, but there followed a delay until July 2011 before the Act was commenced.

extension of the previous law relating to bribery offences save for the possibility that when R[10] extorts some payment or other advantage from P[11] it may be easier under the new law to convict P of a bribery offence. What has changed significantly is the way in which the new offences are drafted. There is no longer the reliance on the evaluative terms 'corrupt' or 'corruptly'. Instead, the new legislation identifies by description situations where financial or other forms of advantage should not be offered or taken. In other words the two new, core offences describe for the purposes of the criminal law what bribery is, confining the role of the jury to finding the facts that constitute the offence and establishing the culpability for the new offences by applying to the facts the less morally freighted concepts of intent, knowledge and belief. While inevitably certain interpretive uncertainties arise when the specifics of these offences are scrutinised, undoubtedly the two core offences capture very well the essence of bribery. Under the terms of the Act, at the core of bribery are inducements or rewards to persons with public or private responsibilities to perform those responsibilities improperly either by acts or omissions done in bad faith, or with partiality, or in breach of trust.[12]

There is just one reservation, alluded to above, about the potential coverage of the offence concerned with, among other things, the payment of a financial or other advantage.[13] Sometimes P, when making a payment to R, will have yielded to the extortionate demands of R, rather than acting corruptly in his own right. Although any criminal liability incurred by R for accepting this payment[14] is well grounded in ethical terms, the same does not necessarily apply for the payment made by P, a victim of extortion. Before UK bribery legislation had extraterritorial

The principal cause of the delay between assent and commencement was concerns raised by commercial interests as to the adverse effect the Act would have on corporate promotional activities and effectiveness in the export trade. Although the Coalition government did not make any changes to the Act despite some intensive lobbying, it published official guidance on the legislation, which included advice on points of interpretation.

10 Used in the Act to denote the recipient of a financial or other advantage.

11 Used in the Act to denote the payer of a financial or other advantage.

12 The core offences should consistently capture conduct that deserves punishment and that is also harmful to the economy and the well-being of public institutions. For an informed discussion of differing rationales for the creation of bribery/corruption offences, see P. Alldridge, 'Reforming Bribery: Law Commission Consultation Paper 185 (1) Bribery Reform and the Law Commission – Again', *Criminal Law Review*, 9 (2008), 671–89, at 674–7 and citations.

13 Bribery Act 2010, s. 1.

14 Bribery Act 2010, s. 2.

applications there was no pressing reason to consider carefully the line between money paid as a bribe and money paid because of an extortionate demand.[15] But, as it will be argued below,[16] where the jurisdictional reach of bribery offences extends to jurisdictions where extortionate demands are commonplace, in some circumstances justice requires the exclusion from the reach of bribery offences of persons who have succumbed to coercive demands for payment or other advantage.

The offence relating to foreign public officials is less complex than the two core offences of bribing and being bribed. In terms of coverage, this offence does not obviously extend beyond the range of the core offence relating to the offer or payment of bribes. Nor does it come with any further jurisdictional reach than that possessed by the core offences. The fourth offence – failure of a commercial organisation to prevent bribery – certainly does break new ground, both in terms of the conduct made criminal and in the extent of its jurisdictional reach.

But before commencing a legal critique of this legislation, something must be said about the current enforcement context.[17] The number of prosecutions for bribery offences in the United Kingdom is low.[18] The Bribery Act 2010 has considerable merits in terms of legislative craft. But a political commitment to the effective enforcement of these new laws is necessary if reform is to be truly successful. And here there are grounds for misgiving. Andrew Feinstein's recent and definitive study of the modern arms trade[19] details the pervasive corruption that seems a permanent and ubiquitous feature of this politically safeguarded line of business. Sir Max Hastings, in a review of Feinstein's book, accepts that Feinstein's moral case against the arms trade is wholly convincing: 'the arms trade is a loathsome commerce'.[20] But his review concludes as follows:

> Arms dealing is much more injurious to mankind than prostitution, but every large government is engaged in it, and none is likely to stop. It would be naive to suggest that anything is likely to change, especially when western societies are struggling against odds to sustain their wealth against the rising Asian economic tide.[21]

15 From the nineteenth century onwards there is no evidence of systemic extortion on the part of UK public officials or the representatives of lawful commercial interests.

16 See n. 94 below and associated text.

17 See Monteith, Chapter 9, this volume.

18 See n. 75 below and associated text.

19 A. Feinstein, *The Shadow World: Inside the Global Arms Trade* (London: Hamish Hamilton, 2011).

20 M. Hastings, 'Current Affairs', *Sunday Times*, 30 October 2011, p. 46.

21 Hastings, 'Current Affairs'.

One may cavil at this summary dismissal of Feinstein's well-informed and thoughtful proposals for the international regulation of the arms trade.[22] Yet Hastings' words have great resonance for the United Kingdom, a prominent participant in the arms trade and (at the time of writing) entering recession in a time of great economic challenges complicated by financial uncertainties. Because of these difficult times, the budget of the Serious Fraud Office (SFO), the lead agency in the investigation and prosecution of overseas bribery, has been severely cut.[23] In the practical coinage of prosecutions undertaken and convictions obtained not much may change, at least in the medium term.

Bribing and being bribed: the core offences

The conduct element

Sections 1 and 2 of the Bribery Act 2010 create offences of bribing or being bribed. The sections set down six stated cases where one or other of these offences will be committed:

Case 1: P offers, promises or gives a financial reward or other advantage to another person. P must intend the advantage to act as an inducement for another person (not necessarily the recipient of the advantage) to perform improperly a relevant function or activity or to reward the improper performance of such a function or activity.

Case 2: P promises or gives a financial or other advantage to another person, knowing or believing that the acceptance of the advantage would itself constitute the improper performance of a relevant function or activity.

Case 3: R agrees to receive or accepts a financial or other advantage, intending that in consequence a relevant function or activity should be performed improperly (whether by R or another person).

[22] Feinstein is a former ANC MP and was a senior member of the South African Parliamentary Accounts Committee that examined the financial implications of an arms procurement programme negotiated in 1999 between South Africa's ANC government and various multinational arms suppliers, including Britain's BAE Systems. The ultimate cost of the programme is estimated to be US$6 billion, an estimate that includes US$300 million allegedly paid to senior ANC figures. It is hard to discern any external threat to South Africa that warrants arms expenditure of this magnitude.

[23] The SFO's budget has been cut from £55 million to £39 million, with a further cut of 25 per cent expected: Transparency International (UK), *National Integrity System Assessment: the United Kingdom* (London: Transparency International, 2011), p. 5.

Case 4: R requests, agrees to receive or accepts a financial or other advantage and the request, agreement or acceptance itself constitutes the improper performance by R of a relevant function or activity.

Case 5: R requests, agrees to receive or accepts a financial or other advantage as a reward for the improper performance (whether by R or another person) of a relevant function or activity.

Case 6: in anticipation of, or in consequence of, R requesting or agreeing to receive or accepting a financial or other advantage, a relevant function or activity is performed improperly by R or by another person at R's request or with R's assent or acquiescence.

Common to all six cases is the offer or taking of a 'financial or other advantage'. No limitation is placed on the nature of those advantages that do not take a financial form. This will not cause difficulty where the advantage is tangible and/or has a significant exchange value. But the potential coverage is large. Great concern was expressed by, among others, the CBI about the implications of the new legislation for corporate hospitality and public relations expenditure.[24] These concerns were a significant factor in the delay in the commencement of the Bribery Act 2010 following the Royal Assent.

The Law Commission for England and Wales struggled valiantly to divide up corporate hospitality into acceptable and non-acceptable forms, an exercise which concluded with proposals of great complexity.[25] Predictably these proposals did not later materialise as legislative provisions. Delineating the parameters of legally acceptable hospitality is not made easier by the fact the bribery offences have extraterritorial reach, thereby covering social and commercial interactions between persons from different gift cultures. The bounds of propriety are set by, 'what a reasonable person in the United Kingdom would expect in relation to the performance of the type of function or activity concerned', with, 'local custom and practice to be disregarded'.[26]

[24] M. Raphael, 'A Defining Problem for the 2010 Bribery Act', *The Guardian*, 2 February 2011, available at: www.guardian.co.uk/law/2011/feb/02/bribery-act-monty-raphael?INTCMP=SRCH.

[25] Law Commission, *Legislating the Criminal Code: Corruption*, Law Com. No. 248 (London: The Stationery Office, 1998), paras 5.75–5.82. For critical discussion see G. R. Sullivan, 'Proscribing Corruption: Some Comments on the Law Commission Report', *Criminal Law Review*, August (1998), 547–55.

[26] Bribery Act 2010, s. 5(1) and (2).

Help is now at hand in the form of guidance on corporate hospitality disseminated by the Ministry of Justice.[27] The guidance is unexceptionable, emphasising sound motivation and a sense of proportion. The era of corporate treats, though, is far from over. For instance, attendance at international sporting events is specifically mentioned as an acceptable form of hospitality.[28] Circumspection is advised about first-class flights and five-star hotels: essentially for VIPs only. Facetiousness is hard to avoid when discussing such matters, but in fairness, the limits of acceptable hospitality evade precision. Unless an unrealistic 'no cakes and ale' policy is adopted, circumstantial elements specific to R, such as the duration and importance of the commercial relationship with P, must feature in any application of the law. Importantly, any successful prosecution must prove a link between the provision of specific items of hospitality provided by P and the improper performance of a relevant function or activity by R, a matter considered in general terms directly below. Further, any prosecution must have the consent of the Director of Public Prosecutions, or the Director of the Serious Fraud Office, or the Director of Revenue and Customs.[29] These consent provisions will minimise the risk of speculative prosecutions.

The offer or taking of the bribe must be linked to an improper performance or non-performance of a 'relevant function or activity'. Section 3 of the Act defines relevant functions and activities as functions of a public nature, activities connected with a business, activities performed in the course of a person's employment and activities performed by or on behalf of a body of persons, whether corporate or unincorporated. Additionally, a performance condition must attach to the function or activity for it to be a relevant function or activity. At least one of the following conditions must attach:

(a) a person performing the function or activity is expected to perform it in good faith;
(b) a person performing the function or activity is expected to perform it impartially;
(c) a person performing the function or activity is in a position of trust by virtue of performing it.

27 Ministry of Justice, *The Bribery Act 2010: Guidance about Procedures which Relevant Commercial Organisations can put into Place to Prevent Persons Associated with them from Bribing* (London: Ministry of Justice, 2011), paras 19–20.
28 Ministry of Justice, *Bribery Act 2010: Guidance*, para. 20.
29 Bribery Act 2010, s. 10.

The performance of the function or activity must be 'improper', a matter dealt under section 4 of the Act. Impropriety is established if a 'relevant expectation' attaches to the performance of the function or activity and the expectation is not met. A relevant expectation must consist of one or more of the conditions (a), (b) or (c) listed above. In some cases offering or asking for a financial or other advantage will not of itself suffice. The advantage must be given or sought in order to induce or reward a lack of good faith, or partiality or a breach of trust in the performance of a function or activity. But there are also cases where offering or taking the advantage will, without more, establish impropriety. Recall Case 2 which deals with circumstances where, 'the acceptance of the advantage would *itself* constitute the improper performance of a relevant function or activity'. Additionally, Case 4 contemplates circumstances where 'the request, agreement or acceptance [of a financial or other advantage] *itself* constitutes the improper performance of a relevant function or activity' (emphasis added).

There is no guidance given in the Act as to the circumstances when taking or receiving an advantage suffices by itself as the improper performance of a function or activity. All that we have is section 4, which on the face of it is exhaustive as to what counts as improper performance of a function or activity. It follows that where the offer or taking of an advantage without more is the basis of the prosecution's case, the offer or taking of the advantage must of itself establish bad faith, or partiality or a breach of trust in the performance of a function or activity.[30]

[30] Such findings will be readily made where R takes an advantage from P in advance of some decision that R is due to make as a judge, or a civil servant or an agent acting for a principal, etc. where P has an interest that may be affected by R's decision. Evidence of such advantage-taking may be proof in itself of an improper performance of a function or activity even before R has made his decision, particularly in the form of a breach of a duty to act impartially and/or a breach of trust by way of conflict of interest. Matters may not be so straightforward where R takes an advantage from P after he has made his decision where there is no evidence of an agreement or expectation in advance of the decision that an advantage would be given (in other words, the advantage is given unilaterally and *ex post* by P). The Law Commission provide such an example involving R, a judge who has made *ex ante* a fair and unbiased judgment in favour of P and who takes up *ex post* P's offer to take a holiday at P's ski chalet. The Commission concludes: 'Although this is a marginal case of bribery, it is a case where it is improper for someone, in virtue of the position they hold, to accept an advantage.' (Law Commission, *Reforming Bribery*, Law Com. No. 313 (London: The Stationery Office, 2008), para. 3.164). Of course, it is very ill-advised of R to take up P's offer of free accommodation, just as a serving prime minister should not take free holidays in the homes of the rich and famous but, in either case, it is hard to see impropriety within the terms of section 4.

What is to be expected of the performance of a function or activity is to be tested against what a reasonable person in the United Kingdom would expect, disregarding any local custom or practice.[31] But there is an important qualification. Account can be taken of a local custom or practice if it is permitted or required by the written law of the country or territory concerned.[32] One thinks immediately of jurisdictions where it is permissible or even obligatory[33] to appoint commercial agents, who may receive large commissions based on the gross value of the contract even in the case of what would be regarded as public sector contracts in the United Kingdom.[34] The use of commercial agents appointed under the local law present what is perhaps the most daunting problem in the international regulation of corrupt activity.[35] Obviously, the payment of an agreed rate of commission is readily distinguishable from a bribe; and yet commission payments may be vast, particularly in the areas of military procurement and major infrastructure projects. Once the payment is made to the agent (which might be a locally owned corporate body) others may share in the good fortune. These machinations may well be lawful under the local law. And if the local law is set down in writing it seems that commission payments are not bribes for the purposes of the Bribery Act 2010, even when payments are made in the certain knowledge that they will in large part be paid over to representatives of the other contracting party. If the commission is a lawful payment in the hands of the agent, he is (subject to any restrictions imposed by local law) free to distribute the largesse as he pleases.

31 Bribery Act 2010, s. 5(2).

32 To be written law the permission or requirement must be contained in a written constitution, legislation or any judicial decision evidenced in public written sources: s. 5(3).

33 Under the Foreign Investment Act 2000 of Saudi Arabia, if a non-Saudi contracting party lacks a presence in Saudi Arabia in the form of a company or partnership, the non-Saudi party must obtain temporary commercial registration and as a condition of registration a 'service' agent must be appointed. The agent must be a Saudi national or a wholly Saudi-owned company or partnership. The legislation explicitly provides that contracts where the counter party is the Saudi Government fall within the scope of these provisions.

34 The Al Yamamah contracts set the gold standard in respect of introduction fees and commission payments to commercial agents. These payments would seem to be lawful within the terms of current Saudi Arabian law: see n. 33 above. For an account of the Al Yamamah arms deal and its ramifications see N. Kochan and R. Goodyear, *Corruption: The New Corporate Challenge* (London: Palgrave Macmillan, 2011), pp. 67–73.

35 For an informed account of the questionable nature of some commercial agents and their activities, see Woolf Committee, *Ethical Business Conduct in BAE Systems plc: The Way Forward* (2008), available at: http://ir.baesystems.com/investors/storage/woolf_report_2008.pdf.

The effective regulation of large-scale commission payments is far from straightforward. Local laws cannot simply be wished away. Respect for the legal sovereignty of states is a bedrock principle of international law. Perhaps the best that can be hoped for at present is full transparency. To that end, there is much to be said in favour of imposing a legal duty on commercial organisations subject to UK jurisdiction to report commissions paid to commercial agents if the payments are in excess of some legally defined order of magnitude.

The mens rea

First to be examined are Cases 1 and 2, which comprise the offence of bribing another person contrary to section 1 of the 2010 Act. In Case 1, P must offer, promise or give a financial or other advantage intending to induce a person to perform improperly a relevant function or activity, or to reward a person for improper performance. In Case 2, P must offer, promise or give a financial or other advantage knowing or believing that acceptance of the advantage would itself constitute improper performance of a relevant function or activity. As discussed already, what constitutes improper performance is defined in the Act[36] and hence is a matter of law.[37] It should follow that, where intent is the relevant culpability element, it suffices that P offers an advantage in order to induce a performance of an activity or function that in law is improper. Accordingly, P must contemplate circumstances which would establish impropriety on the part of the person performing the activity or function and offer an advantage in order to induce R to perform a function or activity in such circumstances. Whether P considers that such circumstances constitute impropriety either in ethical terms or within the meaning of the Act seems to be neither here nor there in the absence of any evaluative criteria such as 'corruptly' or 'dishonestly', remembering that ignorance or mistake of law is no excuse.[38] A similar analysis can be made for Case 2, where the relevant culpability is knowledge or belief. P will have a *mens rea* based on knowledge if he had well-founded

[36] Sections 4–5.

[37] Unlike dishonesty in theft which is only partially defined, thereby leaving a normative role for the jury in cases falling outside the partial definitions, s. 4 stipulates what are the "relevant expectations'. Only a breach of a relevant expectation makes for the improper performance of a function or activity.

[38] For a recent affirmation of this long-standing principle see *Christian* v. *R.* [2006] 2 AC 400.

reasons to assume the existence of circumstances that made for impropriety. P will have a *mens rea* based on belief if he had no substantial doubt in the existence of such circumstances.[39] In either case, P's own normative take on the impropriety of what he is inducing the person to do seems not to be in point, nor is any knowledge on his part of what makes for impropriety under the Act.[40]

Turning to the offence of being bribed under section 2, one anticipates that the same analysis as to the *mens rea* required will follow through. Case 3 is where R requests, agrees to receive, or accepts a financial or other advantage intending to perform a function or activity improperly; Case 4 is where R requests, agrees to receive, or accepts a financial or other advantage where the request etc. of itself is the improper performance of a function or activity; Case 5 is where R requests a reward for the improper performance of a function or activity; and Case 6 is where R improperly performs an activity or function anticipating a financial or other advantage.

But the culpability analysis made in respect of section 1 does not seamlessly carry through to section 2. For Case 3 there is a close parallel with Case 1. R must intend that a function or activity be performed improperly. But in the other cases there are no further references to the culpability terms of intent, knowledge or belief. That these cases are different from Cases 1–3 is fortified by section 2(7) which provides: 'in cases 4 to 6 it does not matter whether R knows or believes that the performance of the function or activity is improper'.

During a debate on the Bribery Bill, the Parliamentary Under Secretary of State, Lord Bach drew a distinction between Cases 4–6 and Cases 1–3. The former, he said were cases of strict liability. Somewhat confusingly he explained his notion of strict liability by reference to the crime of corporate manslaughter. But his meaning is clear: 'A person can be

[39] For further elaboration, see S. Shute, 'Knowledge and Belief in the Criminal Law', in S. Shute and A. Simester (eds), *Criminal Law: Doctrines of the General Part* (Oxford University Press, 2002), pp. 171–206, at p. 184, and G. R. Sullivan, 'Knowledge, Belief and Culpability', in Shute and Simester (eds), *Criminal Law*, 2002, pp. 207–26, at p. 207.

[40] Courts have sometimes treated mistakes as to an applicable normative standard as a basis for a mistake of fact. A well-known example is the Court of Appeal's decision in *R.* v. *Scarlett* [1993] 4 All ER 629 (CA), where D's belief that he had used proportionate force afforded him a defence to assault despite a finding at trial by the jury that the force was disproportionate. But decisions since *Scarlett*, such as *R.* v. *Owino* [1996] 2 Cr App R 128 (CA) and *R.* v. *Martin (David)* [2000] 2 Cr App R 42 (CA) assert that D cannot raise a mistake of fact based on his own normative standards.

convicted of gross negligence manslaughter regardless of whether they recognised that their conduct would amount to the breach of the duty to take care.'[41] By extension, Lord Bach is clearly stating that knowledge of the state of the law and any recognition of moral turpitude is irrelevant for Cases 4–6, but by strong implication are matters in play for liability in Cases 1–3. Lord Bach's analysis is sustained by the language of section 2(7), even though the explanatory notes published with the Act make no reference to strict liability and merely reiterate the provision itself.[42] For section 2 cases, seemingly there is one variant (Case 3) of the being bribed offence requiring the high culpability of intention to perform a function or activity in a way that is improper and which, additionally, requires proof that R knows or believes that the performance is improper. By contrast, the other ways of committing the offence make no explicit reference to *mens rea* and are subject to a provision that knowledge or belief in impropriety is irrelevant to liability.

But if, for the moment, we wish section 2(7) away, any practical differences in terms of culpability provable against R as between the variants of the section 2 offences seem minimal. Recall that in Case 4, R must request, agree to receive, or accept an advantage where the request, agreement, or acceptance itself constitutes the improper performance by R of a relevant function or activity. In Case 5, R must request, agree to receive, or accept an advantage as a reward for the improper performance (whether by R or another person) of a relevant function or activity. And finally in Case 6, R in anticipation or in consequence of requesting, agreeing to receive, or accepting an advantage, performs a relevant function or activity improperly, or another person performs the relevant function or activity improperly at R's request, or with R's assent or acquiescence. It is difficult to conceive of circumstances where R's liability could be established in any of these cases unless there was proof that he was aware of the facts that made the actual or contemplated performance of the relevant function or activity improper. How can R act or contemplate acting in bad faith, or with partiality or in breach of trust without an underlying awareness of the facts which constitute those forms of impropriety? If section 2(7) is given full effect, in Case 3 R's mistakes of law and morality provide excuses, but not within Cases 4–6.

41 *Hansard*, HL, vol. 717, col. 122, 2 February 2010.

42 Bribery Act 2010, Ch. 23, Explanatory Notes, at para. 26, available at: www.legislation.gov.uk/ukpga/2010/23/notes/contents.

What implications does this conclusion have for the *mens rea* analysis made for the section 1 bribing offence? Arguably, the implications of section 2(7) should be confined to section 2 itself thereby confining its effect to Case 3. But the very existence of section 2(7) implies that the default *mens rea* for the core bribery offences created by section 1 includes proof of knowledge or belief of impropriety. It is only when we reach Case 4 that the default position is departed from. So, in Cases 1–3 it seems, however surprisingly, that P will not be guilty of a bribery offence if he does not consider that the conduct he is inducing or rewarding is improper despite his awareness of the circumstances that in law constitute impropriety.

The Law Commission very likely took the orthodox view that normative mistakes were irrelevant to proof of *mens rea*.[43] The orthodox view predominated under the previous law, although the latitude given by the terms 'corrupt' and 'corruptly' was used by judges to avoid convictions in what they considered to be hard cases.[44] The new position appears to be that normative mistakes do count in favour of the defendant for certain forms of bribery, but do not count for others, a disjunction that lacks any moral or policy justification.[45] Furthermore, it is likely to give rise to practical difficulties. In any multi-defendant bribery prosecution there

[43] No provision along the lines of s. 2(7) is to be found in the bill offered in Law Com. No. 313. However, there is this somewhat equivocal passage: 'There was strong support [among consultees] for the view that it should be immaterial whether or not R was aware that the relevant action that he or she performed was improper. Consequently, our draft Bill is silent on this issue. There is enough justification for regarding R as guilty of the bribery offence if R fulfils both the basic and the wrongfulness elements of the offence as we have defined them.' (Law Com. No. 313, para. 3.190). The most tenable reading of this passage seems to be that normative mistakes on the part of R are not relevant to liability.

[44] *R.* v. *Smith* [1960] 2 QB 423 exemplifies the predominant approach, but contrast *R.* v. *Calland* [1967] CLR 236.

[45] One example must suffice. Suppose that that P has started a business which desperately requires the services of some highly skilled non-EU nationals. There is a backlog in processing work permits. P originates from a country where it is usual to pay facilitation payments to expedite such matters. He has let it be known to R, a civil servant, that he would pay good money for a quicker service. R says nothing, but departs from usual civil service practice to deal quickly with the permits of concern to A and subsequently receives a large payment from A. If A is charged under s. 1 with a Case 1 offence he might have a defence if he believes that there is nothing improper in what he did. R would be convicted under s. 2 of a Case 6 offence even if he believed that usual civil service practice was dysfunctional and should not be followed, and that civil servants should receive rewards for doing a good job. Even persons who think, unlike the author, that such normative mistakes are relevant for the culpability for bribery would struggle to justify this differential treatment of A and R.

are likely to be charges based on facts which fall within Cases 1–3 and further charges based on facts which fall within Cases 4–6. Jury directions would have to be worded very carefully.

Is there any way out of these difficulties? The position to be argued for here is that the orthodox approach to *mens rea* should prevail, and that *mens rea* should not be confused with normative awareness that one's conduct is wrong. A possible solution would be for a court to construe section 2(7) as a provision for the avoidance of doubt, a provision that merely makes explicit for Cases 4–6 what would normally be taken for granted and which can be taken for granted in Cases 1–3. There is a precedent for this approach if the alternative is to allow indefensible differences in the culpability standards for the same offence.[46] Such an interpretation would be in line with the spirit of Lord Bach's intervention. His concern was to cut off a line of defence which could, he considered, be raised more plausibly in Cases 4–6: 'It would be much easier for the recipient to claim ignorance of the fact that his or her conduct constituted a breach of an expectation than it would be for the prosecution to prove that the recipient was aware that it did.'[47] That observation obtains, however, *mutatis mutandis*, with respect to P or R as the case may be for any variant of the two core offences. Be that as it may, Lord Bach was concerned with excluding a line of defence in Cases 4–6; he was far from advocating the availability of such a defence for Cases 1–3. Section 2(7) should be read in that spirit. It is excluding a defence for variants of the recipient offence without any implication that the defence is available for other variants of the core offences.

If that interpretation is adopted the conduct made criminal by these two core offences seems pretty much the same as the offences they replace, save for the possibility discussed below that for cases where P pays money to R under extortion it may now be easier to find him

[46] It may be recalled that s. 1 of the Criminal Law Act 1977 defines conspiracy without any reference to D's knowledge or awareness of facts or circumstances necessary for the commission of the substantive offence, whereas s. 1(2) makes special provision for such awareness where the substantive offence is a crime of strict liability. A literal interpretation of these provisions would give rise to the 'scandalous paradox' that awareness of such facts or circumstances need not be proved where the substantive offence is a crime of *mens rea*. That dysfunctional outcome has been deflected by reading s. 1(2) as a provision which merely spells out what would otherwise be assumed and without any wider implication than that: *R.* v. *Saik* [2006] UKHL 18, [2007] 1 AC 18, para. 4 (Lord Nicholls).

[47] *Hansard*, HL, vol. 717, col. 122, 2 February 2010.

liable for a bribery offence.[48] Commenting on the Law Commission consultation paper proposals, Peter Alldridge was of the view that any conduct which would have raised a case to answer under the previous law would also go to the jury under the new law, but no new forms of conduct would be made criminal.[49] Generally, that seems the right estimate for the impact of sections 1 and 2 unless a novel mistake of law defence is found to be available for some variants of the bribing and being bribed offences.

Bribery of foreign public officials

Section 6 of the Bribery Act 2010 creates a discrete offence of P bribing F, a foreign public official.[50] In terms of coverage it may be doubted whether this offence adds much to the core offence under section 1 of P offering or paying a bribe to R given that R may well be an official foreign or otherwise. Since 2001, UK corruption legislation has had extraterritorial reach.[51] The section 6 offence is less complex than the section 1 offence: liability arises from an offer or giving of advantage by P to F to obtain or retain business without any requirement of proving impropriety on the part of F. To that extent, section 6 may be preferable for prosecutors when the offence clearly applies on the alleged facts. Yet, at least in terms of the letter of the law applicable in jurisdictions worldwide, it must be rare that taking advantage to favour external commercial interests is not an improper act on the part of a public official. Perhaps the most significant role for this new offence is to flag clearly that UK law is compliant with its obligations under the OECD Convention on Combating Bribery of Foreign Public Officials in International Business Transactions (1997).[52]

Liability under section 6 will arise if P directly, or through a third party, offers, promises or gives to any foreign public official (F) any financial or other advantage (or to another person at F's request, or with F's assent or acquiescence) intending to obtain or retain business, or an advantage in the conduct of business by influencing F in F's capacity as a

[48] See n. 94, below, and associated text. [49] Alldridge, 'Reforming Bribery', pp. 673–4.

[50] F is not exposed to any liability under this provision.

[51] Anti-terrorism, Crime and Security Act 2001, ss. 108–109.

[52] The Joint Parliamentary Committee on the Draft Bribery Bill considered that the clause which became s. 6 was an important signifier of the UK's compliance with the OECD Convention (*Hansard*, HL Paper No. 115-1/HC Paper 430–1, 28 July 2009). To the same effect, see Lord Bach in *Hansard*, HL, vol. 715, col. 1087, 9 December 2009.

foreign public official. F will act in that capacity by using his position as an official even if he acts outside his authority.[53] P will typically be acting on behalf of a commercial organisation, in which case he may expose that organisation to the failure to prevent bribery offence under section 7.

P will not commit an offence if F is required or permitted by the written law applicable to him to be influenced in his capacity as a foreign public official by any offer, promise or gift.[54] Explicit provisions to that effect will be rare. As indicated above, more frequent would be provisions in laws relating to commerce to permit or even require the appointment of a commercial agent. Of course, payment of an introduction fee or even very large commissions to an agent for services is not of itself the direct or indirect giving of a financial or other inducement to a foreign public official. But particularly in Saudi Arabia and the Gulf states there may be very close relationships between agents and prominent public officials.[55] To be liable under section 6, P must intend any payment made to the agent to be transmitted in whole or in part to F or his nominee as a means of influence over F. At the very least P would have to consider that such a transfer of funds between the agent and F will almost certainly be made. It would not be enough for the prosecution to show that P thought such a payment would likely be made unless there was also proof that P made the payment to the agent in order that at least some of the money should be passed on to F or his nominee to influence F.

What role or position amounts to being a foreign public official is not at large, but is defined in the Act.[56] The common thread is that F must exercise a 'public function' on behalf of a country or territory outside the United Kingdom, or on behalf of any public agency or public enterprise of such a country or territory, or on behalf of an international organisation. One assumes that 'public enterprise' does not take in foreign commercial organisations operating in the private sector even where the state is the only or dominating shareholder. Of course, the bribery of directors/managers of such enterprises by P may well engage the other offences created by the Act if the jurisdictional conditions of the Act are met.

Failure of commercial organisations to prevent bribery

Section 7 creates a broad and innovatory offence that can be committed by a commercial organisation that fails to prevent bribery carried

[53] Bribery Act 2010, s. 6(4)(b). [54] Section 6(3)(b).
[55] See n. 33, above, and associated text. [56] Bribery Act 2010, s. 6(6)–(7).

out on its behalf. It should be noted at the outset that this is a crime of unrestrained extraterritorial jurisdiction, a matter examined below in the section on jurisdiction. The principal offender must be the commercial organisation. But unlike the case of the offence of corporate manslaughter where liability is confined to the company (complicity on the part of individuals associated with the company's offence is closed off),[57] the Bribery Act 2010 does not contain any provision insulating persons employed by or associated with the organisation from secondary liability derived from any primary liability on the part of the organisation for the failure of prevention offence. Under the Act, commercial organisations include, but are not limited to, companies and partnerships incorporated or registered under the law of any part of the United Kingdom.[58] A company or partnership wherever incorporated or registered will be a commercial organisation within the purview of the Act if it carries on a business or part of a business in any part of the United Kingdom. Typically, a business based predominantly overseas wishing to have a business presence in the United Kingdom will form a UK subsidiary company or partnership. But that is not necessary for jurisdictional purposes. Conducting business of itself suffices. Moreover, the presence of a subsidiary arguably need not entail a business presence on the part of the subsidiary if it has been formed merely to obtain a London listing for funds to be used outside the United Kingdom: the question will be for the courts to decide.[59]

A commercial organisation (C) will potentially commit the failure offence if a person (A) associated with C bribes another person to obtain or retain business for C or to obtain or retain a business advantage for C. The payment of the bribe must amount to an offence by A under section 1 or section 6 of the Bribery Act 2010. In deciding that question, the fact that A may lack a 'close connection' with the United Kingdom (a condition that otherwise must be met to give sections 1 and 6 extraterritorial effect) is to be disregarded.[60]

[57] Corporate Manslaughter and Corporate Homicide Act 2007, s. 18.

[58] Bribery Act 2010, s. 7(5).

[59] The Ministry of Justice guidance suggests that the formation of a UK subsidiary purely to raise funds for use by other members of the corporate group registered overseas will not necessarily amount to the doing of business in the United Kingdom by the UK subsidiary: Ministry of Justice, *Bribery Act 2010: Guidance*, para. 36. Transparency International criticises this conclusion as being too narrow a view of what doing business may consist of, but it is certainly not illogical to draw a distinction between raising funds for business and doing business.

[60] Bribery Act 2010, s. 7(3)(b).

An associated person[61] is a person who 'performs services for or on behalf of C'.[62] If A is an employee of C, it is to be presumed that A performs services on behalf of C until the contrary is proved.[63] In other cases, the prosecution must prove that A is a service provider for C. That question must be resolved 'disregarding any bribe under consideration'.[64] So, if the only evidence of service provision on the part of A is the bribes he is charged with paying for C, the case must fail. Bribes that are the basis of charges must be 'under consideration'. But what if the prosecution wish to introduce evidence of bribes that are not the subject of charges to establish A as a service provider for C? (Clearly, in functional terms bribing on behalf of another is provision of a service.) However, any bribe relevant to establishing the prosecution's case is presumably a bribe under consideration. And even if a different view were to be taken, to introduce evidence of bribes paid by A for C in addition to those bribes which are the subject of charges would be highly prejudicial and very likely inadmissible unless the prosecution could persuade the judge that reception of the evidence would not only be relevant to issues arising in the case or the accused's credibility, but also fair to the accused and in the interests of justice.[65] As a practical matter it would seem that the prosecution must have evidence that A does things for C in addition to paying bribes on its behalf. This seems an unnecessary restriction on the offence. In any future reformulation of the provision one could allow proof of payment of a bribe by A made ostensibly on behalf of C to raise an inference that by that act alone C must be taken to be a service provider for A unless A can show that the bribe was not an act done on its behalf.[66]

It may be that A is a company rather than a natural person, which makes no difference to the analysis where company A is clearly acting in a representative capacity for C and its only interest (aside from any fee it may receive from C) in making any payment or conferring any advantage is seeking business advantages for C. But if A is bribing R for the sake of

[61] A person can be a subsidiary of C: s. 8(3). [62] Section 8(1). [63] Section 8(5).

[64] Section 8(1). Such a requirement was not a feature in the original Law Commission proposal for a failure to prevent offence. See further G. R. Sullivan, 'Reforming Bribery: Law Commission Consultation Paper 185 (2) Bribery Outside England and Wales: Corporate Liability, Defences, Consent to Prosecution', *Criminal Law Review*, 9 (2008), 687–701, at 696–7.

[65] Criminal Justice Act 2003, ss. 101, 103.

[66] For example, A might be able to show that C was acting mischievously to make trouble for A rather than advance its business interests.

its own business interests, this is no concern for C, at least within the terms of section 7. This may well apply even if A was a wholly owned subsidiary of C and C benefited as a shareholder from profits arising from business opportunities that A obtained by paying bribes to R. The doctrine of the separate personality of companies from their shareholders is very strongly adhered to under English law: even if A is wholly owned by C and C takes all the profits from the business of A by way of distributions, nonetheless, those profits, until distributed to shareholders, belong in law and equity to A.[67] This doctrinaire separation of companies from their shareholders has been upheld where the controlling shareholder has benefited from the illegal activities of the subsidiary. In *Lonhro* v. *Shell Petroleum*,[68] the House of Lords ruled that C was not implicated in the illegal trading activities of A, its wholly owned subsidiary (breach of UN trading sanctions), even though aware that the profits it took from A were derived from that trade. For the House of Lords, the doctrine of separate, corporate personality entailed that the sanction-busting activities of A were all its own work. One would hope that this rigid application of separate personality might be tempered by a more realistic approach for cases where there is evidence that one of the motivations of C in forming A, its wholly owned foreign subsidiary (rather than a more direct presence in the jurisdiction), was to profit as a shareholder from business tainted by bribery.[69]

If a failure offence is proved against C, liability can be avoided if C can prove that it had in place adequate procedures designed to prevent persons associated with C from undertaking such conduct.[70] On its face this defence is based on an evaluation of the company's procedures. Although

[67] *Salomon* v. *Salomon* [1897] AC 22.

[68] *Lonhro Ltd* v. *Shell Petroleum Co. Ltd* [1980] 1 WLR 627 (HL).

[69] To date, English courts have pierced the veil only to prevent the dominant shareholder taking the benefit of illegal activity carried out by the controlled company when the company was set up by the shareholder in order to evade liabilities that had already arisen, as in *Gilford Motor Company* v. *Horne* [1933] Ch 935 and *Kensington International* v. *Congo* [2005] EWHC 2684 (Comm). The corporate form can be used successfully to insulate *ex ante* from liabilities that arise from the marketing of dangerous products such as asbestos; see *Adams* v. *Cape Industries* [1990] Ch 433. A case where there was proof that a motivation of the dominant shareholder in forming the company was to evade criminal liability that might otherwise arise from using illegal methods to obtain business has not arisen before an English court. In *Lonhro*, the subsidiary company was formed to trade and ship oil before the UN sanctions regime was operational or in contemplation.

[70] Bribery Act 2010, s. 7(2).

there is no legal obligation imposed on commercial organisations to set up an anti-bribery process, it may be assumed that to avail itself of this defence even the smallest company must have some ongoing and cyclical process which it can realistically describe as its anti-bribery procedures. Mere ad hoc advice – 'you may be asked for a bribe as an inducement for an order: refuse' – would presumably not suffice to raise the defence.

Any failure on the part of the procedures to improve the actual practices of the organisation would not, as such, entail the failure of the defence. Indeed, the defence comes into play on proof that a bribe has been paid on behalf of the company to gain or retain business. But in forensic contexts one would anticipate a thorough testing of the adequacy of the organisation's procedures against what can be proved about the company's practices. In this context the written guidance provided by the Ministry of Justice is likely to have weight at any trial.[71] It would clearly be helpful in raising a successful defence if C can demonstrate that each of the six guiding principles (proportional procedures, top-level commitment, risk assessment, due diligence, communication, monitoring and review) are reflected in the organisation's express policy and in its consistent practice.

Apart from any intrinsic merits of the organisational failure offence, it is also important for the compliance of the United Kingdom with the OECD treaty on the bribery of foreign officials. The OECD took the view that English law was ineffective in terms of the imposition of the law of bribery on the conduct of limited companies.[72] The narrow doctrine of identification, the doctrine which requires as a condition of corporate criminal liability that the culpability specified for the offence for which the company has been charged be established at the highest level of the corporate decisional pyramid,[73] was the focus of the OECD's concerns. The concern was well-founded. With corporations of any size and complexity, it was difficult to prove to the criminal standard knowledge on the part of its highest officials that bribes had been paid on the company's behalf. As the organisational failure offence is an offence of strict liability (tempered by the adequate procedures defence) the

[71] Ministry of Justice, *Bribery Act 2010: Guidance*, pp. 21–30.

[72] OECD, *United Kingdom: Phase 2 Report on the Application of the Convention on Combating Bribery of Foreign Public Officials in International Business Transactions and the 1997 Recommendation on Combating Bribery in International Business Transactions* (Paris: OECD, 2005), paras 195–206; OECD, *United Kingdom: Phase 2 Follow-up Report on the Implementation of the Phase 2 Recommendations* (Paris: OECD, 2007), para. 21.

[73] *Tesco Supermarkets Ltd* v. *Nattrass* [1972] AC 153 (HL).

doctrine of identification has no application. This should suffice for OECD compliance. Many other OECD jurisdictions do not impose strict liability on companies for failure to prevent bribes. Further, any individual P who pays a bribe on behalf of a UK company will, of course, straightforwardly be personally liable under the Bribery Act 2010, if that takes place in the United Kingdom, and also liable if the conduct takes place anywhere else provided P has a close connection with the United Kingdom. Finally, if the demands of the identification doctrine can be met the organisation will be directly liable for the bribe under section 1, and cannot use the adequate procedures defence.

Territorial application

From 2001, UK bribery legislation was given an extraterritorial dimension.[74] The practical effects of this expanded jurisdiction were minimal. A contrast may be drawn with the increase in enforcement activity recently initiated by the US Department of Justice against companies who have paid overseas bribes.[75] The very considerable cut in the budget of the SFO dampens any expectation that the bringing into force of the new Act will presage a significant increase in enforcement activity by that agency.[76]

A review of the extraterritorial application of the new bribery offences falls into two parts. There is one regime for the offences of bribing, being bribed and bribing foreign public officials. There is a more expansive regime for the commercial organisations failure to prevent bribery offence.

Bribing, being bribed and bribing foreign public officials: territorial application

An offence will be committed under sections 1, 2 or 6 of the Act in England and Wales, Scotland and Northern Ireland if 'any act or

[74] Anti-terrorism, Crime and Security Act 2001, ss. 108–109.

[75] In the decade ending December 2010, three individuals and two companies had been prosecuted in the United Kingdom for corruption offences with an overseas dimension. By contrast, in 2008 the US Department of Justice prosecuted sixteen cases of overseas bribery under the Foreign Corrupt Practices Act (FCPA) 1977. In July 2012 110 FCPA investigations were being conducted. See further N. Cropp, 'The Bribery Act 2010. A Comparison with the Foreign Corrupt Practices Act: Nuance v. Nous', *Criminal Law Review*, 2 (2011), 122–40, at 138–40.

[76] See n. 23, above.

omission which forms part of the offence takes place in that part of the United Kingdom'.[77] This is a formulation already familiar for theft and fraud offences.[78] Jurisdiction over the offence will exist if some part of the *actus reus* of any of these offences takes place in one of the UK's jurisdictions. Conduct within the United Kingdom which is too preliminary to form part of the *actus reus* of one of these offences may yet be covered by the inchoate offences of conspiracy, attempt and encouraging or assisting crimes. Moreover, any agreement made in England and Wales to commit a crime abroad is an indictable conspiracy irrespective of whether the crime agreed to would be an offence if committed in England and Wales.[79]

If no act or omission forming part of the offence takes place in the United Kingdom there may yet be jurisdiction provided that the conduct taking place elsewhere would form part of the offence if done in the United Kingdom, and that the perpetrator of the conduct has a 'close connection' with the United Kingdom.[80] What makes for a close connection is listed in the Act.[81] Comment will be made here only on a notable absentee from the list. Foreign subsidiary companies of UK parent companies, even wholly owned subsidiaries, are absent from the list. This perpetuates in cases of alleged bribery the strict legal separation of the individual companies which form a corporate group. As discussed already, this strict separation policy has held up in cases where a foreign subsidiary has committed crimes resulting in financial benefit to the UK parent company.[82] Even if a court were minded to follow a more flexible policy by developing aspects of the 'piercing the veil' jurisprudence this would not seem possible in this context where the list of connected persons is exhaustive. It is conceivable that on extreme facts a court might find that acts ostensibly done by a subsidiary were done in fact and in law by the parent.

Failure of commercial organisations to prevent bribery: territorial application

An offence will be committed under section 7, 'irrespective of whether the acts or omissions which form part of the offence take place in the

[77] Bribery Act 2010, s. 12(1). [78] Criminal Justice Act 1993, Pt 1.
[79] Criminal Justice and Terrorism Act 1998, s. 5.
[80] Bribery Act 2010, s. 12(2). [81] Section 12(4).
[82] For example, *Lonhro Ltd* v. *Shell Petroleum Co. Ltd* [1980] 1 WLR 627 (HL).

United Kingdom'.[83] In other words, this is an offence of universal jurisdiction. To engage this jurisdictional competence, there must be an act or omission done by a person associated with a commercial organisation, a commercial organisation made subject to the criminal jurisdiction of UK courts by reason of being a 'relevant' commercial organisation within the terms of section 7. Further, the act or omission must constitute an offence falling within section 1 or section 6. As noted already, in deciding whether there has been a section 1 or 6 offence for section 7 purposes, the location of the act or omission is immaterial and so, too, is whether the associated person has a close connection with the United Kingdom.[84]

Recall that an associated person is someone who provides services for and on behalf of the commercial organisation.[85] An associated person can be a subsidiary company of a parent company.[86] A foreign-owned subsidiary registered in the United Kingdom will be a commercial organisation amenable to the criminal jurisdiction of the UK courts. There would, therefore, be jurisdiction over conduct overseas falling within sections 1 and 6 done by any other members of the corporate group to which the UK subsidiary belongs provided a judgment can be made that a bribe was offered or paid in the context of services done on behalf of the UK subsidiary. But merely profiting in the capacity as a shareholder would, on what authority exists, not be enough to establish that the acts were done for the shareholder.[87] Of itself, the presence of a subsidiary will not establish the presence of the parent. Recall, too, that a foreign company will be a commercial organisation within the United Kingdom for the purposes of the Bribery Act 2010 provided it carries on a business or part of a business within the United Kingdom. Where there is no buffer of a subsidiary company it will be the foreign company itself that will be within the purview of the Act. In strict theory any bribery done anywhere on behalf of that company might engage liability under section 7.

Defences

The adequate procedures defence for the corporate failure offence has already been discussed, as has the defence that payments were required or permitted by the local law. Other than these defences, the only other

[83] Bribery Act 2010, s. 12(5). [84] Section 7(3). [85] Section 8(1).
[86] Section 8(3). [87] See n. 69, above, and associated text.

defence provided by the Act is found under section 13 and is confined to what would otherwise be offences under sections 1 and 2. The defence accommodates the special needs of, respectively, the intelligence service and the military.[88] A defence is provided for P and for R on proof by the person charged with the offence that his conduct was necessary for the proper exercise of any function of an intelligence service or for any function of the armed services when engaged on active service.[89] The head of each of the intelligence services must ensure that arrangements are in place to confine the commission of relevant bribery offences to those that are necessary for the exercise of a service function.[90] An equivalent responsibility falls upon the Defence Council with respect to the armed services.[91] These arrangements must be satisfactory in the judgment of the Secretary of State.[92]

The major problem with this defence, which is not based on any recommendation from the Law Commission for England and Wales, is the potential latitude allowed to what may be highly questionable conduct. To be sure, one can think of circumstances where conduct which contravenes the Act would nonetheless be compellingly in the national interest, such as payments to an Iranian nuclear scientist resulting in the acquisition of vital intelligence. One can be sure that *raison d'état* would ensure that such payments were made without risk of any subsequent prosecution for a bribery offence notwithstanding the absence of any provision along the lines of section 13. The danger with a provision such as section 13 is that it might encourage payments made in circumstances far removed from matters of vital national security. Under section 1(2) of the Intelligence Services Act 1994 the duties of the Intelligence Service include safeguarding the economic well-being of the United Kingdom. An intelligence officer might well conclude that if the large armaments contract in the offing from the government of Erewhon were to be awarded to non-UK companies, the economic well-being of the United Kingdom would be diminished. Hence, his authorisation of large payments to Erewhon commercial agents known to have influence over

[88] The offence of bribing a foreign public official is not a 'relevant bribery offence' for the purposes of section 13 because of concerns about compliance with the OECD Convention on Combating Bribery of Foreign Public Officials.

[89] For a full critical discussion of the issues raised by this defence see J. Horder, 'On Her Majesty's Commercial Service: Bribery, Public Officials and the UK Intelligence Services', *Modern Law Review*, 74 (2011), 911–31.

[90] Bribery Act 2010, s. 13(2). [91] Section 13(3). [92] Section 13(4).

Erewhon government ministers and officials, a decision now less fraught than hitherto because of the enactment of section 13.[93]

Whereas section 13 might facilitate the high-end bribery that in a better ordered world would be subject to consistent prosecution and draconian sanctions, there arises an opposing, yet legitimate, concern that the Bribery Act 2010 might make the lot of victims of extortion even harder than it already is. The case of Bill Shaw is illustrative.[94] Shaw, a UK national based in Afghanistan, was a contractor who supplied and maintained high security vehicles for the safe passage of diplomats and other officials. Several of these vehicles were impounded by Afghan security officials on the basis that the vehicles were unregistered. That was indeed the case because the very same officials had declined to carry out the registration process despite repeated requests from Shaw. Shaw made payments to these officials to secure the release of the vehicles, and on account of these payments he was convicted and imprisoned under the Afghan criminal code for bribery offences. If these events were to repeat themselves it is very likely that Shaw would now commit an offence under section 1 of the Bribery Act 2010. An English court would have jurisdiction because of Shaw's UK nationality. Acceptance of payments from Shaw on the part of Afghan officials would likely of itself constitute improper performance of a relevant function on their part. Obviously, Shaw knew of the circumstances which made for this improper performance. Could Shaw make anything of the fact that in making these payments he was motivated by his legal and moral responsibilities for the safety of embassy staff? It might well be the case that an English court would strive to provide a defence of duress of circumstances/necessity, but doctrinal difficulties would present themselves.[95]

Under the previous law, although there would have been jurisdiction to try the case, a jury would have had to find that Shaw was acting corruptly when making these payments. The jurisprudence on the meaning of 'corruptly' was divergent. On a strict approach the jury might have been directed that Shaw's good motives did not matter provided he was

93 Any direct payment to an Erewhon public official would likely contravene s. 6, an offence which falls outside the protection of s. 13. Payments to intermediaries, however, would not fall within s. 6, failing proof that the intermediaries were mere conduits for payments to public officials that the intelligence officer intended to influence.

94 See at: www.bbc.co.uk//news/10500899.

95 They would revolve around the source of the danger, the nature of the danger and timelines.

aware that the recipient of the payment was corrupt.[96] But there was authority which would have allowed the jury to reflect in a more holistic manner on the moral quality of his conduct, authority which would be strongly pressed in a case such as Shaw's.[97] What is certain is that an acquittal was a possibility under the old law but that outcome is far less likely under the new legislation.

It is submitted that an acquittal is the morally correct result in a case such as Shaw's. In large parts of the world, making what are ostensibly legally binding arrangements to establish a business presence and for the delivery of goods and services is only the start of the journey.[98] It is understandable that bodies with a commitment to changing local cultures, such as the OECD and the UN and NGOs such as Transparency International, favour a strict line on incoming investors and businesses who succumb to local practices. But even the most zealous anti-corruption campaigner might consider what practical impact a conviction in a case such as Shaw's will have on the local culture in Afghanistan. And there are examples nearer to home. Citizens of countries who are members of the EU are entitled to receive emergency medical treatment anywhere within the EU on the same terms and conditions as the local population. But frequently payment in excess of what is legally required is demanded as a condition for providing treatment. Persons succumbing to these demands though concern for the health of themselves or their families should not be at risk of incurring liability for a serious criminal offence.[99]

The Bribery Act 2010 does not recognise the borderline between a corrupt payment intended to secure some advantage, and payments extorted as additional imposts on goods one is entitled to keep or repossess and for services that should be rendered without further costs. At one time the Law Commission for England and Wales favoured a defence of conferring an advantage on R in order to avert what P reasonably believed to be an imminent danger of physical harm to P or another: essentially a defence of duress, but extending to non-serious

96 *R.* v. *Smith* [1960] 2 QB 423; *R.* v. *Wellburn* [1979] 69 Cr App R 254.

97 *R.* v. *Calland* [1967] CLR 236; *R.* v. *Lindley* [1957] CLR 321.

98 For accessible accounts of local trading conditions see Kochan and Goodyear, *Corruption*, ch. 5.

99 The question of whether bribery offences under the Act are potentially committed in these circumstances may be complicated by the fact that in some Member States, payments for medical services rendered to temporary visitors are difficult, even impossible, for the service provider to obtain from public funds.

physical harm.[100] The view taken here is that rather than abandoning this idea it should have been extended to cover payments necessary to secure the health and safety of P and anyone else for whom P is responsible; to recover or retain property P is entitled to keep or to repossess; and to obtain the performance of a service to which P has an entitlement. The counter view would be that this would allow too much scope for commercial organisations to pass off payments made on the initiative of P as payments extorted by R. There is certainly some truth in this, particularly in the matter of payment for services. If P pays R to move his planning application to the head of the queue that is a straightforward bribe, but a payment made to prevent his application from being thrown straight into the bin is a case of extortion. The scope for obfuscation is considerable. In the case of a commercial organisation the defence argued for here should be available only if a contemporaneous report of the payment and the reasons for making it was filed with the relevant prosecuting authority. The making of a false report would be an offence in its own right.[101]

Conclusion

The Bribery Act 2010 is better by some distance than the legislation and associated jurisprudence that it supersedes. Only two reservations of substance arise from the analysis made here: the possibility of raising normative mistakes in answer to some variants of the two core offences; and the failure to be more accommodating to the divide between payments offered as bribes and payments that are extorted. But more important than the state of UK legislation is the commitment of politicians and officials to its enforcement, particularly in cases concerning the bribery of persons overseas. Tolerance of large-scale commission payments to commercial agents remain an impediment in the way of the effective enforcement of anti-bribery legislation.

[100] Law Commission, 'Reforming Bribery', Law Com. CP No. 185, 2007, paras 8.14–8.31.

[101] The Joint Prosecution Guidance of the SFO and the DPP offers no concessions to facilitation payments, but does state that self-reporting and vulnerability are factors weighing against prosecution.

2

Official and commercial bribery: should they be distinguished?

STUART P. GREEN*

In a recent study of how the public views the blameworthiness of various white collar crime-related activity, my collaborator, Matthew Kugler, and I asked our subjects to compare the acts described in two seemingly similar scenarios.[1] In one scenario:

> Jones is 'a member of the upper house of the State Legislature, where he serves on an important legislative committee that is choosing the site of a major new state office building'. Larson is 'CEO of a company that owns property adjacent to one of the sites that Jones' committee is considering'. CEO Larson offers Jones, the legislator, $20,000 in return for Jones' agreeing to vote for the site, and Jones accepts the offer.

In the other scenario:

> Heller is 'a board-member of a large private corporation ... currently serving on an important committee within the company that will choose the site of a major new office building that the company plans to build'. Larson is again 'CEO of a company that owns property adjacent to one of the sites that Heller's committee is considering'. Larson offers Heller, the company board member, $20,000 if Heller votes for the site Larson favours, and Heller accepts the offer.

We asked our subjects: (1) to rate the moral blameworthiness of Jones' and Heller's acts; (2) whether their acts should be treated as criminal; and (3) how severely, if at all, they should be punished.

Under prior law in both the United Kingdom and the United States, the actors in the first scenario (involving acceptance of a payment by a *public* official) would have committed bribery, while the actors in the

* For helpful comments, I am grateful to Peter Alldridge, Jeremy Horder and Mike Koehler.

[1] S. P. Green and M. B. Kugler, 'Public Perceptions of White Collar Crime Culpability: Bribery, Perjury, and Fraud', *Law and Contemporary Problems*, 75 (2012), 33–59.

second scenario (involving acceptance of a payment by a *private* actor) would ordinarily have committed no crime at all. But the law in both jurisdictions has been changing – most dramatically in the newly enacted Bribery Act 2010, which criminalises both official and commercial bribery, and draws no distinction between them. Under US law, the traditional distinction between commercial and official bribery remains sharper, though even here there has been a blurring.

Which approach makes more sense? Should acceptance of a bribe by a private employee be treated as a crime at all? Assuming it should, should it be treated as any less serious a crime than acceptance of a bribe by a government official? And what about the *giving* of a bribe to a private employee: how should that be treated in comparison to the giving of a bribe to a government official? In this chapter, I shall argue that accepting or giving a bribe in the commercial context should indeed be a crime, but one that is conceptually separate from accepting or giving a bribe in the government context.

The law of commercial bribery in the United States

American law has traditionally drawn a sharp distinction between official and commercial bribery. Thus, while bribes paid to government officials have always entailed liability for both the donee and donor, bribes paid to employees of a private firm have traditionally involved liability for neither. Over time, however, this sharp division has softened, and there are now numerous statutes at both the federal and state level that make bribery in the commercial sphere a crime, at least in certain limited circumstances.

Federal law

Typical of the traditional approach is 18 USC § 201, the most venerable federal bribery provision, originally enacted in 1962 to consolidate several separate provisions. There are two separate offences contained in section 201: subsection (b) covers 'bribery' (punishable by up to fifteen years in prison, a fine of three times the value of the bribe and disqualification from holding federal office), while subsection (c) covers the lesser offence of illegal 'gratuities' (punishable by up to two years in prison and a fine). What is important for present purposes is that section 201 is limited to bribes accepted by or given to federal government officials or jurors or witnesses in federal trials and does not generally apply to bribe recipients who work for private firms.[2] Even here, however, there is an exception if the private employee occupies a specific position of trust with official federal responsibilities (e.g., employees of a private non-profit corporation that administer a subgrant from a municipality's federal block grant).[3]

A second major federal anti-corruption statute is 18 USC § 666, which was enacted in 1984 to extend the reach of federal bribery law beyond federal officials, witnesses and jurors, to employees of private firms that receive federal money.[4] Section 666 makes it a crime for a person to give or accept something of value 'in connection with [a] business', if the 'the entity for which the defendant acted as an agent received more than $10,000 a year in federal assistance'. It carries a maximum penalty of ten years in prison.

A third important federal anti-corruption provision is the Hobbs Act, 18 USC § 1951, enacted in 1946, as an amendment to the 1934 Anti-Racketeering Act. Although the Act was originally intended to combat racketeering in labour-management disputes, the statute has frequently been used in connection with cases involving public corruption and commercial disputes. The Act criminalises three distinct forms of criminal conduct: (1) robbery; (2) extortion by force, threat or fear; and (3) extortion under colour of official right. Only the third is relevant here. Extortion under colour of official right consists in the offender's use of his official position to extract something of a value from the alleged victim – understood, essentially, as the taking of a bribe. It is punishable by up to twenty years in prison. Like section 201, the Hobbs Act applies only to bribes taken by government officials, though unlike section 201, the Act applies to bribes taken by state and local officials (such as state legislators, city councillors and mayors) as well as federal officials. (Another important difference is that section 201 applies to both bribees and bribers, while the Hobbs Act applies only to bribees.)

A fourth statute is the Foreign Corrupt Practices Act (FCPA), codified in various provisions of 15 USC §§ 78m, 78dd and 78ff. The FCPA was originally enacted in 1977, in the wake of widespread efforts at government reform. Earlier in the decade, the US Securities and Exchange Commission (SEC) had investigated over 400 US companies alleged to have made a total of more than US$300 million in questionable or illegal

[2] 18 USC § 201(b)(3) and (4).

[3] *Dixson* v. *United States*, 465 US 482, 496 (1984).

[4] See generally G. D. Brown, 'Stealth Statute: Corruption, the Spending Power, and the Rise of 18 U.S.C. § 666', *Notre Dame Law Review*, 73 (1998), 247–314.

payments to foreign government officials, politicians and political parties. One leading case involved Lockheed, which paid foreign officials in the Netherlands, Japan and Italy to favour its company's products. Another was the so-called Bananagate scandal, in which Chiquita Brands bribed the president of Honduras to lower its taxes. The Act was enacted despite substantial concern that it would put American businesses at an economic disadvantage in international business.

The FCPA was signed into law in 1977 and amended in 1998 by the International Anti-Bribery Act, which was designed to implement the anti-bribery conventions of the Organisation for Economic Cooperation and Development. The Act makes it a crime to give payments to 'foreign officials' for the purpose of 'obtaining or retaining business for or with, or directing business to, any person', and further mandates corporate record-keeping that would reveal bribe payments.[5] The Act thus applies to the employees of American companies who *give or offer* bribes to foreign officials, but not to the foreign officials who *accept or solicit* those bribes.[6] Nor does the Act currently apply to those who give bribes to employees of private companies abroad, though, as we shall see below, there has been talk of amending the statute to do just that.

In the first twenty years of its existence, the FCPA was used relatively infrequently. It was not until the early part of the last decade, 'owing to a combination of factors that scholars still only partially understand', that the US Department of Justice and SEC initiated a dramatic surge in enforcement.[7] Today, the FCPA is, as one scholar has put it, 'widely regarded as among the most important and fearsome statutes in international business, with fines routinely reaching into the tens or hundreds of millions of dollars'.[8] Recent FCPA investigations have implicated numerous leading companies, including Maxwell Technologies, Sun Microsystems, Morgan Stanley, Avon, Bridgestone, Aon, Johnson & Johnson, United Parcel Service, Bristol Myers Squibb, Alltel, Alcatel Lucent, Xerox, United Defense Industries, Chiquita Brands, Accenture,

[5] The statute originally applied only to payments originating inside the United States, but was extended in 1998 to reach bribes originating outside the country as well. Thus, US companies are now liable for the acts of their domestic *and* foreign employees.

[6] *United States* v. *Blondek*, 741 F Supp 116, 119–20 (ND Tex. 1990). In other words, the statute applies exclusively to bribers. In that sense, it is the converse of the Hobbs Act.

[7] A. B. Spalding, 'The Irony of International Business Law: US Progressivism, China's New Laissez-Faire, and their Impact in the Developing World', *UCLA Law Review*, 59 (2011), 354–413.

[8] Spalding, 'The Irony of International Business Law'.

DaimlerChrysler, Petro-Canada and Eli Lilly.[9] The result is a statute now celebrated by some as helping to 'effectuate a worldwide sea change in attitudes toward bribery', and derided by others as an agent of 'cultural imperialism'.[10]

In addition to federal statutes that criminalise bribes accepted by government employees, there are also several federal statutes that potentially criminalise bribes accepted by private employees. One is the Anti-Kickback Act, 41 USC §§ 51–58, which prohibits both the giving and receiving of 'kickbacks' involving contractors under federal contracts. The term 'kickback' is defined as any:

> money, fee, commission, credit, gift, gratuity, thing of value, or compensation of any kind which is provided, directly or indirectly, to any prime contractor, prime contractor employee, subcontractor, or subcontractor employee for the purpose of improperly obtaining or rewarding favourable treatment in connection with a prime contract, or in connection with a subcontract relating to a prime contract.[11]

The Act includes a criminal penalty of up to ten years in prison.[12] Like section 666, the Anti-Kickback Act is intended to address the problem of bribes that occur in the context of federal contracts, though unlike section 666, it has no monetary threshold.

Another three federal statutes criminalise commercial bribery by incorporating state commercial bribery laws into federal law. For example, the Travel Act 18 USC § 1952, provides that anyone who travels in interstate commerce with the intent to commit, and who commits, 'any unlawful activity' is guilty of a federal crime, with 'unlawful activity' consisting of a wide range of activity that includes 'bribery ... in violation of the laws of the State in which committed or of the United States'. Thus, as long as the state in which the actor is operating has a commercial bribery statute, the federal government can rely upon the Travel Act to prosecute him for engaging in commercial bribery.[13] To date, at least thirty-five states have enacted commercial bribery statutes that could potentially be used by the Department of Justice as the basis for a Travel

[9] M. Ryznar and S. Korkor, 'Anti-Bribery Legislation in the United States and United Kingdom: A Comparative Analysis of Scope and Sentencing', *Missouri Law Review*, 76 (2011), 415–53, at 415, 417.

[10] Spalding, 'The Irony of International Business Law', 18–19.

[11] 41 USC § 52.

[12] 41 USC § 54.

[13] See *United States* v. *Perrin*, 444 US 37 (1979) (holding that Travel Act applies to bribery in both official and commercial sense).

Act prosecution.[14] Nevertheless, prosecutions under the Travel Act for commercial bribery have been extremely rare, presumably because, in comparison with the Hobbs Act, its penalties are relatively lenient (five years' imprisonment, as opposed to twenty years under the Hobbs Act, as long as no violence is involved).

To a similar effect are the federal mail and wire fraud statutes, 18 USC §§ 1341, 1343, and 1346. Section 1341 makes it a crime to use the mail to execute a 'scheme or artifice to defraud' or to obtain money or property through false or fraudulent pretences, representations or promises. Section 1343 makes it a crime to use interstate wire communications, such as telephone, Internet, television or radio transmissions, to do the same. Section 1346, in turn, provides that a 'scheme or artifice to defraud' includes a 'scheme or artifice to deprive another of the intangible right of honest services'. And what is a 'scheme to deprive another of the intangible right of honest services'? In its latest pronouncement, the Supreme Court has said that honest services fraud consists essentially of bribery and kickbacks, including bribes paid to employees of private firms.[15] Thus, a private employee who accepts a bribe, and does so by means of the mail or wire communications, could be prosecuted for mail or wire fraud, respectively.

Also incorporating state commercial bribery laws into federal law is the Racketeering Influenced and Corrupt Organizations Act (RICO), 18 USC § 1962 *et seq.*, enacted in 1970 for the purpose of combating the influence of organised crime in interstate and foreign commerce. Despite its stated aims, however, RICO has played a relatively minor role in the battle against organised crime, apparently because of ineffective law enforcement and botched prosecutions.[16] If RICO has had an effect anywhere, it has been in the context of routine criminal fraud prosecutions and private civil suits (much encouraged by its treble damages provisions). RICO makes it a crime to invest in, acquire an interest in, maintain control over or conduct the affairs of, an 'enterprise', by means of a 'pattern' of 'racketeering activity', defined to include a wide range of federal and state proscriptions, including state law commercial bribery

[14] J. J. Ansley *et al.*, 'Commercial Bribery and the New International Norms', *Bloomberg Law Reports* (October 2009), available at: http://works.bepress.com/cgi/viewcontent.cgi?article=1005&context=don_berthiaume&sei-redir=1#search=%22travel%20act%20bribery%22.

[15] *Skilling* v. *United States*, 561 US (2010).

[16] For a useful history of RICO's early years, see G. E. Lynch, 'RICO: The Crime of Being a Criminal: Part I', *Columbia Law Review*, 87 (1987), 661–764.

law provisions. To date, however, it does not appear that there have been any criminal RICO cases involving allegations of commercial bribery.[17]

Finally, there is a wide range of federal laws that have been used to prosecute commercial bribery in a variety of specific industries and practices. For example, there are federal statutes making it a crime to give or receive bribes in connection with bank loans, sporting events, employee benefit and pension plans, investment advising, television quiz shows, alcoholic beverages, labour unions, railroad operations and radio play lists.[18]

State law

Beyond those provisions criminalising bribery under federal law there is also a complex collection of corruption and bribery laws that applies in the fifty individual states and the District of Columbia. As in the federal system, the main focus of state bribery enforcement is on bribes taken by governmental officials, including judges, legislators and executive officers. Such statutes are exemplified by (and often modelled on) the bribery provision in the Model Penal Code, which is limited to bribes accepted by, or given to, public servants, party officials, voters and those involved in judicial and administrative proceedings.[19]

But most states also have on the books a variety of provisions that can be used to prosecute one or another form of commercial bribery. There are two basic models that have been followed. The first, less common kind of statute, applies to bribery occurring in practically any commercial context. For example, section 32 of the Texas Penal Code makes it a felony for a fiduciary, such as an agent, employee, trustee, guardian, lawyer, physician, officer, director, partner or manager, to accept or agree to accept any benefit from another person 'on agreement or understanding that the benefit will influence the conduct of the fiduciary in relation to the affairs of his beneficiary'.[20] Similarly, section 180 of the New York Penal Law criminalises both the giving and the receiving of a commercial bribe, defined as a 'benefit [conferred] upon an employee ... without the

[17] G. Heine, B. Huber and T. O. Rose, *Private Commercial Bribery* (Freiburg: International Chamber of Commerce, 2003), p. 517.

[18] For example, 18 USC §§ 212–14 (bank loans); 18 USC § 224 (sporting contests); 18 USC § 1954 (employee pension funds); 27 USC § 205(c) (bribery in alcoholic beverage industry); 29 USC § 186 (bribery of labour representatives); 49 USC § 11907 (bribery of railway employees).

[19] § 240.1. [20] Texas Penal Code, § 32.43.

consent of [his] employer or principal, with intent to influence his conduct in relation to his employer's or principal's affairs'.[21] The more common state approach, however, is to define commercial bribery more narrowly, to apply to individuals working in specific fields of endeavour, such as common carrier and telegraph company employees, labour officials, bank employees and participants in sporting events.[22]

The law of commercial bribery in the United Kingdom

Among the many changes effected by the Bribery Act 2010, one of the most radical concerns the way commercial bribery is handled. The Act criminalises bribery by setting out a number of 'cases' in which bribery is said to exist. Section 1 describes the conduct of the offeror/briber, and section 2 deals with the conduct of the offeree/bribee. For example, it is a crime if a person 'offers, promises or gives a financial or other advantage to another person', if the offeror intends the advantage to 'to reward a person for the improper performance of such a function or activity'. Similarly, it is a crime if one 'requests, agrees to receive or accepts a financial or other advantage intending that, in consequence, a relevant function or activity should be performed improperly'.[23]

What is really novel, however, is section 3, which describes the various 'functions and activities' within which bribery can occur. Here the language is strikingly broad. It refers not only to functions of a 'public nature', but also to activities 'connected with a business' (a term defined to include trades and professions), 'performed in the course of a person's employment', or 'performed by or on behalf of a body of persons (whether corporate or unincorporated)'.[24] The only other requirement is that that the person performing the function or activity be 'expected to perform it in good faith', or 'impartially' or be 'in a position of trust by virtue of performing it'.'[25]

Although there is not yet reported case law interpreting these provisions, it seems clear that they would apply to a broad range of cases of what has traditionally been understood as commercial bribery. For example, in the hypothetical scenario described at the beginning of this

[21] NY Penal Law, §§ 180.00, 180.05.

[22] For a helpful listing, see *United States* v. *Perrin*, 444 US 37, 44 nn. 9, 10 (1979) (listing state commercial bribery statutes).

[23] Bribery Act 2010, s. 2. [24] Section 3(2).

[25] Section 3(3)–(5). And see Sullivan, Chapter 1, above, text at n. 12.

chapter, Larson, the company CEO, offered money to Heller, the corporate board member serving on another firm's building committee, in return for Heller's agreeing to vote for the site favoured by Larson; and Heller accepted the offer. In such a case, both Larson and Heller would be guilty of bribery – Larson, for accepting the bribe, and Heller, for offering it. Larson was clearly performing a function or activity 'connected to a business' and 'performed in the course of a person's employment', and it seems likely that he was expected to perform the function 'in good faith' and 'impartially', and to be 'in a position of trust by virtue of performing it'. It is also clear that Larson accepted, and Heller gave, a 'financial or other advantage intending that, in consequence, a relevant function or activity should be performed improperly'.

The Bribery Act thus effects a significant change from prior law, which had confined its reach to bribery of members, officers and servants of public bodies.[26] To be sure, the old law had extended the reach of bribery law to all 'agents', irrespective of whether the agent was employed or serving in the public or the private sector.[27] Despite its language, however, it appears that the 1906 Act was only rarely used in this manner, presumably because the presumption of 'corruptness' created by Prevention of Corruption Act 1916 applied only to gifts given to public officials.[28] In essence, this presumption meant that public officials would continue to be held to a 'higher standard' than private employees.[29]

Given the magnitude of the change effected by the Bribery Act, it is surprising that its framers had relatively little to say about why they decided to include commercial bribery on the same terms as official bribery. The issue is briefly considered in the Law Commission's 2007 Consultation Paper and its 2008 Report, *Reforming Bribery*. According to the Consultation Paper:

> the main objection to having separate offences is that it is very difficult to define with sufficient clarity the distinction between public sector and private sector functions. Increasingly, what were formerly public sector functions are sub-contracted out to private companies while public bodies now frequently form joint ventures with private companies.[30]

26 Public Bodies Corrupt Practices Act 1889.
27 Prevention of Corruption Act 1906; Law Commission, 'Reforming Bribery,' Law Com. CP No. 185, 2007, para. 1.8, p. 3.
28 Prevention of Corruption Act 1916, s. 2.
29 Law Commission, 'Reforming Bribery', para. 1.13, p. 4.
30 Law Commission, 'Reforming Bribery', para. 1.14, p. 5.

In other words, in the eyes of the Commission, the increasingly blurry line between government and the private sector makes the distinction between official and commercial bribery increasingly irrelevant.

A year later, in its 2008 Report, *Reforming Bribery*, the Commission had not changed its position.[31] It pointed out that:

> it is obviously much more difficult now than it was 100 or more years ago to capture what is meant by 'public bodies'. It may be equally difficult to decide, in relation to a public body, whether someone is a member (or officer, or 'servant') of it, or is alternatively a private person contracted to perform the functions the public body is meant to perform.[32]

The Commission went on:

> so many more private individuals and organisations are now contracted to provide public services, or to provide services to the private sector that have a 'public interest' element to them. In the private sector, the acceptance of advantages in doing business may be perfectly acceptable in many contexts. How, then, should such people or bodies be treated, if there is to be a separate bribery-related offence focused on the 'public' sector? The fact that there is now so much more private sector provision of goods and services in the public interest, makes it hard to argue that no one should ever accept advantages in any form, simply because what they do involves a public service dimension.[33]

Thus, based primarily on the supposed difficulty of distinguishing between official bribery and commercial bribery, the Commission, and ultimately Parliament, settled on a single undifferentiated definition of bribery, one which did not distinguish between bribery in the public and private sector. Under the new scheme, either type of bribery would subject the offender to the possibility of as much as ten years in prison and a fine.[34]

There is, however, a certain ambiguity in the Commission's rationale. Was it saying: (1) that the distinction between official and commercial bribery might still matter in the abstract, but, given the recent blurring between the public and private sectors, simply cannot be maintained in

[31] As a consultant to the Law Commission, I tried to get the Commission to think more about this issue, by submitting a comment that objected to treating official and commercial bribery as equivalent without further discussion, but, alas, my objection seems to have had little effect.

[32] Law Commission, *Reforming Bribery, Reforming Bribery: Report*, Law Com. No. 313 (London: The Stationery Office, 2008), para. 3.19, p. 19.

[33] Paragraph 3.216, p. 58 (footnote omitted).

[34] Bribery Act 2010, s. 11.

practice; (2) that even if the distinction could be maintained in practice, it would not matter in the abstract because there is no normative difference between the two kinds of bribery; or (3) that even if the distinction mattered in theory or in practice, it is not a distinction that needs to be maintained in the Bribery Act itself; whatever differences there are between official and commercial bribery can be worked out by prosecutors and judges in the exercise of their discretion to prosecute and to sentence, respectively.

Is the distinction between official and commercial bribery worth preserving?

In the previous section, we observed a dramatic shift in UK law, and a somewhat less significant shift in US law, towards the criminalisation of commercial bribery.[35] The question now is whether this shift makes sense. Should commercial bribery be treated as a crime; if so, should it and official bribery be treated as distinct? We begin by considering an empirical study that tested people's attitudes towards the two kinds of offence. We then look at the merits of non-differentiation from a conceptual and policy standpoint.

Empirical study of public attitudes concerning bribery

As part of a larger project on public attitudes regarding various issues in white collar crime, my collaborator, Matthew Kugler, and I conducted an empirical study that examined how the 'man in the street' views the relative blameworthiness of various bribery-related acts.[36]

Procedure followed

The study (described in more detail in our previous article) involved fifty-two participants (all Americans: fifteen male, thirty-seven female) recruited from Amazon's Mechanical Turk service. Data from three were discarded due to abnormally fast completion times (< ½ the median) or incorrectly answering a question intended to screen inattentive participants.

[35] Something similar can be observed in a host of other jurisdictions as well. See Heine *et al.*, *Private Commercial Bribery* (surveying Czech Republic, France, Germany, Italy, Japan, Korea, the Netherlands, Poland, Spain, Sweden and Switzerland, in addition to the United States and England and Wales).

[36] Green and Kugler, 'Public Perceptions of White Collar Crime Seriousness'.

Of the remaining forty-nine (fifteen male, thirty-four female), the median age was thirty-three. Fifty-one per cent of participants had college degrees. Participants were also asked a range of questions about their political orientation, faith in various public institutions, and beliefs regarding the extent to which the world is a competitive place.[37]

The basic procedure consisted of giving participants a core 'story' with multiple possible 'endings' and asking them to make distinctions, if any, where relevant. After each scenario, participants were asked three questions. First, they were asked to rate the moral blameworthiness of the described act on a scale ranging from 1 (not at all blameworthy) to 7 (very blameworthy). Secondly, they were asked whether the act should be treated as criminal (yes/no). Thirdly, they were asked how severely, if at all, the person should be punished on a scale ranging from 1 (no punishment) to 7 (severely punished).

Basic demographics (age, sex, occupation, educational attainment and state of residence) were collected at the end of the study. Participants were also asked whether they had ever run for public office, held a position of responsibility at a larger firm, worked at a company with a gifts policy, been involved in lobbying or given money to a political candidate.

Among other issues, we wanted to know how our subjects would regard a bribe paid to a government official in comparison to a bribe paid to a business person. As described in the introduction to the chapter, several of the scenarios were intended to test this distinction. In one scenario, an offer of money was accepted by a member of the state legislature in return for his agreeing to vote for a building being placed at a particular location. In the other scenario, the offer of money was accepted by a board member of a large private corporation who would be voting on a similar issue. In both cases, the amount of money offered was the same. Alternative scenarios also involved 'gratuities' being given to a retiring official and to an official with no plans to retire.

Results of the study

An overwhelming majority of subjects regarded both cases of receiving a bribe as blameworthy and deserving of significant punishment (see Table 2.1). But the case involving official bribery was rated as more

[37] C. G. Sibley and J. Duckitt, 'Big-Five Personality, Social Worldviews, and Ideological Attitudes: Further Tests of a Dual Process Cognitive–Motivational Model', *Journal of Social Psychology*, 149 (2009), 545–61.

Table 2.1 *Ratings of public versus private scenarios in terms of blameworthiness, deserved punishment and percentage of the sample criminalising the activity*

	Blameworthiness	Punishment	Per cent Criminalising
Payment accepted by public official	6.67_a (1.05)	5.90_a (1.37)	$95.9\%_a$
Payment accepted by private employee	6.06_a (1.72)	4.88_a (1.88)	$79.6\%_b$

For each variable, numbers sharing subscripts are not significantly different from each other.
Standard deviations are in parentheses. Blameworthiness and punishment scores are on scales ranging from 1 to 7.

blameworthy than that involving commercial bribery. When the bribe was accepted by the public official, almost 96 per cent of respondents said that it should be treated as a crime. When the bribe was accepted by the board member of a large company, nearly 80 per cent of our subjects said that this should be treated as a crime – less than in the context of official bribery, but still substantial. With respect to blameworthiness judgments and amount of punishment recommended, we found a similar pattern. Acceptance of a bribe by a public official was rated as 6.67 on the blameworthiness scale, while acceptance of a bribe by a private employee was rated as 6.06.[38] And with respect to punishment deserved, official bribery was rated as 5.90, while commercial bribery was rated as 4.88.

[38] The individual differences analysis for this study created separate composites for the private and the public bribee cases, combining the bribery and gratuity cases for each. Two individual difference factors emerged as significant. When the receiver of funds was a private official, a participant who had worked at a company that had a gift policy was more likely to criminalise the private official's actions ($\beta = 0.27, p = 0.05$) and rate them as blameworthy ($\beta = 0.36, p < 0.05$) and assign higher punishments ($\beta = 0.37, p < 0.05$). Participants high in competitive world beliefs, a measure of support for social Darwinist dog-eat-dog attitudes, were somewhat less likely to criminalise a private official accepting money ($\beta = 0.27$, $p = 0.05$), but there was no effect on the other measures. When the receiver of funds was a public official, the same two factors were relevant. Again, if the participant had worked at a company that had a gift policy, they were more likely to criminalise the official's actions ($\beta = 0.32, p < 0.05$) and rate them as highly blameworthy ($\beta = 0.34$, $p < 0.05$). If the participant was high in competitive world beliefs, they were

Why citizens' intuitions matter

The question being tested in the empirical study was whether people's intuitions about the blameworthiness of different forms of bribery are consistent or inconsistent with how such offences are treated by modern law. What citizens think about such issues matters, as I have discussed elsewhere, for a number of reasons.[39]

Most scholars agree that society's ability to enforce compliance with the law lies less in the power to impose sanctions than it does in the norms by which people direct their lives. Generally, people refrain from committing crimes not because they fear sanctions if they do, but because they believe it is morally wrong to do so.[40] Thus, it is important that the law be consistent with moral norms. As Paul Robinson and John Darley have put it:

> The criminal justice system's power to stigmatise depends on the legal codes having moral credibility in the community. The law needs to have earned a reputation for accurately representing what violations do and do not deserve moral condemnation from the community's point of view. This reputation will be undercut if liability and punishment rules deviate from a community's shared intuitions of justice.[41]

Where the criminal law is viewed as offering a reliable statement of what the community regards as wrongful citizens are more likely to follow its lead in cases which are unclear. When criminal codes deviate from the norms of the community, citizens may be less likely to cooperate with or acquiesce to the system's demands.[42]

again less likely to criminalise the official's actions ($\beta = 0.39$, $p < 0.01$) or rate them as highly blameworthy ($\beta = 0.39$, $p < 0.01$). There were no effects of either factor on punishment for the public official.

39 The discussion in this section borrows from Green and Kugler, 'Public Perceptions of White Collar Crime Seriousness', and S. P. Green, *Thirteen Ways to Steal a Bicycle: Theft Law in the Information Age* (Cambridge, MA: Harvard University Press, 2012).

40 See, e.g., T. Tyler, *Why People Obey the Law* (New Haven, CT: Yale University Press, 1990).

41 P. H. Robinson and J. M. Darley, 'Intuitions of Justice: Implications for Criminal Law and Justice Policy', *Southern California Law Review*, 81 (2007), 1–67, at 21. See also P. H. Robinson and J. M. Darley, *Justice, Liability, and Blame: Community Views and the Criminal Law* (Boulder, CO: Westview Press, 1995); P. H. Robinson and J. M. Darley, 'Testing Competing Theories of Justification', *North Carolina Law Review*, 76 (1998), 1095–143; J. M. Darley *et al.*, 'Community Standards for Defining Attempt: Inconsistencies with the Model Penal Code', *American Behavioral Scientist*, 39 (1996), 405–20.

42 E. Mullen and J. Nadler, 'Moral Spillovers: The Effect of Moral Mandate Violations on Deviant Behavior', *Journal of Experimental Social Psychology*, 44 (2008), 1239–45;

It is not merely the case that social norms play a role in shaping the criminal law. The criminal law also plays an important role in informing, shaping and reinforcing societal norms. Children and adults learn what is wrong in part from what the law says is wrong. Where the law deviates too far from existing norms, its instructive function is impaired as well.

Maintaining consistency between the law and social norms is important not only in connection with deciding *which* conduct should or should not be criminalised; it is also vital in deciding *how much* to punish. If the legal system imposes more, or less, punishment on some crimes than citizens believe is deserved, the system seems unfair; it loses its credibility, and ultimately its effectiveness.

What is ultimately at stake here is what Andrew Ashworth has called the 'principle of fair labelling' – the idea that 'widely felt distinctions between kinds of offences and degrees of wrongdoing are respected and signalled by the law, and that offences should be divided and labelled so as to represent fairly the nature and magnitude of the law-breaking'.[43] As Ashworth puts it, 'one of the basic aims of the criminal law is to ensure a proportionate response to law-breaking, thereby assisting the law's educative or declaratory function in sustaining and reinforcing social standards'.[44] Where people consistently regard two or more types of conduct as different in terms of blameworthiness, the law ought to reflect those differences. Other things being equal, it ought to punish the more blameworthy act more severely and the less blameworthy act less severely.

All of these considerations would seem to apply in the case of bribery. If the law treats some kinds of bribery more, or less, harshly than people believe they should be treated, it seems unjust and out of step, and likely is to lose some of its moral authority and effectiveness.

I should be clear, however, about what I believe is, and is not, the value of studying community attitudes regarding crime seriousness.[45] First, I do not mean to suggest that the criminal law should always follow popular opinion, or that people's moral intuitions are necessarily

J. Nadler, 'Flouting the Law', *Texas Law Review*, 83 (2005), 1399–441; Robinson and Darley, 'Intuitions of Justice', p. 23; W. Stuntz, 'Self-Defeating Crimes', *Virginia Law Review*, 86 (2000), 1871–900.

43 A. Ashworth, *Principles of Criminal Law*, 4th edn (Oxford University Press, 2003), pp. 89–90. For a critique, see J. Chalmers and F. Leverick, 'Fair Labelling in Criminal Law', *Modern Law Review*, 71 (2008), 217–46.

44 Ashworth, *Principles of Criminal Law*, p. 90.

45 This paragraph borrows from my book, *Thirteen Ways to Steal a Bicycle*.

correct.[46] Secondly, I do not mean to imply that empirical studies of this sort should provide a substitute for serious normative reflection about deontological desert.[47] Thirdly, I acknowledge that giving subjects relatively brief descriptions of fictional crimes and asking them to make blameworthy judgments is not the only, and perhaps not even the most accurate, way to assess their views regarding the relative blameworthiness of criminal acts.[48] Fourthly, while I do believe that the prohibition of at least certain kinds of bribes is probably universal, I make no claim that the distinction between official and commercial bribery is also universal.[49] Rather, I view empirical studies regarding community views of crime seriousness as a *supplement* to normative analysis, a way for the analyst (in this case, me) to check the validity of his or her own intuitions, and as a means for assessing the likely effectiveness of offence grading.

The dangers of over-particularism

To say that the law should, to some degree, reflect widely felt distinctions between kinds of wrongdoing is not to deny the potential for *over*-particularism. As James Chalmers and Fiona Leverick have argued, 'not only does [very specific crime labelling] over-complicate the law, running the risk of needless arguments about the appropriate charge in respect of indisputably criminal conduct, it also runs the risk that novel conduct will not be covered at all because offences have been drawn up with too high a degree of specificity'.[50] For example, it could be the case that mutually exclusive statutes criminalising official and commercial bribery

46 Cf. A. J. Kolber, 'How to Improve Empirical Desert', *Brooklyn Law Review*, 75 (2009), 433–61, at 436 (even if a large majority of people believed that 'it is immoral to permit people of the same sex to marry each other, we might resist the idea that such intuitions alone, even if they represent a consensus view, provide *any* moral support for prohibiting same-sex marriage').

47 Cf. M. Sigler, 'The Methodology of Desert', *Arizona State Law Journal*, 42 (2011), 1173–202; C. Slobogin, 'Is Justice Just Us? Using Social Science to Inform Substantive Criminal Law', *Journal of Criminal Law & Criminology*, 87 (1996), 315–33; K. W. Simons, 'The Relevance of Community Values to Just Deserts: Criminal Law, Punishment Rationales, and Democracy', *Hofstra Law Review*, 28 (2000), 635–66 (all criticising empirical desert approach on this ground).

48 Cf. Kolber, 'How to Improve Empirical Desert', pp. 441–3 (criticising the work of Paul Robinson on this ground).

49 Cf. Z. R. Calo, 'Empirical Desert and the Moral Economy of Punishment', *Arizona State Law Journal*, 42 (2011), 1123–40, at 1136–7 (discussing the relationship between empirical desert and universal moral judgments).

50 Chalmers and Leverick, 'Fair Labelling in Criminal Law', p. 239.

statutes would create a situation in which a defendant charged with one offence could avoid conviction by arguing that he had actually committed a different offence. Something similar was said to have occurred under the common law of theft, where a defendant charged with, say, embezzlement, could avoid conviction by showing that he had actually committed false pretences, or vice versa.[51] The solution of twentieth-century law reformers was to treat most previously distinct forms of theft as undifferentiated and, in effect, to leave it to sentencing courts to sort out which kinds of theft should be punished more or less severely.

The Bribery Act has followed a similar approach, making no distinction between official and commercial bribery, though presumably leaving to prosecutors and judges (at sentencing) the discretion to do so. As I have argued with respect to theft law itself, however, I am sceptical that such legislative levelling is necessary or appropriate. Given the reduction in indeterminate sentencing and increased reliance on strict sentencing guidelines that have occurred in the United States and to a somewhat lesser extent in the United Kingdom, it seems unlikely that courts will have the discretion to make the kinds of distinction that arguably need to be made. And, even if judges and prosecutors could differentiate in ways that Parliament has chosen not to, this would not resolve the basic issue: namely, whether there is a moral difference between commercial and official bribery; and, if so, is that difference, balanced against concerns about the law's administrability, sufficient to justify treating them as separate offences?

Conceptual and policy analysis

What explains the fact that, while a large number of respondents believed that both official bribery and commercial bribery should be treated as a crime, most people also believed that official bribery was the more serious offence? Were they right? To answer that question, it is necessary to examine the moral content of official and commercial bribery, as well as some of the policy concerns that underlie the criminalisation of such practices. We begin by considering the moral content of bribe-accepting, and then turn to the moral content of bribe-giving.

[51] This problem is dealt with at length in Green, *Thirteen Ways to Steal a Bicycle*.

Accepting a bribe

As I have explained in earlier work, the acceptance of a bribe involves, at its core, the misuse of the bribee's position for personal gain.[52] It reflects a kind of disloyalty: rather than serving the interests of the principal to whom he owes a fiduciary duty, the bribee serves his own interests instead.

Consider again the hypotheticals used in the empirical study: in both, money was given by CEO Larson 'under the table' in return for a favourable vote on the siting of a new office building. In one case, the bribe was taken by a state legislator (Jones). In the other, the bribe was taken by a board member of a private corporation (Heller). Both Jones and Heller put their own interests before those of their principals: in Jones' case, before those of his constituents, his public office and the community at large; in Heller's case, before those of his firm, its management and its shareholders.

The question, then, is whether breach of a duty to a public office is any more (or less) harmful or wrongful than, or qualitatively different from, breach of a duty to a private employer.

In an age in which corporate entities have a greater reach into our lives than ever before, there is no reason to assume that the corrupt decisions of company employees will necessarily cause less harm than the corrupt decisions of public officials. Indeed, a corrupt decision made by a bribe-taking executive of a Fortune 500 company might adversely affect the lives of many more victims than a corrupt decision made by a bribe-taking judge, city councillor or even a member of Congress. The real question, then, is whether, *ceteris paribus*, the wrongs and harms of official bribery differ qualitatively from those of commercial bribery.

Bribery, in both the public and commercial sphere, is said to 'corrupt' political and commercial life by inviting inappropriate grounds for decision-making.[53] It makes the decision-maker unable or unwilling to determine what is in the best interest of his principal. (This is not to say that every act of bribery will necessarily lead to any actual bad decisions: a legislator or judge, corporate executive or department store buyer can be bribed into making the same, objectively 'correct' decision she would

[52] See S. P. Green, *Lying, Cheating, and Stealing: A Moral Theory of White Collar Crime* (Oxford University Press, 2006), pp. 193–211.

[53] See generally A. J. Heidenheimer, M. Johnson and V. T. LeVine (eds), *Political Corruption: A Handbook* (New Brunswick, NJ: Transaction Publishers, 1989).

have made absent the bribe. All that is required is that the decision-making process itself be corrupted by the payment of the bribe.[54])

But beyond that similarity there are significant differences. Those who hold public office have duties that are qualitatively different from those held by employees of private firms. In a democracy, they typically hold their jobs either because they were directly chosen by the people or because they were appointed by, and serve at the pleasure of, those who were popularly elected. They are frequently charged with 'serving', 'protecting', 'preserving' or 'defending' the public interest, and doing so 'truly' and 'faithfully'. To accept a bribe is to violate that trust, to betray one's office and the polity, to commit a kind of 'treason'.[55] Public officials, at whatever level they function, are charged with representing and working on behalf of the public good. They are supposed to represent all their constituents, not just those who pay them money under the table. When public officials accept bribes, they undermine a process in which all their constituents theoretically have an interest. For example, in the hypothetical described above, Jones' constituents had the right to expect their legislator to decide how to vote on the site of the building based on his assessment of what was in the best interest of those constituents or perhaps of society at large.

Bribes in the private sphere reflect a quite different dynamic. Private employees who accept bribes also violate a trust, but it is a trust owed to a private firm, to their superiors, colleagues, customers or shareholders. No matter how large their companies might be, and how many 'victims' their conduct might ultimately affect, such employees are engaged in a process that is at its core a private one. Their internal decision-making procedures are not governed by public law in the same way that public officials' decision-making procedures are. Private company officials ordinarily have no obligation to the general public other than that specifically imposed on them by law.

Customers who buy goods from a private firm have no right to expect that the company makes its decisions about the products and services it sells in any particular way, or to expect that the company's decisions have been made in their best interest. As long as the company does not misrepresent the products it is selling, or violate laws concerning safety, public health or other regulatory matters, it has not violated any legal

[54] The issue is dealt with in more detail in Green, *Lying, Cheating, and Stealing*, pp. 205–7.

[55] See D. H. Lowenstein, 'Political Bribery and the Intermediate Theory of Politics', *UCLA Law Review*, 32 (1985), 784–850, at 806.

duty in selling a lower quality product. If the company is to be punished for its inferior product or service, it is the market that will do the punishing. Nor do customers normally have any legitimate expectation regarding the 'process' by which the company makes its decisions. Even shareholders of the firm have no right to assume that the company will make its decisions in a certain way, unless such procedures have been specified.

Whether a private employee is expected to perform his duties 'impartially' (in the language of section 3(4) of the Bribery Act) will depend on the norms of the particular industry in which he works. For example, David Mills and Robert Weisberg, citing Jonathan Klick, have suggested that in dealings between auto repair shops and the insurance industry, commercial bribes and kickbacks are sometimes viewed as akin to 'performance bonds' in the sense that they operate to ensure the continuing quality of the work being performed.[56] Imagine that an insurance company recommended particular auto repair shops to its policyholders seeking to have insured work performed. If the insurance company received an upfront payment or a discount, but paid above-market prices as the repair shops proved the high quality of their work, a performance bond would be created. If the shop failed to continue providing high quality service, then the insurance company would presumably steer its policyholders elsewhere and the repair shop would lose its bond. Although the performance bond would be fostering above-market pricing, it would nevertheless create competition among repair shops to provide the best service. It might thereby provide better protection from low-quality repairs than the prohibition on steering itself.[57]

[56] D. Mills and R. Weisberg, 'Corrupting the Harm Requirement in White Collar Crime', *Stanford Law Review*, 60 (2008), 1371–445, at 1413 (citing J. Klick, 'Performance of Bond Pooling: An Efficiency Argument for Insurance Steering', unpublished manuscript, 2004).

[57] Mills and Weisberg, 'Corrupting the Harm Requirement in White Collar Crime', pp. 1413–14. Something similar, they say, occurs with respect to 'soft dollar' arrangements in the institutional financial services industry. *Ibid.* p. 1414 (citing S. Horan and D. B. Johnsen, 'Does Soft Dollar Brokerage Benefit Portfolio Investors: Agency Problem or Solution?', *George Mason Law & Economics Research Paper No. 04–50*, March (2004), available at SSRN: http://ssrn.com/abstract=615281 or doi:10.2139/ssrn.615281. According to Mills and Weisberg, soft dollars are essentially a kickback from a broker to a portfolio manager, and, as in the case of the insurance industry, can serve as a kind of performance bond that ensures the quality of brokerage service. For the contrary view that commercial bribery has no 'redeeming pro-competitive attributes', see F. A. Gevurtz, 'Commercial Bribery and the Sherman Act: The Case for Per Se Illegality', *University of Miami Law Review*, 42 (1987), 365–400, at 393.

In the case of public employees, it is hard to imagine that such practices would be tolerated. Whatever benefits they confer upon the public through the exercise of their duties is supposed to be done on the basis of some impartial and objective criteria, determined in accordance with law or the public interest, rather than on the basis of their own personal enrichment. The idea that public officials might provide better 'service' in return for payment under the table is anathema to the idea of good government. Government is not, in the normal course of affairs, a competitive industry. In the American context, local town councils typically have a monopoly over trash pick-up, law enforcement, public schools and public parks; state governments have a monopoly over state parks and state courts; the federal government has a monopoly over national defence, social security, customs and immigration. It is simply implausible to suggest that money paid to a congressman or judge could somehow function as a 'performance bond' to ensure high-quality performance. (This is not to say that there are not cultures in which it is common practice for citizens to give 'grease payments' to, say, police officers or customs agents in return for special treatment. But, at least in Western democracies, which tend to put a high value on legality, procedural regularity, equal treatment and transparency, such practices are highly disfavoured.)

Finally, it should be noted that the argument offered here in some respects parallels an argument made by Peter Alldridge, though it follows from a very different premise.[58] Alldridge argues that the problem with bribery derives not from a breach of trust, but rather from the deleterious effects of corruption on the proper functioning of governments and markets. According to this account, bribery in the private sphere 'distorts[s] the operation of a legitimate market', whereas bribery in the public sphere creates 'a market in things that should never be sold'.[59] (For this reason, Alldridge has also been critical of the Law Commission's tendency to conflate public and private bribery.) Elsewhere, I have explained why I prefer a breach-of-trust-based account of bribery to a market-based one.[60] Nevertheless, Alldridge's idea that there is

[58] P. Alldridge, 'The Law Relating to Free Lunches', *Company Lawyer*, 23 (2002), 264–73, at 267.

[59] Alldridge, 'The Law Relating to Free Lunches'.

[60] See Green, *Lying, Cheating, and Stealing*, p. 196 n. 13; S. P. Green, 'Broadening the Scope of Criminal Law Scholarship', *Criminal Justice Ethics*, 20 (2001), 55–62.

something *qualitatively* different about dealing in government and private services is very much consistent with my own views.

Blurring the public–private distinction

Even if the distinction between bribery in the public sphere and bribery in the private sphere were accepted in the abstract, it might still be contended that the distinction does not reflect the reality of modern life in the industrialised world today, in which public and private functions have been blurred. The argument, I take it, is not that the public–private distinction is meaningless or irrelevant in theory (though a long line of legal realists and critical legal scholars have come close to arguing just that[61]), but rather that the distinction has become so hazy in practice that it is no longer worth preserving. According to this view, the Heller and Jones scenarios themselves would be regarded as artificial in that they draw an unrepresentative picture of the spheres in which bribery actually takes place.

As noted above, it is the belief that public and private have become thoroughly blurred that was a major motivation behind the Law Commission's decision to do away with the distinction between commercial and public bribery. Similar concerns have also been expressed in the context of the FCPA. For example, in June 2011, the House Judiciary Committee's Subcommittee on Crime, Terrorism, and Homeland Security held a hearing on the reform of the FCPA. During the hearing, the Chair of the Committee, Representative James Sensenbrenner, pressed Greg Andres, the Justice Department official whose office oversees FCPA enforcement, about confusion with respect to the question of what constitutes a 'public official' under the Act.[62] Sensenbrenner asked: '[would] the Department approve an amendment to the Foreign Corrupt Practices Act to use the statute on bribing somebody in a commercial contract to apply to any type of bribery and forget about this debate on who a foreign official is, because bribery is bribery?'[63] Anders responded

[61] The *locus classicus* is R. L. Hale, 'Coercion and Distribution in a Supposedly Non-Coercive State', *Political Science Quarterly*, 38 (1923), 470–94.

[62] Foreign Corrupt Practice Act: Hearing before the Subcommittee on Crime, Terrorism, and Homeland Security of the Committee on the Judiciary, House of Representatives, 112th Congress, First Session (14 June 2011), Serial No. 112-47, available at: http://judiciary.house.gov/hearings/hear_06142011.html. Thanks to Mike Koehler for bringing these proceedings to my attention.

[63] Foreign Corrupt Practice Act: Hearing before the Subcommittee on Crime, Terrorism, and Homeland Security, p. 75.

that, 'obviously the Department is more than willing to work with Congress on any possible changes', to which Sensenbrenner replied, 'Okay. Well, the invitation is there, and we are going to be drafting a bill.'[64]

Certainly, recent years have seen a significant trend in this direction. Functions that were once thought of as exclusively governmental – such as operating prisons, schools, the post office and various utilities – have increasingly been taken over by private entities. Meanwhile, functions once viewed as predominantly private – such as banking and insurance – have in many instances become 'nationalised', or at least subject to extensive government involvement. And there is a host of positions that truly straddle the line, such as political party leaders (who may hold no public office themselves, but who clearly have influence over public officials), and private trustees of government employee pension funds.[65]

The extent to which the public and private have been blurred is, of course, an empirical question that could not be resolved without extensive research. My own sense is that the claim of blurring has been overstated. In a significant percentage of cases, we should still be able to say quite clearly whether the recipient of a given bribe is a public actor or a private actor. And where bribees are acting in a purely private capacity, I see no reason to subject them to the same legal standard as bribees acting in a public capacity. For example, in the scenario used in the empirical study, Heller was a board member of a large private corporation, while Jones was a member of the state legislature. Both took bribes in return for agreeing to vote for the briber's favoured location for the building. The effects of their votes on the community at large would presumably be similar. But the character of the bribes is quite different. Jones has betrayed the public trust in a way that Heller simply has not.

And what of those cases in which we genuinely cannot distinguish between public and private? It seems to me reasonable to say that, where private firms take on significant public functions, they should be regarded as 'public' for the purposes of bribery law. For example, in the *Dixson* case, a private social services corporation was given the responsibility of administering a federal housing and urban development programme. Officers of the corporation, responsible for the expenditure of federal funds, were alleged to have used their positions to extract

[64] Foreign Corrupt Practice Act: Hearing before the Subcommittee on Crime, Terrorism, and Homeland Security, p. 75.

[65] Mills and Weisberg, 'Corrupting the Harm Requirement in White Collar Crime', p. 1401.

kickbacks from contractors seeking to work on housing rehabilitation projects.[66] Inasmuch as the employees of the firm were performing a 'governmental' role, it makes sense to say that they were acting in a 'public' capacity and that, in taking kickbacks, they breached a duty they had to the public at large.

The converse, however, is not true. Where government officials act in 'proprietary'-type roles, it does not follow that the bribes they accept should thereby be treated as private. A government official who works for an agency that buys or sells scrap metal, provides health care, or runs a railroad is still a government official. He still has a duty to the public, and there is no reason to exempt him from the special obligations that such officials have.

Giving a bribe

Having considered the distinction between official and commercial bribery on the bribe-*acceptance* side, we now need to consider the distinction between official and commercial bribery on the bribe-*giving* side. Before we do that, however, we need to consider the difference between bribe-taking and bribe-giving more generally.

Most of the leading statutes in the United States and the United Kingdom treat the giving and acceptance of a bribe as equivalent. (There are, however, exceptions: as we saw above, under the FCPA only the giving of a bribe is actionable, while under the Hobbs Act only the acceptance of a bribe is.) Does it make sense to treat bribe-giving and bribe-taking in this manner?

In the empirical study described above, after subjects were asked for their views on various scenarios involving the acceptance of a bribe by a government official, they were then asked for their views on the official's bribe-giving. (We did not ask subjects about the wrongfulness of a bribe given to a private employee.) The differences were not as significant as we had anticipated. Almost all of our subjects said that both the acceptance of a bribe by, and the offering of a bribe to, a public official should be treated as a crime, though acceptance was viewed as slightly more blameworthy and deserving of greater punishment than giving (see Table 2.2).[67]

[66] *Dixson* v. *United States*, 465 US 482 (1984).

[67] An earlier study by the National White Collar Crime Center had also addressed this issue, asking respondents to compare the seriousness of a bribe accepted by a public official to a bribe offered by a private citizen. Seventy-four per cent of respondents said it was more

Table 2.2 *Ratings of accepting versus giving bribe scenarios in terms of blameworthiness, deserved punishment and percentage of the sample criminalising the activity*

	Blameworthiness	Punishment	Per cent Criminalising
Payment accepted by public official	6.67_a (1.05)	5.90_a (1.37)	$95.9\%_a$
Payment given to public official	$6.45(1.32)_a$	5.57_a (1.73)	$93.9\%_a$

For each variable, numbers sharing subscripts are not significantly different from each other.
Standard deviations are in parentheses. Blameworthiness and punishment scores are on scales ranging from 1 to 7.

The results were somewhat surprising. We had thought that our subjects would perceive a more decisive difference between accepting and giving a bribe. As previously suggested, soliciting or accepting a bribe seems to involve a kind of disloyalty. Both public officials and private employees are supposed to work in the best interests of their constituents or institutions, rather than in the interest of third parties who tempt them. Offering or giving a bribe, by contrast, seems to involve a very different dynamic: in contrast to the bribee, the briber normally has no duty of loyalty to violate.

So why was the offering of a bribe viewed as blameworthy and deserving of criminal punishment by so a high percentage of respondents? I can think of two possible explanations. The first is that the briber was seen as inducing the bribee to be disloyal. As such, he was acting as an accomplice: influencing, encouraging or persuading another to do wrong. What is unclear is whether, other things being equal, inducing another to do a wrongful act should be regarded as more or less wrongful than doing the wrongful act oneself.[68] One can certainly imagine a reading of the scenario in which the bribe-offerer

serious for a public official to accept a bribe; 12 per cent said it was more serious for a private citizen to give a bribe; and 12 per cent said they were equally serious. National White Collar Crime Center, *National Public Survey on White Collar Crime* (Fairmont, VA: National White Collar Crime Center, 2000), p. 13.

[68] I address the issue in Green, *Lying, Cheating, and Stealing*, p. 203.

was seen as a more active, and therefore more blameworthy, player than the relatively passive bribe-taker.

A second possibility is that the offering of a bribe involves a kind of unfair competition or 'cheating'. In the typical case, the briber is seeking to obtain an unfair advantage over his non-bribe-paying 'competitors'. For example, a defence contractor gives a bribe to a procurement officer with the understanding that his bid will be viewed more favourably than his competitors' bids, despite the fact that it is no better in terms of quality, price or other material qualities. A gambler gives a bribe to a referee with the understanding that the referee will use his position to help the gambler's favoured team win the game. By seeking and obtaining an unfair advantage over his competitors, the briber in each case does them harm and wrong.

The question here, though, is whether we should treat those who 'cheat' in the public sphere (by giving a bribe to a congressperson or procurement officer) the same as those who 'cheat' in the commercial context (by giving a bribe to a basketball referee or department store buyer). It seems to me that, in the ordinary case, there is an important difference – one that parallels the difference in the context of accepting a bribe. A constituent who gives his congressperson a bribe for the purpose of inducing her to vote for legislation he favours is wronging not just his political adversaries, but also the political process and perhaps his fellow citizens. Rather than working through legitimate channels to rally public opinion and persuade the legislator of the correctness of his views on the merits, the briber of a public official attempts to short-circuit the process, to the detriment of the public at large. By contrast, the salesman who gives a bribe to the department store buyer presents a quite different profile. He is harming not the political process, but, rather, the market process. Rather than competing, as he should, on the basis of quality and price, he is attempting to circumvent the market by means of a bribe. As for the government contractor who bribes the procurement official at the Defence Department, and in many ways resembles the wholesaler who bribes the department store buyer, he nevertheless undermines a governmental process in which the broader public has a significant interest.

My claim is not that one form of bribe-giving is necessarily more wrongful or harmful than the other. My claim is simply that these acts involve quite distinct kinds of harm and wrong, and that under the principle of fair labelling the law should therefore treat them as distinct offences.

Conclusion

For most of its long history, 'bribery' meant official bribery: it was a crime for a judge or a legislator to accept money in return for an official act, but not for a private employee to do the same.[69] In recent years, prohibitions on commercial bribery have become increasingly widespread. There is a growing recognition that bribery in the business sphere impedes good decision-making, wastes resources, harms consumers and creates anti-competitive conditions. It makes sense to treat commercial bribery as a crime. But it is a crime the moral and political character of which justifies treatment as distinct from official bribery.

[69] For an interesting, if somewhat idiosyncratic, treatment of official bribery from an historical perspective, see J. T. Noonan, Jr., *Bribes: The Intellectual History of a Moral Idea* (Berkeley, CA: University of California Press, 1984). In more than 800 pages of historical analysis, Noonan has virtually nothing to say about commercial bribery.

3

Countering corrupting conflicts of interest: the example of Hong Kong

DAVID C. DONALD*

Introduction

This chapter views corruption as arising from a conflict of interests, in which the corrupt actor pursues a private interest at the expense of an official or professional duty. In this way, conflicts of interest are at the root of corrupt behaviour in both the public and the private sector. Such conflicts can be countered by structural strategies that subject the agent to limited discretion, increased supervision or transparency. An independent anti-corruption agency is a powerful check of this type. Conflicts of interest can also be combated by increasing the cost of pursuing the private interest, whether that cost be monetary or in the form of a loss of freedom or reputation. Increasing the probability that such cost will be incurred augments the deterrent factor, and thus the quality of oversight, investigation and prosecution will increase the cost of corruption to potential actors and reduce the frequency of its occurrence. The Hong Kong anti-corruption regime combines all of these techniques in exemplary fashion. This chapter uses the example of Hong Kong to analyse how corrupting conflicts of interest can be countered through law and related programmes.

Conflicts of interest and corruption

The undesirable acts referred to with the term 'corruption' display conflicts of interest at their core.[1] Organisations like governments and corporations

* The author thanks Justice Ian McWalters, Jeremy Horder, Lutz Wolff, Aletheia Donald and Liu Lianlian for their comments on an earlier draft of this chapter.

[1] 'Although there is no universal or comprehensive definition as to what constitutes corrupt behaviour, the most prominent definitions share a common emphasis upon the abuse of public power or position for personal advantage.' Asian Development Bank (ADB), *Anticorruption and Integrity* (Manila: Asian Development Bank, 2007), p. 29.

operate by delegating the governing power of collective citizens, owners or their respective leaders to managing agents, whether these be ministers, directors, officials or officers.[2] The organisation thus becomes a network of delegated duties and assigned rights, whether of principals and agents, fiduciaries and beneficiaries or some less well-defined relationship of trust and reliance. These 'delegations' of power usually exist without a formal agency relationship, as in the type of fiduciary duties that corporate directors owe to shareholders, or the type of behaviour that investors legitimately expect from the 'gate-keeping' rating agencies trusted to rate the safety of investment products.[3] When exercising delegated power, every agent has a duty to his principal, whether such principal be the state, its citizens or a private employer. When the person charged with such a duty breaches it by serving a private, conflicting interest, the system built on delegated power and trust runs amok, no longer serving the ends for which it was designed, but organically disparate and even conflicting ends.[4]

The outside boundaries of this problematic can be seen as existing even in relationships incapable of being conceived, even analogically, as principal–agent. The recent example of a mortgage crisis caused in part by lending banks that passed their credit risk on to the market by securitising their loans shows the potentially disastrous effects of disrupting a balanced network of incentives and interests. From the crisis, it became clear that society had depended on lenders' incentives to act in a

[2] See e.g., R. H. Coase, 'The Nature of the Firm', *Economica* (N.S.), 4 (1937), 386–405, at 403 *et seq.* and M. C. Jensen and W. H. Meckling, 'Theory of the Firm: Managerial Behavior, Agency Costs and Ownership Structure', *Journal of Financial Economics*, 3 (1976), 305–60, at 305.

[3] In corporate law, the concept of 'agency cost' is well established, yet used analogically. No major corporate statute provides for a group of shareholder/principals to issue daily instructions to director/agents. There is, legally speaking, no strict agency relationship between the two parties. Rather, the concept of agency is used figuratively to indicate that shareholders ultimately have the power to appoint directors, and directors must act in the best interests – although not always the sole interests – of those shareholders. Directors have fiduciary duties to the company and to the shareholders. The UK Bribery Act 2010 attempts to capture the improper behaviour it would prevent without recourse to the agency analogy – rather, it defines the improper behaviour in part as a breach of a 'relevant expectation': s. 4. On the whole, this attempt to make a clean break from existing concepts by formulating a new, tailor-made category of behaviour that case law will flesh out, could be wise. For the purposes of the analytical model set forth in this chapter, I will continue to use the traditional concepts of 'agent' and 'fiduciary' to express the dutiful relationship that is breached by pursuit of private interest in a corrupt act. This by no means restricts the relationships I am addressing to those strictly contained within law of agency.

[4] See e.g., J. R. Macey, *Corporate Governance: Promises Kept, Promises Broken* (Princeton University Press, 2008), p. 1.

manner complementary to the greater interests of a healthy credit system, and it was assumed that the interest of the entire system to avoid excess defaults was aligned with the interest of the lenders. When this alignment was broken through securitisation, the network of interlocking interests was distorted.[5] In response, reform laws have been 'designed to reshape some of the perverse regulatory incentives that contributed to the financial crisis'.[6] In complex social systems built on interlocking duties, law thus acts to channel and adjust behaviour, whether the undesired behaviour will merely cause collateral damage to bystanders (such as when credit risk is passed on), deceive persons reasonably relying on expertise (such as when credit ratings are faulty), breach a fiduciary duty (such as when directors are disloyal to companies) or constitute corrupt behaviour.

In each of the cases mentioned above, the systemic texture of delegated responsibility on which a specific organisation or a larger system depends for its wholesome operation becomes 'corrupted', to use a different, but related, meaning of our key term. When the delicate texture of interlocking interests in a society or organisation is corrupted, law can step in to repair and prevent such corruption. As Rose-Ackerman observes:

> Self-interest and the public interest frequently conflict … Corruption scandals can then be a sign of a country's growing political maturity. They show that citizens are beginning to recognize the difference between the public and the private spheres and to complain when the border is crossed. Citizens concerns over bribes paid in return for favors indicate that people recognize norms of fair dealing and competent administration and are beginning to demand that government serve general public purposes.[7]

'Corruption', as the effect of a private, conflicting interest working against the proper exercise of delegated power and duty, can be combated by eliminating, overcoming or at least countervailing the private, conflicting interest.[8] Thus, for example, if a public transport official has a

[5] J. E. Stigliz, *Freefall: America, Free Markets, and the Sinking of the World Economy* (New York: W. W. Norton, 2010), p. 14.

[6] D. Skeel, *The New Financial Deal: Understanding the Dodd–Frank Act and its (Unintended) Consequences* (Hoboken, NJ: John Wiley, 2010), p. 110.

[7] S. Rose-Ackerman, *Corruption and Government: Causes, Consequences, and Reform* (New York: Cambridge University Press, 1999), p. 225.

[8] This argument benefits greatly from the line of analysis that Rose-Ackerman has for decades pursued by focusing on economic interest at the heart of corrupt activity. See e.g., S. Rose-Ackerman, 'The Economics of Corruption', *Journal of Public Economics*, 4 (1975), 187–203; S. Rose-Ackerman, 'The Political Economy of Corruption', in K. A. Elliott (ed.), *Corruption and the Global Economy* (Washington, DC: Institute for International Economics, 1997), pp. 40–1; and Rose-Ackerman, *Corruption and Government*, pp. 39–68.

duty to select the lowest priced bidder of high quality to construct a bridge, but is offered a bribe to select another contractor, the official has a private interest to enrich himself, which likely runs counter to the public's interest that he select the best bidder. This conflicting interest can be combated with a number of techniques: the state can compensate the official so well that he has no interest in receiving a bribe;[9] or it can create punishments severe enough that – even when discounted by the likelihood of being caught – accepting the bribe would be more expensive than refusing it.[10] The state can also appoint another, independent official whose compensation is tied to detecting and punishing bribes, so that the interest of the policing official countervails the temptation of the transport official.[11] It can also create an ethical atmosphere that increases the reputational value of lawful behaviour and lowers that of pursuing illicit, private interest. A successful anti-corruption regime would employ a combination of these techniques.[12] The overall result is to lessen the attractiveness of the agent's conflicting interest, so that the agent perceives continued pursuit of his principal's interests as the more desirable option. Moreover, if the selection process used by the transport official is fair and efficient, this could make it cheaper for potential bidders to compete by means of the quality of their service rather than the largesse of their bribes.[13] These measures can be combined in a number of ways to increase the relative cost, and thereby decrease the probability, of corrupt behaviour.

Thus, corruption can be viewed as the result of conflicting interests, and its cures can be conceived as measures that reduce the attractiveness and increase the cost of illicitly serving private interests.[14] 'Cost', however, is a relative value that depends on a position within a system of currency, whether monetary or ideal. One US dollar is more expensive than one HK dollar, and the same relational relevance also applies to cultural values. If a

[9] The United Nations Convention against Corruption (UNCAC) recommends that 'adequate remuneration and equitable pay scales' be established for civil servants. See Art. 7(c) of the UNCAC.

[10] The OECD's Convention on Combating Bribery of Foreign Public Officials in International Business Transactions recommends that the sanctions imposed on bribery be 'effective, proportionate and dissuasive criminal penalties'. See Art. 3(1) of the OECD Convention.

[11] See e.g., Art. 6 of the UNCAC.

[12] See e.g., Art. 13(1)(c) of the UNCAC.

[13] The UNCAC requires that states 'establish appropriate systems of procurement, based on transparency, competition and objective criteria in decision-making, that are effective, *inter alia*, in preventing corruption'. See Art. 7(c) of the UNCAC.

[14] Rose-Ackerman, 'The Political Economy of Corruption', p. 46.

married French political leader were found to have extramarital contact, it might well have much less impact on his or her political career than a similar action would for a US politician. Cultural values determine the reputational 'cost' of prohibited behaviour. Because a change in the cultural valuation of a certain behaviour can significantly reinforce the strength of a rule seeking to eliminate such behaviour, conditioning the moral opinions of an environment can be an effective technique to make the cost of pursuing illicit private interest in such an environment greater than the potential gain. Public education unambiguously characterising corruption as personally destructive and detrimental to the good of society is thus another effective tool with which to combat corrupt behaviour.

While still one of the last remaining outposts of the British Empire, Hong Kong put in place laws and institutions to educate against, discourage, prohibit, investigate and punish corrupt behaviour, whether in public office or in private dealings.[15] In Hong Kong, public education against corruption begins early, is extensive and is widespread.[16] This helps to create an atmosphere in which the value of serving the public interest is appreciated and the value of exploiting office for private gain is depreciated. The acts prohibited in Hong Kong extend beyond the public sector into private agency relationships, thus cultivating a culture in which fiduciary duties generally, not just those of the civil service, are seen as essential to society.[17] The costs imposed on perpetrators by Hong Kong's legal penalties are high.[18] The creation of a separate education, investigation and prosecution body, the Independent Commission Against Corruption (ICAC), guarantees that the interests of at least one body of regulatory officers in Hong Kong are aligned perfectly with those of the public good and against the illicit private interests of individual agents, public and private.[19] The investigative powers of the ICAC are as broad as respect for human rights and civil liberties allow.[20]

15 An excellent history of anti-corruption and anti-bribery law in Hong Kong is presented in I. McWalters, *Bribery and Corruption Law in Hong Kong*, 2nd edn (Hong Kong: LexisNexis, 2010), pp. 3–45.

16 See the third section, 'Teaching the value of the public interest', below, for the educational activities of the ICAC in Hong Kong.

17 See the Annotated Ordinances of Hong Kong (Cap. 201), Prevention of Bribery Ordinance (POBO), s. 9.

18 POBO, s. 12 provides for imprisonment of up to ten years.

19 See the Annotated Ordinances of Hong Kong (Cap. 204), Independent Commission Against Corruption Ordinance (ICACO).

20 These will be discussed in the second section, 'Turning interest against interest', below.

Presumptions, such as treating a public official's unexplained excessive income as a refutable index of corrupt behaviour,[21] assist the ICAC to overcome the considerable asymmetries of information that hinder the prosecution of corruption. Hong Kong has in this way created an array of initiatives that increase the value to an agent of dutiful behaviour in the principal's best interest, while decreasing the value of pursuing illicit private gain.

This chapter will use the alignment of interests and the costs of behaviour to analyse the anti-corruption laws and institutions of the Hong Kong Special Administrative Region (SAR) of the People's Republic of China. Singling out Hong Kong as an example is a valid choice, as the SAR enjoys one of the world's most effective anti-corruption regimes,[22] while it is also a region of the People's Republic of China (PRC), which is both the world's second largest national economy[23] and widely believed to suffer from extensive corruption.[24] In a best case scenario, Hong Kong could serve as the incubator for China's future anti-corruption regime. Looking at Hong Kong's anti-corruption regime as channelling, preventing and punishing interest conflicts allows anti-corruption studies to draw on an older and deeper legal tradition. Courts have addressed the conflicted interests of corporate officers for over 100 years, and the fiduciary duties of agents and trustees for much longer than that.[25] Legislation in the field of 'corporate governance' has for decades sought to prevent corporate officers from pursuing their own interests at the expense of the company by dictating prohibitions, creating presumptions, imposing penalties, inserting independent supervisory bodies, raising ethical standards and aligning the interests of officers with those of the ultimate beneficiaries of their action, the corporate

21 This is provided for in POBO, s. 10.

22 In its 2009 Corruption Perception Index, Transparency International had Hong Kong tied with Luxembourg at twelfth place with a score of 8.2, while the United Kingdom tied with Japan for seventeenth place with a score of 7.7. See at: www.transparency.org/policy_research/surveys_indices/cpi/2009/cpi_2009_table.

23 See the International Monetary Fund, Data and Statistics, World Economic Outlook Database, select 'Gross domestic product, current prices' and 'Gross domestic product based on purchasing-power-parity (PPP) valuation of country GDP', available at: www.imf.org, accessed 26 October 2012.

24 The PRC tied with Burkina Faso, Swaziland and Trinidad and Tobago for seventy-ninth place in the 2009 Transparency International Corruption Perception Index. See, n. 22, above.

25 See, e.g., *Aberdeen Railway Co.* v. *Blaikie Brothers* [1854] 1 Macq 461 (HL Sc), at 471.

shareholders.[26] These strategies have been applied rather mechanically and quite effectively in company law. A similar attempt to guide behaviour is at work in laws combating public and private corruption, and so these methods of company law may benefit anti-corruption studies.

This chapter is arranged as follows: the section 'Turning interest against interest' examines the institutional structure that turns interest against interest in combating corruption. An independent ICAC has the sole interest of deterring, detecting and disciplining corrupt behaviour in the public and the private sectors, so that its employees' interests are diametrically opposed to the private interests tempting officials and agents towards corruption. The ICAC is not only independent, but it has extensive powers of investigation and prosecution; it also contains a subunit whose sole purpose (and thus the interest of its employees) is to detect and punish corrupt behaviour in the ICAC itself.[27] This resembles the basic system of checks and balances used as the ultimate safeguard against abuse of power in many democratic constitutions.[28] The next section, 'Teaching the value of the public interest', will examine efforts to shape the value system in which the price of corrupt behaviour is assessed, focusing on the ICAC's conditioning of the ethical environment through education. The following section, 'The discounted net value of corrupt behaviour in Hong Kong', will estimate the net price of corrupt behaviour in Hong Kong by examining the penalties imposed on the guilty, the presumptions used to increase the probability of their actually being imposed, and the transaction costs entailed by fully complying with the law. The final section will draw conclusions and speculate on the possibility of transferring the Hong Kong anti-corruption regime to other countries.

[26] These legal strategies for reducing agency costs have again been recently mapped out very well in R. Kraakman *et al.*, *The Anatomy of Corporate Law: A Comparative and Functional Approach*, 2nd edn (New York: Oxford University Press, 2009), pp. 37–45. The debate about exactly to whom corporate directors owe duties is long-standing, and some scholars advocate replacing 'shareholder primacy' with duties to a much larger field of stakeholders, including employees, creditors, suppliers and the community at large. See, e.g., Companies Act 2006, s. 172.

[27] See McWalters, *Bribery and Corruption Law*, p. 83.

[28] See e.g., J. Madison, 'The Structure of the Government Must Furnish the Proper Checks and Balances Between the Different Departments', in A. Hamilton, J. Madison and J. Jay, *The Federalist Papers* (Kindle edition, 2011), No. 51, location 5451: 'This policy of supplying, by opposite and rival interests, the defect of better motives … We see it particularly displayed in all the subordinate distributions of power, where the constant aim is to divide and arrange the several offices in such a manner as that each may be a check on the other that the private interest of every individual may be a sentinel over the public rights.'

Turning interest against interest: an independent commission against corruption

Jon Quah argues that: 'The most important strength of an independent anti-corruption agency is that its *raison d'être* is the investigation of corruption cases without political interference.'[29] If an independent anti-corruption agency is established, the organisation and its employees have one interest: to combat corruption, and this interest is diametrically opposed to the interests of those who would exploit their positions of public trust or as private agents to enrich themselves illicitly. Perhaps the clearest converse to an independent anti-corruption agency is the use of the police to combat corruption. The unique position of the police, usually instilled with significant power that may be exercised on a discretionary basis while inserted in situations where the gain from bribery can be large, subjects police officers to considerable tension between their duty to keep the public order and the tug of their private interest. While entrusted to uphold the law, they are given the power and relative freedom from supervision that is necessary to extract rents from lawbreakers. The term 'police force' itself expresses this tension: force that, although exercised by fallible humans, should be applied towards serving the polity's good order. A look at one peculiar circumstance where high pubic and mean private interests are fully aligned can perhaps help highlight the tension suffered by the enforcement officer foregoing private temptation for public duty. Maitland and Montague tell us that primitive policing of some crimes in pre-Norman England simply aligned self-interest with the desired violence against the accused through the tool of 'outlawry': 'The contumacious offender is put outside the peace; he becomes a foe of all law-abiding men. It is their duty to waste his land and burn his house, to pursue him and knock him on the head as though he were a beast of prey.'[30] In 2010, the United States Congress introduced a popular updated form of this outlaw bounty by providing that any 'whistle-blower' who supplies the regulatory authority with information leading to successful prosecution under the US securities laws and imposition of a penalty exceeding US$1 million on the

[29] J. S. T. Quah, 'Combating Corruption in the Asia-Pacific Countries: What do We Know and What Needs to be Done', *International Public Management Review*, 10 (2009), 5–33, at 25.

[30] F. W. Maitland and F. C. Montague, *A Sketch of English Legal History* (Boston, MA: Adamant Media Corporation, 2001), p. 19.

wrongdoer shall receive 10–30 per cent of the spoils.[31] 'Wasting' the property of the accused becomes 'corrupt' only when it contradicts the mandate received from the state, such as when no violation has occurred, or more relevant for our purposes, a countervailing duty to 'police' the public order with restraint is imposed on the actor, an enforcing official. Then, self-interestedly pursuing a desire to take the property or life of the accused conflicts with another interest: that of the public in seeing justice done, and seeing it done in an orderly fashion. Self-interested behaviour then corrupts as the alignment of public and private interests diverge. This tension has repeatedly shown itself to be problematic. Indeed, it was concrete acts of police corruption that prompted the creation both of Singapore's Corrupt Practices Investigation Bureau (CPIB) and Hong Kong's ICAC.

In Singapore, in 1951, at a time when corruption was investigated by a special branch within the Singapore Police Force, certain police detectives used information and connections gained from their offices to hijack S $400,000 of contraband opium.[32] Although investigating police officers did later name and accuse these detectives of corruption, an independent special investigation 'uncovered evidence of widespread police corruption', so that in 1952 the British colonial government decided to establish the CPIB as an independent agency outside the police force.[33] Approximately twenty years later, in Hong Kong, the director of the police force's Anti-Corruption Office received information that a chief superintendent of the Hong Kong Police, Peter Godber, had remitted over HK$1 million abroad.[34] Godber was informed that he was under investigation, but was not detained, when investigating officers confronted him with a request to search his car and house, and subsequently his name was put on an immigration watch list at the borders of Hong Kong.[35] One step ahead of his investigating colleagues, Godber used his special police security clearance, which had not been revoked, to circumvent the immigration check points and board a flight to Singapore,[36] from where he continued

[31] Dodd–Frank Wall Street Reform and Consumer Protection Act, Pub. L. No. 111–203, §922 (2010), to be codified at 15 USC 78a *et seq.*

[32] J. S. T. Quah, 'Defying Institutional Failure: Learning from the Experiences of Anti-corruption Agencies in four Asian Countries', *Crime Law and Social Change*, 53 (2010), 23–54, at 23.

[33] Quah, 'Defying Institutional Failure', p. 24.

[34] MacWalters, *Bribery & Corruption Law*, p. 26.

[35] MacWalters, *Bribery & Corruption Law*, p. 27.

[36] MacWalters, *Bribery & Corruption Law*, p. 27.

on to the United Kingdom.[37] The fact that a chief superintendent of police had used his special police credentials to escape the Hong Kong authorities and, as it appeared, prosecution for corruption, caused a public outcry, and the colonial government created a commission of inquiry, headed by Judge Sir Alastair Blair-Kerr, to investigate.[38] The Blair-Kerr Commission produced two reports, the first exposing the legal loopholes through which Godber had escaped – such as the police's lack of power to detain a suspect under investigation – and the second expressing their finding that the Hong Kong police force suffered from extensive, syndicated corruption.[39] Beyond strengthening the existing anti-corruption law to make it more difficult for cases like Godber's to reoccur, the colonial government decided to create an independent investigative body, the ICAC, which came into existence in early 1974.[40]

The ICAC is indeed independent, funded directly out of the general revenue of the Hong Kong SAR,[41] and answerable only to its chief executive,[42] while its independence from the latter is strengthened by an express power to investigate and prosecute the chief executive for corruption.[43] The ICAC's mission as stated in the ICACO rests on three prongs: investigation, prevention and education, each performed by a separate department of the Commission.[44] To perform its investigative mission, the ICAC has extensive powers, including limited authority to search, seize and arrest without prior judicial oversight.[45] It can, on its own authority, access all types of financial books and records held with intermediaries before naming a specific person as a suspect,[46] although after its investigation begins to target a specified suspect, it requires approval from the HK Court of First Instance to access confidential

[37] Independent Commission Against Corruption (ICAC), 'The Landmark Case: Godber's Downfall', 2010, available at: www.icac.org.hk. Godber was eventually imprisoned in the United Kingdom when evidence was obtained that he took a HK$25,000 bribe in Hong Kong; he was extradited back to Hong Kong for further trial in 1975, and sentenced to four years in prison. MacWalters, *Bribery & Corruption Law*, p. 27.

[38] MacWalters, *Bribery & Corruption Law*, p. 27.

[39] MacWalters, *Bribery & Corruption Law*, p. 29.

[40] MacWalters, *Bribery & Corruption Law*, p. 33.

[41] ICACO, s. 4.

[42] 'The Commissioner shall not be subject to the direction or control of any person other than the Chief Executive': ICACO, s. 5(2).

[43] POBO, ss. 4(2A), (2B); 5(3), (4); 10(1A).

[44] See ICACO, s. 12 and MacWalters, *Bribery & Corruption Law*, p. 79.

[45] As for other law enforcement officers, an ICAC official may conduct a search and seize contraband and evidence when making an arrest or an application to the court for a warrant 'would seriously impede an investigation'. See ICACO, s. 10C and POBO, s. 17(1B).

[46] POBO, s. 13(1).

accounts.[47] The ICAC can also obtain an order from the Court of First Instance instructing the HK Inland Revenue Department to provide it with investigation-relevant information that is otherwise protected and confidential.[48] Thus, the ICAC has all the powers of a normal law enforcement agency, plus some quasi-judicial powers that it may exercise in instances where the Legislative Council found the Commission needs freedom to act quickly.

The Prevention of Bribery Ordinance (POBO) also gives the ICAC a rather unusual presumption, reversing the burden of proof in the prosecution of corruption, which helps it to overcome informational asymmetries. Pursuant to section 10 of the POBO, if a current or retired public official lives or maintains assets incompatible with her 'official emoluments' and fails adequately to explain how she manages to do so, she will be guilty of an offence, which under section 12 of the POBO can result in a fine of up to HK$1.0 million and ten years' imprisonment. In this way, the ICAC need merely present numerical proof of assets significantly exceeding emoluments in order to shift the burden to the accused, forcing the person in possession of information, whose existence may be difficult to ascertain, to produce it if he or she can. This tool is bolstered by the ICAC's power to inspect any type of books or accounts evidencing the suspect's wealth,[49] and to obtain confidential information held by the HK Inland Revenue Department on a given suspect if there are reasonable grounds to suspect that an offence under the POBO has been committed.[50] Understandably, the reversal of the burden of proof in a criminal case, bringing with it incarceration of up to ten years, presents a significant challenge to guarantees offered by human and civil rights.

The UK Law Commission charged with reforming the Bribery Act addressed a comparable presumption found in the Prevention of Corruption Act 1916. That presumption stated that once it is 'proved that any money, gift or other consideration' is conveyed to a public official, it 'shall be deemed to have been paid or given and received corruptly'.[51] Consideration was given to whether this and other presumptions of guilt were in contravention of Article 6(2) of the European Convention on

[47] POBO, s. 13(1A). [48] POBO, ss. 13, 13(A).

[49] POBO, s. 13. [50] POBO, s. 13(A).

[51] Prevention of Corruption Act 1916, s. 2, discussed in the Law Commission, *Reforming Bribery*, Law Com. No. 313 (London: The Stationery Office, 2008), para. 2.18, available at www.justice.gov.uk.

Human Rights.[52] Presumptions of this sort were ultimately not carried forward into the Bribery Act 2010, which carefully requires an element of intent or knowing action and prosecutorial proof of such element in connection with an offence of bribery.[53]

The UK Law Commission certainly did not have the task of viewing the 1916 Act's presumption in an abstractly conceptual, essentially functional, manner, but when so viewed we can see that the Hong Kong POBO's presumption differs significantly. The UK presumption *characterises* the *quality* of an advantage conferred (i.e., legitimate or corrupt) and must be rebutted with evidence establishing the true quality, which like a finding of innocence itself, can require complex evaluation of many elements. The POBO's presumption is triggered by a simple, mathematical formula (assets significantly exceeding official remuneration equal corruption) and can be rebutted by the simple proof of an alternative source of the excess, such as inheritance or capital gains.[54] Thus, while the 1916 presumption requires qualitative proof of legitimacy to rebut a presumption of guilt, the POBO presumption merely requires the production of a source of income. A further element for comparative study is the effect of the European Convention on Human Rights, which like European law in general, has resulted in newly arising distinctions between UK law and the laws of Commonwealth countries and other common law jurisdictions, such as the United States. When the POBO's presumption was challenged as a violation of Hong Kong's Bill of Rights, the courts have repeatedly found it to withstand judicial scrutiny.[55] In one well-known Court of Appeals case, Bokhary JA observed:

> Where corruption is concerned, one can readily see the need – within reason of course – for special powers of investigation and provisions such as ones requiring an accused to provide an explanation. Specific corrupt acts are inherently difficult to detect let alone prove in the normal way. The true victim, society as a whole, is generally unaware of the specific occasions on which it is victimised … Before the prosecution can rely on

52 See, e.g., House of Lords and House of Commons, Joint Committee on the Draft Bribery Bill 2009, *First Report of Session 2008–09*, p. 58, available at www.publications.parliament.uk.

53 See Bribery Act 2010, ss. 1, 2, 6.

54 Perhaps interesting to note in this context is that under s. 6 of the UK Proceeds of Crime Act 2002, once a defendant has been convicted of or committed for sentence with respect to an offence, the court may order the seizure of the defendant's unjust gains and the recoverable amount is determined in part by presumption. This would apply to the proceeds of all crime, not just bribery.

55 MacWalters, *Bribery & Corruption Law*, p. 395.

> the presumption that pecuniary resources or property were in the accused's control, it has of course to prove beyond reasonable doubt the facts which trigger it ... Section 10(1) is Bill consistent. It is dictated by necessity and goes no further than necessary. The balance is right.[56]

This clearly demonstrates that Hong Kong has the 'political will' to fight corruption, which Quah describes as an essential element of a successful anti-corruption regime.[57] It also shows that a combination of informational asymmetry ('corrupt acts are inherently difficult to detect') and well defined elements of the offence (emoluments for a civil servant are precisely defined) allow an important political goal to be served by a presumption. The same type of presumption is used to prevent corporate directors subjected to conflicts of interest from breaching their fiduciary duties in the secrecy of the boardroom. Under the laws of many countries, including the United Kingdom and the United States, as well as the Hong Kong SAR, if a director has a direct or indirect economic interest in a transaction the company enters into, he is presumed to have committed an offence unless he discloses the matter to the other directors and those directors or shareholders approve the transaction.[58] Both in corporate governance and in combating corruption, the desire to eliminate the abuse, the difficulty of detecting it in specific cases, and the probable causal nexus between the economic element and a resulting abuse – under the POBO the source of excess wealth and under company law the loss of disinterested judgment – support the creation of a presumption. The accused suffering from the presumption is in the best position to produce the information necessary to rebut it. Another angle from which to view the similarities is that in both cases, the offence is committed by a person whose office, duties and compensation are well defined, allowing a presumption to be created when factors (such as conflicting interests or excessive assets) reach a dimension at which there is a high probability that a duty will be breached.

The ICAC's powers are significant and its independence is guaranteed, but Hong Kong does not depend on deterrence and enforcement

[56] *Attorney General* v. *Hui Kin-Hong* [1995] 1 HKCLR 227, 235–36.

[57] Quah, 'Combating Corruption', p. 21.

[58] See, e.g., as to the United Kingdom, Companies Act 2006, ss. 182, 190, as to the United States, *Cooke* v. *Oolie*, 1997 WL 367034 (Del.Ch., 23 June 1997); A. Cahn and D. C. Donald, *Comparative Company Law: Text and Cases on the Laws Governing Corporations in Germany, the UK and the USA* (Cambridge University Press, 2010), ch. 12; and as to Hong Kong, the Annotated Ordinances of Hong Kong (Cap. 32), Companies Ordinance, s. 157H.

alone. In reviewing 'the practices and procedures of Government departments and public bodies, in order to facilitate the discovery of corrupt practices and to secure the revision of methods of work or procedures which, in the opinion of the Commissioner, may be conducive to corrupt practices',[59] the ICAC's Corruption Prevention Department battles corrupting conflicts of interest in a manner very similar to those bodies that seek to improve corporate governance in business corporations. Codes or rules of 'best practices' in corporate governance attempt to separate decision-making from conflicts of interest, introduce independent directors to provide unbiased supervision, give such independent directors sufficient funds to act independently, and ensure that they are indeed qualified enough to fulfil their obligations.[60] This introduction of structural safeguards is a preventative and pre-emptive activity that supplements deterrence through investigation and punishment.[61] The ICAC has likewise studied the processes of government decision-making and isolated points at which safeguards and supervision against conflicts of interest should be introduced, such as in the process of tendering for public sector contracts.[62] Structural measures introduced at high-risk bottlenecks reduce the probability that private and public interests will interact, conflict and lead to corrupt action in the administration of official business.

The ICAC also undertakes a significant conditioning of the cultural environment in Hong Kong, which has the effect of raising the reputational cost of engaging in corrupt activity, and educating potential actors about the missteps that can lead to such loss of reputation. This cultural backdrop that the ICAC attempts to create adds an additional layer of prevention beyond the deterrence offered by the threat of fines and loss of freedom. In the next section, after briefly outlining the extent of the ICAC's community outreach programmes, I provide an aesthetic analysis

[59] ICACO, s. 12(d).

[60] See, e.g., the Financial Reporting Council, *The Combined Code on Corporate Governance*, 2006, applicable to companies listed on the London Stock Exchange on a voluntary basis, available at: www.frc.org.uk; and the New York Stock Exchange, *Listed Company Manual*, ss. 303A and 307, available at: nysemanual.nyse.com. Cahn and Donald, *Comparative Company Law*, ch. 15.

[61] For a general discussion of this technique in corporate law, see D. C. Donald, 'Some Observations on the Use of Structural and Remedial Measures in American and German Law after Sarbanes–Oxley', *German Law Journal*, 4 (2003), 127–35, at 127.

[62] MacWalters, *Bribery & Corruption Law*, p. 86.

of the television series the ICAC co-produces to provide pedagogical entertainment for the people of Hong Kong.[63]

Teaching the value of the public interest

The Community Relations Department of the ICAC conducts significant conditioning of the Hong Kong environment to increase the reputational cost of corrupt behaviour, or, as the ICAC Ordinance expresses it, to 'educate the public against the evils of corruption; and enlist and foster public support in combating corruption'.[64] In addition to staging information sessions at schools, universities, professional associations and other organisations, the ICAC co-produced a television drama with Hong Kong's leading television provider, Television Broadcasts Ltd, for fifteen years. The series, entitled *ICAC Investigators*, does for Hong Kong's ICAC and its struggle against corruption much of the same work that the James Bond films and *Mission Impossible* performed for the Cold War or Fox Television's *24* performed for the post-9/11 fight against terrorism, but with significantly less dramatic appeal and substantially more pedagogical focus. A reader who enjoys the moral reinforcement provided in Henry Fielding's *Tom Jones* would perhaps also appreciate *ICAC Investigators*.

Each episode of *ICAC Investigators* is based on an actual ICAC investigation. All the episodes of *ICAC Investigators 2007* I viewed are set in Hong Kong, so that viewing citizens see the everyday icons of their cultural environment as the backdrop to the film's moral lessons. The language is Cantonese, but it is also possible to view the series synchronised into Mandarin or with English subtitles. The episodes usually present cases of public and private corruption that have an immediate and tangible impact on the quality of life in Hong Kong. The episodes I viewed all used a cathartic, pedagogical approach where one of the main protagonists of the drama gradually succumbs to corruption and is then

[63] The analysis draws heavily from a method developed by Wolfgang Iser, in which a given text is seen to interact with the expected preconceptions ('repertoire') of an audience in order to stage a creative activity in the reader's mind that can simply reinforce a given ideology (propaganda), impart knowledge and techniques of judgment (pedagogy) or make the reader aware of his or her own projections and prejudices (liberating 'estrangement'). Iser's method views texts in an Aristotelian (experiential) and phenomenological perspective. See W. Iser, *Der Akt des Lesens: Theorie ästhetischer Wirkung*, 4th edn (Munich: Wilhelm Fink, 1994), pp. 175 *et seq.*

[64] ICACO, s. 12(g)–(h).

apprehended by the ICAC, questioned and, if necessary, incarcerated. The filming focuses on the pivotal decision, the point at which the suspect chooses either to fulfil public duty or to serve private interest. Each episode of the series brings viewers vicarious participation in this fateful decision, including the hollow pleasure of ill-gotten gain and the painful regret that inevitably follows.

In the episode 'Empty Wagons', a middle-aged man of modest income, Mr Leung, has a loving wife and son, and a good job at the Kowloon Canton Railway Company. He is seduced into smuggling by a crafty merchant through the medium of an attractive *femme fatale* who works with the merchant to ensure that Leung takes the bribes and assists in smuggling. What is remarkable about this episode is that the contraband being shipped to China in unglamorous, rusty railway cars are seemingly innocuous *cigarette filters*, not components for a neutron bomb or vital crown secrets. In this way, *ICAC Investigators* drives home that point that we, dear viewers, are not the judges of what is legal or illegal, important or unimportant, but rather we must look to and follow the law. The personal cost of breaking the law is starkly revealed during the majority of the episode: first, Leung is apprehended in front of his wife and son, and the disgrace that his criminal activity should rightly trigger is shown in the pain on his son's face as he stares with disbelief at his father being taken into custody. The investigators later uncover evidence of the relationship between Leung and the *femme fatale*, which Leung's wife sees, and when Leung leaves his family one evening for a tryst with this woman, his wife decides to leave him. In a very dramatic closing scene, Leung chases his wife and son to the Lo Wu border crossing into China, following a tip his son sends him by SMS, and pleads through tears for his wife to stand by him while he is in prison, affirming between sobs that he never should have taken the money, and he only sought to secure a more comfortable life for his family, particularly a larger flat – something most Hong Kong residents desire. The wife nevertheless abandons him, but the son aged about fifteen stands by his dad, his eyes welling with tears of anguish at his father's downfall and his family's destruction. This scene has the potential for heavy cathartic impact on Hong Kong's adolescent viewers. While the very humane and sympathetic ICAC agents who tracked Leung to the border crossing prepare to lead him away, the picture turns to grainy grey and the camera freezes on the face of a broken man who made a terrible mistake. In that instant we as viewers have no doubt that crime – even if only allowing cigarette filters to cross a border between two regions of the same country – does not pay.

In addition to the straightforward message that crime does not pay presented with maximum cathartic impact, *ICAC Investigators* also presents some very sophisticated symbolism and character analysis in connection with corruption. The episode 'Sand Castle' is about a construction company that saved money by skimping on the foundations of two high-rise buildings, which then had to be demolished at an exorbitant cost. The clear message is that in society, as in construction, if the foundation is not solid, the entire structure will collapse. If this episode were to be broadcast in a region with a majority Christian culture, which Hong Kong is not, it could certainly be seen as a reference to the New Testament parable of building one's moral house on sand rather than on rock, the latter being able to withstand the storm of temptation and the former crumbling at great cost to the builder. The symbolism packed into the episode goes further, as the two main figures present doppelgangers of each other, a kind of Dr Jekyll and Mr Hyde of the Hong Kong young professional set. They were university classmates who studied engineering at the same university, one with solid moral integrity, but rather wooden and dull, and the other confidently outgoing, but not very strong on ethics. During university they had competed for the same girl, and the honest engineer has won her at the episode's outset, although the dishonest engineer reclaims her at the height of his ill-gotten success. They both find employment with the same construction company. At this company they are befriended and advised by a series of either honest or dishonest co-workers at various levels of the company, basically dividing the visible portion of the workforce into two, mirroring camps. The narrative clearly distinguishes between the character traits of the two camps at various levels of the company, perhaps trying to give young viewers a guide to ethically navigating the workplace.

As in many stories of this type, the dishonest cadre pulls ahead at the beginning, as the bad engineer wines and dines the building inspectors so they do not notice his cost-saving shortcuts, which the highly budget-conscious CEO greatly admires. After the good engineer's expected promotion goes to the bad engineer, the latter also reclaims the college sweetheart, driving the good engineer to attempt suicide. At this point, his life broken, he briefly goes over to the dark side, helping the CEO out of a budget crisis with advice to use compressed water to support the buildings' foundations, which fatally compromises its structure. When the ICAC swings its investigation into motion, it is made very evident, both in this and in other episodes, that we are being shown a force that must be respected: they are cool and efficient, and even appear omniscient and omnipresent as they photograph every suspect at every incriminating moment, an all-seeing eye from which one cannot hide. This may well have an impact on the average viewer's estimation of the risk connected with corrupt behaviour. Also typical for the series is that the ICAC apprehends the bad engineer at his attractive flat eating breakfast with his pretty new bride, having reached the peak of happiness, yet this happy house is built not on the rock of lawfulness but on the sand of corruption, and crumbles at the sight of the ICAC badge.

The good engineer is also apprehended, for in that great moment of crisis mentioned above, he agreed to sign a pile of receipts for concrete that was never bought or used, but as in 'Empty Wagons' and other episodes of *ICAC Investigators*, we are shown a powerful cathartic moment, an existential crisis that decides his entire life. In the ICAC's interrogation room, when faced with the signed receipts, he begins to sob and scream, and we see a flashback of the good engineer running in a cold sweat through Hong Kong until he reaches land's end and the harbour in anguish and tears; we then see him bursting back to the construction firm, knocking papers to the floor, accusing the CEO of putting lives in danger and, most decisively, in the presence of his evil doppelganger, exclaiming 'I am I, not the person who approved this; I never go against my conscience, and I quit this job!' As the credits roll at episode's end, a factual statement on the persons convicted and their prison sentences makes clear that the good engineer was not charged with a crime. He repented in time, chose the right side of the conflict, and this teaches the viewer that he or she too can repent and be saved in his or her company or agency. This important message of repentance and forgiveness will certainly encourage potential whistle-blowers to contact the ICAC.

The five episodes I viewed to prepare this brief analysis all focus on the decision to abandon public or professional duty for private gain. The choice to behave corruptly is, of course, always shown to be disastrous. However, the ICAC is always depicted as showing sympathy for the weak protagonist who goes astray, and the investigative officer is always ready to receive him back into the fold of responsible citizens. The office culture of the ICAC as depicted in the episodes is also interesting: it appears based on fairness, reason and teamwork, and superiors deserve respect because they are more able, more dedicated and more experienced than the bright, young professionals who work under them. On the other hand, in the criminal organisations and businesses run in a corrupt manner, authoritarian figures control their cronies through greed and fear. They are usually shown in shadowy light, often consuming alcohol, unlike the officers of the ICAC, who are inevitably seen in well-lit offices or bright daylight, consuming water, tea or coffee. In another episode, entitled 'Prison Courier', the television drama draws on popular lore surrounding the ICAC, as the warden of Stanley Prison jokes with an ICAC inspector who visits his office that the tea at the warden's office is quite good, but of course the ICAC has the best coffee. In popular Hong Kong parlance, being 'invited to drink a coffee' at the ICAC means being under investigation. Here the work of the ICAC's Community Relations Department draws on and reaffirms the same popular culture that it has conditioned in preceding decades. Pedagogical art and popular culture become one.

In a population of approximately 7 million, the ICAC's educational activity has had a significant impact on the perception of corruption. The reputational cost of corruption is seen as very high, particularly for employees in the public sector, and its potential gains are seen as of uncertain value. This conditioning of the cultural environment has worked in complement with the ICAC's actual investigative prowess and respected independence to greatly increase the perceived cost of breaching the public trust.

The discounted net value of corrupt behaviour in Hong Kong

If the problem of corruption can be understood as a conflict between an official or agent choosing dutifully to fulfil his obligations as society expects or choosing to exploit his position to pursue a private interest, the value of the two competing options may determine the agent's choice. It is therefore possible to view a successful strategy against corruption as one that increases its cost to the offender, discounted by the probability of being successfully prosecuted for an offence, to a quantum exceeding the value of corrupt behaviour, thereby giving corrupt behaviour a negative net value. There is nothing novel about this view of deterrence. As Richard Posner has observed, a crude form of such calculus can been seen in deterrent-oriented damage payments such as '*wergeld*' employed in pre-Norman England to punish acts that would now be regarded as criminal.[65] Rose-Ackerman has expressly applied such a calculus to the field of corruption with the following formula: 'The expected cost of

[65] R. Posner, 'An Economic Theory of the Criminal Law', *Columbia Law Review*, 85 (1985), 1193–231, at 1203.

bribery is the probability of being caught times the probability of being convicted times the punishment levied.'[66] Novel or not, a formula of this type well captures the impact an anti-corruption regime must achieve in order to be effective.

Cost would include a number of quantifiable elements, such as fines, loss of employment and loss of consortium with family and friends (in the case of imprisonment), as well as some non-quantifiable elements, such as loss of reputation. The potential value of corrupt behaviour would be limited to the value of decisions made by agents acting against the best interests of those persons to whom their duty runs. For example, if an agent with delegated decision-making power to award contracts is constrained to decide within set price bands for the service, detailed quality guidelines are set for the purpose of assessing the competing contractors, and the procurement process is transparent and fair, this would reduce the value of the agent's corrupt influence to a potential bidder. The bidder might see competing purely on the quality of products or services as the less expensive route. The converse is also true: if a procurement process is opaque and the agent has a free hand in deciding the best contractor and setting the price, that agent would be able to give the bidding contractor great value in return for a bribe.

As this chapter has explained, the laws and institutions of Hong Kong have reduced the value of corrupt behaviour and increased its cost in a number of interlocking and complementary ways. Under the POBO, the maximum fine is HK$1.0 million and the maximum prison term is ten years.[67] Although at about £83,000, the value of the fine discounted by the probability of conviction would likely not outweigh the gains of more significant forms of corrupt behaviour, the potential prison sentence certainly presents a substantial deterrent. *ICAC Investigators* and the extensive educational programmes of the ICAC's Community Relations Department have significantly shaped the Hong Kong cultural view of ethical behaviour so as greatly to increase the reputational cost of corrupt behaviour. This is substantiated by a recent public poll in which 98 per cent of respondents said the ICAC deserved their support.[68] Thus, the

[66] Rose-Ackerman, 'The Political Economy of Corruption', p. 40.

[67] POBO, s. 12. These penalties would be applicable to a civil servant convicted of holding assets well above her income. Other forms of corruption involving civil servants have much lower fines, but prison terms that are either equivalent or still significant (i.e., seven years).

[68] Hong Kong SAR Information Services Department, *Hong Kong: The Facts* (2010), p. 2, available at: www.gov.hk/about/abouthk/factsheets/docs/icac.pdf.

maximum cost of corrupt behaviour for a civil servant in Hong Kong could be HK$ 1.0 million, a prison term of ten years and social ostracism. To understand its actual impact on decision-making, this must be discounted by the probability of conviction.

If a corrupt actor has a 1 per cent chance of being forced to pay a HK $1 million dollar fine and serve ten years in prison, the discounted value of that fine is thus 1 million multiplied by 0.01 or only HK$10,000, and the discounted prison term, using the same formula, is only about thirty-six days. Increasing the probability of conviction is therefore a very important part of making corruption too costly to undertake. As discussed above, the ICAC has investigatory powers as extensive as the law enforcement agencies in most developed countries, particularly when it comes to accessing financial and tax records. Moreover, the presumption of guilt in the case of civil servants holding assets significantly above their emoluments reverses the burden of producing otherwise unavailable financial information, eliminating a substantial asymmetry of information between the ICAC and the suspect.[69] As discussed above, similar presumptions may not be available in other, comparable jurisdictions. Through application of these powers in trials before Hong Kong's courts, which are generally considered to be of high quality, the conviction rate for completed prosecutions based on ICAC investigations in 2009 was 85 per cent.[70] Assuming that effective detection powers allow prosecution of at least 50 per cent of all instances of corruption, this conviction rate increases the discounted value of the maximum fine from HK$10,000 in the hypothetical example given above to HK$425,000, and lengthens the prison term from thirty-six days to 4.25 years. These figures should also be slightly increased for the bias created in the public mind by the investigative prowess put on display in *ICAC Investigators* and the high reputation for efficiency the ICAC enjoys in Hong Kong's public mind.

The value of corrupt behaviour to an official or agent will equal the advantage this official or agent can offer the person who would purchase his breach of duty, minus a profit margin for the latter. Thus, as said, this quantum will depend on the potentially corrupt actor's freedom to reach a decision without external constrains or supervision and the efficiency of the decision-making process. To this end, the ICAC's Corruption Prevention Department examines the Hong Kong Government for red

[69] The presumption found in POBO, s. 10 is discussed above, in the section 'Turning interest against interest'.

[70] Information Services Department, *Hong Kong: The Facts*, p. 2.

flags like excessive discretion and insufficient supervision or transparency, as well as for red tape such as unnecessary procedures and outdated or excessive instructions, so as to promote structural change to prevent corruption.[71] By increasing efficiency and subjecting discretion to transparency and accountability, the resulting changes reduce the value of corrupt behaviour to the buyer of disloyalty. Transactional efficiency is tied to the general business practices of a jurisdiction, and those practices thus influence the value of corrupt behaviour to a participant: the more cumbersome the bureaucratic hurdles, the more valuable the corrupt detour around them. The Hong Kong Government is, of course, famously diligent in promoting efficient bureaucracy and low barriers to business dealings.[72] Indeed, it has remarkably retained the title of the world's freest economy for eighteen years in a row against a field of over 180 other contenders.[73]

The result is a high, discounted net price for corrupt activity. When faced with a choice of whether to pay for a shortcut, an unearned privilege or a favourable decision, or compete legally on the basis of quality, the potential corrupt actor will be faced with a fairly clear choice. On the one hand, business dealings and regulatory approvals in Hong Kong are carried out in an efficient manner on the basis of quality, even if the economy itself might be tilted towards the large corporate groups that dominate its economy. In short, the system works well and at a reasonable cost. On the other hand, an independent agency watches for corrupt behaviour in Hong Kong using solid investigatory techniques, benefiting from presumptions of guilt in some cases, and achieving an 85 per cent conviction rate in the cases that go to trial. Moreover, an ethical atmosphere has been created in which corruption has been clearly marked out as unacceptable among the population, and, as observed above, the ICAC enjoys near unanimous support from the population. Using financial terminology, one might say that the option to commit corruption in Hong Kong is 'under water', so that it is very unwise to exercise it. For fifteen years the foolishness of the

[71] See MacWalters, *Bribery & Corruption Law*, p. 86.

[72] Yasheng Huang calls Hong Kong 'the most laissez-faire economic system ... a safe harbour for some of the talented Chinese entrepreneurs ... an alternative to China's poorly functioning financial and legal systems'. Y. Huang, *Capitalism with Chinese Characteristics: Entrepreneurship and the State* (New York: Cambridge University Press, 2008), pp. 228–30.

[73] The Heritage Foundation, *2012 Index of Economic Freedom*, p. 8, available at: www.heritage.org.

decision to engage in corruption in Hong Kong has been painted on the faces of those tragic protagonists of *ICAC Investigators* who traded sailing in capitalism's safe harbour for sinking in the quicksand of corruption, and the sobs of their remorse are tucked among the various mental impressions that will figure in a Hong Kong citizen's decision-making.

A matter of culture: is the Hong Kong anti-corruption regime transferable?

No discussion of law in Hong Kong would be complete without addressing at least in passing its chance of future survival in and impact on the massive mother country into which it is being absorbed day by day: the People's Republic of China. Pursuant to its Basic Law, Hong Kong's legal system will remain separate from that of the PRC at least until 2047.[74] However, Shenzhen, the free trade zone city that borders Hong Kong immediately to the northwest, has now reached a population of approximately 9 million, and its economy is increasingly integrating with that of Hong Kong.[75] The transfer of Hong Kong's manufacturing to the mainland,[76] and the steady increase of RMB-denominated products in Hong Kong,[77] indicate that the amalgamation of Hong Kong and Shenzhen into a 'Greater Hong Kong' of about 16 million souls could be on the medium-term horizon. The gem that Hong Kong can offer its young bride will certainly be the rule of law, a great example of which is its anti-corruption regime. However, as we have seen, law is only one institution that orders a society; law interacts with the political, economic, social and cultural context in which it is found. Although law can be a causal factor in a society taking a particular shape, it is also a product of the same society, and thus the characteristics of a given legal regime will be complementary and congruent with the society in which it is

[74] The Basic Law of the Hong Kong Special Administrative Region of the People's Republic of China, art. 5.

[75] The Shenzhen Government website offers general demographic and economic information on the city and the Pearl River Delta region, available at: http://english.sz.gov.cn/gi.

[76] See K-W. Li, *The Hong Kong Economy: Recovery and Restructuring* (Singapore: McGraw-Hill, 2006), pp. 304 *et seq.*

[77] The Hong Kong Monetary Authority regularly publishes updated statistics on the development of the Renminbi business in Hong Kong, see, e.g., the Hong Kong Monetary Authority, *Half-Yearly Monetary and Financial Stability Report*, September 2011, p. 8, available at: www.hkma.gov.hk.

embedded.[78] Thus, it is not only the Chinese Communist Party (CCP) that offers a possible impediment to transplanting the Hong Kong legal system. Not every legal technique can be effective in all cultural circumstances. For this reason, it is not unproblematic to transplant any set of laws, including an anti-corruption regime, from one country to another.

In discussions of business ethics, corruption and bribery, much is made of the unique characteristics of Asian culture, particularly the centrality of *guanxi*, as presenting greater challenges than the culture of Western societies.[79] The specifically Asian understanding of personal relationships referred to with this term, particularly the notion that private obligations can be owed to friends and family so as to override public duties, is seen as a cultural catalyst for corruption.[80] Under the pressure of these cultural values, when a private obligation to a friend or family member conflicts with a duty to serve the public good, the private will gain and the public will wane in significance, thus lowering the net price of corrupt behaviour to the actor considering it. Moreover, a related culture of gift-giving can help to transform an act we might otherwise see as bribery into a traditional gesture of respect and friendship. These elements of Asian culture can thus both increase the motivation to purse private interests and camouflage acts of bribery.

In evaluating whether the Hong Kong anti-corruption regime is transferable to the PRC, the Asian culture of *guanxi* and custom of gift-giving, discussed above, would not present obstacles to a transplant. Hong Kong and the PRC share a common cultural heritage. They do not, however, share a common history during the twentieth century or a common political system, and these are significant factors in shaping their cultures in relation to congruence with laws and techniques to combat corruption. These factors are thus relevant for evaluating the transplant of an anti-corruption regime. Of particular importance for the acceptance of corrupt behaviour is whether a given population lives under a government

[78] See C. Milhaupt and K. Pistor, *Law and Capitalism: What Corporate Crises Reveal about Legal Systems and Economic Development around the World* (University of Chicago Press, 2008), pp. 516 *et seq.*

[79] A leading comparative jurist well summarises a widely held conception: 'Most importantly, a society of relations, or guanxi, may easily slide towards cronyism, the ongoing cultivation of reciprocal, unjustified advantage, to the exclusion of considerations of the outside world': H. P. Glenn, *Legal Traditions of the World: Sustainable Diversity in Law*, 4th edn (New York: Oxford University Press, 2010), p. 341.

[80] C. Provis, 'Guanxi and Conflicts of Interest', *Journal of Business Ethics*, 79 (2007), 57–68, at 58.

whose laws it can respect. Take, for example, the case of a people under the laws of an occupying foreign power, such as was the case in much of Europe during the Second World War:

> To live normally in occupied Europe meant breaking the law: in the first place the laws of the occupiers (curfews, travel regulations, race laws, etc.) but also conventional laws and norms as well. Most common people who did not have access to farm produce were obliged, for example, to resort to the black market or illegal barter just to feed their families ... In occupied Europe authority was a function of force alone ... Violence bred cynicism.[81]

When a government or the rules it imposes are widely perceived to violate natural law or popular custom, the subject population may well create a parallel code of behaviour and a black market that contravenes the government's rules. Persons who practice such defensive, clandestine civil disobedience for extended periods of time are naturally marked by it. A continuity bias would carry forward an expectation that corrupt behaviour is acceptable, regardless of whether it was a behaviour adopted in protest or one expected by the government itself. Much of the corruption during the first 130 years of the Hong Kong colony could be seen as European cynicism when faced with a Chinese culture they did not fully understand, and Chinese cynicism when faced with an English culture they did not fully understand. Accurately or inaccurately, Hong Kong's second governor, John Francis Davis, saw the Chinese of Hong Kong as:

> Born and bred in the universal belief of official venality and corruption from the undisguised habits of their native magistrates, who avowedly receive only a nominal pay from Government, and make up the bulk themselves. So indelible is this habitual conviction, that many of them in this Colony will never believe that the fines imposed by our Magistrates, under the Police and other Ordinances, are not for those Magistrates' own benefit; whereas in this Colony there is not even a fee in existence that is not paid into Her Majesty's Treasury.[82]

On the other side, as Munn observes, 'there is little doubt ... that European and other non-Chinese police were quite prepared to exploit their positions, and were perhaps restrained from certain sophisticated forms of extortion more by linguistic handicaps than by moral

[81] T. Judt, *Postwar: A History of Europe since 1945* (London: Heinemann, 2005), p. 37.

[82] Correspondence of 9 August 1847, cited in C. Munn, *Anglo-China: Chinese People and British Rule in Hong Kong, 1841–1880* (Hong Kong University Press, 2001), p. 294.

inhibitions'.[83] By 1859, Chief Magistrate and Colonial Secretary William Caine had been credibly charged with, *inter alia*, dispensing justice for fees and sexual favours, operating a private pirate network, falsely registering land in his own name, accepting bribes in administering the opium monopoly, profiting from a prostitution protection scheme and covering up the crimes of other officials.[84] The gradual consolidation of Hong Kong society on the edge of an imploding Chinese empire and through decades of hot and cold war led to the creation of a people of Hong Kong, which might be thought of as a Chinese culture with Western characteristics.[85] This may well be a factor in the success of numerous legal measures taken to create an anti-corruption regime in Hong Kong. The growing awareness that Hong Kong offered a viable, societal alternative to the mainland could support a sense of 'national' pride in establishing a clean Hong Kong. Another factor is simply a prescient policy that consequently removed opportunities for profitable corruption. As Goodstadt has argued, a reason for Hong Kong's famed *laissez faire* policy was to reduce the opportunities for business to seek favours from government.[86] The simple absence of government from most business activity may be another pillar supporting the growth of Hong Kong's strong anti-corruption culture.

Returning to China, and its own culture vis-à-vis corruption, there is little dispute that at least by 1976, many Chinese found themselves under a form of government that seemed to breed lawlessness and be driven by irrationality.[87] Indeed, a major target of the Cultural Revolution was the rule of law itself.[88] Under these circumstances, it is quite normal that many Chinese people would have turned to parallel systems of private ordering even if they violated the official rules imposed by the CCP; it also appears normal that this resort to private

[83] Munn, *Anglo-China*, p. 296. [84] Munn, *Anglo-China*, p. 300.

[85] As Steve Tsang remarks, 'the rule of law is more than an Anglo-Saxon political idea or legal concept. It is a way of life. It diverts completely from the Chinese legal tradition and remains an alien concept in the PRC, where it is routinely confused with "rule by law". It took Hong Kong a long time to understand and appreciate its value. By the 1990s, this idea had generally been accepted among the people of Hong Kong as a great gift from the British. They were proud that the rule of law prevailed in Hong Kong': S. Tsang, *A Modern History of Hong Kong* (London: I. B. Tauris, 2004), p. 274.

[86] L. F. Goodstadt, *Uneasy Partners: The Conflict between Public Interest and Private Profit in Hong Kong* (Hong Kong University Press, 2010), pp. 13, 121.

[87] See, e.g., R. Peerenboom, *China's Long March Toward Rule of Law* (New York: Cambridge University Press, 2002), pp. 55–6, 169–70.

[88] Peerenboom, *China's Long March*, p. 56.

ordering would have continued under and even be confused with the official sanction of private enterprise that began in 1978. As Luo observes, 'In the 1970s and 1980s, guanxi largely meant to obtain scarce consumer goods or to find a better job for one's children through the "back door".'[89] Luo argues that the Chinese Government has offered no widely accepted moral norms to accompany China's economic growth, so that 'although guanxi is not necessarily an origin or a source of corrupt behavior, it is a critical facilitator of corruption in a demoralized society. In a demoralized environment, the general principle of guanxi is shifted from favor exchange toward power exchange and gain sharing without obligating formal laws and informal relational norms.'[90] Unlike Hong Hong's *laissez faire* economy, moreover, the structure of China's state-managed commercial environment injects government officials into every aspect of business in China, from granting licences or allowing an IPO to go forward, to the appointment of corporate directors in most of China's largest companies. This offers ample opportunity to profit from breaches of duty. As McGregor observes, 'this combination – of wide administrative discretion amidst unprecedented economic opportunity – means that on-the-ground officials can make or break businesses, especially in localities far from larger cities, where there is less scrutiny and accountability. The potential for corruption is obvious.'[91]

In evaluating the transferability of the Hong Kong anti-corruption regime to the PRC, the question is thus whether the current structural promotion and pervasive acceptance of corrupt behaviour in China could be reversed through a comprehensive and powerful system designed to educate against, investigate into and prosecute corruption. Given the current structure of the PRC economy, the opportunities for corrupt behaviour by public officials are significantly greater than under Hong Kong's *laissez faire* regime. In future, it may well be that if the CCP were to be perceived as being unable to provide necessary services, a fair employment market, a safe environment and some mechanism for redistributing the excess wealth of the country's most fortunate

[89] Y. Luo, 'The Changing Chinese Culture and Business Behavior: The Perspective of Intertwinement between Guanxi and Corruption', *International Business Review*, 17 (2008), 188–93, at 192.

[90] Luo, 'The Changing Chinese Culture and Business Behavior', p. 189.

[91] R. McGregor, *The Party: The Secret World of China's Communist Rulers* (London: Allen Lane, 2010), pp. 934.

citizens, strong anti-corruption measures would not be enough to stem the tide of private self-help. Anti-corruption measures would inevitably catch in their net private attempts by frustrated citizens to counterbalance governmental failures, amplifying an existing conflict between public order and human rights. Gradual retreat of the public sector involvement in commercial dealings would reduce the opportunities of public officials to profit from corrupt behaviour, but could lead to a corresponding increase in the corrupt behaviour of private agents unless a culture of trust in the rule of law and duty to the general good is satisfactorily introduced. As such, unless accompanied by the broad reforms many citizens see as necessary, a campaign against corruption might well meet with the kind of cynical avoidance that Judt describes as dominating occupied Europe at mid-twentieth century. Even significant increases in the cost of corruption through China's liberal application of capital punishment might still have insufficient impact to reverse the tide of corruption. Anti-corruption measures could then be seen as just another tool 'used by the political leaders against their political rivals'.[92]

Beyond the difficulties brought by China being a state-managed, high-growth, transition economy with no real culture of civic society, it is also a nation of very large geographical expanse and massive population. Recent studies have shown some correlation between corruption and country size.[93] If size and population are relevant for a nation's people to commit themselves seriously in the fight against corruption, then these two factors will be very relevant in any transfer from Hong Kong to China. Size and population could tie in with the other determinants of corruption discussed above, allowing a citizen of a small, less populous country more easily to see his or her personal interests as aligned with those of the general good, or bring the breaches of bad actors in the nation emotionally and geographically closer to home. Negative information distributed within a smaller population can also have a greater impact on the reputation of that population's individual members. Indeed, all but two of the top ten ranked countries in Transparency International's Corruption Perception Index 2011 have populations of under 10 million and territories with a relatively small geographical

[92] Quah, 'Combating Corruption', p. 45.

[93] See, e.g., M. Amin, 'Is there More Corruption in Larger Countries? Evidence Using Firm-level Data', September 2011, available at: works.bepress.com, with further citations.

area.[94] In this context, it is relevant that Hong Kong's population constitutes about only about 0.5 per cent of China's and its geographical expanse is less than 0.02 per cent of the PRC.[95] In such a small area, even word of mouth might be able to spread reputational information to damage a known corrupt actor, but this dissemination is significantly amplified by Hong Kong's numerous, uncensored press and media outlets. The differences of history, political system, civic culture and education discussed above may well be amplified by the simple, physical proximity of a Hong Kong citizen to the seat of government and the speed with which reputational information can spread its deterring impact. All this indicates that transplanting to China the manner in which Hong Kong's anti-corruption regime successfully counters corrupting conflicts of interest will be no easy task.

[94] The top ten countries listed are New Zealand, Denmark, Finland, Sweden, Singapore, Norway, the Netherlands, Australia, Switzerland and Canada – and the next three are Luxembourg, Hong Kong and Iceland. See Transparency International, *Corruption Perception Index 2011* (London: Transparency International, 2011), available at: http://cpi.transparency.org. Number 14 on the list, Germany, with a population that is more than double that of Canada, the largest of the top ten, presents an exception to this rule as it does to many other rules, given its ability to achieve substantial uniformity in standards of behaviour amid significant political and geographical diversity.

[95] Hong Kong has a population of about 7 million, while that of China is about 1.35 billion. Hong Kong has a geographical expanse of about 1,000 km^2 while that of China is about 9.5 million km^2. See United Nations Department of Economic and Social Affairs, available at: http://esa.un.org and *Encyclopedia of the Nations*, available at: www.nationsencyclopedia.com.

PART II

Bribery without borders: tackling corruption in the EU and beyond

4

Bribery in Italy: an outlook on present laws and perspectives on reform

ROBERTO GUERRINI AND DARIO GUIDI

Introduction

In Italy, for some time now corruption has assumed the characteristics, both in its proportions and qualitative features, of a 'systemic' phenomenon, that contaminates vast sectors of administration and public life, not to mention a non-negligible part of business and finance.[1] As it turns out from the data supplied by the Court of Auditors at the inauguration of the judicial year, during the last few years, the number of sentences passed by the accounting magistracy against public employees for offences related to corrupt practices has registered an exponentially increasing trend. In 2010 alone, there was an increase of 30 per cent in comparison to the preceding year. The increase has been so great that, according to the attorney general of the same court, corruption today represents one of the main sources of damage to the Italian Government's revenue.[2]

Recently, moreover, the Italian press has given great prominence to the last report drafted by the non-governmental organisation, Transparency

[1] Italian scholars are in substantial agreement regarding the structural character of the 'corruption phenomenon', cf. G. Fiandaca, 'Esigenze e prospettive di riforma dei reati di corruzione e concussione', *Riv. it. dir. e proc. pen.* (2000), 883 *et seq.*; M. G. Vivarelli, 'Il fenomeno della corruzione', *Foro amm.* (2008), at 2928 *et seq.*; G. Forti (ed.), *Il prezzo della tangente. La corruzione come sistema a dieci anni da "mani pulite"* (Milano: Vita e Pensiero, 2003); P. Davigo and G. Mannozzi, *La corruzione in Italia, percezione sociale e controllo penale* (Bari: Laterza, 2007). As fairly observed by Romano, corruption is a practice, 'common and endemic in many countries, not at all excluded from those with a higher rate of civilization'. M. Romano, *Comm. sist. c.p., I delitti contro la pubblica amministrazione* (Milan: Giuffrè, 2006), p. 128.

[2] The data can be consulted in the report written by the Attorney General Mario Ristuccia, *Cerimonia di inaugurazione dell'anno giudiziario 2001*, 22 February 2011, available at: www.corteconti.it.

International (a global network with headquarters in Berlin to which more than ninety associations are members on a national basis), that every year compiles a ranking of the most corrupt countries based on the so-called CPI.[3] This index measures the level of 'perceived corruption' by several categories of citizen in each country, taking as its main reference point the opinion of managers, entrepreneurs, businessmen and political analysts.[4] In this ranking, Italy is not only placed in the 'lower part' of the list, it is also one of the few Western countries to have lost further ground in the last three years.[5] However, the scientific reliability of the data coming from this organisation is not incontrovertible. As we have said, it is an index that measures not the corruption actually present in a country, but the perception that the citizens have of this phenomenon. In this regard, it should be emphasised that among analysts and within the international community more and more doubts are being expressed regarding the foundation criteria adopted for measurement by Transparency International.[6]

However, the situation in Italy is alarming, above all when one considers that corruption is a phenomenon 'with a high degree of concealment' and therefore difficult to quantify.[7] In truth, as asserted with an effective metaphor in the first Servizio Anticorruzione e Trasparenza report (SaeT) to the Italian Parliament, 'corruption is like an iceberg of which we see only the tip emerging from the surface of the water'.[8] In effect, while we know with good approximation the dimensions of 'discovered corruption', forecast on the basis of the number of advanced

[3] Acronym of Corruption Perceptions Index.

[4] See the tables published in Transparency International Italy, at the section 'Indici corruzione', available at: www.transparency.it.

[5] Today Italy is positioned in sixty-seventh place, having dropped four positions since 2009, and as many as twelve positions since 2008.

[6] It is enough to consider, in this regard, that in October 2010, the OECD published a study in which the index *de quo* is censured for the insufficient reliability of the survey methods: C. P. Oman and C. Arndt, *Measuring Governance, Policy Brief No. 39* (Paris: OECD Development Centre, 2010). Of the rest, even the founder of this index, Johann Lambsdorff, who carried out the measurements with his collaborators at the University of Passau in recent years, abandoned the organisation in September 2009, claiming that Transparency International persists in maintaining 'artificially' live indexes that are no longer in a position to represent the truth. See the communication of 18 September 2009 published on the www.globalintegrity.org site.

[7] Davigo and Mannozzi, *La corruzione in Italia*, p. 4.

[8] The Servizio Anticorruzione e Trasparenza (SAeT) has operated as part of the Ministry for Public Administration and Innovation since 2 October 2008. It replaced the previous Office of the High Commissioner Against Corruption, established in 2003. The cited report to the Parliament is available at: www.innovazionepa.gov.it.

complaints and the sentences effectively passed, we know nothing of the real scope of the 'submerged part', conspicuous but presumably destined to remain beneath the surface. Also, beyond the mere statistical data, it is easy to see how the recent level of attention to the phenomenon of corruption has grown remarkably in Italy, both at the governmental–institutional level and in the sensibility of public opinion. In truth, from the end of 2008, the already-mentioned SAeT has been active within the Ministry for Public Administration and Innovation. In the first years of its existence it was engaged full-time in the difficult activity of collection and analysis of the data coming from several areas of the administration, the judiciary and the police. It was also responsible for preparing instruments of communitarian and international coordination, finalised to confront the phenomenon in a more homogeneous and effective manner. Italy, moreover, has still not actuated the Council of Europe Criminal Convention on Corruption,[9] ratified in September 2000, and the two 1997 conventions on fighting against corruption involving civil servants of the European Communities (EU) and foreign public officials in international business transactions (OECD). In August 2009, Italy also ratified the more recent United Nations Convention Against Corruption, adopted by the General Assembly meeting 31 October 2003 in Merida. This Convention – received integrally also with the aim of its execution together with Article 2 of the law it ratifies – has as its object, 'the promotion and the strengthening of the measures used to prevent and to fight corruption in the most effective way', alongside the 'promotion, facilitation and support of international cooperation and technical assistance with the aim of preventing corruption, including the recovery of assets'.[10]

Finally, in June 2010, the Senate of the Republic approved a bill of law of government initiative, entitled, 'Dispositions for the Prevention and the Repression of Corruption and Abuse in Public Administration'. Such a plan, currently under examination by the Justice Commission of the Chamber of Deputies, proposes more energetically to combat with greater effectiveness the corruption phenomenon through a 'differentiated strategy' that it is articulated in a series of measures destined to operate both through prevention (upgrading, in particular, the

[9] The Convention of Strasbourg of 27 January 1999 has been undersigned but not ratified by Italy.

[10] United Nations Convention Against Corruption, Art. 1 (the text of the Convention, in Italian translation, is available at: www.transparency.it site, in the section 'Pubblicazioni internazionali').

transparency of the administrative activity) or by repression (focusing on an increase in the sanction applied). This point will be explored below.

Legally protected interest and criminological dimension of the crimes of corruption

From a survey of the main doctrinal opinions, and from an analysis of the jurisprudence, emerges the absolute centrality of referring to Article 97, Codicil 1, of the Italian Constitution. This has the aim of securing a correct and up to date identification of protected legal assets within the 'Crimes of the public officials against the Public Administration' (Book II, Title II, heading I of the Criminal Code). This constitutional norm provides, that, 'public offices are organised according to legal dispositions so that the proper conduct[11] and the impartiality of the administration are guaranteed'.[12] The role played by this norm in the interpretation of criminal typologies, such as the above-mentioned Book II, Title II of the Penal Code, has been highlighted by our doctrine beginning from the second half of the 1960s. An authoritative direction assigns to the principles of proper conduct and impartiality the twofold importance of 'the theological restriction of the organization of public offices', and of 'the essential connotation of the administrative action'. This formulation has subsequently received further impetus with the organic reform of the system of crimes of public officials against the Public Administration, put into effect on 26 April 1990.[13] The main rationale of this law consisted in adapting the original system, *in parte qua*, to the new order of values emerging from the Constitution, moving the axis of protection from the (formalistic–authoritarian) sphere of the relationship between the state and its public civil servants to the (substantial–functional) sphere of the relationship between these two and the citizen.

[11] According to the translation of the Italian 'buon andamento' used by A. J. Peaslee, *Constitutions of Nations*, vol. III (The Hague: Martinus Nijhoff, 1968), p. 515.

[12] F. Bricola, 'Tutela penale della pubblica amministrazione e principi costituzionali', *Temi* (1968), 568 *et seq.*; R. Rampioni, *Bene giuridico e delitti dei pubblici ufficiali contro la pubblica amministrazione* (Milan: Giuffrè, 1984), pp. 257 *et seq.*; G. Vassalli, 'Corruzione propria e corruzione impropria', *Giust pen*, 2 (1979), 326; P. Nuvolone, 'Norme penali e principi costituzionali', in P. Nuvolone (ed.), *Trent'anni di diritto e procedura penale*, vol. I (Padova: CEDAM, 1969), pp. 678 *et seq.*

[13] This brought 'modifications on the topic of crimes of public officials against the Public Administration', constituting one of the main new interventions of a systematic character, made in the special section of the Rocco Code by the state legislator.

In the last two decades, Article 97 of the Constitution has carried out the fundamental role of 'polar star', influencing the immense extra-penal reforms in the matter of the civil service and the functional activities of the Public Administration. Such an apparatus of reforms has had as its common denominator the basic inspiration of the constitutional principles of 'proper conduct' and 'impartiality'.[14] These concepts, in fact, if correctly interpreted and developed in all of their potential implications, indicate to the legislator and the interpreter a model of modern and efficiently organised Public Administration according to the criteria of functionality and transparency. In truth, according to an opinion now widely shared, 'proper conduct' is not to be interpreted as a mere synonym of 'regular' operation of the administrative action, but more fully to mean the 'maximum adhesion to the public interest', designating the ability of the Public Administration to realise the purposes assigned to it by regulations.[15] Therefore, we are dealing with a parameter of measurement relating to the 'merit' of the administrative action that imposes an evaluation of the actions in terms of yield, productivity and efficiency.

The same can equally be said with reference to 'impartiality', given that the principle of impartiality is intended, in its traditional 'negative' meaning, as a prohibition on public civil servants taking advantage of their own position in order to illicitly benefit themselves or other private citizens to the detriment of the community. 'Impartiality' is also intended, though, to have a 'positive' meaning, as an obligation on the administration to proceed to identify and evaluate with equidistance and adequate weighting all of the interests involved in the administrative procedure, in order then to reach a final choice exclusively according to the criterion of the 'better public interest'.

The legally protected interest within the category of crimes against the Public Administration is thus defined in the master plan. However, it should be noted that if one observes more specifically the crimes of corruption, the identification of the focus of the scope of protection turns out to be anything but easy. The problem originates from the fact that in

[14] This can be cited with regard to the Law on Administrative Procedure, 7 August 1990, No. 241; the three laws of Bassanini of 1997; and the more recent d.lgs. of 27 October 2009, No. 150 (the so-called 'Brunetta law'); without forgetting the so-called 'Codice dei contratti pubblici', d.lgs. No. 163, 2006.

[15] See for all, Romano, *I delitti contro la pubblica amministrazione*, p. 10, and Rampioni, *Bene giuridico*, pp. 257 et seq.

the Italian penal system the concept of corruption, far from being identified in a single criminal typology, turns out to be fragmented in several subtypes divided on the basis of the type of action bought or sold and the moment in which the pact is stipulated (*pactum sceleris*). First, the Code distinguishes between corruption *propria*, which has as its object the fulfilment of an action contrary to the office duties, or the delay or the omission of an action; and *impropria*, which has as its object the fulfilment of an action in compliance with the office duties. A distinction then becomes relevant between *antecedent* corruption, which occurs when the criminal agreement is concluded prior to and based on the fulfilment of the action; and *subsequent* corruption, which is shaped when such agreement takes effect after the fulfilment of the action.

This complex configuration of the disciplinary code of corruption is reflected unavoidably in the topic of enucleating what are the legally protected goods. Italian doctrine is today essentially divided in this respect between two main interpretations. On one side, there are those who, albeit with subtle differences between them, incline towards a unitary reconstruction of the legally protected interest in the crimes of corruption. On the other side, are those who favour a differentiated reconstruction.

The first viewpoint cannot ignore the importance of the criteria defining proper conduct and impartiality in the hermeneutical recognition of the legal object of the cases of corruption; but it relegates such values to the background of protection. It considers them on the basis of a 'teleological frame' of reference, within which the legal interest is specifically protected, and identified singularly with 'the exclusive inspiration of the public function in the public interest'. In other words, it is identified with the interest that the actions of office do not constitute the object of a private sale.[16] Through the cases of corruption, therefore, 'the venality of the public subject and trade of the office or of the service are punished as real or potentially polluting factors of the administrative action'.[17]

[16] C. F. Grosso, 'Corruzione', *Dig disc. pen.*, 3 (1989), 153; A. Pagliaro, *Principi di diritto penale, parte speciale, vol. I: delitti contro la pubblica amministrazione* (Milano: Giuffrè, 2000), p. 150; Romano, *I delitti contro la pubblica amministrazione*, pp. 133 *et seq.*; D. Fornasari, 'Delitti di corruzione', in A. Bondi, A. di Martino and G. Fornasari (eds), *Reati contro la pubblica amministrazione* (Turin: Giappichelli, 2004), pp. 191 *et seq.*

[17] See, textually, Romano, *I delitti contro la pubblica amministrazione*, p. 134.

According to the alternative viewpoint, by contrast, the object of protection should be reconstructed in a way that is differentiated according to the various types of corruption.[18] The supporters of this point of view see the values of 'proper conduct' and 'impartiality' as the common denominator for enucleating the legally protected interest in all crimes against the Public Administration. However, they then draw analytical distinctions according to how such assets come into relief jointly or alternatively, that is, they form the object of direct or indirect protection in individual cases. More precisely, within this line of thought, one first distinguishes between corruption *propria* and *impropria*. The first form of corruption would be undoubtedly damaging to both proper conduct and to impartiality, because the public agent receives money or accepts its promise in exchange for an action contrary to the office duties (or to delay or to omit an office action). However, the second form of corruption prejudices only the good of impartiality. In this case, the *intraneus*, even though he or she is under a duty to maintain a totally extraneous position and an equidistance towards the interests involved in the procedure, accepts the payment or the promise of money or other profit for the execution of an action 'consistent' with the office duties and therefore does not create damage to the functionality of the administrative action. The conformity to office duties, in fact, implies, at least in general, a correct execution of the function and a correspondence to the best public interest. Indeed, as all sides agree, it can be presumed that the illicit retribution notably induces the public agent to carry out his activity with greater zeal, fulfilling more quickly his duties of office in relation to the bartered action.[19]

In the present context, and in light of the distinction in wording, it is necessary to distinguish further between *antecedent* and *subsequent* corruption. While in relation to the first of these an offensive action has already been carried out, things are more complex with regard to the second. In a case in which the *intraneus* receives money or other profit after having completed an action in compliance with his duties of office, even impartiality does not seem prejudiced since, at the moment at which

[18] G. Fiandaca and E. Musco, *Diritto penale, parte speciale, vol. I: delitti contro il patrimonio* (Bologna: Zanichelli, 2002), p. 217; Rampioni, *Bene giuridico*, pp. 305 *et seq.*; A. Segreto and G. de Luca, *Delitti dei pubblici ufficiali contro la pubblica amministrazione* (Milan: Giuffrè, 1999), p. 280.

[19] Vassalli, *Corruzione propria*, p. 58; Fiandaca and Musco, *Diritto penale*, p. 227; Romano, *I delitti contro la pubblica amministrazione*, p. 133.

the undue reward is given, the action has already occurred without any preventative external interference. In such a case, therefore, the *ratio* of the indictment would reside not only in the protection of the constitutionally important values of proper conduct and impartiality, but also 'in the requirement to prevent the occurrence of a kind of criminal progression from the reception of money for lawful activity to recompense for illicit interference'.[20] However, this form of corruption also turns out to be teleologically correlated to the fundamental principles of Article 97 of the Constitution. It concludes, in fact, by assigning to the *subsequent impropria* corruption a function of the anticipated protection of the values of proper conduct and impartiality, punishing the *intraneus* who receives money for having basically completed a correct action in compliance with his or her duties, and aiming to strike the corruption phenomenon at its origin in order to prevent the risk that in future the repetition of the trade of the functional activity becomes a consolidated praxis for the public agent, fatally extending itself over time to the execution of actions contrary to the duties of office.

Additionally, in spite of the variety of opinions seeking to reconstruct the exact objectivity of the protection referred to by corruption, there is unanimous acknowledgement that this criminal phenomenon constitutes a real obstacle to the progress and economic development of contemporary democracies, and not merely a factor instrumental in strong social destabilisation. It is not by chance that the fight against corruption and the crimes closely correlated to it (fiscal crimes, false social communications, money laundering, etc.) today constitutes one of the most shared-priority political–criminal objectives at domestic, European and international levels. All the agreements, conventions and doctrines during the last few years *in subiecta materia* express preoccupation with the ominous implications of generalised corruption in practice: serious alteration of the rules of competition; illicit interference in the allocation of public resources; regressive fiscal systems; reduction of foreign investments; and social destabilisation.

In synthesis, there is by now a diffused knowledge that corruption, in its inexorable tendency to extend itself to a systemic level, risks damaging the benchmarks of modern democracy by eroding, in its extreme development, the foundation of the *Rechtsstaat* and the social cohesion of its people. In this regard, it is enough to consider what is happening today in

[20] Fiandaca and Musco, *Diritto penale*, p. 229.

some North African and Middle Eastern countries (Algeria, Egypt, Libya, Syria, Bahrain), where the diffuse and chronic practice of corruption has worn away the vital ganglia of institutions and public administrations to such point as to generate a real 'short-circuit' in the operation of the state and the distribution of resources, hindering economic growth and engendering an inflationary tendency of enormous capacity. This has provoked widely diffused social dissatisfaction that, in the absence of democratic instruments to channel it, has recently led to public protests and violent forms of popular uprising against the government of the moment. The phenomenon of social disintegration existing today in countries in which the 'cancer' of corruption is rooted and diffused, therefore testifies that the last, if not diagnosed and combated in a timely manner and with suitable instruments, can represent a serious threat to democracy and to the resilience of state institutions.

The state of enforced legislation in Italy

As we have already remarked, in Italy the *codicistica* discipline of corruption is articulated in numerous cases that form a kind of 'unitary minisystem'.[21] Markedly, in our current Penal Code, the following criminal typologies are present: (a) corruption for an act of office (so-called '*impropria*': Article 318); (b) corruption for an action contrary to the duties of office (so-called '*propria*': Article 319); (c) corruption in legal proceedings (Article 319*ter*); (d) instigation to corruption (Article 322); (e) corruption and instigation to corruption of members of the organs and the civil servants of the European Communities (Article 322*bis*). Articles 320 and 321 complete this normative picture by extending the application of Articles 318 and 319, in which only the public official figures as an active subject, to the person responsible for the public service and to the private corruptor.

The basic distinction between *propria* and *impropria* corruption has already been covered (see section above). Turning now to the other hypotheses outlined above, we should first note the corruption in legal proceedings offence that applies when the facts bring the offence within Articles 318 and 319 (more precisely, corruption for an act of office or an action contrary to the office duties) and is committed in order to favour or to damage a party in a civil, penal or administrative proceedings.

[21] The expression is from Romano, *I delitti contro la pubblica amministrazione*, p. 128.

This criminal typology, introduced in the actual formulation of Article 9 within the already-mentioned law No. 86 of 1990, is characterised by a very severe sanctioning framework (imprisonment from three to eight years). Further, among the active perpetrators of the crime endowed with public qualifications, only the most important of these is contemplated, the public official: the person in charge of a public service is not contemplated (Article 320 does not contain any reference to Article 319*ter*). Both of these features are easily explained when one considers first, on one side, the amplitude of the sphere of protection of Article 319*ter*, that touches on the correct exercise of the judicial function. Secondly, on the other side, there is the different nature of the respective powers attributed by the legislator to the two subjective typologies, respectively, of the public official and the person responsible for the public service; only the first one is in a position to influence the content of a judicial decision. As for the cases of instigation to corruption, it punishes, in its first two codicils, the private party that offers or promises money or other undue profit to a public agent to entice him or her to complete an act of office or to delay, or omit, an act of office, or to complete an action contrary to the duties of office in the case of not-accepted instigation, and, in the third and fourth codicils, the public agent that solicits from a private party payment of money for the same purposes and with the same result (non-acceptance of the instigation). Finally, Article 322*bis* extends the application of the main criminal typologies included in the so-called Penal Charter of Public Administration (those dealing with corruption) to a series of subjects, operating at a communitarian and international level, listed in the same Article (the members of the European Parliament or the Court of Law of the European Union).

Such a complicated arrangement of the discipline, even having been the object of some important modifications to law No. 86/90, has not suffered distortion and, indeed, has remained faithful, at least in its essential outline, to the original strategy delineated by the Rocco Code (1930). The subsequent reforms of 1990 have not affected the structure base and the types of corruption crimes. Reform was limited to the modification of the sanctioning treatment (eliminating the pecuniary penalty in relation to all the corruption crimes; increasing the minimum penalty for corruption *impropria*; equalising *quoad poenam* of the corruption *propria* subsequent to that antecedent), extension of the cases of instigation to corruption (Article 322 c.p.), and also to cases in which the instigating conduct comes from the public official or from the person in charge of the public service. Moreover, the already-described instance of corruption in legal proceedings, originally configured by the Penal Code as an aggravating circumstance of corruption, has been rendered independent – with the contribution of modifications to the configuration of the typical facts[22] – and today constitutes an incriminating case of its own.

There has been confirmation, therefore, of the basic choices available to the legislator of 1930 not only, as already pointed out, with respect to the structure of the crime and to the *summa divisio* between corruption for an act of office and corruption for an action contrary to the duties of office, but also with regard to the mechanism of extending the ability to punish subjects other than the public official. Under this last profile, two things remain unchanged. First, the equalisation between the public agent and *extraneus* established by Article 321 c.p., according to which the penalties foreseen for the several varieties of corruption are applied also to the private party that gives or promises money or other profit to the public official or the person in charge of the public service (with the only exception represented by the subsequent *impropria* corruption of that paragraph of Article 318 c.p., in relation to which the private party is not punishable), and the attenuation of the penalty for the case in which the subject *intraneus* applies to the role of a person in charge of a public service rather than to a public official. In this case, according to Article 320 c.p., Codicil 2, 'the penalties are reduced to not more than a third'. The same Article 320, finally, restricts the application of corruption *impropria* to the person in charge of a public service that also holds a public employee qualification.

In the past, it was thought that the norms of the Penal Code in reality shaped two distinct crimes of corruption, one having as its author a private party (c.d., 'active corruption'), the other having as its author the public official (c.d. 'passive corruption').[23] Today, the unitary

[22] According to the existing text of Art. 319 c.p., an increased penalty is foreseen in the event where, from the facts derived, 'the favour or the damage of one of the parties in a civil, penal or administrative trial' is possible. Today, vice versa, it returns to the figure of corruption in legal proceedings 'if the facts indicated in arts. 318 and 319 are committed in order to favour or to damage a party in a civil, penal or administrative trial'. There has, therefore, been an important anticipation of the indictment threshold.

[23] N. Levi, 'I delitti contro la pubblica amministrazione', in E. Florian (ed.), *Trattato di diritto penale* (Milan: Giuffrè, 1935), p. 264; S. Riccio, 'Corruzione', *Noviss Dig. It.*, vol. IV (Turin: UTET, 1959), p. 899. More recently, in a substantially analogous sense: A. Pagliaro, *Principi di diritto penale, parte speciale, I delitti contro la pubblica amministrazione* (Milan: Giuffrè, 2000), pp. 155 *et seq.*

reconstruction prevails almost unanimously, or rather the thesis according to which corruption, regardless of its specific form of manifestation (*propria*, *impropria*, antecedent, subsequent, etc.), always assumes the appearance of a single crime, reflecting a bilateral crime contract focused on the agreement of the parties, and on the perpetration of a complementary and closely interdependent conduct between them.[24] In truth, beyond the mere difference in terminology, in corruption we always find ourselves confronting two forms of conduct in which a 'give' and a 'take' exist on both sides. First, the public agent receives the payment or the promise of money or other profit and gives in exchange an action consistent with, or contrary to, the duties of his office. Secondly, the private party receives the action and in exchange gives or promises money or other profit. We are therefore dealing with a single crime with necessarily multiple subjects, a typology that occurs in our system when it is the same incriminating norm of a special section that demands the presence of two or more subjects to constitute the crime (in this specific case: public agent, so-called *intraneus*, and private citizen, so-called *extraneus*). It appears, therefore, opportune to analyse singularly, albeit briefly, some basic ideas that occur in the various varieties of corruption.

Fundamental, first of all, is the concept of 'act of office'.[25] This expression designates the legitimate action that figures within the functional competence of the public agent and represents the execution of the powers inherent in the office or the service. It is commonly held, however, that the act of office does not necessarily figure within the specific competence of the public agent: it is sufficient that the act can be traced to the generic competence of the office to which the *intraneus* belongs.[26] Moreover, the expression 'act of office' should not be understood in the technical-restrictive sense as a synonym for a formal action of an

[24] Cf., *ex plurimis*, Fiandaca and Musco, *Diritto penale*, p. 215; Romano, *I delitti contro la pubblica amministrazione*, p. 134.

[25] On this point, cf., *amplius*, M. Pellissero, 'La nozione di atto d'ufficio nel delitto di corruzione tra prassi e teoria', in *Dir pen proc*, No. 8 (Milan: Ipsoa, 2000), pp. 1011 *et seq*.

[26] See, the last case, Cass. pen., sez. VI, 2 March 2010, No. 20502, *Ced Cass*, 2010, in which it is asserted explicitly that, 'to the aim of establishing the crime of corruption, either *propria* or *impropria*, it is not determining the fact that the act of office or contrary to the duties of office is compensated within the confines of the specific duties of the public official or the person in charge of a public service, but it is necessary and sufficient that it features an action that is a part of the competences of the office to which the subject belongs and in relation to which he exercises, or can exercise, some form of interference, or also of mere fact'. In a consistent manner: Cass. pen., sez. VI, 4 May 2006, n. 33435, *Cass pen.*, 2006, p. 3578; Cass. pen., sez. I, 27 October 2003, No. 4177, *ibid.*, 2005, p. 449.

administrative, legislative or judicial nature, but rather as a broader notion including any action that constitutes a concrete execution of the powers inherent in the office, including the material behaviour used by the public agent in the exercise of his or her own duties.

The correct interpretation of the normative formula 'act of office' assumes preliminary importance when seeking to understand the parallel concept of 'contrariety to the duty of office'. On this point, two different interpretations are currently in contention. According to one formalistic interpretation, imprinted perhaps with excessive rigour, the expression *de qua* would be extended to embrace every conduct of the public agent who places himself in conflict with any legal norm or with the good use of the discretionary power of the Public Administration.[27] It follows that as actions contrary to the duties of office should be considered not only illegitimate or illicit actions in a limited sense, but also those which, albeit formally in compliance, contrast with the generic duties of conduct of the public official (fidelity, prestige, obedience, secrecy, etc.).

According to the other interpretation, the appraisal of the action must be targeted not at the generic duties of conduct correlated to the role covered, but at the single and specific duties that in concrete terms govern the exercise of the function.[28] This interpretation is inspired by the constitutional dictate according to which the 'contrariety to the duty of office' is reconstructed in light of the requirements of proper conduct and impartiality. From this angle, the 'contrariety to the duties of office' would restrictively be understood as a synonym for the 'illegitimacy' of the action similar to norms that discipline the typical defects of the administrative action.

Another notion of pre-eminent importance in the Code's definition of corruption is that of 'recompense'. Markedly, according to Article 318 c.p., the public agent who receives money or other profit, or accepts its promise

[27] F. Antolisei, 'Manuale di diritto penale', in L. Conti (ed.), *Parte speciale*, vol. II (Milan: Giuffrè, 2003), p. 333; Pagliaro, *Principi di diritto penale*, p. 191; Segreto and de Luca, *Delitti dei pubblici ufficiali*, p. 360. This stance is still clearly prevalent within jurisprudence: Cass. pen., sez. VI, 18 June 2010, No. 24656, *Guida dir*, 2010, 43, p. 98; Cass. pen., sez. VI, 14 May 2009, n. 30762, *Ced Cass*, 2009; Cass. pen., sez. VI, 15 May 2008, No. 34417, *Cass pen*, 2009, p. 1420; C. App. Milano, 20 November 2008, No. 3359, *Guida dir*, 2009, 14, p. 79.

[28] Fiandaca and Musco, *Diritto penale*, p. 224; C. F. Grosso, 'Dazione o promessa di denaro al pubblico ufficiale in ragione delle funzioni esercitate: corruzione punibile o fatto penalmente atipico?', *Foro it.*, 2 (1996); C. Benussi, 'Art. 319', in G. Marinucci and E. Dolcini (eds), *Codice penale commentato* (Milan: Giuffrè, 2006), p. 2263.

in the form of 'undue recompense' is punishable. This means that between the payment or the promise of money from a private party and the fulfilment of the action by the public agent, there must exist a synallagmatic relationship, that is, the money received by the *intraneus* must constitute an exchange for the fulfilment of the action. The concept of recompense goes back therefore to that of 'proportion', in the sense that between the 'performance' of the private party and the 'counter-performance' of the public agent there must always exist a relationship of (at least in tendency) symmetry.[29] This does not happen, for instance, in the event of donation of small advantages (the so-called *munuscula*): for example, when the profit given by the private party is of such small value, like a box of chocolates or a bunch of flowers, as not to be able to play the role of authentic 'counter-performance' regarding the fulfilment of the action from the *intraneus*.

Such a relationship of proportion, however, would also seem to characterise the other form of corruption. Even if in the text of Article 319 c.p. (corruption *propria*) there is no explicit reference to 'recompense', in fact, the prevailing opinion is that this concept must be considered in these cases.[30] In effect, the nexus of reciprocity (*do ut des*) that characterises 'synallagmatic' relationships and actions exists also in corruption, precisely from the moment that the payment of money from the private party is nothing if not the 'equivalent' of the fulfilment of an action contrary to the duties of office by the public agent. In other words, the private party 'gives recompense' to the civil servant in order to receive a counter-performance of value usually correspondent to his own (contrary action to the duty of office or omission or delay of an action of office). So, a relationship of similar proportions must also exist between the two corresponding actions in this form of corruption.

A third common element to the several typologies of corruption is constituted in the 'utility or profit' that, in alternative to money,

[29] In this sense, among many cases, see Cass. pen., sez. VI, 15 July 2008, No. 46065, in *CED Cass* 2008; Cass. pen., sez. VI, 5 September 2002, Rossi, *Riv pen*, 2003, p. 666; Cass. pen., sez. VI, 25 March 1999, Di Pinto, *Cass pen*, 2000, p. 1223.

[30] Fiandaca and Musco, *Diritto penale*, p. 222; Grosso, 'Corruzione', p. 153; Pagliaro, *Principi di diritto penale*, p. 172. Romano is placed at an intermediate position as, according to him, corruption *propria*, even if not being able to speak of real and proper 'retribution', 'introduces the essential synallagmatic relationship between extra compensation and the action future or past'. A clean disproportion between the corresponding performances would also exclude the configuration of the crime here. Romano, *I delitti contro la pubblica amministrazione*, p. 183

represents, in Articles 318, 319 and 322 c.p., the correspondence to the fulfilment of the action by the public agent. Regarding the semantic capacity of such a concept, the doctrine was in the past essentially divided between two interpretations. The first interpretation, the majority one, was inclined towards a wider notion of utility, suitable to include any action advantageous to the official, be it patrimonial or non-patrimonial, material or moral.[31] According to the second interpretation, the minority one, the application of such a notion was limited to the single advantage of a patrimonial or rather material nature.[32] The dispute can be said to have been overcome today, in the sense that the doctrine and jurisprudence currently dominant are substantially in agreement in thinking that the utility concept should be reconstructed, not in reference to the patrimonial or non-patrimonial nature of the advantage, but with regard to the existence or not of a synallagmatic connection between the action of the *intraneus* and the counter-action of the *extraneus*. In this view, an advantage of a non-patrimonial nature, such as a sexual favour, can without doubt constitute a corrupt benefit, provided that such advantage, in its concrete actualisation, assumes the role of 'correspondence' to the fulfilment of the action by the public agent and therefore represents to all intents and purposes the 'recompense'.[33]

To complete the picture sketched so far of the state of the current legislation *in subiecta materia*, an additional variety of corruption deserves to be considered. This is a species placed outside the Penal Code, but included within the range of the so-called 'corporate crimes' in Title XI, Book V of the Civil Code ('Penal dispositions in the matter of companies and consortia'). It refers to the cases contemplated by Article 2635 c.c., called '*private corruption*' by the first commentators.[34] This crime punishes with up to three years' imprisonment the administrators, general manager, managers at the head of the company's accounting records, mayors and liquidators who, as a result of payment or promise of profit, perform or omit actions in violation of the obligations inherent

[31] G. Maggiore, *Diritto penale*, vol. II (Bologna: Zanichelli, 1950), pp. 155 *et seq.*; Riccio, *Corruzione*, p. 901; R. Venditti, 'Corruzione (delitti di)', *Enc dir*, 10 (1962), 757.

[32] Levi, 'I delitti contro la pubblica amministrazione', p. 250; R. Pannain, *I delitti dei pubblici ufficiali contro la pubblica amministrazione* (Naples: Jovene, 1966), pp. 138 *et seq.*

[33] As such, in doctrine, Fiandaca and Musco, *Diritto penale*, p. 223; Romano, *I delitti contro la pubblica amministrazione*, p. 111; Pagliaro, *Principi di diritto penale*, p. 181. In jurisprudence, from the last Cass. pen., sez. VI, 18 June 2010, No. 24656, *Cass pen*, 2011, p. 1780.

[34] Listed as 'infidelity as a result of payment or promise of profit'.

in their office causing damage to the company. The same penalty is applied, based on a paragraph of the same Article 2635 c.c., to one who gives or promises the profit, confirming that this form of corruption is configured as a single crime involving agreement. We also find ourselves here facing two actions mirrored and interdependent: that of the *extraneus*, that gives or promises money or other form of profit, and that of the *intraneus* that, as a result of such payment or promise, performs or omits actions in violation of the obligation inherent in his or her office. From this exchange of 'synallagmatic' actions must stem 'damage to the company'.

Obviously, the group of the active subjects is, in this case, more limited with respect to the macro-category of the public agent (public officials and individuals in charge of a public service) that characterises the cases of corruption contemplated within the Penal Code. Moreover, in the 'private corruption' variety there must be a damaging event, the harm to which the company is subjected, not included in the other forms of corruption. Beyond the important differences, among other things, easily explicable with the peculiar configuration of corporate crimes, the structure of the crime under investigation introduces numerous points of similarity with 'traditional' cases of corruption.

The season of '*mani pulite*' and the so-called 'Cernobbio plan'

Prior to the reform of the penal charter of the Public Administration, there was already evidence of defects and inadequacies in the 1990 reforms. First, the reforms did not introduce truly meaningful modifications to the penal repression of corruption and the abuses committed in the execution of public economic activity. The reforms showed themselves to be intrinsically weak precisely in a field in which the requirement for a totally new order of discipline was most clear.[35] Secondly, the absence of a complete strategy of institutional reform was criticised, insofar as it could, 'affect the perverse circuits that render the Public Administration too permeable to the interests of a private party and to easy profiteering'.[36] The absence of an all-encompassing strategy emphasised how a reform limited to penal norms could not represent an effective obstacle to the spread of illegality and corruption.

[35] For a summarising account of such critiques see Fiandaca and Musco, *Diritto penale*, pp. 159 *et seq*.

[36] Fiandaca and Musco, *Diritto penale*, p. 161.

The serious limits to law No. 86/90 were dramatically revealed in the space of a few years with the outbreak of the so-called phenomenon of '*Tangentopoli*'. In the period immediately following the reform, a famous wide-ranging judicial inquiry, called '*mani pulite*', brought to light an immense amount of corruption, consolidated and systemic, that involved politicians, entrepreneurs, financiers and high-level civil servants of the state.[37] Such a system was centred around 'agreements of a stable character that assured a constant flow of illicit financing to the parties from the enterprises that came into contact with the Public Administration for the execution of activities and services, through the practice of side-payments'.[38] In other words, a generalised phenomenon of misbehaviour in the relationships between the political system and the economic world, in which side-payments for the award of public contracts, the concession of building licences, the realisation of institutional financial operations, etc. were seen as an obligatory route to success, and in some way intrinsic to the transactions, came to the surface for the first time.

The season of '*mani pulite*' started with investigations led by a pool of magistrates of the attorney general of the Republic of Milan, guided by Francesco Saverio Borrelli and his deputy Gerardo D'Ambrosio. It continued in successive years, extending to substantial part of the national territory.[39] From the beginning, the enquiry quickly became prominent in the media (unsurprisingly, given the importance and the number of subjects involved) and had a shattering impact on public opinion and on the main centres of power at the time; revolutionising, in fact, the Italian political–institutional scene. In truth, the clamour provoked by the many warnings of guarantee and decrees of precautionary custody towards eminent political exponents, together with the economic crisis of the early 1990s, led quickly to the disintegration of the old ruling class and to the consequent exit from the political scene of the traditional parties, marking the epochal passage to the so-called 'second Republic'.

From the strictly judicial point of view, the season of '*mani pulite*' concluded with a small number of sentences (in Milan, the epicentre of the inquiry, little more than 1,000 between abbreviated trial and ordinary

37 Cf. R. Guerrini, 'The Crimes of Civil Servants against the Public Administration in Italy: Perspectives of Reform', *Studi Senesi* (1997), 411 *et seq.*

38 Vivarelli, 'Il fenomeno della corruzione', p. 2935.

39 The beginning of *Tangentopoli* is traditionally dated to 17 February 1992, the date of the arrest of Mario Chiesa, the famous exponent of the Milan PSI and president of the Pio Albergo Trivulzio.

trial): all together a rather meagre return, considering the size of investigations and the number of registrations in the crime registry.[40] It can easily be asserted, therefore, that it constituted a judicial experience now historically placed and circumscribed in a relatively short temporal arc. Nevertheless, once popular support in Italy for the 'moralising' action of the magistrates weakened, a remarkable 'lowering of the guard' regarding the phenomenon developed with respect to corruption, both at the level of public opinion and towards the plan of the basic political choices in the *sujecta material*.[41] From this last angle, a substantial do-nothing policy on the part of Italian legislators can be recorded during the last few years, which has been counterbalanced by an excessive dynamism in the jurisprudence developed from the requirement to adapt in an interpretative way the Code's system to the new 'morphology' of the corruption facts. The character of these facts has changed deeply over the course of time, to the point that today we cannot speak of side-payments in the traditional sense, since 'new' corruption resorts to other instruments of recompense, and has metamorphosed, in more general terms, into a network of exchanges of favours and utility or profit.[42] In the majority of the cases, moreover, the corruption does not have as its object a single action bought or sold, but an entire functioning relationship.

Not by chance, a recent direction of reform on the topic of fighting corruption, asserted both at the supranational level (see the already-mentioned Convention of Strasbourg 1999) and at the internal level (see below, 'New models of protection and future perspectives'), postulates the introduction of a wider offence having for its object, alternatively or cumulatively, 'the sale of the action, the function or the position'. The basic idea is to replace a plurality of criminal typologies subdivided on the basis of *criterium individuationis* of the type of action bought or sold with a single more general typology generated in the

[40] See the so-called 'effect funnel', represented graphically in Davigo and Mannozzi, *La corruzione in Italia*, p. 137, on the basis of a completed elaboration of the data supplied by the Procura della Repubblica di Milano.

[41] Cf. Vivarelli, 'Il fenomeno della corruzione', p. 2936. According to him, in the successive years to *Tangentopoli* there was 'a certain reduction in the comparisons of the corruption phenomenon, consisting in the tendency to underrate its seriousness, through reducing the economic capacity of the patrimonial dimension of the tangent to the illicit exchange between the corrupted and the corruptor'.

[42] Regarding the criminological evolution of the corruption phenomenon from 1930 to today, see F. Palazzo, 'La tutela penale della pubblica amministrazione e il rapporto tra politica e legalità', in S. Vinciguerra and F. Dassano (eds), *Scritti in onore di G. Marini* (Naples: ESI, 2010), p. 631.

period of *Tangentopoli*. This is part of a plan elaborated by a group of experts on the matter, composed of magistrates of the attorney general's office of Milan, university professors and lawyers. This initiative involves a proposal to strengthen the instruments to fight the corruption phenomenon through a twofold strategy.[43] First, stimulating the individual propensity towards denunciation through providing a so-called 'strategy of rewards'. It was proposed to introduce a special clause of impunity for:

> anyone who denounced spontaneously, and before anyone else, an episode of corruption (*impropria* or *propria*) within three months from the realisation of the illicit action and before the news of a crime was inserted in the general registry under the subject's name, having supplied useful indications for the identification of the other persons responsible.[44]

The application of such impunity was subordinated to the previous realisation of reparatory conduct by the active subjects of the crime, that is, in particular, the restitution of the sum received as a side-payment from the corrupt party and the disposition of a sum equal to the amount given by the corrupting party.

The second part of the strategy focused on the coexistence in the Italian ordering of two contiguous criminal typologies: corruption and 'concussione'.[45] To date this distinction has produced more breakdowns than advantages in relation to both trial and evidence. So, it was proposed to eliminate this distinction by reformulating corruption as macro-cases of the most general capacity with consequently increasing penalties. On that view, the indicted conduct would no longer have to centralise itself on the action of the office, but on the relation between the promise or the acceptance of undue profit and the 'quality, functions or activity' of the public official or the person in charge of a public service.

Thus, the distinction between corruption *impropria* and *propria* and antecedent and subsequent was lessened, and within the concept of corruption intended in this wider sense was also included concussione

[43] The text of the project, entitled, 'Proposte in materia di prevenzione della corruzione e dell'illecito finanziamento ai partiti', but commonly known as 'Progetto Cernobbio', can be found in *Riv. it. dir. proc. pen.* (1994), 1025 *et seq.* For an *excursus* on the various bills of law presented to overcome the corruption emergency, see also C. Longobardo, 'I progetti per uscire da "Tangentopoli"', *Riv. trim. dir. pen. econ.* (2000), 288 *et seq.*

[44] 'Proposte in materia di prevenzione', p. 1027 (*sub* Art. 10).

[45] The crime of 'concussione' is a peculiarity of the Italian Criminal Code. It represents an extortion committed by civil servants in two ways: by constriction or by induction.

by induction. On the other side, the hypotheses of the overpowering of the private party by the public agent who acts with violence or threats, currently traceable to concussione by constriction, was made to merge with all the general cases of extortion with an aggravation of penalty correlated to the subjective qualification and the modalities of the conduct (abuse of the qualities or the powers). This last proposal for reform, aside from every appraisal of merit, carries great importance because, as pointed out above, in Italy it has returned to current relevance within some of the bills introduced during the last few years by the opposition forces that are still waiting in Parliament (of which, see section 'New models of protection and future perspectives', below).

The concrete instruments at the disposition of the Italian system

Corruption, both for the intrinsic characteristics of the basic crime and for the variety of forms that it can concretely assume, is a phenomenon of the highest obscured numbers, or, as it can also be said, of the highest rate of concealment. This is easily explained if it is considered, on one side, that corruption does not leave the usual direct traces or witnesses and, from the other side, that the perpetrators, a public agent and an *extraneus*, are joined by a tie of mutual convenience and have therefore a common interest to cover each other with the aim of avoiding the emergence of the *pactum sceleris* that binds them. In corruption, in other words, the classic carrier of the denunciation is missing, that is, the physical victim who, having been victimised, has an interest in the intervention of a judicial authority. When single episodes of corruption arise not from the effective collaboration of one or more of the involved subjects or from the correct operation of some virtuous administrative control system, but rather from an inner short-circuit to the criminal exchange, if the rules of the agreement are aborted, 'the possibility increases that someone is induced or more motivated to denounce the fact or in any case to collaborate with the investigators'.[46]

Quite commonly, thus, the only operating instrument available to the investigators to uncover the secret agreement on which the fact of corruption rests is represented by 'interceptions of communications or conversations' (Article 266 ss. c.p.p.). These enter in the 'means of

[46] Davigo and Mannozzi, *La corruzione in Italia*, p. 5.

research for evidence' (Title III, Book III of the c.p.p.) and they are divided into two types: (a) wiretaps, that have as their object telephone conversations or communications and other forms of telecommunication (Article 266 c.p.p.), including computer communications or data transmissions (Article 266*bis* c.p.p.); and (b) 'open' interceptions, that have for their object communications between the parties present (Article 266, Codicil 2, c.p.p.). In the case of the latter, however, if the communication happens in certain places (a room or other space of a private dwelling, Article 614 c.p.), the interception is permitted only if there is a good reason to think that the criminal activity is being carried out there. An indispensable condition common to all the cases is the third-party nature of the operator with regard to the interlocutors: the subject that carries out the interception must be a stranger to the conversation and operate in a clandestine way. On the other side, if a person who participates actively in a conversation, or is admitted to witness it, carries out a recording, the relevant tape is not subject to the law governing interceptions but assumes the nature of a 'document', and as such is usable in the process.

In the Italian system, the possibility of carrying out interceptions is subordinated to limits and conditions so as to mitigate the investigative requirements with the constitutional demand, according to which 'the freedom and the secrecy of correspondence and of every other form of communication are inviolate' (Article 15 Cost.). From the combined dispositions of Articles 266 and 267 c.p.p. a triple order of conditions applies. First, the interceptions are permitted in the proceedings only relative to the crimes enumerated in Article 266, Codicil 1, c.p.p. Secondly, they must be authorised by a judge upon the request of the prosecuting attorney. Thirdly, such authorisation can be given only when the interception operations are absolutely indispensable to the prosecution in their investigation and there exist serious indications of crime. For the aims of this analysis, the first condition is of the most interest, given that between the cases enumerated in Article 266 c.p.p. there is also that of 'crimes against the Public Administration punished with a penalty not inferior to the maximum five years' (Codicil 1, lett. b). This means that interceptions are not admitted for all cases of corruption, but only for the most serious ones, that is, in relation to the *propria* corruption and corruption in legal proceedings. It is necessary to keep in mind, in fact, than in *impropria* corruption, that has as its object an action in compliance with the duties of office, the range of sanctions is placed well below the limit indicated by the code of criminal procedure, extending itself from six months to three years in the event of antecedent corruption, and up to one year in the event of subsequent corruption. Vice versa, the *propria* corruption (that has as its object an action contrary to the duties of office or the omission or the delay of an action of office) is punished with confinement of two to five years. The interceptions are permissible also with reference to the crime of corruption in legal proceedings, whose sanctioning framework consists of confinement of three to eight years.

Recently, the topic of the reform of the regime for interceptions has provoked a heated debate between the political forces of the majority and those of the opposition. The object of contention is represented by the proposal, advanced many times over by the government in the course of the last year, further circumscribing the number of the crimes for which it is possible to effect interceptions and to introduce strict penalties for the journalists who publish the content of these before the so-called 'audience filter'. The political tension reached its apex at the beginning of October 2011, when the president of the Justice Commission to Parliament, Giulia Bongiorno, announced her resignation from her assignment as reporter of the interceptions for examination by the Commission. This was as a result of an amendment introduced by a representative of the majority (Enrico Costa), which extends further the time frame in which publication is prohibited and increases the sanctions for transgressors. With the increasing importance of the economic crisis, the process of approval of this bill has been interrupted abruptly, for the moment damping down the bitter controversies unleashed from more recent developments. Nonetheless, it remains a basic question of difficulty to find a point of equilibrium between the right to confidentiality, often seriously damaged by the anticipated publication of conversations of a intensely private character that are then demonstrated to be insignificant in relation to the true object of the proceedings, and the investigative requirements to use the most effective means for the search for evidence that can sometimes be satisfied only with the use of interceptions. However, it is hoped that a problem this important and delicate will be confronted in the future in a more serene and constructive climate, requiring a relationship of effective collaboration between all political forces.

In the fight against corruption, it is important to keep in focus at all levels (investigative, preventive, repressive) the so-called 'satellite' crimes correlated to corruption crimes, such as corporate crimes or fiscal crimes. Emblematic in this regard are crimes involving false social communications (Articles 2621 and 2622 c.c.),[47] which punish the administrators, general managers, managers in charge of the company accounting records, mayors and liquidators who act with the intention of defrauding the associates or the public and with the aim of achieving for themselves or others an unjust profit. So, in the balance sheet, the reports or the other social communications required by law, directed to the associates or the public, expose material facts not corresponding to the truth or omit communication of information which is required by the law regarding the economic, patrimonial or financial institution of the company or the group to which it belongs. In many cases, such a situation is manufactured with the principal aim of keeping hidden from the associates and the public prior reserves and successive management of financial reserves not accounted for, to employ them in the illicit distribution of money within corrupt exchanges.

In this regard, it is considered that one of the maxi-processes that the season of '*mani pulite*' started had as its object the wrongdoing involved in the creation, concealment and management of extra-budget funds (so-called 'secret funds'). A well-known example is the Enimont trial that, even having as its main culprit a figure of secondary importance, a mere intermediary, saw the involvement of important political exponents of the 'first Republic'.[48] In this case, the crime of balance sheet fraud was merely instrumental to the realisation of other, more serious crimes. This was so from the moment that the hidden supplies, previously set aside by the administrators of the company, were used to carry out undocumented payments to suppliers in order to conclude corrupt agreements with officials of the Financial Police and in order to finance political parties and journalists in exchange for favours. In this case, as in other similar cases, therefore, the discovery of the 'satellite crime' allowed the investigators to force into the open the facts of correlated corruption.

[47] 'Fraud in the balance sheet', according to journalistic jargon. As a result of the reform of trading crimes, put into effect with d.lgs. 11 April 2002, No. 61, the balance sheet of fraud today is subdivided into two criminal types: a '*delitto*' and a '*contravvenzione*', respectively. These are distinguished by the presence or not, in the typical scheme, of an event of patrimonial damage towards the company.

[48] The 'Enimont' was a joint venture derived from the fusion between two petrochemical colossi: Eni and Montedison. For a fuller account of such controversial vicissitudes, see S. Monari, 'Utilizzo di somme extrabilancio tra distrazione e appropriazione indebita (nota a Cass. pen. V, 21 gennaio 1998, Cusani)', *Giust pen.*, 3 (1999), 145 *et seq.*

Analogous considerations apply also to fiscal crimes (on which, see d.lgs. 10 March 2000, No. 74). Quite often, the setting aside of huge sums of money, which then flow into the secret funds to which we have just made reference, happens through tax evasion. Irregular corporate accounting and fraudulent or incorrect fiscal declaration is, in fact, closely correlated to corruption, and helps to form a kind of 'vicious criminal circle'. The omitted registration in the balance sheet or other company accounting records of the setting aside of accumulated sums allows the company to indicate in the annual income tax declarations or on the added-value elements an amount inferior to the effective value. At the same time, it is precisely through this systematic underestimation of the assets that the company can continue to set aside sums destined not to be accounted for. From this angle, therefore, tax evasion and counterfeiting of the budget represent various stages in the realisation of the same criminal design, that is, they are two essential passages on the whole *iter criminis* followed by company administrators in order to amass hidden reserves that will then be used in order to corrupt.

In light of the considerations made up to this point, if we intend to combat the corruption phenomenon on all fronts, strengthening the penal control on corporate and fiscal crime, and interrupting at its origin the supply chain of illicit resources that habitually reaches the corruptors, it is necessary to strengthen the strategy to fight 'satellite' crimes. A new normative intervention in the matter would be hoped for, which, starting from a consciousness of the common incidence of 'satellite' crimes within the genesis and the spread of the corruption phenomenon, accepts the need to strengthen the general preventive effectiveness of the incriminating typologies of such crimes by means of their extensive redefinition and a correlated increase in the sanctioning response.

New models of protection and future perspectives

The generalised spread of corruption now represents an ethical emergency. Obviously, the moralisation of public life and the daily actions of citizens cannot be enforced by law. However, neither can one trust in the hope of a spontaneous ethical-social redemption. In order to try to check the continuous advance of corruption, an ever-more pervasive phenomenon, it is necessary therefore to take stock of the real dimensions and the new morphology of this phenomenon, and to react by introducing the necessary normative modifications to the law and more effective actions to fight corruption. The reforms that have been witnessed in Italy attest to three main directions: (a) the modernisation of sanctions, with the introduction of criminal liability of corporations; (b) the reorganisation and rationalisation of the incriminating cases in the penal code; and (c) the strengthening of the preventative controls of an administrative nature.

The first important direction in which Italian legislators have moved in this effort to strengthen the fight against corruption was taken by an important reform that has introduced an organic system of sanctions for legal entities: the criminal liability of corporations. For some time a debate has been continuing as to whether to extend the law to include such sanctions, in order to get to the decisional heart of criminal policies matured within the company. The prohibition maxim *societas delinquere non potest* that dominated a good part of continental Europe ended in avoiding the serious argument on the criminological foundations of a direct indictment of legal entities, especially within the sphere of economic crimes, as a fundamental moment of modernisation of the Italian sanctioning system. Unfortunately, the discussion of the matter was slowed by the dubious compatibility of a pure system of corporate liability with the penal principles contained in the Italian Constitution; but, this issue has been overtaken by supranational developments. Italy has found itself needing to ratify a series of international conventions regarding instruments that foresee the introduction of a system of direct sanctions applicable to companies (without being restricted to precise form, administrative or penal).[49]

We have arrived therefore at the approval of law No. 300 of 29 September 2000. The successive legislative decree of 2001 No. 231/01 has now put into effect the aforesaid principles, thus introducing the Italian Charter of Sanctioning Responsibility of Legal Entities (Corporate and Unincorporated). This is a code of sanctions equipped with general rules, and a special section containing the list of crimes to which the sanctions to the entity apply, together with the traditional sanctions against the physical person who has committed the crime in the interest or advantage of the entity. This is not the proper place to expound on this important legislative text that has clearly revolutionised Italian penal

[49] These are, among others, the II Protocol of the Convention for the protection of the financial interests of the European Community (PIF), undersigned in Brussels, 29 June 1997, and of the OECD Convention on the Bribery of Foreign Public Officials in International Business Transactions, signed in Paris, 17 December 1997.

tradition. However, the sanctions have not been expressly called penal; they instead speak of the 'administrative responsibility for crime' of the entities. Beyond this normative label, the sanctioning system is equipped with significant instruments of intervention: severe pecuniary sanctions in most cases, accompanied by disqualifying sanctions and strongly invasive judicial intervention into corporate activity that centres on the introduction (voluntary) of compliance programmes with a preventive scope in respect of the commission of crimes. If one adds that the recognition of the responsibility of the entities is rooted in the criminal trial, it is easy to understand how the substance with which we are confronted is a powerful system of sanctions within the penal environment towards the entities.

This reform, which began with reference to a rather limited number of crimes, has today grown progressively. Originally, next to the crimes typical of the criminality of profit,[50] the crimes of concussione and corruption have been inserted into Article 25 of the aforesaid legislative decree No. 231/01. This testifies clearly that at the top of the agenda of the intervention for reform and modernisation the inescapable aim for Italian legislators was to strengthen legal protection in the face of ever-more pervasive corruption. Crimes of corruption have thus constituted the starting base of the liability of corporations in Italian law, providing an important initial test case.[51]

The aforesaid Article 25 of d.lgs. No. 231/01 foresees three different levels of gravity of behaviour in which corruption is embodied. First, there are the crimes of corruption with respect to an act of office, extending also to the corruptor (Articles 318 and 321 c.p.), and instigation to corruption for an act of office (Article 322, Codicils 1 and 3). Secondly, there are the crimes of corruption for an action contrary to the duties of office (Article 319 c.p.), and corruption in legal proceedings, extending also to the corruptor (Article 319*ter*, Codicil 1), and also the

[50] Crimes such as embezzlement from the state; improper obtainment of contributions from the state; defrauding the state or other public agencies; aggravated fraud aimed at obtaining public funding; computer fraud. They are a group of crimes that are placed in the area of crime for profit, 'consisting in the more or less fraudulent acquisition of patrimonial advantages to the damage of the State, other public agencies, or the European Communities': G. de Vero, *La responsabilità penale delle persone giuridiche* (Milan: Giuffrè, 2008), § 26.3.

[51] In fact, the first judicial decisions in execution of d.lgs. 231/01 include some comments on bribery: Trib. Milano, Ufficio G.i.p., 27 April 2004, *Soc*, 2004, p. 1275; Trib. Milano, Ufficio G.i.p., 20 September 2004, *Corr merito*, 2005, p. 85.

instigation to corruption for an action contrary to the duties of office (Article 322, Codicils 2 and 4). Thirdly, and the most serious level, are crimes of concussione (Article 317 c.p.), crimes of corruption for an action contrary to the duties of office, aggravated (former Article 319*bis*) in a case where the entity has achieved a significant profit, and the crime of corruption in legal proceedings, aggravated (Article 319*ter*) with an extension to the corruptor.

The foreseen sanctioning response from the law for the entities responsible for crimes of corruption leaves no doubt regarding the severity of the crimes in question. In the more serious cases, pecuniary penalties imposed on entities will be much closer to the maxima foreseen by the law, and there will be, in addition, the complex and frightening arsenal of disqualifying sanctions listed in Article 9, Codicil 2, of the d. lgs. No. 231/01.[52] These are applicable in order to prevent any 'absorption' of the sanction, as could happen in the case of the imposition of a single pecuniary penalty if applied to entities of immense economic–patrimonial capacity. The application of disqualifying sanctions also opens up the possibility of arranging the publication of the condemning sentence, which will carry a strong element of adverse publicity particularly feared by the more commercial companies.

Let us now leave the area of the already enacted modernising norms and consider the planned legislative interventions to deter corruption. From the vast assortment of bills lying in Parliament concerning the fight against corruption, there emerge two various perspectives of reform, which are not incompatible with each other. From one side, comes a proposal to implement the penal Convention on corruption adopted in Strasbourg in January 1999 (the so-called 'European Anti-corruption Convention'), that draws inspiration from the already described 'Cernobbio plan'. This aims to bring radical innovations to the Penal

[52] The foreseen disqualifying sanctions towards entities for corruption cases, ranging from one year to an unlimited duration, are therefore: (a) debarment from exercising the activity; (b) suspension or revocation of the authorisations, licences or concessions functional to the commission of the offence; (c) prohibition on contracting for work with the Public Administration, except in order to obtain the provision of a public service; (d) exclusion from public aid, financing, grants and subsidies, and the eventual revocation of those already granted; and (e) prohibition on advertising assets or services. It is easy to understand how a single one of these drastic endorsements can affect the economic life of the entity in a lethal way, not turning out in some 'calculable' way or metabolisable from it like any other cost of a criminal enterprise. For a discussion of this issue, see, *amplius*, R. Guerrini, *La responsabilità da reato degli enti, sanzioni e loro natura* (Milano: Giuffrè, 2006), pp. 131 *et seq.*

Code modifying *ab imis* the structure of crimes of corruption.[53] From the other side, there are bills that, without significantly affecting the code definitions of corruption, propose to strengthen the system of prevention and extra-penitentiary control, and to improve transparency in the operation of the Public Administration.[54]

With regard to the first path of reform, the basic logic of the proposed bill is to modify more incisively the actual order of corruption crimes under the Code. It proposes to intensify penal repression, widening the applicable borders of the corruption base, introducing new criminal typologies and increasing penalties. It also embodies new examples of non-punishment or penalty attenuation for those who are disposed to break the *pactum sceleris* by collaborating with justice. In parallel, it is proposed to valorise the rewards of corruption, assuming a special cause of impunity in favour of the subject that within three months, or in any case prior to the beginning of the penal procedure, denounces the fact of corruption and collaborates with the judicial authority, making available a sum correspondent to that which was given or received. From such reform would come, according to its proponents, remarkable practical advantages and relevant probative simplifications. Every undue action that the private party carries out towards the public official would involve the liability of both (with the exception of violent or threatening requests from the public official, which would constitute concussione and therefore the liability of the single public official), without the necessity of further investigation to clarify the mutual position and the different psychological attitudes of the subjects involved. The impunity granted to the collaborating corruptor, moreover, would pull down the wall of conspiracy of silence that often renders corruption agreements impenetrable, hindering or preventing the discovery and the punishment of the guilty.

Always with a view to innovations in the Penal Code, the introduction of a new criminal typology is contemplated, constituted by the 'traffic of illicit influences'. Such cases, addressed by the European Anti-corruption

[53] See, in particular C. 4159 (Garavini); C. 3859 (di Pietro); S. 2174 (Finocchiaro). The projects cited can be consulted on the website of the Senato della Repubblica at: www.senato.it in the section 'Leggi e documenti'.

[54] The more important of these plans, also because it has reached an advanced phase of the *iter* parliamentarian, is C. 4434 (governmental initiative), approved in the Senate on 15 June 2011, transmitted to the Chamber of Deputies the following day and now under the examination of the Constitutional Commission of Justice and Transactions; in partially analogous sense: S. 2854 (Oliva).

Convention through Article 12 (trading in influence), is directed at punishing the conduct of subjects that propose themselves as intermediaries in the settlement of matters of corruption, alongside those who seek out collaboration. The indicted conduct is that of:

> anyone, boasting credit with a public official or a person in charge of a public service, or rather alleging to be able to buy the favour or to satisfy the request, who requires the receipt or promise of money or other profit to himself, as the price for his mediation or as remuneration for the public official or the person in charge of the public service.[55]

The introduction of this new typology of crime becomes necessary in order to adapt the outline of the doctrine to the recent changes in the corruption phenomenon. The traditional bilateral form of corruption has been in many cases supplanted by a more complex agreement: the recompense is received by the intermediary, while the illicit administrative activity is carried out by a different subject. On another occasion, then, the intermediary will return the favour by guaranteeing the activity of the public official. In other words, we have passed from the classic duality of corruption to a more articulated 'triangular' system. In the corruption agreement, a new figure of the intermediary – the subject that receives the recompense – is different from the person who completes the administrative activity (the object of the agreement). Corruption agreements now assume more and more often the form of a virtual spider's web of mutual opacities, based on little and great gifts or exchanges of favours that, while they may not amount to a classic 'bribe', involve an enormous rise in the costs of public works, falsifying the free market, nullifying competition and overturning meritocracy in democracy.[56]

Coming at last to administrative controls, it is by now a widely shared opinion that the unavoidable point of departure for a really effective provision against corruption is represented by the strengthening of the internal control mechanisms within the Public Administration.[57] From this perspective, the various proposals that have been advanced over the

[55] The proposed normative formulation is almost identical to those in the already-mentioned plans, C. 3859 (Di Pietro); S. 2174 (Finocchiaro).

[56] The affirmation of the text is contained in C. 3859 (di Pietro), p. 6.

[57] F. Palazzo, 'Corruzione: per una disciplina "integrata" ed efficace', *Dir. pen. proc.* (2011), 1177 *et seq.*; Vivarelli, 'Il fenomeno della corruzione', p. 2941 *et seq.*; A. di Nicola, 'Dieci anni di lotta alla corruzione in Italia: cosa non ha funzionato e cosa può ancora funzionare', in M. Barbagli (ed.), *Rapporto sulla criminalità in Italia* (Bologna: Zanichelli, 2003), p. 124.

course of the years in order to prevent the phenomenon *de quo* at its origin – partially received in the already-mentioned bill of governmental initiative C. 4434 – are fundamentally traceable to a three-point line of intervention. First, valorisation of the transparency of the *modus operandi* of the Public Administration (consistent regulation of the procedures; identification of the responsible person; publication on the institutional websites of the person responsible for dealing with the information relevant to the procedures; following criteria of easy accessibility, etc.). Secondly, strengthening vigilance with respect to potential conflicts of interest, both within the administration and in the relationships between the private and public sectors. Thirdly, adopting models for the appraisal of the risk of corruption in relation to every administrative sector, and strengthening internal control systems, with a correlated responsibility placed on management to make such models effective.

We have seen how Italian legal culture and a good part of the political class clearly understand the serious dangers that are hidden in the spreading phenomenon of corruption. Italian legislators have not abandoned themselves to a desolate contemplation of a vision of degradation that infects to varying degrees many other Western countries. On the contrary, the parliamentary initiative has set in motion many strategies for intervention at all levels. Some of these interventions, such as the managerial corporate responsibility for crimes of corruption, have already been an operating reality for many years. The anticipated reform of crimes of corruption by the Penal Code is also on the table for discussion, and the interventions are not limited only to the field of penal sanctions. They also involve crucial strengthening of the internal control mechanisms of the Public Administration and of the transparency of their procedures. However, we cannot forget the warning from an important protagonist of the Italian legal and economic scene, who years ago doubted 'the saving' power of rules and sanctions, observing, a little sceptically, that, 'cathartic ethics are not launched by decree'.[58] We would like to specify that, of course, such catharsis cannot derive only from the saving action of new laws and new rules, even if such knowledge should not in any way induce us to give up, or refrain from proposing and identifying different models for combating corruption to keep pace with the changing face of the criminological phenomenon of corruption. In reality, the effort itself produced with regard to the topic of corruption

[58] G. Rossi, 'Per un'etica degli affari. Se le regole vengono trasgredite', *La Repubblica*, 18 June 2003.

in order to bring innovation to the penal law and the sanctioning mechanisms is something that reaffirms and testifies to the absolute priority of the values protected here in the way that they relate to the structural mechanisms of a modern democracy. Such efforts seek to reorient civic conscience regarding the spread of corrupt misbehaviour; misbehaviour that perversely anesthetises individual sensibility. The continuous reaffirmation of the values in the arguments and the new laws can stimulate the internalisation of proper values, and maybe even a collective conscience in the sense of a spontaneous conformation to the concepts behind the laws.

5

Development, business integrity and the UK Bribery Act 2010

INDIRA CARR

Introduction

The impact of corruption on the interface of private and public sector dealings on economic growth is by now well established in the economic literature. According to Tanzi, corruption results in a reduction in the flow of foreign direct investment (FDI).[1] This decrease is attributable to increases in costs for the investor, and to the undermining of the productivity of public investment, infrastructure and investment generally. This inevitably impacts on a nation's economic growth and infrastructural development. In Tanzi's view, neither does corruption contribute to raising living standards of the poor. Shleifer and Vishny,[2] the World Bank (WB),[3] and Kaufmann and Wei[4] also arrived at similar conclusions. However, according to Wheeler and Mody the relationship between corruption and FDI is not that significant.[5] The problem with the Wheeler and Mody study, as Wei states, is that they 'combined corruption with twelve other variables to form a composite indicator', which therefore is not helpful in exposing the link.[6] More recent studies still seem to support the commonly held view that corruption does affect

[1] V. Tanzi, 'Corruption Around the World', *Staff Papers International Monetary Fund*, 45 (1998), 559–94.

[2] A. Shleifer and R. W. Vishny, 'Corruption', *Quarterly Journal of Economics*, 106 (1993), 599–618.

[3] World Bank, *World Development Report: The State in a Changing World* (New York: Oxford University Press, 1997).

[4] D. Kaufmann and S. Wei, 'Does "Grease Money" Speed Up the Wheels of Commerce?', NBER Working Paper No. 7093 (Cambridge, MA: NBER, 1999).

[5] D. Wheeler and A. Mody, 'International Investment Location Decisions: The Case of US Firms', *Journal of International Economics*, 33 (1992), 55–76.

[6] S. Wei, 'Local Corruption and Global Capital Flows', *Brookings Papers on Economic Activity*, 2 (2000), 303–54.

inward investment. Al-Sadig's study sought to test the link between corruption and FDI flows by employing data covering the period 1984–2004 from 117 states.[7] Employing two econometric methodologies – different panel data sets and control variables – the study found that corruption does deter foreign investors, but also highlighted that the negative impacts of corruption are not present where there are high-quality institutions. Recent evidence is also supportive of such a view. To illustrate, India had a reduction in FDI due to widespread allegations of corruption, especially during the preparation for the Commonwealth Games and the anti-corruption campaign carried out by activists after the furore over these Games.[8] It has also seen a reduction in economic growth.[9] By comparison, FDI in Singapore, perceived as a state with low levels of corruption[10] and good institutions, has gone up.[11] According to a WB survey measuring bribery from the private sector to the public sector the cost of bribery worldwide is estimated to be US$1 trillion per annum.[12] As Kaufmann has observed, 'the main point is that [bribery] is not a relatively small phenomenon of a few billion dollars – far from it'.[13]

7 A. Al-Sadig, 'The Effects of Corruption on FDI Flow', *Cato Journal*, 29(2) (2009), 267.

8 T. Yenamandra, 'Corruption in India's Commonwealth Games, Kalmadi Arrested', 26 April 2011, available at: www.2point6billion.com/news/2011/04/26/corruption-in-indias-commonwealth-games-9163.html.

9 See table available at: www.google.co.uk/publicdata/explore?ds=d5bncppjof8f9_&met_y=bx_klt_dinv_cd_wd&idim=country:IND&dl=en&hl=en&q=foreign+direct+investment+india.

10 The Corruption Perceptions Index (CPI) published annually by Transparency International has always given a high score (indicating low corruption) for Singapore. The methodology for collecting these scores has been criticised widely for being unreliable (see I. Carr, 'Fighting Corruption through Regional and International Conventions: A Satisfactory Solution?', *European Journal of Crime, Criminal Law and Criminal Justice*, 15 (2007), 121–53). Nevertheless, the scores seem to be viewed seriously. The favourable scores given by the CPI do not mean that Singapore does not approve of corruption. Despite its reputation as a state with low levels of corruption it is regarded as an offshore tax haven and has gained popularity as such. It is well known that tax havens are often used for illicitly obtained assets and for tax evasion. See Shelter Offshore, 'OECD Update on Offshore Tax Havens', 2011, available at: www.shelteroffshore.com/index.php/offshore/more/oecd-update-on-offshore-tax-havens.

11 See FDI by Country available at: http://greyhill.com/fdi-by-country.

12 Undated interview with Daniel Kaufmann, available at: http://web.worldbank.org/WBSITE/EXTERNAL/NEWS/0,contentMDK:20190295~menuPK:34457~pagePK:34370~piPK:34424~theSitePK:4607,00.html; see also World Bank, 'Costs of Corruption', 8 April 2004, available at: http://web.worldbank.org/WBSITE/EXTERNAL/NEWS/0,contentMDK:20190187~menuPK:34457~pagePK:64003015~piPK:64003012~theSitePK:4607,00.html.

13 Interview with Daniel Kaufmann.

This figure relates to bribery alone. Losses from other forms of corrupt activities, such as embezzlement, informal arrangements relating to bid manipulation and over-invoicing to accommodate kickbacks are not included. Inclusion of these losses would raise the estimation considerably.

The contribution of the private sector to the current levels of corruption globally cannot be overestimated.[14] Business corruption is to be found in all the activities they undertake – from a straightforward sale transaction to the public sector (e.g., sale of military aircraft to a foreign state) to FDI, within infrastructure projects and improvement programmes (e.g., building of schools, dams and vaccination programmes), and humanitarian aid[15] funded by international and national financial institutions, such as the WB and the UK Department for International Development (DFID). It is not as if cases of bribery and bid manipulation are confined to one business sector, though some sectors, such as construction, defence,[16] pharmaceutical and natural resources, are highly prone to it. Yet academic writing in the general area of business corruption does not normally give prominence to the involvement of the private sector as supplier of bribes and their engagement with other corrupt activities in development aid projects. The reason for this, as Cremer, writing as recently as 2008 states, is that:

> For a long time corruption has been a taboo subject among the institutions of development co-operation, in particular corruption within their very own work … Until the recent past, aid organisations seldom made an issue of bribery or embezzlement as a hindrance in carrying out the project and programs they fund.[17]

Any discussion of combating bribery and injecting integrity into business behaviour would be incomplete without highlighting corruption

[14] Much of the literature on business corruption focuses on bribes flowing from the private sector to the public sector. It must be added that many ex-colonies and socialist countries have engaged, and continue to engage, in trade activities through state trading organisations. Such public sector undertakings are also likely to supply bribes when engaging in business transactions abroad. The issue of public sector to public sector corruption has not yet been studied in any detail.

[15] See S. Breau and I. Carr, 'Humanitarian Aid, Human Rights and Corruption', in M. Odello and S. Cavandoli (eds), *Emerging Areas of Human Rights in the 21st Century* (New York: Routledge, 2011), pp. 149–75.

[16] In some countries the manufacture of arms and other defence equipment is part of the public sector (e.g., India's Bharat Electronics Ltd and Hindusthan Aeronautics Ltd). More recently, there is a move towards opening up manufacturing of defence equipment to the private sector. On India, see http://mod.nic.in/product&supp/welcome.html.

[17] G. Cremer, *Corruption and Aid Development: Confronting the Challenges*, trans. Elisabeth Shüth (London: Lynne Reinner, 2008).

in the context of development and the 'leakage' of funds in development-related projects. DFID's bilateral aid, excluding humanitarian assistance, was £3,903 million in 2010/11, up from £3,524 million in 2009/10 (an 11 per cent increase). India (£279 million), Ethiopia (£245 million) and Bangladesh (£171 million) were the largest recipients of bilateral aid excluding humanitarian assistance.[18] It must be said that all of these countries are highly corrupt in Transparency International's (TI) Corruption Perception Index; and DFID is not alone in providing loans to highly corrupt countries. The questions that any taxpayer would naturally ask are: 'how much of these funds really help in promoting development and help towards alleviating poverty?', and, 'what do donor countries do to increase business integrity?'.

This chapter's focus therefore is twofold: first, to show the link between development aid and corruption and the need to promote business integrity as a legal imperative; and, secondly, to examine how the Bribery Act enacted by the United Kingdom in 2010 promotes business integrity. The first section, examines development aid and corruption, and the kinds of opportunities for engaging in corrupt activities that present themselves to businesses in development projects. This section also provides a brief discussion of regulatory and self-regulatory developments in respect of business corruption to provide the context for the next section. The following section concentrates on the Bribery Act 2010, in particular section 7(2) and the *Guidance about Procedures which Relevant Commercial Organisations can Put into Place by Persons Associated with them from Bribing* (Guidance) issued by the Ministry of Justice to see whether they have the potential to raise business integrity.[19]

Development aid and corruption

The World Bank is a major international financial institution that provides both low interest and interest-free loans to countries for infrastructure development.[20] Since its inception, the WB has provided funds that

[18] SID 2011 Statistics, available at: www.dfid.gov.uk/About-us/How-we-measure-progress/Aid-Statistics/Statistics-on-International-Development-2011/Key-Statistics.

[19] Available at: www.justice.gov.uk/downloads/guidance/making-reviewing-law/bribery-act-2010-guidance.pdf.

[20] Reconstruction and poverty reduction are important parts of their work. For more on the history and evolution of the World Bank see: http://web.worldbank.org/WBSITE/EXTERNAL/EXTABOUTUS/0,contentMDK:20653660~menuPK:72312~pagePK:51123644~piPK:329829~theSitePK:29708,00.html.

run into billions of US dollars. In 2011, the total for International Bank for Reconstruction (IBRD) and International Development Association (IDA)[21] lending was US$43 billion, with south Asia receiving 24 per cent; the Middle East 5 per cent; Latin America and the Caribbean 22 per cent; Africa 16 per cent; east Asia and the Pacific 19 per cent; and central Asia 14 per cent.[22] The total IBRD and IDA lending by sector was water, sanitation and flood protection receiving 8 per cent; transportation 20 per cent; public administration 22 per cent; agriculture, fishing and forestry 5 per cent; education 4 per cent; energy and mining 14 per cent; finance 2 per cent; health and other social services 16 per cent; industry 5 per cent; and information and communications 1 per cent.[23] These data provide a picture of the amounts of money that change hands between the donor and the borrowing states, and the variety of sectors and activities where the monies lent are put to use. By way of illustration, India, the WB's largest borrower in 2011, received funds for a variety of infrastructure projects which include the prime minister's Rural Roads Programme, Mission Clean Ganga and the Eastern Dedicated Freight Corridor to be run as a 'freight-only rail line'.[24] All of these infrastructural improvement projects will, without doubt, involve both public sector authorities, such as the railways and environment authorities, and the private sector, both domestic and international. Given the recent news on how millions of dollars were squandered in the Commonwealth Games held in India[25] and the subsequent civil movement by the Indian anti-corruption activist, Anna Hazare,[26] the question that immediately comes

[21] The World Bank comprises two development institutions – the IBRD and the IDA – and three affiliate agencies – the International Finance Corporation (IFC), the Multilateral Investment Guarantee Agency (MIGA) and the International Centre for the Settlement of Investment Disputes (ICSID).

[22] Information derived from Figure 3, World Bank Annual Report 2011, available at: http://siteresources.worldbank.org/EXTANNREP2011/Resources/8070616-1315496634380/03TheRoleofIBRDandIDA.pdf.

[23] Figure 4, World Bank Annual Report 2011.

[24] The World Bank Annual Report 2011, p. 24, available at: http://siteresources.worldbank.org/EXTANNREP2011/Resources/8070616-1315496634380/SouthAsia.pdf.

[25] See 'Commonwealth Games: Corruption, Chaos and a Race to Avert a Crisis', *The Independent*, 20 August 2010, available at: www.independent.co.uk/sport/general/others/commonwealth-games-corruption-chaos-amp-a-race-to-avert-a-crisis-2057234.html; 'India Orders Probe into Commonwealth Games Corruption', *Voice of America News*, 16 October 2010, available at: www.voanews.com/english/news/asia/south/India-Orders-Probe-into-Commonwealth-Games-Corruption-105097774.html.

[26] See J. Burke, 'Indian Activist Anna Hazare Refuses to End Hunger Strike', *The Guardian*, 7 April 2011, available at: www.guardian.co.uk/world/2011/apr/07/anna-hazare-hunger-

to mind is how much of the monies that are borrowed from the WB actually reach the projects for which they are ear-marked. Many of the WB-funded projects have fallen prey to allegations of corruption, and the media is replete with stories about the squandering of aid monies by politicians and civil servants to serve their own purposes: as, for example, in Kenya,[27] and Lesotho.[28] According to a news item dated 2004, a US Senate Committee is reported as saying that, since 1946, the WB has lost US$100 billion, nearly 20 per cent of its lending portfolio, in corruption.[29] It was not as if the WB was unaware of the high exposure to corruption when they lent monies for various projects from road building to health provision. So why did the WB take no action? Its inaction until the 'cancer of corruption' speech in 1999 by the then President Wolfensohn was justified on the basis of its Articles of Agreement. These Articles did not provide the WB with a mandate to make lending decisions on the basis of political considerations or to intervene in the political structures and matters of a state.[30] And the WB saw corruption as a political matter.

The WB may also have been greatly influenced by the functionalist theory which viewed corruption as performing functions that could bring about modernisation to post-colonial states and better the economic state of a society. Among functionalist theorists we can count Leys,[31]

strike; J. Burke, 'Indian Activist Anna Hazare on Hunger Strike as MPs Debate Anti-graft Bill', *The Guardian*, 27 December 2011, available at: www.guardian.co.uk/world/2011/dec/27/indian-anti-graft-hunger-strike.

[27] Bank Information Centre, 'World Bank Accused of Tolerating Corruption in Kenya', 3 April 2008, available at: www.bicusa.org/en/Article.3717.aspx.

[28] For examples of corruption in DFID-funded projects see Appendix I, Select Committee on International Development, available at: www.publications.parliament.uk/pa/cm200001/cmselect/cmintdev/39/39ap06.htm.

[29] E. Mekay, 'Poorest Pay for World Bank Corruption: US Senator', *Common Dreams*, 14 May 2004, available at: www.commondreams.org/headlines04/0514-07.htm.

[30] The exclusion of politics is clearly stated in Art. III, s. 5(b) and Art. IV, s. 10 of the IBRD Articles of Agreement which read: Art. III, s. 5(b): 'The Bank shall make arrangements to ensure that the proceeds of any loan are used only for the purposes for which the loan was granted, with due attention to considerations of economy and efficiency and without regard to political or other non-economic influences or considerations.' Article IV, s. 10: 'The Bank and its officers shall not interfere in the political affairs of any member; nor shall they be influenced in their decisions by the political character of the member or members concerned. Only economic considerations shall be relevant to their decisions, and these considerations shall be weighed impartially in order to achieve the purposes stated in Article 1.'

[31] C. Leys, 'What is the Problem about Corruption?', *Journal of Modern African Studies*, 3 (1965), 215–30.

Leff[32] and Nye.[33] A common problem in many of the newly independent states was excessive bureaucracy and complex tax systems, along with labour laws that made it extremely difficult for businesses and entrepreneurs to enter the market and kick-start economies that were stagnating due to the state trading organisations (parastatals) that largely controlled international trade, as in Tanzania and in India.[34] The reason for adopting the state trading model was justified by the example set by the Soviet Union, which had transformed itself from a 'backward country to a country of extensive industrialisation and modern technique at an unprecedented tempo … effected under the guidance and control of a national economic plan'.[35] Against this context of centralised control and the red tape, bribery was seen as a means of inducing economic growth through investment from the private sector. For Nye, corruption also had the potential to bring about political development through economic development. It is possible to support this functionalist view with illustrations such as the example from India widely known as the Licence Raj,[36] where extensive red tape procedures made it virtually impossible for investors to bring their expertise and capital to fuel economic growth. However, there are serious drawbacks to the functionalist theory. From an economic perspective the very corruption that induces the economy to stir can also act as a disincentive, resulting in donors refusing aid and foreign investors not providing their capital or know-how. There is also the danger of corruption becoming embedded within the value system of a state such that any attempts to bring about anti-corruption reforms are difficult, if not impossible. Equally, corruption creates an elite class, largely consisting of politicians, civil servants and businessmen, creating a huge gap between the rich and the poor, leaving scope for civil unrest and loss of legitimacy of the government in the eyes of the citizens who

[32] N. H. Leff, 'Economic Development through Bureaucratic Corruption', *American Behavioral Scientist*, 8 (1964), 8–14.

[33] See J. S. Nye, 'Corruption and Political Development: A Cost–Benefit Analysis', in A. Heidenheimer (ed.), *Political Corruption: Readings in Comparative Analysis* (New York: Holt, Reinhart & Wilson, 1970), pp. 564–78.

[34] For instance, the State Trading Corporation of India was set up in 1956. It still exists, though it does not have the monopoly on international trade. For more on this entity see: http://stc.gov.in.

[35] M. Dobb, *Soviet Economic Development since 1917* (London: Routledge & Kegan Paul, 1948), p. 2.

[36] P. Aghion *et al.*, 'The Unequal Effects of Liberalization: Evidence from Dismantling the Licence Raj in India', *CEPR*, 22 December 2005, available at: www.cepr.org/meets/wkcn/2/2360/papers/Burgess.pdf.

are left behind in poverty. Nepotism and cronyism become part and parcel of such a system, with no room for recognising merit. The recent Arab Spring provides a good illustration.[37] From a governance perspective, corruption is likely to increase red tape, since it is a convenient method of extracting fees from those who wish to engage in business transactions. In extreme forms the state becomes a financial predator.

The functionalists had their critics, among whom were Klitgaard and Rose-Ackerman.[38] They did not see corruption as fuelling economic growth in the long term. Neither did they see it as alleviating poverty, or as enabling development, since corruption affected projects from reaching their optimum objective or of reaching the citizens by providing them with much-needed infrastructure and services. Corruption supported and promoted poverty. Both critics put forward what has come to be known as the principal–agent–client (PAC) model, according to which corruption is the betrayal of the principal's (P) interest by the agent (A) in pursuit of his own interests by accepting or seeking a benefit from the client (C) who is the service seeker. For corruption to occur, P must be in a powerful position, the agent must have some discretion in administering the services, and there must be a lack or near lack of accountability.[39] The solution to reducing corruption according to this model is through greater competition, improving the environment within which discretion is allowed and exercised – so that it imparts confidence in the way the discretion is exercised – and introducing greater accountability and transparency.[40] As we will see in the following

[37] See L. Anderson, 'Demystifying the Arab Spring', in *The New Arab Revolt*, Foreign Affairs/CFR eBook, May/June 2011, summary available at: www.foreignaffairs.com/articles/67693/lisa-anderson/demystifying-the-arab-spring.

[38] R. Klitgaard, *Controlling Corruption* (Berkeley, CA: University of California Press, 1988); S. Rose-Ackermann, *Corruption and Government: Causes, Consequences, and Reform* (New York: Cambridge University Press, 1999).

[39] This is also often called the Weberian rational–legal model of administration. According to this model, the public and private sphere of officials are separate and this separation has to be maintained (M. Weber, *The Theory of Social and Economic Organization* (New York: Free Press, 1947). Until recently (the nineteenth century) in much of Europe the rule was of a patrimonial type and did not follow the Weberian rational–legal model. The transition to the Weberian model was a gradual one. For more on this gradual evolution from patrimony where all assets, personal and public, are owned by the leader, to the modern Weberian model, see D. C. North and R. P. Thomas, *Rise of the Western World: A New Economic History* (Cambridge University Press, 1996).

[40] For more on this see I. Carr, 'Corruption, the Southern African Development Community Anti-corruption Protocol and the Principal–Agent–Client Model', *International Journal of Law in Context*, 5 (2009), 147–77. While this model is used by both Klitgaard

section, it was this model that influenced the measures adopted by the WB to combat corruption.

Opportunities for corruption within development projects

The private sector is presented with ample opportunities for engaging in bribery and other corrupt activities in development projects from the stage of inception to completion. The decision as to which project is to be prioritised (e.g., whether to build a dam or to implement a vaccination programme) normally involves civil servants and politicians. Lobbying of these individuals by activists, citizen groups and the private sector is not uncommon. The private sector, companies and their agents, and other intermediaries such as lobbyists, through bribes and agreed kickbacks (were the project to be awarded to them) influence the decision-making. This means that it is the private rewards that drive the choice of projects rather than the needs of the state and its citizens. A state with bountiful rainfall and a good irrigation system may decide to propose a project for the building of a dam, as opposed to funding for a vaccination programme to eradicate the high incidence of tuberculosis and other childhood diseases, if the rewards from the construction industry are far greater than that offered or promised by the pharmaceutical industry.

Similarly, there are numerous opportunities for offering bribes at the implementation stage. Bribes may be given to influence the drawing up of the specifications that favour a particular company. There may also be an understanding at this stage that if the tenderer wins the contract kick-backs are to paid to the state officials. The end result is likely to be overpricing of the project to accommodate the kick-backs or the use of substandard materials. During the performance of the contract, other mechanisms may be used to siphon off funds informally, such as over-invoicing, employment of phantom contractors and workers, favourable tax deals and other forms of misappropriation. The following illustration relating to cyclone shelters along the Bay of Bengal by Cremer is illuminating:

> Just a few years after construction, the shelters are in such terrible condition that any further use should be prohibited … Bearing in mind the mechanisms behind the deviation of funds, it is difficult to accept that the

and Rose-Ackerman to explain corruption in the public–private interface, it could be easily adapted to explain corruption in the private sector, which has also more recently caught the attention of policymakers.

> failure in this type or similar types of government-run projects is merely a matter of administrative incompetence. It is safe to say that economic conditions underlie most cases. Civil servants or officials of para-govermental organisations accept inadequate building materials and neglect inspections in exchange for kickback[s] or bribe[s] from the contractor, who gains added income from providing lower quality.[41]

As stated above, the media is replete with stories of corruption in projects funded by the WB and other bilateral agencies, DFID amongst them. A well-publicised case of bribery is the Lesotho Highland Water Project for bringing water from Lesotho to South Africa. A consortium of companies which included the UK construction company Balfour Beatty[42] was reported to have paid over US$2 million in bribes used to manipulate various processes.[43] A report from the WB-funded project in Indonesia conveys how public procurement processes are manipulated and the difficulties faced in obtaining information to establish 'leakages'. In the review, the fiduciary practices in procurement, implementation and financial management systems were found to be weak and the 'winners were pre-arranged in a majority of the contracts'.[44] The review also exposed shortcomings both on the part of the government and the

[41] Cremer, *Corruption and Aid Development*, pp. 39–40.

[42] Balfour Beatty has been implicated in other bribery cases. See D. Leigh and R. Evans, 'Balfour Beatty agrees to pay £2.25m over allegations of bribery in Egypt', *The Guardian*, 7 October 2008, available at: www.guardian.co.uk/business/2008/oct/07/balfourbeatty.egypt. See also Ilisu Dam Campaign, *2000: Balfour Beatty's Annus Horribilis* (Oxford: Ilisu Dam Campaign, 2000), available at: www.thecornerhouse.org.uk/sites/thecornerhouse.org.uk/files/balfour.pdf.

[43] Both civil and criminal proceedings were brought against Mr Sole, the Chief Executive of the Lesotho Highlands Developments Authority. Mr Sole was charged with bribery and fraud and was imprisoned for eighteen years, which was reduced to fifteen years on appeal. The civil proceedings were for recovery of funds. See Energy Probe Research Foundation, 'M12 Million Bribery Scam on Sole', 16 July 2010, available at: http://eprf.probeinternational.org/node/9016. A number of companies involved in the consortium were also found guilty of corruption and fined various amounts. See 'Lesotho Fines Second Dam Firm', BBC News Channel, 27 August 2003, available at: http://news.bbc.co.uk/1/hi/business/3185145.stm. The WB has debarred two firms, the Canadian firm Acres International and the German firm Lahmeyer. See 'Corrupt Lahmeyer Debarment Welcome but Late: NGOs', International Rivers, 7 November 2006, available at: www.internationalrivers.org/en/africa/lesotho-water-project/corrupt-lahmeyer-debarment-welcome-late-ngos.

[44] World Bank, *Indonesia: Fiduciary Review of the Second Sulawesi Urban Development Project Overview Report* (Washington, DC: World Bank, 2002), available at: www1.worldbank.org/publicsector/anticorrupt/PoliticalEconomy/PREMCourse07/Amit%20background%20material/Fiduciary%20review%20Indonesia.pdf.

consultants who were supposed to help the government in implementing and supervising the project.

Another WB internal memorandum lists the typology and the amounts of informal payments that are made in funded projects. At the pre-project stage 5–10 per cent is set aside for payments to various authorities, including planning to place a project on the priority list; during the procurement process 5–35 per cent is set aside for being included in the approved bidders list, signing of the contract with the bid winner; and during the course of the project bribes are also paid towards obtaining inspection certificates for work done and so on.[45]

Given the prevalence of leakage of funds raised in various memoranda, in 1999 the WB brought corruption squarely within its agenda. Its then President James D. Wolfehnson said that 'the "C" word [being corruption] was not [to be defined] as a political issue but as something social and economic'.[46] Subsequent documents have regularly highlighted the negative impact of corruption on development. For instance in the WB Annual Report of 2004, its then President stated that:

> It is not just the financial damage from fraud and corruption that should be of concern … It is the fact that corruption sets in motion a chain of events that wreak havoc on a development project. The money to pay a bribe must come from some part of the project; as a result, prices may be raised, and/or quality and performance lowered. Less qualified bidders win by bid-rigging while qualified bidders become discouraged and stop bidding. In addition, citizen awareness of unchallenged corruption undermines trust and in government and public institutions.[47]

The WB, since entering the anti-corruption drive, has tried to further the improvement of governance and public administration structures in donee states, calling for transparency and accountability influenced by

[45] 'World Bank Memoranda on Corruption in Indonesia Confidential: Indon Resident Staff Views re "Leakage", Staff Bank Dunia di Jakarta Augustus, 1997', reproduced as Appendix 2, Select Committee on International Development, available at: www.publications.parliament.uk/pa/cm200001/cmselect/cmintdev/39/39ap07.htm.

[46] J. D. Wofensohn, 'Remarks at a Global Forum on Fighting Corruption', World Bank, 24 February 1999, available at: www.worldbank.org. Many of the WB-funded projects have fallen prey to corruption. See, e.g., A. Tricarico, 'Dams on Trial: The World Bank and the "Cancer of Corruption": Donor Governments, Financial Institutions and TNCs' Responsibilities in the Lesotho Case' (Rome: Reform the World Bank Campaign, 2000), available at: www.odiousdebts.org/odiousdebts/publications/DamsOnTrial.pdf.

[47] World Bank, *Report on Investigation and Sanctions of Staff Misconduct and Fraud and Corruption in Bank Financed Projects Fiscal Year 2004* (Washington DC: World Bank, 2005).

the PAC model. In furthering changes the WB resorted to the use of 'conditionalities' whereby donees were expected to introduce measures such as openness in the public procurement systems, adopt or amend existing anti-corruption laws, ratify regional or international anti-corruption conventions, and improve public sector governance generally. Whether such conditionalities have contributed greatly to a reduction in corruption is highly debatable. Much has been written both about the success and lack of success of such programmes in academic literature.[48] However, as a result of these conditionality-induced pressures, many developing countries introduced measures for improving governance structures by adopting codes of conduct for civil servants, procedures for transparency in government institutions and public procurement processes, as well as ratifying regional and international conventions. Many new laws were passed and existing laws were amended to better reflect the increasing convergence of the mechanisms devised for preventing and combating corruption. The WB has also introduced a debarment procedure, with the aim of initiating ethical behaviour in WB-funded projects. There is evidence that this is being used by the WB. In the Lesotho Highland Project, one of the companies, Acres International, was debarred by the Sanctions Committee of the WB for three years. This is seen as a sign that the WB is sending out a clear message, although there have been a number of questions raised about the delay in starting the enquiry and also the length of debarment.[49]

The developments and steps initiated by the WB and other financial institutions are not sufficient in themselves. Not all commercial transactions take place within the framework of a funded development project. Companies from both developed and emerging countries still seem to engage in corrupt practices. Even a quick survey of the daily newspapers from the English-speaking world reveals that there is at least one corruption story reported every day which involves a business.[50] Corruption

[48] P. Collier, 'The Failure of Conditionality', in C. Gwin and J.M. Nelson (eds), *Perspectives on Aid and Development* (Washington, DC: Overseas Development Council, 1997), pp. 51–77; P. Collier, P. Guillaumont, S. Guillaumont and J. W. Gunning, 'Redesigning Conditionality', *World Development*, 25 (1997), 1399–407.

[49] See F. Darroch, *The Lesotho Corruption Trials: A Case Study* (Berlin: Transparency International, 2003), available at: www.ipocafrica.org/index.php?option=com_content&view=article&id=71&Itemid=66.

[50] J. Phenal, 'India Journal: Companies Need to Ride the Anticorruption Wave', *The Wall Street Journal*, 13 September 2011, available at: http://blogs.wsj.com/indiarealtime/2011/09/13/india-journal-companies-need-to-ride-the-anticorruption-wave; D. Swallow,

also needs to be tackled from the business side, that is, from the supply side, if corruption is to be reduced. At this juncture it would be appropriate briefly to introduce the developments at the international scene to set the context for the second part of this chapter.

The international community response

Anti-corruption conventions

The response of the international community took two separate but inter-related routes: regulation and self-regulation. Even before the WB took an interest in corruption in 1999, inter-governmental organisations had already started tackling corruption from the supply side with the adoption of the Organisation for Economic Cooperation and Development (OECD) Convention on the Bribery of Foreign Public Officials in International Business Transactions (Anti-Bribery Convention). This Convention was the result of consistent pressure from the United States, which had taken measures to eradicate business corruption as long ago as 1977 with the enactment of the Foreign Corrupt Practices Act (FCPA).[51] The reason for the intolerance towards corruption was fuelled by two events: first, the Watergate scandal which exposed corruption at the highest levels,[52] and, secondly, a survey by the US Security Exchange Commission (SEC)[53] which found that:

> more than 400 corporations have admitted making questionable or illegal payments. The companies, most of them voluntarily, have reported paying out well in excess of $300 million in corporate funds to foreign government officials, politicians, and political parties. These corporations have included some of the largest and most widely held public companies and over 117 of them rank in the top Fortune 500 industries. The abuses

'Russia: Bribery, Corruption & the High Price of Bad Business', 24 May 2010, available at: www.deborahswallow.com/2010/05/24/russia-bribery-corruption-the-high-price-of-bad-business; 'Leaked Report on Quebec Construction Industry Corruption Shows Sickness in the System', available at http://canadians4accountability.org/blog/2011/09/16/leaked-report-on-quebec-construction-industry-corruption-shows-sickness-in-the-system.

51 Text available at: www.justice.gov/criminal/fraud/fcpa.

52 This scandal exposed the illegal contributions made towards the re-election campaign of President Richard Nixon. The investigation revealed cash slush funds in US corporations. For more on the Watergate scandal, see K. W. Olson, *Watergate: The Presidential Scandal that Shook America* (Lawrence, KS: Kansas University Press, 2003); B. Sussman, *The Great Coverup: Nixon and the Scandal of Watergate* (USA: Catapulter Books, eBook Store, 2010).

53 This institution regulates publicly traded companies.

> disclosed run the gamut from bribery of high foreign officials in order to secure some type of favorable action by a foreign government to so-called facilitating payments that allegedly were made to ensure that government functionaries discharge certain ministrial [sic] or clerical duties. Sectors of industry typically involved are: drugs and health care; oil and gas production and services; food products; aerospace, airlines and air services, and chemicals.[54]

Soon after the enactment of FCPA, the United States started exerting pressure on other developed states to adopt legislation similar to the FCPA which criminalised the corrupt activities of their businesses while conducting transactions abroad. In June 1977, the US Ambassador to the United Kingdom said that President Carter was 'taking the issue of corruption very seriously'.[55] The response on the part of the United Kingdom, to say the least, was not at all enthusiastic.[56] The United Kingdom felt that the importance of the export market for the economy meant that they could not take the moral tone adopted by the United States.[57] While there is no record of this, there may also be another reason for the UK Government's reluctance. Adopting the technique of 'long-arm' jurisdiction (which was a recent legal development) along US lines could have undermined the United Kingdom's relationship with its former colonies. If adopted, such a technique had the potential to be seen as meddling in the internal affairs of the newly independent states. Further, the ex-colonies were still important for trade, as economic growth as a result of joining the European Economic Community (EEC) was yet to be established. Besides, the ex-colonies had laws modelled on the common law, which should have been sufficient to act as a deterrent for public sector employees and were sufficiently robust for them to be prosecuted under their national laws.

The pressure from the United States nonetheless continued, and during the process of introducing amendments to the FCPA through the Omnibus Trade and Competitiveness Act 1988 (OTCA),[58] the International Agreement Negotiations Report to Congress included in the OTCA stated that 'the President should pursue the negotiation of an

54 House Report 95-640, 95th Congress, 1st Session, US House of Representatives, 12 May 1976, available at: http://10.173.2.10/criminal/fraud/fcpa/history/1977/houseprt.html.

55 See http://image.guardian.co.uk/sys-files/Guardian/documents/2007/05/29/ch06doc03.pdf.

56 See www.guardian.co.uk/baefiles.

57 See http://image.guardian.co.uk/sys-files/Guardian/documents/2007/05/29/ch06doc1.pdf.

58 For criticisms of the FCPA see M. Maris and E. Singer, 'Foreign Corrupt Practices Act', *American Criminal Law Review*, 43 (2006), 575–601, at 583.

international agreement, among the members of the Organization of Economic Cooperation and Development'.[59]

However, the international scene suddenly underwent a change in the 1990s, and there was more willingness to adopt legislation along the lines indicated by the United States. The reason for this sudden change of tone can be attributed to at least two factors: the geopolitical scene; and the end of the Cold War. As Hotchkiss says:

> The conjunction of five trends and events caught the attention of voters and policymakers around the world, giving a new sense of urgency to efforts to combat corruption: (1) the end of the Cold War, (2) the arrival of the information revolution, (3) the global acceptance of the ideology of free trade, (4) the worldwide explosion of the volume and scale of corruption, and (5) a significant change in the US government policy …
>
> Possibly the most significant precondition for the renewal of multilateral efforts to curb corruption was the end of the Cold War. The collapse of the former Soviet Union and its economic allies related directly to the later development of the movement against corruption. It began with Gorbachev's glasnost and perestroika initiatives. The new openness allowed public criticism and individual expression, and the restructuring that began in Gorbachev's era exposed the inherent bankruptcy and corruption of the Soviet system. The impact of Gorbachev's actions extended far beyond the Soviet Union, making possible the reforms and revolutions throughout Central Europe.[60]

It is also possible that the end of the Cold War brought a change in attitude towards corruption on the part of lending agencies, and greater willingness to demand more from the donee states to improve governance.

Soon after the creation of the Anti-Bribery Convention, a number of other anti-corruption conventions were adopted by intergovernmental organisations such as the African Union and the Council of Europe. Of these the most comprehensive convention is the United Nations Convention against Corruption (UNCAC), which has received 150 ratifications.[61] It covers bribery and other corrupt activities in both the public

[59] OTCA, Title V, Subtitle A, Part I, s. 5003(d), 102 Stat. 1424 as cited in B. Earle, 'The United States' Foreign Corrupt Practices Act and the OECD Anti-Bribery Recommendation: When Moral Suasion Won't Work, Try the Money Argument', *Dickinson Journal of International Law*, Winter (1996), 207–42.

[60] C. Hotchkiss, 'The Sleeping Dog Stirs: New Signs of Life in Efforts to End Corruption in International Business', *Journal of Public Policy and Marketing*, 17 (1998), 108–15, at 109.

[61] Came into force 14 December 2005. The text of this convention is available at: www.unodc.org. For further on this see I. Carr, 'The United Nations Convention on

and the private sector, from the supply side and the demand side, and has innovative provisions on asset recovery.[62] By contrast, the Anti-Bribery Convention addresses only bribery, and even then only bribery of foreign public officials in the context of international business transactions. Its main features in brief are:

(a) states required to make it a criminal offence for any person to offer, promise or give any undue pecuniary or other advantage to a foreign public official in order to obtain or retain business or other improper advantage in the conduct of international business (Article 1(1));
(b) provides an extensive definition of foreign public official sufficiently wide to include civil servants, Members of Parliament, the judiciary and those working in public undertakings (Article 1(4));
(c) states to have sanctions that are effective and proportionate (Article 3); and
(d) states required to put in place measures regarding liability of legal persons, in accordance with their legal principles (Article 2).

Self-regulation

The private sector is no stranger to self-regulation. Self-regulation through voluntary codes, it was felt by organisations such as the International Chamber of Commerce (ICC), would be a useful means of inducing responsibility in corporate behaviour. This self-regulatory approach to corruption is traceable to 1977 when the ICC published a *Report on Extortion and Bribery in International Trade*.[63] It called upon states and intergovernmental institutions to combat extortion and

Corruption: Improving the Quality of Life of Millions in the World?', *Manchester Journal of International Economic Law*, 3 (2006), 3–44. See also Daniel and Maton, Chapter 11, this volume.

62 The other conventions in force are: Organisation of American States Inter-American Convention Against Corruption 1996 (OAS Convention), came into force on 6 March 1997, available at: www.oas.org; Council of Europe Criminal Law Convention on Corruption 1999 (COE Criminal Convention), came into force on 1 July 2002, available at: www.coe.int; Council of Europe Civil Law Convention on Corruption 1999 (COE Civil Law Convention), came into force on 1 July 2002, available at: www.coe.int; and the African Union Convention of Preventing and Combating Corruption 2003 (AU Convention), came into force on 5 August 2006, available at: www.africa-union.org. For more on this Convention, see I. Carr, 'Corruption in Africa: Is the African Union Convention on Combating Corruption the Answer?', *Journal of Business Law*, March (2007), 111–36.

63 ICC, *Report on Extortion and Bribery in Business Transactions* (Paris: ICC, 1977). See also A. Argandona, 'The 1996 ICC Report on Extortion and Bribery in International Business Transactions', *Business Ethics: A European Review*, 6 (1997), 134–46.

bribery in the context of overseas trade. In this it mirrored the US message to the developed nations to combat bribery in international business. Alongside the Report, the ICC published its Rules on Extortion and Bribery which provided the framework for good commercial practice to be adopted by companies. These Rules underwent amendment in 2005 and then in 2011 when it was published as the Rules on Combating Corruption.[64] In brief, the Rules prohibit bribery and extortion, be they direct or indirect, and the indirect acts of bribery and extortion cover not only the acts of agents (the usual indirect means of engaging in bribery), but other intermediaries who may act as a conduit, such as consultants, lawyers and accountants. Facilitation payments are permitted only if a managerial review indicates that they cannot be eliminated.[65] If facilitation payments are to be made they should be small and paid to low-level officials for actions that are routinely undertaken. Businesses are also expected not to cloak bribery as charitable payments.[66] The importance of training employees and the extension of the code to subsidiaries, besides appropriate accounting and auditing standards, are also advocated by these Rules. They also promote in Part III the implementation of:

> an efficient Corporate Compliance Programme (i) reflecting these Rules, (ii) based on the results of a periodically conducted assessment of the risks faced in the Enterprise's business environment, (iii) adapted to the Enterprise's particular circumstances and (iv) with the aim of

[64] Text available at: www.iccwbo.org/uploadedFiles/ICC/policy/business_in_society/Statements/ICC_Rules_on_Combating_Corruption_2011edition.pdf.

[65] It is unfortunate that the OECD Anti-Bribery Convention does not require member states to criminalise facilitation payments. This means that bribes can be passed off as facilitation payments. Subsequent pressure has come from various quarters including the ICC and in the Recommendations of the Council for Further Combating Bribery adopted in 2009, paragraph VI, which states: 'In view of the corrosive effect of small facilitation payments, particularly on sustainable economic development and the rule of law that member countries should: (i) undertake to periodically review their policies and approach on small facilitation payments in order to effectively combat the phenomenon; (ii) encourage companies to prohibit or discourage the use of small facilitation payments in internal company controls, ethics and compliance programmes or measures, recognising that such payments are generally illegal in the countries where they are made, and must in all cases be accurately accounted for in such companies' books and financial records.'

[66] Most countries have special tax rules when it comes to charitable payments. If bribes are cloaked as charitable payments this means that businesses are getting a tax advantage for paying bribes.

> preventing and detecting Corruption and of promoting a culture of integrity in the Enterprise.[67]

It is widely recognised that whistle-blowers (informants from within an organisation) are important actors in revealing malpractices within an organisation. Their role in the context of corruption has been well publicised by organisations such as Public Concern at Work.[68] But for whistle-blowers to come forward in the face of ostracisation from others in the workplace, it is important that they are protected and that there are avenues for safe and confidential reporting of their concerns. The ICC's *Guidelines on Whistleblowing*[69] sit alongside the Rules to strengthen business integrity. The ICC views them as a positive force with the potential to contribute to and enhance the reputation of a company.[70]

Through its *Guidelines for Multinational Enterprises* (Guidelines),[71] the OECD also promotes all aspects of business ethics, including measures against corruption. These Guidelines arguably carry more weight than the ICC Rules, since governments that adhere to them have a National Contact Point (NCP) which maintains a link with businesses, employees and civil society organisations (CSOs). There are no available statistics to establish the effectiveness of NCPs, but there are accounts of responses to reported instances of bribery and corruption by NCPs that have resulted in behaviour change.[72] A downside of these Guidelines is their limited impact, in that many of the emerging economies do not adhere to them. Against this background, the United Nations Global Compact (UNGC) has wider geographical reach and provides a platform for companies to commit themselves to social and ethical principles. Its tenth principle requires companies to commit themselves to work against corruption in whatever form. It has been launched in a number of states

67 Rules on Combating Corruption, Art. 10.

68 For more on the organisation visit: www.pcaw.co.uk.

69 *Guidelines on Whistleblowing*, 2008, text available at: www.iccwbo.org/uploadedFiles/ICC%20Guidelines%20Whistleblowing%20%20as%20adopted%204_08(2).pdf.

70 The Council of Europe recognises the importance of protection for whistle-blowers as an aid to exposing malpractices including corruption within the corporate and public sectors. See I. Carr and D. Lewis, 'Combating Corruption through Employment Law and Whistleblower Protection', *Industrial Law Journal*, 39 (2010), 51–81.

71 Guidelines for Multinational Enterprises, 2011, available at: www.oecd.org.

72 For a list of cases visit www.oecdwatch.org (an international network of CSOs that promote corporate accountability and responsibility).

(e.g., Nigeria, Ghana, South Africa) and it seems that there are a number of collaborative projects between companies and CSOs.[73]

Business integrity and corporate social responsibility

The aim of the initiatives described above is clearly to infuse social and ethical values into the behaviour of businesses. The importance of embedding integrity within a business is not a new idea. A survey of company codes of conduct indicates widespread use of the word 'integrity' and of the phrase 'business integrity'. In the absence of a definition it makes sense to examine the concept within the context of the codes of conduct. An examination of a number of codes of conduct indicates that they expect employees to behave in an ethical and responsible manner that closely follows the company policies on health and safety, environment, corruption and so on.[74] Business integrity, it could be said, is a reflection of corporate social responsibility (CSR), a concept that emerged in the capitalist world in the mid twentieth century.[75] CSR since then has expanded to include not only health and safety issues, but also labour, sustainability and, more recently, corruption. Unlike business integrity, CSR is defined, but on the downside there are too many definitions to give a commonly accepted definition. Modern CSR literature also uses a variety of terms such as 'corporate responsibility', 'corporate accountability' and 'corporate citizenship'.[76] Regardless of these diversities, CSR promotes a shift in the focus of companies to include people and the planet besides profit (commonly referred to as the 'triple

[73] Further information on the progress made by these networks and a list of participants (which include small- and medium-sized enterprises and large enterprises) are available at: www.unglobalcompact.org. See the Global Compact Regional Learning Forum, 'Creating a Culture Intolerant of Fraud and Corruption in Total South Africa (PTY Ltd)', in UNGC, *Businesses Fighting Corruption: Experiences from Africa* (New York: UNGC, 2007), available at: www.unglobalcompact.org/docs/news_events/8.1/bfc_web.pdf.

[74] See, e.g., Shell's 'Business General Principles', available at: www-static.shell.com/static/aboutshell/downloads/who_we_are/sgbps/sgbp_english.pdf; Bristow's 'Code of Business Conduct', available at: www.bristowgroup.com/pdf/IntegrityCode.pdf.

[75] In his interesting article, Spector compellingly argues that the broad responsibilities on the part of companies to go beyond shareholders to include customers, employees and the public is a means of defending capitalism from the dangers of communism: B. Spector, 'Business Responsibility in a Divided World: The Cold War Roots of Corporate Social Responsibility', *Enterprise and Society*, 9 (2008), 314–36.

[76] See, e.g., H. R. Bowen, *Social Responsibilities for the Businessman* (New York: Harper, 1953); A. B. Carroll, 'A Three-Dimensional Conceptual Model of Corporate Performance', *Academy of Management Review*, 4 (1979), pp. 497–505; P. W. Maclagan, *Management and Morality* (London: Sage, 1998), p. 147.

bottom line').[77] There is also the expectation that companies will not just assume responsibility, but also ensure that the responsibilities assumed are met. There is an implicit requirement that companies will adopt codes and put in place mechanisms to ensure that their employees, contractors and suppliers will adhere to the social and ethical policies adopted by the company. However, there are disadvantages to codes of conduct. They are entirely voluntary in nature, and there is no way of ensuring that the company follows the standards that it says it has set for itself. So, there is a case for being prescriptive with codes of conduct by including them within a formal regulatory framework, but the common response to such an intrusive approach is that it would place businesses under the stresses that regulation brings with it. Further, voluntary codes have the advantage of speedy adaptability, a feature not found in formal regulations. While there is some credibility in this argument, the drawback of bringing about business integrity through voluntary codes nonetheless remains: it may turn out to be nothing more than a public relations exercise; and there is no certainty that the philosophy as enshrined in the company's code of conduct is being applied and followed by the company executive management, employees, contractors and others in the supply chain. Against this background, and given the corrosive effect of business corruption on economic growth and the well-being of the public at large, it does make sense to include at the very least a framework for business integrity within anti-corruption laws. As we will see in the following part of this chapter the Bribery Act 2010 has brought the element of business integrity within it in respect of bribery through sections 7 and 9.

Business integrity in the Bribery Act 2010

Background to the Bribery Act

Before proceeding to ask whether and how the Bribery Act (BA) 2010 tackles business integrity, it seems appropriate to provide a background,

[77] The notion of 'triple bottom line' was developed by J. Elkington, *Cannibals with Forks: The Triple Bottom Line of 21st-Century Business* (Hoboken, NJ: John Wiley, 1999). See also P. Yeoh, 'The Direction and Control of Corporations: Law or Strategy?', *Managerial Law*, 49 (2007), 37–47; F. Robbins, 'Why Corporate Social Responsibility should be Popularised but not Imposed', *Corporate Governance*, 8 (2008), 330–41; C. Holliday, S. Schmidheiny and P. Watts, *Walking the Talk: The Business Case for Sustainable Development* (Sheffield: Greenleaf, 2002).

albeit brief, to the Act.[78] As with other areas of English law, the law relating to corruption was dispersed among common law and statute law. Apart from the common law offence of bribery, the offences of corruption were created by the Prevention of Corruption Acts 1889–1916 and Part 12 of the Anti-Terrorism, Crime and Security Act 2001 (ATCSA). While the focus of the common law offence of bribery and the 1889 Act was the public sector, the 1906 Act focused on public and private sector corruption and dealt with corruption by agents. Since it was unclear whether the existing offences covered corruption involving foreign public officials, Part 12 of the ATCSA was enacted to ensure that the United Kingdom met with its implementation obligations as a result of ratifying the OECD Convention on Bribery of Foreign Public Officials in International Business Transactions 1997 (Anti-Bribery Convention), thus imparting jurisdiction over corruption of foreign public office officials. However, the OECD, which operates a peer review system to monitor the implementation of its Anti-Bribery Convention, had consistently raised a number of criticisms in its Reports,[79] which included the way the anti-corruption laws were spread across statutes and common law, the low number of prosecutions, and the unsuitability of the 'directing mind' principle for establishing liability of legal persons.[80] Recommendations were made for reform and these took on an energetic tone when, on grounds of national security, the Serious Fraud Office (SFO) dropped its investigation into the allegation of bribery by British Aerospace (BAE) in the al-Yamamah arms deal with Saudi Arabia. It was felt widely that the decision to drop the investigation, albeit on grounds of national security,

78 See further Sullivan, Chapter 1, this volume.

79 See, e.g., OECD, *United Kingdom: Phase 2 Report on the Application of the Convention on Combating Bribery of Foreign Public Officials in International Business Transactions and 1997 Recommendation on Combating Bribery in International Business Transactions* (Paris: OECD, 2005), available at: www.oecd.org/dataoecd/23/20/41515077.pdf.

80 This is the principle of the active and directing will of the company 'in the person of somebody who for some purposes may be called an agent, but who is really the directing mind and will of the corporation, the very ego and centre or the personality of the corporation' (*Lennards' Carrying Co. Ltd* v. *Asiatic Petroleum Co.* [1915] AC 502). This principle, which has been adopted by a number of common law jurisdictions, has been variously applied ranging from the narrow to the wide. The English courts have adopted a narrow application, which means that the act of a person lower down the command structure of a company will not be viewed as the act of a directing mind. To illustrate, in *Tesco Supermarkets Ltd* v. *Nattrass* [1972] AC 153 (HL), it was held that a manager could not be a directing mind. A wider application would find the directing mind further down the command chain; e.g., the Canadian case as illustrated by *Canadian Dredge & Dock Ltd* v. *The Queen* (1985) 19 CCC (3d) 1 (SCC).

showed reluctance on the part of the United Kingdom to take corruption seriously. This also strengthened the widely held view that the United Kingdom was unwilling to prosecute despite its ratification of the Anti-Bribery Convention. Under intense pressure from the OECD the United Kingdom finally enacted the BA.[81]

There are two general offences of bribery created by the Act: section 1 criminalises the supply side of bribery ('active bribery'); and section 2 criminalises the demand side ('passive bribery'). This section is pertinent for our purposes since businesses are the suppliers of bribe. According to this section, the offering, promising or giving of a financial or other advantage by a person P to another is an offence where:

- P intends the advantage to induce a person to perform improperly a relevant function or activity (section 1(2)(a));
- P intends to reward a person for the improper performance of such a function or activity (section 1(2)(b)); or
- P knows or believes that the acceptance of the advantage would itself constitute the improper performance of a relevant function or activity (section 1(3)(c)).

Sections 6 and 7 deal with business bribery specifically. Section 6 relates specifically to bribery of a foreign public official. A person (P) who bribes such a foreign official (F) would have committed an offence provided it was P's intention to influence F in F's capacity as a foreign public official and P intended to obtain or retain business or an advantage in the conduct of business.[82] However for the purposes of section 6, P's offers, promises or the giving of a financial advantage will be regarded as a bribe only if the written law applicable to F does not permit or require F to be influenced by the offer, promise or gift. This might not

[81] Bribery Act 2010, Chapter 23. It received Royal Assent on 8 April 2010. It abolishes the common law offences of bribery and embracery in the law of England, Wales and Northern Ireland (s. 17(1)) and the offences of bribery and accepting a bribe in Scotland (s. 17(2)). It also repeals the Prevention of Corruption Acts 1889–1916 and ss. 108–110 of ATCSA. It must also be added that there had been other attempts to pass legislation on corruption.

[82] As opposed to s. 1, which is directed at 'improper performance', the s. 6 offence is aimed at influencing decision-making. The scope of 'improper performance' is to be gathered from ss. 3, 4 and 5, and, briefly, it 'amounts to a breach of an expectation that a person will act in good faith, impartially or in accordance with a position of trust' (Ministry of Justice, *The Bribery Act 2010: Guidance about Procedures which Relevant Commercial Organisations can put into Place to Prevent Persons Associated with them from Bribing* (London: Ministry of Justice, 2011), para. 18.

be difficult to establish given the level of harmonisation due to the 150 state ratifications of the UNCAC, subject to the proviso that there has been effective implementation of this Convention by the ratifying state. The UNCAC in its Article 15 requires state parties to make passive bribery when committed intentionally a criminal offence. Passive bribery as envisaged in Article 15(b) is 'the solicitation or acceptance by a public official, directly or indirectly, of an undue advantage, for the official himself or herself or another person or entity, in order that the official act or refrain from acting in the exercise of his or her official duties'.

Section 7 is more interesting for the purposes of this chapter. It creates a new offence of failure of a commercial organisation to prevent bribery.[83] This has the potential to improve business integrity within organisations. According to sections 7(1) and (3), a commercial organisation (C) is guilty if a person (A) associated with C bribes another person intending to (a) obtain or retain business for C, or (b) to obtain or retain an advantage in the conduct of business for C as long as A is or would be guilty of bribery under sections 1 or 6 of the BA. However, the Act also imparts a defence in section 7(2) to the commercial organisation to prove that it 'has in place adequate procedures designed to prevent persons associated with it from undertaking such conduct'. The phrase 'commercial organisation' is defined widely in section 7(5) and the central feature is 'carrying on business' in the United Kingdom.[84] Circumstances will

[83] This offence perhaps does not really address the OECD recommendation to extend the narrow principle of 'directing mind'. However, the Law Commission recommends that 'the extension of the scope for imposing direct liability on companies should form part of a general review of corporate liability' (para. 6.39). In support they cited the Council of HM Circuit Judges which said that: 'We agree that this should be seen as part of a much larger review of corporate liability for criminal offences. The topic is potentially difficult and the consequences far-reaching … Thus we agree that consideration of the law relating to direct liability of legal persons (incorporated and unincorporated bodies) should be deferred until the Law Commission's wider review of this area' (Law Commission, *Reforming Bribery*, Law Com. No. 313 (London: The Stationery Office, 2008), para. 6.29).

[84] 'Relevant commercial organisation' is defined in s. 7(5) as: (a) a body which is incorporated under the law of any part of the United Kingdom and which carries on a business (whether there or elsewhere); (b) any other body corporate (wherever incorporated) which carries on a business, or part of a business, in any part of the United Kingdom; (c) a partnership which is formed under the law of any part of the United Kingdom and which carries on a business (whether there or elsewhere); or (d) any other partnership (wherever formed) which carries on a business, or part of a business, in any part of the United Kingdom, and, for the purposes of this section, a trade or profession is a business.

determine whether a particular commercial organisation is carrying on business in the United Kingdom or not. Whether 'a body or partnership is carrying on business will be answered by applying a common-sense approach'.[85] The Guidance provides some examples which indicate that mere trading on the London Stock Exchange is insufficient to say that a company is carrying on business in the United Kingdom. Other factors are likely to be relevant, such as whether the company has an office or employees in the United Kingdom.

Section 7 also makes a company liable for the acts of persons associated with it. The meaning of 'persons associated with' is provided in section 8 to include an employee, agent or subsidiary. The definition, however, has its limitations. Subcontractors within a supply chain (third parties) who have no contact with C would not be regarded as persons associated with C, since C is unlikely to be in a position to exercise control over them, or even know their identity. The Guidance does highlight this issue and suggests that:

> the principal way in which commercial organisations may decide to approach bribery risks which arise as a result of a supply chain is by employing the types of anti-bribery procedures referred to elsewhere in this guidance (e.g., risk-based due diligence and the use of anti-bribery terms and conditions) in the relationship with their contractual party, and by requesting that counterparty to adopt a similar approach with the next party in the chain.[86]

However, such a device is unlikely to be effective. There is no way that C can ensure, apart from a contractual clause, that subcontractors further down the supply chain are going to include such clauses and will be bound by the clause. At some point the anti-bribery contractual clause chain is likely to be breached, especially where the counterparty is working with subcontractors in a country with endemic corruption. Many of the subcontractors are also likely to be small- to medium-sized enterprises, and they may find it difficult to resist the demands for bribes in states with a highly corrupt public sector. In the current climate of global recession, resistance on the part of businesses may not meet the desired value-driven expectations.

As stated earlier, the OECD had previously criticised the rather limited approach to corporate liability through the use of the 'directing mind'

[85] Ministry of Justice, *Bribery Act 2010: Guidance*, para. 35.
[86] Ministry of Justice, *Bribery Act 2010: Guidance*, para. 39.

principle, and in its most recent document[87] it has noted that the earlier criticisms in relation to this principle and the identification theory adopted by the United Kingdom in respect of corporate liability applies equally to the BA. While the BA has not directly said anything about the 'directing mind' principle it must be emphasised that it has widened corporate liability for its purposes. Section 7(1) makes C liable where an associated person bribes with the intention of obtaining or retaining business for C or to obtain or retain an advantage in the conduct of business for C. The provision defining 'associated person' does not make any reference to the status of an employee within C. Further, section 8(5) states that 'if A is an employee of C it is to be presumed unless the contrary is shown that A is a person who performs services for or on behalf of C'. While it is correct that the United Kingdom did not take the opportunity to visit the 'directing mind' principle when drafting the BA (despite the OECD's recommendations to do so), it has certainly relaxed the grip on the principle in the context of bribery in its section 7.[88]

As stated earlier, section 7(2) does allow a defence of having adequate procedures in place to prevent associated persons from engaging in corrupt activities. The question of what procedures are to be in place is addressed in section 9, indicating that the Secretary of State will publish guidance and that the guidance may be revised from time to time. The current Guidance sets out six principles:

Principle 1: 'Proportionate Procedures', sets out that: 'A commercial organisation's procedures to prevent bribery by persons associated with it are proportionate to the risks it faces and to the nature, scale and complexity of the commercial organisation's activities. They are also clear, practical, accessible, effectively implemented and enforced.'

Principle 2: 'Top-Level Commitment', sets out that: 'Top level management in a commercial organisation (be it board of directors, the owners or any other equivalent body or person) are committed to preventing bribery by persons associated with it. They foster a culture within the organisation in which bribery is never acceptable.'

87 See OECD, *United Kingdom: Phase 1 Report on the Application of the Convention on Combating Bribery of Foreign Officials in International Business Transactions and the 2009 Revised Recommendation on Combating Bribery in International Business Transactions* (Paris: OECD, 2009), para. 37, available at: www.oecd.org/dataoecd/58/43/46883138.pdf.

88 See OECD, *United Kingdom: Phase 3 Report on Implementing the OECD Anti-Bribery Convention in the United Kingdom.*

Principle 3: 'Risk Assessment', sets out that: 'The commercial organisation assesses the nature and extent of its exposure to potential external and internal risks of bribery on its behalf by persons associated with it. The assessment is periodic, informed and documented.'

Principle 4: 'Due Diligence', sets out that: 'The commercial organisation applies due diligence procedures, taking a proportionate and risk-based approach, in respect of persons who perform or will perform services on behalf of the organisation, in order to mitigate identified bribery risks.'

Principle 5: 'Communication (including Training)', sets out that: 'The commercial organisation seeks to ensure that bribery prevention policies and procedures are embedded and understood throughout the organisation through external and internal communication, including training, that is proportionate to the risks it faces.'

Principle 6: 'Monitoring and Review', sets out that: 'The commercial organisation monitors and reviews procedures designed to prevent bribery by persons associated with it and make improvements where necessary.'

To some extent there is a degree of overlap between the principles. For instance, top level commitment highlighted in Principle 2 is also of relevance and related to Principle 5. Each principle is followed with a commentary. It is not the intention here to examine the commentary in great detail, but to provide the key features highlighted by the commentaries in pursuing anti-corruption policies within the organisation. Principle 1 stresses the importance of having policies and procedures in respect of bribery prevention. The Guidance clearly indicates that it is not promoting a one-size-fits-all approach and is appreciative that procedures will be dependent on factors such as size and the risks faced in the operations undertaken by the organisation. A small organisation with five employees, for instance, is unlikely to have the extensive procedures adopted by large companies. The Guidance expects the anti-bribery policies and procedures to span the entire spectrum of functions, internal and external. The second principle, in focusing on commitment from top level management (e.g., directors, owners) to anti-bribery policies, promotes the need to convey zero tolerance to bribery, both internally and externally. Communication through information technology is seen as an important tool in conveying the anti-bribery policy by the Guidance. As part of this commitment to integrity, it is expected that the anti-corruption procedures adopted for incident reporting, rules on payments to political campaigns, political parties or gifts, due diligence of associated persons, transparency of information and transaction, decision-making processes, financial controls, and processes for disciplining those who have breached the organisation's anti-bribery policies are communicated. Principle 3 promotes risk assessment by the organisation. It is recognised that risks are dependent on factors such as sector, countries of operation, the scale of activities, types of transactions and business relationships. Top level management is expected to oversee risk and due diligence enquiries. Under Principle 3, active leadership is expected from top level involvement in bribery prevention and a continuous assessment and regular reviews of the policies and procedures that have been put in place. Due diligence, which is closely linked to risk assessment, is addressed in Principle 4 and the Guidance sees this as an important element of good governance. Due diligence is to ensure that persons associated with commercial organisations do not bribe on their behalf. In countries with high levels of corruption associated persons pose a problem and their selection will require considerable care. This may require vetting of the associated person thoroughly through background checks such as proximity to politically exposed persons (PEPs),[89] tax evasion, debarments by WB, business experience and market reputation.[90] Some of these checks may indeed prove difficult. The Guidance also under this Principle emphasises the importance of assessing internal factors which may also contribute to risk, such as bonuses for high risk-taking activities, failure to promote the anti-bribery policies clearly and effectively across the organisation, and the lack of financial controls. Due diligence is also expected to be exercised in respect of employment policy, but it is meant to be proportionate to the associated risk of the post.[91]

[89] PEP is commonly defined as an individual who is or has been entrusted with a prominent public function; examples include heads of state, senior politicians, government, judicial or military officials, senior executives of state-owned corporations and political party officials. The definition is not intended to cover middle ranking or more junior individuals, see www.spectator.co.uk/coffeehouse/3435556/rbss-definition-of-a-politically-exposed-person.thtml. The identification of a PEP can indeed be a difficult task. There are also ambiguities as to whether relatives and friends should be included within the class of PEPs. For more on this, see T. S. Greenberg *et al.*, *Politically Exposed Persons* (Washington DC: World Bank, 2010).

[90] See also Ministry of Justice, *Bribery Act 2010: Guidance*, para. 4.5. (Principle 5), which suggests direct interrogative enquiries, indirect investigations or general research on associated persons.

[91] Surprisingly, due diligence in relation to employees is dealt with under Principle 5 instead of Principle 4.

So, serving staff within a canteen are likely to be regarded as low-risk posts as opposed to the manager in charge of preparing tenders in infrastructure projects. Principle 5 highlights the importance of communication, internally and externally, which was also, for instance, promoted in Principle 2. Inclusion of anti-bribery policies within codes of conduct are promoted: this is intended to 'reassure existing and prospective associated persons and can act as a deterrent to those intending to bribe on a commercial organisation's behalf'.[92] Training[93] is another aspect covered by Principle 5 as well as by the final Principle 6, which addresses monitoring and review, and highlights the kinds of activities that may help to 'deter, detect and investigate and monitor the ethical quality of transactions'.[94] External verification of procedures and certification through external bodies such as industry associations are also recommended though the Guidance. This does point out very clearly that 'such certification may not necessarily mean that a commercial organisation's prevention procedures are "adequate" for all purposes where an offence under section 7 of the Bribery Act could be charged'.[95]

As indicated earlier, whistle-blowers have an important role to play in alerting others to the presence of corrupt practices within an organisation. There is no mention in the BA of whistle-blowers and this silence could be explained by the already well-established whistle-blower protection law in the United Kingdom. It is one of the few states with whistle-blower protection legislation in the form of the Public Interest Disclosure Act 1998 (PIDA) which seems to be working well according to the statistics published by Public Concern at Work.[96] However, whistle-blower protection is also addressed in Principles 2 and 5. Under Principle 2, in communicating commitment to 'zero tolerance' to bribery internally and externally it is expected that the organisation will put in place procedures and protection for confidential reporting of bribery or

[92] See Ministry of Justice, *Bribery Act 2010: Guidance*, para. 5.4 (Principle 5).

[93] The ICC, along with Transparency International, UNGC and the World Economic Forum have developed a toolkit called RESIST (Resisting Extortions and Solicitations in International Transactions) to raise 'employee awareness of how to prevent demands from being made, and sets out practical measures on how to respond to dilemmas in the most efficient and ethical manner when they cannot be avoided'. The text of RESIST is available at: www.iccwbo.org/uploadedFiles/RESIST2_Oct2010.pdf.

[94] Ministry of Justice, *Bribery Act 2010: Guidance*, para. 6.2 (Principle 6).

[95] Ministry of Justice, *Bribery Act 2010: Guidance*, para. 6.4 (Principle 6).

[96] Public Concern at Work (PCAW), *Where is Whistleblowing Now?* (London: PCAW, 2010), available at: www.pcaw.co.uk/policy/policy_pdfs/PIDA_10year_Final_PDF.pdf.

whistle-blowing. Under this Principle it is also expected that there will be procedures for 'speak-up' or 'whistle-blowing'. Under Principle 5, reference is again made to the usefulness of speak-up procedures as an important management tool for improving detection and prevention of bribery, and that if such a tool was to be used, adequate protection must be given to those who report such concerns. If one is looking to the Guidance to provide greater detail on how whistle-blowers are to be protected or the procedures that a whistle-blower has to follow to raise concerns, that is missing. But this is understandable to some extent. As the Guidance itself notes, in being addressed to all commercial organisations, it is flexible and of general application. The expectation of the Guidance document is outcome-oriented in that 'the outcome should always be robust and effective anti-bribery procedures'.[97] Since the emphasis is on effective anti-bribery procedures, then whistle-blowing procedures and whistle-blower protection should form important aspects of anti-bribery procedures in virtually all relevant commercial organisations.

There is no doubt that, through section 7 and the Guidance published under section 9, the BA has sought to embrace business integrity within its fold. The Guidance reflects the practices normally understood as essential for bribery prevention: adopting a policy of zero tolerance of bribery; communication of the policy internally and externally; procedures to ensure compliance with organisation's anti-bribery policies; risk assessment; due diligence and continuous monitoring and review of procedures and processes; and protection of whistle-blowers.

The approach to business integrity taken by the BA is open to criticism. Why give a defence to commercial organisations in section 7(2) at all? Admittedly, criminal law has the advantage of bringing about changes in behaviour or deterring persons from behaving in a certain manner due to the punishments associated with an offence. But its success is dependent on enforcement and in a clandestine activity such as bribery the level of enforcement is likely to be low. Against this, in practical terms, section 7(2) is likely to result in organisations reflecting on their policies and practices and embedding them within the psyche of their organisations and of those they deal with. This may be a gentle approach, but it is far better than using criminal law to its full extent. The Guidance also notes that the objective of the BA:

[97] Ministry of Justice, *Bribery Act 2010: Guidance*, p. 20.

> is not to bring the full force of the criminal law to bear upon well run organisations that experience an isolated incident of bribery on their behalf. So in order to achieve an appropriate balance, section 7 provides a full defence. This is in recognition of the fact that no bribery preventing regime will be capable of preventing bribery at all times. However, the defence is also included in order to encourage commercial organisations to put procedures in place to prevent bribery by persons associated with them.[98]

It must also be said that many of the larger companies already have well-developed codes in place for issues such as labour and the protection of the environment as part of their CSR drive. They should be able to incorporate anti-bribery policies and procedures with ease. The BA's definition of a commercial organisation is such that a number of institutions which hitherto might not have reflected on anti-bribery policies will be forced to take note. These include educational establishments and charities.

The generality of the Guidance also raises questions. Instead of indicating in broad terms the areas to be addressed, could it not have been more specific? Could it have indicated clearly what a sole trader needs to put in place as opposed to a small- to medium-sized enterprise or a multinational? Such an approach (even if it would have been feasible) would have created rigidity and would have made a number of assumptions that would not have applied to a particular organisation. As the Guidance itself states, the question of procedures is led by the context in which an organisation operates. So, for an organisation that deals with New Zealand only, one of the least corrupt countries, it is unlikely that their risk assessment procedures are to be as extensive as those of an organisation engaging in business in India.

The Guidance in its Appendix A does provide a number of case studies which may be of help to all organisations including the small- and medium-sized. But these are illustrative, and as the Guidance itself states, they are not to be seen as 'standard setting'. Recently, the British Standards (BSI) published its Anti-Bribery Management System (ABMS).[99] It came into effect on 30 November 2011 and is designed for all sectors, private, pubic and voluntary, to implement anti-bribery policies. However, BSI sees the standard as being of particular relevance to the gas, oil,

[98] Ministry of Justice, *Bribery Act 2010: Guidance*, para. 11.

[99] Anti-Bribery Management System (ABMS) BS 10500-2011. For more on BSI, visit http://bsigroup.com.

mining, defence, engineering[100] and construction sectors. The standard addresses the areas covered by the Guidance and is more detailed than the Guidance. By way of illustration, ABMS has extensive provisions on management responsibility, which include within it day to day responsibility for compliance and the role and duties of the compliance managers.[101] There is also provision on implementation of ABMS by controlled organisations and business associates.[102] The advantage of implementing the ABMS within an organisation is that it would help in showing stakeholders, internal and external, that appropriate procedures to combat bribery are in place. However, as the Introduction itself notes, 'compliance with this standard cannot provide assurance that no bribery has occurred or will take place in relation to the organisation'.

The beauty of the BA is that it has through a regulatory route brought business integrity, often regarded as a self-regulatory CSR issue, within its embrace. It will at the very least result in commercial organisations engaging with and prioritising anti-bribery policies.[103] It is hoped that this will reduce the incidence of bribery, but the adoption of anti-bribery policies itself is no guarantee that businesses will stop engaging in bribery.

Conclusion

This chapter started with a discussion of the impact of corruption through the lens of corruption within development aid and suggested that business integrity should be promoted as a legal imperative. Against this context this chapter explored in the second part the issue of how the United Kingdom addresses and incorporates business integrity within its recent anti-bribery legislation. The BA does not take a prescriptive approach to business integrity by creating, for instance, an offence of not having an anti-bribery policy. Instead, it tackles the issue in a subtle manner by creating an offence of failure by a commercial organisation to

[100] It has recently been endorsed by the World Federation of Engineering Organisations.

[101] ABMS, clause 4.4. [102] ABMS, clause 4.8.

[103] A recent survey of publicly listed companies as published by *The Times* found that corruption, when compared with equality, anti-discrimination, and health and safety, was low on the list of CSR priorities. This could perhaps be explained due to the robust legislative intervention in respect to equality, anti-discrimination, and health and safety. See I. Carr and O. Outhwaite, 'Controlling Corruption through Corporate Social Responsibility and Corporate Governance: Theory and Practice', *Journal of Corporate Law Studies*, 11 (2011), 299–341.

prevent bribery on its behalf and providing a defence in section 7(2) that is more than likely to result in the adoption of policies and procedures in respect of bribery by commercial organisations. Hopefully, this will result in a noticeable shift in the way business is conducted, both at home and abroad, the net result of which will improve the quality of life of millions globally.

6

The aims and limits of European Union anti-corruption law

VALSAMIS MITSILEGAS

Introduction

The question of how best to tackle corruption by legal means has proven to be far from straightforward, as demonstrated by the recent debates surrounding domestic law reform in the field. The question becomes even more complex when one looks at the European Union. For the European Union to legislate, it is not enough to simply establish a justification for the adoption of legislation; it is also necessary, in the light of the EU's constitutional structure, to establish in advance that the European Union has the competence to legislate and that power has been conferred to the EU by the Member States. It is essential in this context to establish the appropriate legal bases in the EU treaties, which are linked to specific EU policies and objectives. It is from this, constitutional, perspective that this chapter will attempt to map and evaluate the emergence of EU anti-corruption law. The content of EU law in the field will be assessed in the light of the constitutional aims it has been designed to achieve. In doing so, the constitutional limits to the development of anti-corruption law will also be highlighted, with the underlying questions being how has EU anti-corruption law been shaped in the light of the evolving EU constitutional law? and what are the prospects for the future? Emphasis will be placed on the changes brought forward by the Lisbon Treaty and related policy developments in the field of EU criminal and internal market law, as well as on the relationship between internal and external EU action against corruption.

The aims of EU anti-corruption law

A key challenge when legislating on corruption is to locate a concrete justification and need for the adoption of anti-corruption law. This is particularly evident in the field of criminal law, where opinions on why it is necessary to criminalise corruption (attempting to locate the harm in corruption) diverge considerably. The justification of anti-corruption law as necessary to protect a variety of different legal interests (a justification linked to the different views on the harm caused by corruption) is particularly relevant at the level of the European Union, where legislation on corruption has been linked to safeguarding a variety of EU objectives, ranging from the protection of the EU budget to the rule of law. This holistic, catch-all view of the harm in corruption has been confirmed by the European Commission in its recent Communication on Fighting Corruption in the EU,[1] where it is stated that:

> Although the nature and extent of corruption vary, it harms all EU Member States and the EU as a whole. It inflicts financial damage by lowering investment levels, hampering the fair operation of the internal market and reducing public finances. It causes social harm as organised crime groups use corruption to commit other serious crimes, such as trafficking in drugs and human beings. Moreover, if not addressed, corruption can undermine trust in democratic institutions and weaken the accountability of political leadership.[2]

The Commission's statement will be assessed in the light of the various aims put forward to adopt EU anti-corruption standards, followed by an analysis of the legislative outcomes in the field.

Aim 1: defending the EU budget

The protection of the budget of the European Union has been a key policy objective since the 1980s, pursued by judicial intervention by the Court of Justice (which, in the late 1980s, established the assimilation principle obliging Member States to treat fraud against the (then) Community budget in a manner equivalent to the way they treat fraud against their domestic budget), policy intervention by the Commission (in particular, by funding the *Corpus Juris* project, an academic study which produced a mini criminal code for Europe) and legislative intervention by Member States (in particular, by the adoption of criminal law conventions on fraud and the establishment of an EU anti-fraud office).[3]

[1] *Fighting Corruption in the EU*, COM (2011) 308 final, Brussels, 6 June 2011.
[2] COM (2011) 308 final, p. 3.
[3] For details, see V. Mitsilegas, *EU Criminal Law* (Oxford: Hart, 2009).

Defending the EU budget via institutional steps: the establishment of OLAF

The EU Anti-Fraud Office (*Office lutte anti-fraude*, OLAF) is the product of a major political crisis in the European Union, resulting from allegations of mismanagement of Community funds internally. Such allegations led eventually to the fall of the Santer Commission in 1999.[4] One of the responses to this crisis has been internal institutional reform – with existing internal EU anti-fraud mechanisms being replaced by a new unit, OLAF[5]: as it has been noted, the latter is thus 'the fruit of exceptional circumstances in the aftermath of a scandal' and 'reflects the necessity of restoring credibility'.[6]

OLAF was established by a Commission Decision in April 1999.[7] The Decision confirms that OLAF's tasks would include the conduct of both external and internal administrative investigation[8] – with OLAF exercising the Commission's powers to carry out external investigations.[9] It also confirms the independence of OLAF's investigative function.[10] The Decision also calls for the establishment of a 'surveillance committee' responsible for monitoring such investigative function[11] – the latter will also have a role in the appointment of OLAF's director, who will be nominated by the Commission after consulting in the European Parliament and the Council.[12]

[4] See P. Craig, 'The Fall and Renewal of the Commission: Accountability, Contract and Administrative Organisation', *European Law Journal*, 6 (2000), 98–116; A. Tomkins, 'Responsibility and Resignation in the European Commission', *Modern Law Review*, 62 (1999), 744–65; and D. Georgakakis, 'La démission de la Commission européenne: scandale et tournant institutionnel (octobre 1998–mars 1999)', *Cultures et Conflits*, Nos 38–39 (2000), available at: www.conflits.org.

[5] For a brief chronology, see the Report by the French Assemblée nationale, *Rapport d'information déposé par la délégation de l'Assemblée nationale pour l'Union européenne sur l'Office européen de lutte anti-fraude (OLAF)*, No. 1533, 8 April 2004, pp. 9–10, available at: http://www.assemblee-nationale.fr/12/europe/rap-info/i1533.asp.

[6] V. Pujas, 'The European Anti-Fraud Office (OLAF): a European Policy to Fight against Economic and Financial Fraud?', *Journal of European Public Policy*, 10 (2003), 778–97, at 792.

[7] OJ 1999 No. L136, 31 May 1999, p. 20.

[8] The Court of Justice resisted attempts to limit the powers of OLAF with regard to Community bodies, by annulling Decisions of the European Central Bank and the Management Committee of the European Investment Bank aiming to exclude to a great extent these bodies from OLAF's remit. See Case C-11/00 *Commission* v. *European Central Bank* ECR [2003] I-7417; and Case C-15/00 *Commission* v. *European Investment Bank* ECR [2003] I-7281.

[9] Article 2(1). For such powers, see in particular Council Regulation (Euratom, EC) No. 2185/96 concerning on-the-spot checks and inspections carried out by the Commission in order to protect the European Communities' financial interests against fraud and other irregularities, OJ 1996 No. L292, 15 November 1996, p. 2.

[10] Article 3. [11] Article 4. [12] Article 5(1).

The Decision is complemented by a Regulation fleshing out rules concerning OLAF investigations.[13] The Regulation contains the rules applicable to the conduct of OLAF's external (primarily by reference to pre-existing EC law rules concerning Commission powers) and internal investigations.[14] The Regulation also includes specific rules on the opening[15] and the procedure of investigations,[16] and emphasises the need for confidentiality.[17] Central to the conduct of investigations is also the provision calling for forwarding of information by OLAF to the competent (including judicial) authorities of Member States,[18] and the provision stating that OLAF will draw a report on completion of its investigations.[19] As will be seen in the part on the limits of EU anti-corruption law below, these provisions raise a number of questions concerning the relationship of OLAF's activities with the domestic criminal procedure systems of Member States, in particular as regards the impact of the use of information forwarded by OLAF on defence rights[20] and the use of the OLAF investigation report as evidence in domestic criminal proceedings.[21]

Defending the EU budget via substantive criminal law

Another tool for the EU to tackle fraud against the EU budget has been the criminalisation of corruption in the public sector, stemming from the view that corruption at this level contributes to fraud. The first instance of the criminalisation of corruption in the public sector at EU level was the adoption of two protocols to the 1996 EU Fraud Convention.[22] The First Protocol to the Convention[23] recognises from the outset that:

13 Council Regulation (EC) No. 1073/1999 concerning investigations conducted by OLAF, OJ 1999 No. L136, 31 May 1999, p. 1.

14 Articles 3 and 4, respectively. 15 Article 5. 16 Article 6. 17 Article 8.

18 Article 10. 19 Article 9.

20 For an analysis, see V. Covolo, 'The Legal Framework of OLAF Investigations', *New Journal of European Criminal Law*, 2 (2011), 201–19.

21 The OLAF Regulation states that the Reports 'constitute admissible evidence in administrative or judicial proceedings of the Member State in which their use proves necessary, in the same way and under the same conditions as administrative reports drawn up by national administrative inspectors': Article 9(2).

22 Convention drawn up on the basis of Article K.3 of the Treaty on the European Union, on the Protection of the European Communities' Financial Interests, OJ 1995 No. C316, 27 November 1995, p. 49.

23 Protocol drawn up on the basis of Article K.3 of the Treaty on European Union to the Convention on the Protection of the European Communities' Financial Interests, OJ 1996 No. C313, 23 October 1996, p. 2

> the financial interests of the European Communities may be damaged or threatened by other criminal offences, particularly acts of corruption by or against national and Community officials, responsible for the collection, management or disbursement of Community funds under their control.[24]

The Protocol criminalises passive corruption in the public sector, defined as:

> the deliberate action of an official, who, directly or through an intermediary, requests or receives advantages of any kind whatsoever, for himself or for a third party, or accepts a promise of such an advantage, to act or refrain from acting in accordance with his duty or in the exercise of his functions in breach of his official duties in a way which damages or is likely to damage EC financial interests.[25]

It also criminalises active corruption in the public sector, defined as:

> the deliberate action of whosoever promises or gives, directly or through an intermediary, an advantage of any kind whatsoever to an official for himself or for a third party for him to act or refrain from acting in accordance with his duty or in the exercise of his functions in breach of his official duties in a way which damages or is likely to damage EC financial interests.[26]

In addition to criminalising corruption, the Second Protocol to the Fraud Convention[27] criminalises the laundering of proceeds of corruption,[28] and made legal persons potentially liable for fraud, active corruption and money laundering.[29] Legal persons do not necessarily incur criminal liability under the Protocol, but they must be punished by 'effective, dissuasive and proportionate sanctions'.[30]

Aim 2: protecting the internal market

The establishment of the internal market is a key and long-standing European Union objective touching upon a plethora of secondary EU measures. Anti-corruption standards have been deemed essential to protect the internal market, and have been adopted in a variety of fields ranging from criminal law to public procurement law. As will be seen

[24] Preamble, Recital 4. [25] Article 2(1). [26] Article 3(1).
[27] Second Protocol, drawn up on the basis of Article K.3 of the Treaty on the European Union, to the Convention on the Protection of the European Communities' Financial Interest, OJ 1997 No. C221, 19 July 1997, p. 12.
[28] Article 2. [29] Article 3. [30] Article 4.

below, this is a field where criminal law meets internal market law and where various policy objectives overlap.

Protecting the internal market by criminalising corruption in the private sector

The second level of the EU's criminal law strategy against corruption has been to criminalise corruption in the private sector. In this context, a post-Maastricht Joint Action adopted in 1998[31] was replaced in 2003 by a more clearly legally binding Framework Decision.[32] While the Framework Decision is a third-pillar instrument,[33] its adoption was justified for a number of reasons: the need to improve judicial cooperation after the abolition of dual jeopardy for corruption in the European Arrest Warrant Framework Decision[34] was coupled with the acknowledgement that 'along with globalisation, recent years have brought an increase in cross-border trade in goods and services. Any corruption in the private sector within a Member State is thus not just a domestic problem but also a transnational problem, most effectively tackled by means of a European Union joint action.'[35] In this light, criminalising corruption (in both the public and private sectors) is considered necessary in order to protect a variety of interests ranging from the market to economic development and the rule of law. According to the Preamble to the Framework Decision: 'Member States attach particular importance to combating corruption in both the public and the private sector, in the belief that in both those sectors it poses a threat to a law-abiding society as well as distorting competition in relation to the purchase of goods or commercial services and impeding sound economic development.'[36]

The Framework Decision criminalises both active and passive corruption in the private sector. Article 2 calls upon Member States to criminalise the following intentional acts, if committed *in the course of business activities*:

> promising, offering or giving, directly or through an intermediary, to a person who in any capacity directs or works for a private sector entity, an *undue advantage* of any kind, for that person or for a third party, in order

[31] Joint Action 98/742 on corruption in the private sector, OJ 1998 No. L358, 31 December 1998, p. 2.

[32] Council Framework Decision 2003/568/JHA on combating corruption in the private sector, OJ 2003 No. L192, 31 July 2003, p. 54.

[33] Adopted under Articles 29, 31(1)(e) and 34(2)(b) TEU.

[34] Preamble, Recital 5, see below. [35] Preamble, Recital 1. [36] Recital 9.

> that that person should perform or refrain from performing any act, *in breach of that person's duties*; and directly or through an intermediary, requesting or receiving an *undue advantage* of any kind, or *accepting the promise* of such an advantage, for oneself or for a third party, while in any capacity directing or working for a private sector entity, in order to perform or refrain from performing any act, *in breach of one's duties*.[37]

'Breach of duty' is to be construed in accordance with national law, but should cover as a minimum 'any disloyal behaviour constituting a breach of a statutory duty, or, as the case may be, a breach of professional regulations or instructions, which apply within the business of a person who in any capacity directs or works for a private sector entity'.[38] Criminalisation applies to business activities in both profit and non-profit entities,[39] and also extends to instigating, aiding and abetting.[40] The Framework Decision also includes standard provisions on the liability of legal persons[41] and on jurisdiction.[42]

The Framework Decision has introduced a broad criminalisation of corruption in the private sector.[43] As in the public sector, promising or requesting (or accepting the promise of) an undue advantage is enough to constitute criminal liability: no further action is required. The only limitation is that the offence must be carried out in the course of business activities. Further limitations on the harmonisation of criminal liability (and harmonisation in this field) may stem from the fact that owing to the broad criminalisation adopted by the Framework Decision (which as a third-pillar measure was adopted unanimously), the latter allows Member States to declare that they will limit its scope to conduct which involves, or could involve, a distortion of competition in relation to the purchase of goods or commercial services.[44] A further obstacle to harmonisation may be the fact that the definition of the concept of 'breach of duty' is left to the national law of Member States. The definition of what constitutes disloyal behaviour will be crucial in this context. However, it

[37] Emphasis added. [38] Article 1. [39] Article 2(2). [40] Article 3.
[41] Articles 4 and 5. [42] Article 7.
[43] Convictions for corruption may also involve the exclusion of applicants from making tenders under EU public procurement law and exclusion under the Financial Regulation from public contracts involving EU funds. See P. Szarek-Mason, *The European Union's Fight Against Corruption: The Evolving Policy towards Member States and Candidate Countries* (Cambridge University Press, 2010), pp. 94–7.
[44] Article 2(3). According to the Commission's report on the implementation of the Framework Decision, Germany, Italy, Poland and Austria have lodged declarations under Article 2(3) (COM (2007) 328 final, Brussels, 18 June 2007, p. 7).

is noteworthy that EU legislation itself sets out quite extensive minimum criteria for defining breach of duty and extends it to breach of professional regulations or instructions. This is indeed a very broad definition, since it criminalises the mere breach of professional guidelines.[45] The limitations on liability included in the definition of corruption in the private sector in the Framework Decision may not be adequate to stop the risk of over-criminalisation as a consequence of transplanting the concept of breach of duty to the private sector in an extensive manner.[46]

Protecting the internal market by establishing corruption as a money laundering predicate offence

A complementary approach to the criminalisation of corruption as such has been its treatment as a predicate offence of money laundering. As far back as 1991, and before the entry into force of the Maastricht Treaty which introduced the third pillar into the EU constitutional framework, Member States, acknowledging the potentially adverse impact of money laundering on the stability of the financial system and internal market, agreed the so-called First Money Laundering Directive.[47] The Directive was adopted under free movement and internal market legal bases in order to sidestep the fact that at the time of adoption the Community was not granted express competence to legislate in criminal matters: it prohibited the laundering of the proceeds of drug trafficking, while giving Member States discretion to add further predicate offences to the list.[48] The adoption of the Directive was followed by calls to extend the scope of predicate offences. In this light, the Second Protocol to the Fraud Convention extended the predicate offences of money laundering to the proceeds of (serious) fraud and of active and passive corruption.[49] Having been adopted under the third pillar, which granted the European Union express criminal jurisdiction, the Protocol required Member States to take the necessary measures to establish money laundering as

[45] On this point, see M. Kaiafa-Gbandi, 'The Penal Repression of Corruption in the Public and Private Sector' (in Greek), *Poinika Chronika* (2010), 3 *et seq.*

[46] V. Mitsilegas, 'Corruption and the European Union', in U. Cassani and A. Héritier Lachat (eds), *Lutte contre la corruption internationale: The Never Ending Story* (Zurich: Schulthess, 2011), pp. 83–106.

[47] Council Directive of 10 June 1991 on Prevention of the Use of the Financial System for the Purpose of Money Laundering, OJ 1991 No. L166, 28 June 1991, p. 77.

[48] For an analysis see V. Mitsilegas, *Money Laundering Counter-Measures in the European Union* (London: Kluwer, 2003).

[49] Article 1(e).

a criminal offence.[50] The treatment of corruption as a money laundering predicate was further 'normalised' by the Second Money Laundering Directive,[51] which amended Article 1(e) of the 1991 Directive to include 'corruption' in the list of predicates. This wording was retained in the text of the third money laundering Directive, which repealed the two earlier instruments.[52]

It is noteworthy that the Money Laundering Directives refer to 'corruption' in general as a predicate offence for money laundering, without referring to the definition of corruption in specific EU law instruments, such as the 1997 Corruption Convention or the 2003 Framework Decision on corruption in the private sector.[53] This indicates a broad approach to corruption, covering both the public and the private sectors. It also indicates a disassociation of corruption from fraud against the EU's financial interests.[54] While this approach may reflect the willingness of the legislator to create flexibility in the implementation of the Directives and to adopt a broad approach with respect to the criminalisation of the laundering of proceeds from corruption, the lack of any further definition of corruption in the Money Laundering Directives may create considerable legal uncertainty and significant divergences in their implementation and interpretation. As we will see below, the impact of such uncertainty on judicial cooperation in criminal matters in the EU may be significant.[55]

[50] Article 1(2).

[51] Directive 2001/97/EC of the European Parliament and of the Council amending Council Directive 91/308/EEC on Prevention of the Use of the Financial System for the Purpose of Money Laundering, OJ 2001 No. L344, 28 December 2001, p. 76.

[52] Directive 2005/60/EC of the European Parliament and of the Council on the Prevention of the Use of the Financial System for the Purpose of Money Laundering and Terrorist Financing, OJ 2005 No. L309, 25 November 2005, p. 15. Now Article 3(5). For an overview of the third money laundering Directive see V. Mitsilegas and B. Gilmore, 'The EU Legislative Framework against Money Laundering and Terrorist Finance: A Critical Analysis in the Light of Evolving Global Standards', *International and Comparative Law Quarterly*, 56 (2007), 119–41.

[53] See Mitsilegas, 'Corruption and the European Union'.

[54] On the legislative history of this provision, see Szarek-Mason, *The European Union's Fight Against Corruption*, p. 119. She notes that initially two possibilities were examined in negotiations: to take 'corruption' as something damaging to EC financial interests, or to refer to corruption as defined in the EU Anti-Corruption Convention and the OECD Convention. It was eventually decided to view 'corruption' in a broad sense covering all forms of corruption, whether or not they are damaging to the financial interests of the EU, and to stress the seriousness of the offence.

[55] See section, 'Aim 3: Facilitating judicial cooperation in criminal matters', below.

The introduction of corruption as a money laundering predicate offence reflects the trend towards the extension of the money laundering predicates to all serious crime.[56] This extension is alleged to be necessary in order to enhance the effectiveness of anti-money laundering law – which, at EU level, has been justified largely on the grounds that it protects free movement and the internal market. However, the insertion of anti-corruption considerations into anti-money laundering law may also be intended to enhance enforcement and the rule of law. These aims are particularly apparent in the fact that the Third Money Laundering Directive requires private companies and professionals covered by the Directive to exercise enhanced due diligence in respect of transactions or business relationships with 'politically exposed persons residing in another Member State or in a third country'. This includes taking 'adequate measures to establish the source of wealth and source of funds that are involved in the business relationship or transaction'.[57] The focus on politically exposed persons signifies a shift of money laundering law towards pursuing rule of law anti-corruption objectives. This shift is confirmed by the broad definition of politically exposed persons in the Directive as: 'natural persons who are or have been entrusted with prominent public functions and immediate family members, or persons known to be close associates, of such persons'.[58]

Protecting the internal market by including anti-corruption standards in EU public procurement rules

In addition to the criminalisation of corruption at EU level (both in the form of the criminalisation of corruption in the private sector and in the form of using corruption as a money laundering predicate offence), achieving the protection of the internal market from corruption has been attempted via the indirect use of criminal law in the domestic systems under EU public procurement rules. The two major EU public procurement Directives – which have been adopted under free movement and internal market legal bases – contain certain provisions dealing with corruption. Directive 2004/18/EC on the coordination of procedures for the award of public works contracts, public supply contracts and public service contracts[59] contains a general Preambular statement according to which the award of public contracts to economic operators who have participated in a criminal organisation, or who have been

[56] Mitsilegas, *Money Laundering Counter-Measures*, chs 2 and 3.

[57] Article 13(4). [58] Article 3(8). [59] OJ 2004 No. L134, 30 April 2004, p. 114.

found guilty of corruption or of fraud to the detriment of the financial interests of the European Communities, or of money laundering should be avoided.[60] Article 45 of the Directive fleshes out this commitment further by stipulating as an exclusion criterion from public contracts a conviction by final judgment of which the contracting authority is aware for corruption, as defined in Article 3 of the Council Act of 26 May 1997 and Article 3(1) of Council Joint Action 98/742/JHA, respectively.[61] A similar approach was put forward by Directive 2004/17/EC coordinating the procurement procedures of entities operating in the water, energy, transport and postal services sectors[62] both as regards the Preamble[63] and as regards the exclusion criteria.[64] Current EU law on public procurement thus uses corruption in a limited manner as an express ground of exclusion from public contracts.

In its recent Green Paper on the modernisation of EU public procurement policy,[65] the Commission opened up a consultation on whether to extend the ambit of Article 45 in the light of the entry into force of the Lisbon Treaty by the development of minimum standards for criminal sanctions at EU level in particular circumstances, such as corruption or undeclared conflicts of interest.[66] It remains to be seen whether the legal basis for such legislation – should it be tabled in the future – will be Article 83(1) TFEU, which contains an express reference to corruption as one of the areas of crime for which the European Union has competence to harmonise substantive criminal law if they are particularly serious and have a cross-border dimension, or Article 83(2) TFEU, which confers competence on the EU to harmonise substantive criminal law when EU legislation proves essential to ensure the effective implementation of an EU policy in an area which has been subject to harmonisation measures (in this case the protection of the internal market). A key question in this context is whether the potential criminalisation of conflicts of interest

[60] Recital 43.

[61] Article 45(1)(b). It is noteworthy that the Directive cross-refers to the 1998 Joint Action on corruption in the private sector, although at the time of its publication in the *Official Journal* the 2003 Framework Decision on corruption in the private sector had already been adopted.

[62] OJ 2004 No. L134, 30 April 2004, p. 1.

[63] Recital 54.

[64] According to Article 53(3) of the Directive, the criteria and rules for qualification referred to in paragraph 2 may include the exclusion criteria listed in Article 45 of Directive 2004/18/EC on the terms and conditions set out therein.

[65] *Towards a More Efficient European Procurement Market*, COM (2011) 15 final, Brussels, 27 January 2011.

[66] COM (2011) 15 final, Brussels, 27 January 2011, p. 53.

falls within the scope of 'corruption' under Article 83(1) or whether a specific link with the internal market must be made under Article 83(2). This debate over the legal basis may mask the broader debate of whether criminal law is the optimal way of legislative intervention to regulate conflicts of interest in the procurement process.

Aim 3: Facilitating judicial cooperation in criminal matters

Criminal law on corruption at EU level has thus far been adopted primarily under the so-called 'third pillar' of the EU Treaty (now largely abolished by the entry into force of the Lisbon Treaty). The third pillar legal bases conferred criminal law competence upon the European Union largely on the grounds of facilitating judicial cooperation in criminal matters. As seen above, the facilitation of judicial cooperation has coexisted with a series of other Treaty objectives. There have been cases, however, where legislation on corruption is targeted more expressly towards facilitating judicial cooperation. Such legislation has taken the form of both the harmonisation of substantive criminal law on corruption and the inclusion of corruption offences within the scope of the operation of the principle of mutual recognition in criminal matters at EU level.

Facilitating judicial cooperation by establishing a self-standing criminalisation of corruption in the public sector

The adoption of the EU Fraud Convention and its Protocols was followed by the adoption of EU legislation devoted specifically to establishing a criminal law framework against corruption in the public sector. Another Maastricht third-pillar Convention, the 1997 EU Convention on Corruption,[67] was justified on the grounds that it was necessary to go further than the Fraud Convention in order to improve judicial cooperation in criminal matters of this nature.[68] While keeping the emphasis on the fact that acts of corruption involving national or Community officials are likely to damage EC financial interests,[69] the Convention went a step further than the Protocol to the Fraud Convention as regards the criminalisation of corruption in the public sector: while the main elements of

[67] Convention, drawn up on the basis of Article K.3(2)(c) of the Treaty on the European Union, on the Fight against Corruption Involving Officials of the European Communities or Officials of Member States of the European Union, OJ 1997 No. C195, 25 June 1997, p. 2.

[68] Preamble, Recitals 2 and 4. [69] Preamble, Recital 3.

the offences of passive and active corruption remained the same as in the Protocol, criminalisation of public sector corruption in the Corruption Convention was no longer conditional upon the acts in question being such as to 'damage or be likely to damage EC financial interests'.[70] Thus, the Convention broadens the criminalisation of corruption in the public sector by disassociating it from fraud against EU financial interests and, thus, arguably creating free-standing corruption offences.[71]

The 1997 EU Convention on Corruption thus introduced a broad criminalisation of public sector corruption. Not only has it removed the need for corruption to be linked expressly to fraud against the EU budget, but, moreover, criminalisation (as with the Protocol to the Fraud Convention) is not conditional upon obtaining a specifically business advantage; the focus is on 'advantages of any kind whatsoever' and on the breach of official duty itself. This is a departure from the criminalisation of corruption in the OECD Convention on the Bribery of Foreign Public Officials, of which Article 1 criminalises such bribery 'in order to retain business or other improper advantage *in the conduct of international business*'.[72] For passive corruption to be criminal, a *request* for an advantage is enough; for active corruption to be criminal, the *promise* of an advantage is enough. No further action is required. The Explanatory Report on the Convention[73] also adopts a broad interpretation of the criteria for criminal liability, pointing out that the Convention makes no distinction between direct and indirect means of corruption, or between passive and active corruption.[74] The Convention adopts a similarly broad interpretation of the concept of 'advantages of any kind whatsoever', the offer or acceptance of which is a key element in criminal corruption. According to the Explanatory Report, this 'is a deliberately broad concept, embracing not only material objects ... but also anything that might represent an indirect interest, such as settlement of the corrupted person's debts, work on property belonging to him, etc. This list is not exhaustive. The concept of advantage, requested, received or promised, covers all kinds of material or intangible advantages.'[75]

[70] Article 2 on passive corruption and Art. 3 on active corruption.

[71] The Convention also includes a provision on the criminal liability of company directors.

[72] Article 1(1) *in fine*, emphasis added. For a commentary see I. Zerbes, 'The Offence of Bribery of Foreign Public Officials', in M. Pieth, L. A. Low and P. Cullen (eds), *The OECD Convention on Bribery. A Commentary* (Cambridge University Press, 2007), pp. 45–172, at 150 *et seq*.

[73] OJ 1998 No. C991, 15 December 1998, p. 1.

[74] Points 2.2 and 3.2, respectively.

[75] Point 2.4.

The 1997 EU Convention on Corruption confirms the broad criminalisation of corruption in the public sector at EU level and provides the basis for the harmonisation of Member States' criminal law in this field. However, two major obstacles to the achievement of meaningful harmonisation can be discerned: one involving the substance of the Convention and one involving its form. With respect to the substance, considerable leeway is left to Member States to define the *ratione personae* scope of the Convention. According to Article 1(c) of the Convention, 'national official' means an 'official' or 'public officer' as defined in the *national* law of the Member State in which the person in question performs that function for the purposes of application of the criminal law of that Member State. The provision adds that in the case of proceedings initiated by one Member State against an official of another Member State, the former shall not be bound to apply the definition of 'national official' except insofar as that definition is compatible with its own national law. This leaves plenty of room for divergent definitions of who, in each Member State applying the Convention, is or is not a national official. The right of each Member State to define the term is confirmed by the Explanatory Memorandum to the Convention.[76] Moreover, the *ratione personae* scope of the Convention is substantially curtailed by the fact that, as noted in the Explanatory Report to the Convention, members of Community institutions are not covered by the definition of Community officials, but rather come under Article 4 of the Convention.[77] The latter introduces the principle of assimilation as regards acts of government ministers, elected members of parliament, the members of the highest courts of Member States and the members of their courts of auditors in the exercise of their functions.

[76] According to the Explanatory Report on the Convention: 'Where a national official of the prosecuting Member State is involved, this clearly means that its national definition is applicable. Where, however, an official of another Member State is involved, this means that the definition in the law of that Member State should normally be applied by the prosecuting Member State. If the person concerned would not have had the status of official under the law of that State, that definition may not be decisive … It should be noted that in general the reference to the law of the official's Member State means that due account can be taken of specific national situations regarding the status of persons exercising public functions' (Point 1.4).

[77] Point 1.2.

Facilitating judicial cooperation via mutual recognition: the European Arrest Warrant

Not only is corruption criminalised in many sectors at EU level, it is also one of the offences meriting enhanced judicial cooperation via mutual recognition among EU Member States. The aim of the application of the principle of mutual recognition in criminal matters is for judicial cooperation between competent national authorities to take place on the basis of quasi-automaticity, a minimum of formality and speed: under mutual recognition *in extremis*, a competent authority in the executing Member State should recognise and execute a judgment by the authority in the issuing Member State without asking questions and without looking beyond the form submitted to it by the issuing authority.[78] The key instrument in this context is the European Arrest Warrant Framework Decision,[79] which simplified surrender proceedings among Member States and further developed the relevant provisions on extradition in the sectoral anti-corruption instruments analysed above. A key element in the European Arrest Warrant Framework Decision is the abolition of the dual criminality requirement for a list of thirty-two offences if these are punishable by a custodial sentence for a maximum period of at least three years in the issuing state.[80] Corruption is included in the list of the offences for which dual criminality is abolished. However, as with the Money Laundering Directives, the European Arrest Warrant Framework Decision does not define corruption by reference to existing EU law in the field, but rather contains a general reference to 'corruption'. This raises the question of whether the Framework Decision on the European Arrest Warrant leaves the definition of 'corruption' entirely to the national law of Member States – which may cast serious doubt on the legality of European Arrest Warrant requests for conduct which may not be an offence in the executing state. While the Court of Justice has ruled that the principle of legality is to be defined according to the law of the issuing Member State,[81] European Arrest Warrants for corruption may, in practice, become highly politicised in view of the potential link

78 On the application of mutual recognition in criminal matters see V. Mitsilegas, 'The Constitutional Implications of Mutual Recognition in Criminal Matters in the EU', *Common Market Law Review*, 43 (2006), 1277–311.

79 Council Framework Decision 2002/584/JHA on the European Arrest Warrant and the Surrender Procedures between the Member States, OJ 2002 No. L 190, 18 July 2002, p. 1.

80 Article 2(2).

81 Case C-303/05, *Advocaten voor de Wereld VZW* v. *Leden van de Ministerraad*, ECR [2007] I-3633.

between corruption allegations and the political process in Member States. Similar considerations apply with regard to the abolition of dual criminality in the European Arrest Warrant Framework Decision for the offence of money laundering – especially since (as we have seen) corruption is not defined as a predicate offence for money laundering in the Third Money Laundering Directive.

Aim 4: Safeguarding the rule of law

The harm that corruption may pose to the rule of law has been highlighted on a number of occasions in the development of internal EU anti-corruption standards. However, it is in the field of EU external action where safeguarding the rule of law has emerged as a key objective justifying an emphasis by the European Union on the adoption of and compliance with anti-corruption standards. The emphasis on anti-corruption measures as a rule of law safeguard in external relations may be explained by the fact that the European Union has limited competence internally to legislate on rule of law issues – with the rule of law being a *condition* and *prerequisite* of EU membership, rather than a separate EU policy as such. However, as will be seen below, this approach may lead to allegations that the European Union is employing double standards as regards anti-corruption measures by insiders (its Member States) and outsiders (candidate countries and neighbours). This section will analyse how these challenges have been addressed in the context of the enlargement of the European Union (both pre- and post-accession), as well as in the context of the European Neighbourhood Policy.

Safeguarding the rule of law in the context of the enlargement of the European Union

A key external aspect of EU anti-corruption strategy is the requirement for countries seeking accession to the European Union to comply with EU *acquis* on corruption.[82] Compliance with anti-corruption requirements in this context was deemed necessary not only in order to ensure the protection of EU financial interests and the internal market, but also to achieve institutional stability and to promote the rule of law in candidate countries. Compliance with anti-corruption standards is thus

[82] For a detailed analysis, see Szarek-Mason, *The European Union's Fight Against Corruption*.

inextricably linked to fulfilment of the Copenhagen criteria which underlie the very start of accession negotiations, in particular, the criteria relating to democracy and the rule of law. Compliance with anti-corruption standards and rules is a prerequisite for the assumption by candidate countries of the obligations of EU membership. This applies in particular to the current candidate countries, in the light of the rapid growth of the EU *acquis* in areas of law (such as criminal law) which are highly relevant to the protection of fundamental rights and the rule of law.

Developing a comprehensive anti-corruption framework has been central in the negotiations for the accession to the European Union of new Member States in the recent past. In the accession process that led to the EU enlargements of 2004 and 2007, candidate countries were required to comply with a series of specific anti-corruption standards, including both measures relating to internal EU criminal law on corruption and anti-corruption measures developed outside the EU in international fora. However, as has been noted, pressure to comply with anti-corruption standards decreased after accession, with the former candidate countries no longer being monitored as rigorously as they were during the accession process, leading to claims that 'paradoxically, anti-corruption standards actually diminished once the CEE countries acceded to the EU'.[83] Concerns of this kind prompted the insertion into the Accession Act, following the (largely eastward) enlargement of the European Union in 2004, of a 'safeguard clause' to cover potential shortcomings in the implementation by newcomers of EU instruments relating to mutual recognition in criminal matters. In case of serious shortcomings, or an imminent risk of such shortcomings, in these matters, the Commission may, after consulting the Member States, introduce safeguards including temporary suspension of the provisions on judicial cooperation in criminal matters.[84] The safeguard clause could have been invoked for three years after accession, but this never happened and the period has now expired.

Concerns about the implementation of the EU criminal law *acquis* by new Member States persisted in the context of the sixth EU enlargement, which saw Bulgaria and Romania joining the European Union in

[83] Szarek-Mason, *The European Union's Fight Against Corruption*, p. 220.

[84] Article 39 of the Accession Act. For an overview, see Ch. Hillion, 'The European Union is Dead. Long Live the European Union … A Commentary on the Treaty of Accession 2003', *European Law Review*, 29 (2004), 583–612, at 605–7.

2007.[85] In its pre-accession monitoring reports, the Commission was consistently critical of progress in the fields of justice and home affairs; more generally, gaps in institutional capacity cast doubt on the feasibility of the 2007 accession date for both countries.[86] Nearer the accession date, the Commission published a critical monitoring report which pointed out continuing shortcomings in the two countries' judicial systems and anti-corruption measures; Bulgaria was also said to be deficient in measures against organised crime and money laundering.[87] The Commission recommended a safeguard clause allowing the unilateral suspension of Member States' obligations with regard to judicial cooperation in civil and criminal matters vis-à-vis Bulgaria and Romania, plus the introduction of a mechanism to verify the newcomers' progress after accession. The Commission's recommendations were taken up by Member States: the Act of Accession included a safeguard clause in criminal matters similar to the one used in 2004,[88] and the Commission adopted, on the legal basis of the Accession Treaty and the safeguard clauses in the Accession Act, two Decisions establishing 'a mechanism for co-operation and verification of progress' to check specific benchmarks in the areas of judicial reform and the fight against corruption (in Bulgaria and Romania) and organised crime (Bulgaria only).[89]

The benchmarks themselves are annexed to the Commission Decisions and betray anxieties about the preparedness of Bulgaria and Romania to fully assume their EU obligations in the criminal law field. They focus on compliance with anti-corruption standards and on strengthening the rule of law. Romania is asked to develop a 'more transparent and efficient judicial process'; to combat corruption by establishing an integrity agency which will conduct 'professional, non-partisan investigations' into allegations of high-level corruption; and to take 'further measures' to prevent and fight corruption, particularly in

[85] From a wide range of academic articles in the field, see M. A. Vachudova, 'Corruption and Compliance in the EU's Post-Communist Members and Candidates', *Journal of Common Market Studies*, 47 (2009), 43–62; D. Bozhilova, 'Measuring Success and Failure of EU-Europeanization in the Eastern Enlargement: Judicial Reform in Bulgaria', *European Journal of Law Reform*, 9 (2007), 285–319.

[86] For a background, see A. Lazowski, 'And Then They Were Twenty-Seven … A Legal Appraisal of the Sixth Accession Treaty', *Common Market Law Review*, 44 (2007), 401–30.

[87] European Commission, *Monitoring Report on the State of Preparedness for EU Membership of Bulgaria and Romania*, COM (2006) 549 final, Brussels, 26 September 2006, pp. 4–5.

[88] Articles 37 and 38.

[89] OJ 2006 No. L354, 14 December 2006, pp. 56 and 58, respectively.

local government. This benchmark (which includes corruption at the borders) also applies also to Bulgaria, as do the benchmarks relating to corruption investigations and the development of a more transparent and efficient judicial process. The benchmark list for Bulgaria is somewhat more extensive: it includes the independence of the judiciary (a call to adopt constitutional amendments 'removing any ambiguity' regarding the independence and accountability of the judicial system, and to continue the reform of the judiciary); together with a strong recommendation to implement a strategy to fight organised crime, focusing on serious crime, money laundering and confiscation. It is thus evident that the benchmarks are essentially targeted towards broader institutional changes, rather than implementing specific legislation forming part of the EU criminal law *acquis*.[90] Even the benchmarks relating to specific areas of EU action in criminal matters (such as corruption) refer to broader measures aimed at changing the culture and practices of the administration and judiciary.

Bulgaria and Romania are required to report once a year to the Commission on progress made in addressing each of these benchmarks.[91] The Commission may gather and exchange information on the benchmarks and organise expert missions for that purpose.[92] The evaluation by the Commission is far-reaching, covering fields which fall outside of the competence of the European Union.[93] If Bulgaria and Romania fail to address the benchmarks adequately, the Commission may apply safeguards based on Articles 37 and 38 of the Accession Act, including the suspension of Member States' obligation to recognise and execute, under the conditions laid down in Community law, judicial decisions from the two countries 'such as European arrest warrants'.[94] However, the progress verification decisions do not preclude the

[90] For a general criticism on the EU requiring compliance with standards which are not part of the EU *acquis* and thus leading to difficulties in implementation see A. L. Dimitrova, 'The New Member States of the EU in the Aftermath of Enlargement: Do New European Rules Remain Empty Shells?', *Journal of European Public Policy*, 17 (2010), 137–48. EU anti-corruption requirements have also been criticised for being unclear, see Vachudova, 'Corruption and Compliance'.

[91] Article 1, first indent of each Decision.

[92] Article 1, second indent of each Decision.

[93] See, e.g., the recent Commission Report on Bulgaria, where it is noted that 'responding to the Council of Europe's Group of States against Corruption (GRECO) recommendations on transparency in political party funding, Bulgaria included 11 out of 16 recommendations in the new Electoral Code adopted in January 2011', COM (2011) 459 final, Brussels, 20 July 2011, p. 7.

[94] Preamble, Recital 7 in each Decision.

adoption of safeguards at any time, if the conditions for such measures are fulfilled.[95] The Commission has been publishing regular progress reports.[96] It has stopped short of recommending the suspension of the relevant criminal law *acquis*, but with respect to Bulgaria, it has coupled benchmark compliance with the issue of administration of EU funds and decided to suspend certain funds until the Bulgarian authorities are able to demonstrate that sound financial management structures are in place and operating effectively.[97]

The design of the progress verification process is noteworthy from a constitutional perspective. This is an *ex post* monitoring mechanism which did not come into operation until after the entry of the new Member States into the European Union. This means that, for the time being, Bulgaria and Romania are subject to more detailed evaluation and monitoring in the criminal law sphere than the other twenty-five EU Member States. One might describe this as applying 'double standards' to the two newcomers. On the other hand, one cannot help but notice the *content* of the benchmarks. Not only do they address the implementation of specific EU criminal law standards, they also take us back to the fulfilment of fundamental Copenhagen criteria – the institutional stability which guarantees the rule of law – and concern themselves with the institutional and judicial systems of the assessed states as a whole.[98]

It appears that the perceived lack of preparedness to fulfil the fundamental Copenhagen criteria – or at least those relating to the functioning of criminal law in the 'area of freedom, security and justice' – was not deemed sufficient to change the political decision to admit Bulgaria and Romania into the European Union in 2007.[99]

95 Preamble, Recital 8 in each Decision.

96 See the recent *Report on Progress in Bulgaria under the Co-operation and Verification Mechanism*, COM (2011) 459 final, Brussels, 20 July 2011, and *Report on Progress in Romania under the Co-operation and Verification Mechanism*, COM (2011) 460 final, Brussels, 20 July 2010.

97 See, in this context, the additional Commission *Report on the Management of EU Funds in Bulgaria*, COM (2008) 496 final, Brussels, 23 July 2008.

98 For further details see Mitsilegas, *EU Criminal Law*, ch. 6.

99 However, the perceived lack of compliance with EU anti-corruption standards has significant political consequences. At the time of writing, the Netherlands is blocking the full membership of Bulgaria and Romania to the Schengen border-free area. It is reported that the Netherlands wants to see two consecutive 'positive' Reports on Bulgaria and Romania's anti-corruption efforts prior to lifting its veto to their Schengen

In light of the serious shortcomings revealed in assessments of the progress of these 2007 newcomers, the same decision may not be repeated in future EU enlargements. The emphasis EU institutions place on the development of sound anti-corruption standards by candidate countries is reiterated in the recent Commission Communication on enlargement strategy,[100] where the fight against corruption is identified as one of the 'key challenges'. According to the Commission:

> The fight against corruption is one of the key challenges for the rule of law in most enlargement countries. Corruption remains a serious problem, affecting not only citizens' every day life in vital areas such as healthcare and education. It also has serious negative impacts on investments and business activities and damages national budgets, especially concerning public procurement and privatisation. The Commission has sharpened its focus on the fight against corruption in the enlargement countries in recent years.[101]

Candidate countries' compliance with anti-corruption standards will assume growing importance in this context. This seems to be confirmed by the Commission's strategy in current accession negotiations, whereby compliance with anti-corruption standards is examined in the framework of the chapter on the political criteria for membership, in particular, democracy and the rule of law,[102] as well as, in cases where negotiations are advanced, in the framework of the chapter on the ability to assume EU membership obligations (under the part on the judiciary and fundamental rights).[103]

membership. See V. Pop, 'Dutch Insist on Anti-Corruption Measures in Border Row', *euobserver.com*, 14 December 2011, available at: http://euobserver.com/22/114629.

[100] European Commission, Communication to the European Parliament and the Council, *Enlargement Strategy and Main Challenges 2011–2012*, COM (2011) 666 final, Brussels, 12 October 2011.

[101] COM (2011) 666 final, p. 5.

[102] See Albania 2011 Progress Report, SEC (2011) 1205 final, Brussels, 12 October 2011; Bosnia and Herzegovina 2011 Progress Report, SEC (2011) 1206 final, Brussels, 12 October 2011; Croatia 2011 Progress Report, SEC (2011) 1200 final, Brussels, 12 October 2011; FYROM 2011 Progress Report, SEC (2011) 1203 final, Brussels, 12 October 2011; Kosovo 2011 Progress Report, SEC (2011) 1207 final, Brussels, 12 October 2011; Turkey 2011 Progress Report, SEC (2011) 1201 final, Brussels, 12 October 2011; and Iceland 2011 Progress Report, SEC (2011) 1202 final, Brussels, 12 October 2011, available at: ec.europa.eu/enlargement/index_en.htm.

[103] See the Reports on Albania, Croatia, FYROM, Turkey and Iceland, available at: ec.europa.eu/enlargement/index_en.htm.

Safeguarding the rule of law in the context of the European Neighbourhood Policy

Similar considerations relating to the use of anti-corruption law to promote democracy and the rule of law apply to relations between the European Union and its neighbours. Although the European Neighbourhood Policy does not carry with it the promise of EU membership, and there is considerable differentiation among the 'neighbours', compliance with anti-corruption standards is central to the EU strategy. This is evident from the 2010 Progress Report of the European Commission,[104] which, under the heading 'Improving governance and addressing protracted conflicts', stresses the importance of tackling corruption, noting that 'the need to encourage good governance remains pressing, both as a goal in itself, and because it ultimately underpins political stability and economic growth', adding that 'progress on political reform will be a core element for the development of enhanced relations with the partners'.[105] Moreover, the recent Joint Communication by the High Representative of the Union for Foreign Affairs and Security Policy and the European Commission[106] stresses the need to support what is called 'deep democracy', and notes that:

> While reforms take place differently from one country to another, several elements are common to building deep and sustainable democracy and require a strong and lasting commitment on the part of governments. They include the rule of law administered by an independent judiciary and fighting against corruption.[107]

Compliance with anti-corruption standards is central to a number of specific Action Plans drawn up in the framework of the European Neighbourhood Policy: as with current enlargement negotiations, anti-corruption requirements are grouped, along with presidential elections, public administration reform, judicial reform and the rule of law, under the chapter on 'Political dialogue and reform: democracy and the rule of law'.[108] In the latest Commission Report on the Implementation of the

[104] European Commission, Communication to the European Parliament and the Council, *Taking Stock of the European Neighbourhood Policy*, COM (2010) 207, Brussels, 12 May 2010.

[105] COM (2010) 207, p. 4.

[106] *A New Response to a Changing Neighbourhood*, COM (2011) 303, Brussels, 25 May 2011.

[107] COM (2011) 303, Point 1.1, p. 3.

[108] See, e.g., European Commission, *Implementation of the European Neighbourhood Policy in 2009. Progress Report Ukraine*, SEC (2010) 524, Brussels, 12 May 2010. Compliance

European Neighbourhood Policy,[109] compliance with corruption measures appears under the part on cooperation on justice, freedom and security. The importance of compliance of neighbours with international anti-corruption standards is stressed in this context.[110]

The limits of EU anti-corruption law

As seen in the discussion of the aims of EU anti-corruption law, EU legislators have evoked a multitude of objectives to adopt and develop a variety of anti-corruption standards touching upon a range of EU policies. However, the actual impact of EU anti-corruption law may be limited. The limits of EU anti-corruption law can be traced at the limits of and controversy regarding the extent of EU competence in the field of corruption in particular, and in the field of criminal law more generally. Limits to competence have had a considerable impact on the form and nature of EU legislative intervention, as well as on the implementation of EU anti-corruption standards in Member States. While the EU criminal law competence and action has been largely 'normalised' after the entry into force of the Lisbon Treaty, political constraints as regards EU 'hard law' action on corruption remain. The limits of internal EU anti-corruption law appear increasingly at odds with the emergence of the European Union as a global actor in the development of international law anti-corruption standards and mechanisms for ensuring compliance with these standards.

with anti-corruption requirements, including the ratification of the Council of Europe and UN Conventions on corruption and more structural requirements such as cooperation with civil society and the establishment of an anti-corruption agency, is also covered in the revised EU–Ukraine Action Plan on Freedom, Security and Justice.

[109] Joint Staff Working Paper, *Implementation of the European Neighbourhood Policy in 2010. Sector Progress Report*, SEC (2011) 645, Brussels, 25 May 2011.

[110] According to the Commission Report: 'All partner countries except Syria completed ratification of the 2005 UN Convention against Corruption. As a complement to their international obligations under the above Convention, Egypt and Tunisia have yet to sign the 2003 African Union Convention on Preventing and Combating Corruption. Cooperation with civil society in the implementation of national anti-corruption plans remains critical in all partner countries in order to fight corruption in both the public and private sectors. Enhanced vigilance is required in relation to transparency in public procurement, in order to guarantee the accountability of public officials.' SEC (2011) 645, pp. 11–12.

The limits of EU competence

As seen thus far, action against corruption touches upon a wide range of legislative and policy areas to which the existence and extent of EU competence varies. In a number of areas, including the protection of the internal market and the EU budget, the European Union has long-standing competence. The Area of Freedom, Security and Justice is another policy area where competence was conferred to the European Union to act (as regards criminalisation and judicial cooperation in criminal matters) gradually from the early 1990s (the Maastricht Treaty) to the entry into force of the Lisbon Treaty in December 2009. The question of the extent of EU competence becomes more complicated when one looks at the rule of law. Compliance with the rule of law is a prerequisite of EU membership.[111] However, it is not a distinct policy area with a legal basis for the EU to legislate upon. This places limits on EU action and may explain why the European Union has attempted to link anti-corruption action with the rule of law in the context of its *external*, rather than its *internal* action. In the context of enlargement, the aim has been for anti-corruption standards to strengthen the rule of law *before* accession. While a number of rule of law aspects (such as the independence of the judiciary) are related to specific EU policies (such as the operation of the principle of mutual recognition in criminal matters via the execution of European Arrest Warrants), other rule of law related issues fall far beyond the EU competence to legislate, and would constitute an undue influence on state sovereignty and independence. By way of an example, the recent Commission Communication on corruption[112] contains a part on 'preventing and fighting political corruption' where the Commission calls upon the Member States, the national parliaments and the European Parliament 'to ensure more transparency and allow effective supervision of the financing of political parties and other interest groups', and urges Member States 'to take all necessary measures to ensure effective implementation of the existing legal framework guaranteeing the independence and freedom of the media, including of media funding'.[113] While tackling corruption at the level of political party financing may constitute a key part of a holistic anti-corruption strategy, competence limits mean that this is an area where not a lot can be expected from the European Union in terms of legislative action at the

[111] See the Copenhagen criteria and Article 2 TEU.
[112] COM (2011) 308 final.
[113] COM (2011) 308 final, p. 14.

domestic level. This explains the calls from the Commission to Member States to ensure adequate standards in the field.

Institutional and legislative limits

The competence question is linked to the extent and nature of EU powers to act. In sensitive areas with a potential impact on state sovereignty, competence has been conferred upon the European Union, but accompanied by limits as to how it can legislate. This has been the case, in particular, as regards criminal law. The Maastricht Treaty conferred limited competence on the European Union to legislate, with very weak legal instruments – the main instruments being Joint Actions (the legal effects of which are still contested) and conventions (requiring, as with international law, ratification by Member States). The Amsterdam Treaty introduced Framework Decisions (similar to Directives, but without direct effect), which formed the main instrument of EU legislative intervention in criminal law. But the powers of EU institutions to scrutinise instruments in the field remained limited: the Commission was not granted the right to institute infringement proceedings against Member States before the Court of Justice for inadequate or non-implementation of EU law; and the Court's jurisdiction was limited not only with regard infringement proceedings, but also with regard to the ability to receive questions of interpretation of EU law (preliminary references) from national courts. All this has changed after the entry into force of the Lisbon Treaty, where any new legislation on criminal law will take the form of 'traditional' EU law instruments (most notably Regulations and Directives), and the EU institutions will have, with some exceptions, full powers of scrutiny of EU criminal law.[114]

The historically limited powers of the European Union to legislate in criminal matters have had an impact on the EU criminal law on corruption. The legal instrument of criminalising corruption in the public sector at EU level has been a post-Maastricht Convention. The form of legislative intervention, via the quintessentially intergovernmental legal instrument of a Convention (which, unlike first-pillar instruments and post-Amsterdam third-pillar Framework Decisions, requires subsequent ratification by Member States before it can enter into force) complicates the required harmonisation. In its second report on implementation of

[114] Mitsilegas, *EU Criminal Law*, ch. 1.

the Fraud Convention, the Commission[115] noted in this context that '*De facto* the current system of protection, based on conventions, creates a multi-speed situation. It results in a mixture of different legal situations in terms of the binding effect of the PFI instruments in the individual Member States' internal legal order.'[116] This assessment would apply equally to the relevant corruption instruments (two of which are, in fact, covered by the Commission's Report). It is striking that no legislative action was undertaken by EU institutions after the entry into force of the Amsterdam Treaty to replace or consolidate the existing anti-corruption legal framework with a stronger and more coherent legal instrument under the third pillar. This contrasts starkly with the practice of replacing a number of weak Maastricht third-pillar instruments (Joint Actions or Conventions) with stronger, binding legal instruments such as Framework Decisions and Decisions after Amsterdam.

The European Union did replace a Maastricht Joint Action on corruption in the private sector with an Amsterdam Framework Decision. However, what is striking in both cases of criminalisation of corruption in the public and private sector is that the entry into force of the Lisbon Treaty has not resulted in calls to replace these 'old' and limited instruments with post-Lisbon Directives. Further 'hard' criminal law on corruption under Article 83(1) TFEU was not a priority under the Stockholm Programme.[117] The European Council merely called upon the Commission to 'develop indicators, on the basis of existing systems and common criteria, to measure efforts in the fight against corruption ... and to develop a comprehensive anti-corruption policy, in close cooperation with the Council of Europe Group of States against Corruption (GRECO)', and to increase 'coordination between Member States in the framework of the UN Convention against Corruption, GRECO and the OECD work in the field of combating corruption'.[118] The emphasis, therefore, is on the development of soft law mechanisms and best practice exchange, and on prioritising external action, rather than developing further internal anti-corruption standards. The Commission followed up on this call with its recent Communication on corruption where it was stated that the main way forward as far as EU internal anti-corruption policy is concerned is further monitoring:

[115] COM (2008) 77 final, Brussels, 14 February 2008. [116] COM (2008) 77 final, p. 4.

[117] European Council, *The Stockholm Programme: An Open and Secure Europe Serving and Protecting Citizens*, OJ (2010) No. C115, 4 May 2010, p. 1, Point 3.3.1.

[118] OJ (2010) No. C115, Point 4.4.5.

> The Commission will set up a new mechanism, the *EU Anti-Corruption Report*, to monitor and assess Member States' efforts against corruption, and consequently encourage more political engagement. Supported by an expert group and a network of research correspondents, and the necessary EU budget, the Report will be managed by the Commission and published every two years, starting in 2013. It will give a fair reflection of the achievements, vulnerabilities and commitments of all Member States. It will identify trends and weaknesses that need to be addressed, as well as stimulate peer learning and exchange of best practices. Alongside this mechanism, the EU should participate in the Council of Europe Group of States against Corruption (GRECO).[119]

According to the Commission, the aim of this mechanism is 'to prompt stronger political will in the Member States and enforcement of the existing legal and institutional tools'.[120] New legislation on corruption is not envisaged immediately: the Commission will 'consider in the medium and long term, based on the findings of the EU Anti-Corruption Report, the need for additional EU policy initiatives, including the approximation of criminal law in the field of corruption'.[121] In sharp contrast to developments in other areas of EU criminal law post-Lisbon,[122] the strategy on corruption seems to prioritise an emphasis on monitoring rather than an emphasis on consolidating and developing the 'hard law' *acquis* in the field. While the emphasis on monitoring may lead to a more extensive debate on the criminalisation of corruption at EU level, the approach by the EU institutions has resulted – at least in the short term – in the maintenance of an extremely complex and fragmented legal framework on corruption at EU level, a great part of which stems from the antiquated instrument of a Convention. Extensive 'soft law' monitoring may not alleviate the gaps in the implementation of EU anti-corruption law resulting from the very format of the current legal instruments.[123] The reluctance to embark on further legislative action in the field seems to betray a lack of political will by EU institutions and Member States alike to embark on a new debate on the content of EU

[119] COM (2011) 308 final, p. 2. [120] COM (2011) 308 final, p. 6.

[121] COM (2011) 308 final, p. 8.

[122] A new post-Lisbon Directive on trafficking in human beings, consolidating and expanding existing legislation, has already been adopted (Directive 2011/36/EU, OJ 2011 No. L101, 15 April 2011, p. 1). The Commission's Work Programme for 2012 envisages the revision of the third money laundering Directive and the replacement of the 2002 Framework Decision on drug trafficking by a new instrument (COM (2011) 777 final, Brussels, 15 November 2011, p. 18).

[123] See also the next section on the implementation limits.

anti-corruption law and to adopt new 'hard law' instruments which will ensure the introduction of a clear supranational compliance framework in cases of perceived non-implementation.[124]

The reluctance to develop a comprehensive legally binding EU anti-corruption framework is coupled with persisting institutional constraints with regard to the powers of OLAF in investigating corruption. OLAF's complex legislative framework has led to the justified conclusion that OLAF's status is 'hybrid and ambiguous'.[125] OLAF was set up as a response to grave allegations of financial irregularities within the Commission, in order partly to investigate any such irregularities independently – yet it is not an independent Community agency, rather it remains a department of the Commission itself, under the Commission's control. The paradox – and potential conflict of interest – with regard to OLAF's role in *internal* investigations is glaring: the office that was set up to 'clean up' the financial affairs of the Commission is basically – with some added safeguards of independence – in essence the Commission itself. This paradox may account for what is deemed as the 'increased politicisation' of OLAF investigations.[126] In this light, OLAF's hybrid status, along with its extensive investigative powers, may have significant implications for the position of individuals under investigation. This is in particular the case in view of the inevitable politicisation of cases involving alleged irregularities within the European Commission, where OLAF's zeal in pursuing the matter along with its extended avenues of communication with national investigative authorities may lead to the

[124] The reluctance to legislate further is also reflected in the recent Green Paper on public procurement. In the part on fighting favouritism and corruption, the Commission states that: 'The procurement rules of many Member States contain mechanisms specifically designed to prevent and combat corruption and favouritism. In the same way as for the issue of conflict of interest, an analysis must be made as to whether certain specific safeguards should be integrated in the EU public procurement legislation, on the condition of not creating disproportionate administrative burdens. However, it should be borne in mind not only that corruption is a highly sensitive issue for Member States but also that the actual problems in this field and also the potential solutions depend on the – widely diverging – national administrative and business cultures. Consequently, it might be difficult to find "one size fits all" solutions to be put in place at EU level.' COM (2011) 15 final, 27 January 2011, p. 50.

[125] Assemblée nationale, 'Un statut hybride et ambigu', *Rapport d'information déposé par la délégation de l'Assemblée nationale pour l'Union européenne sur l'Office européen de lutte anti-fraude*, pp. 9–10, at 10.

[126] Assemblée nationale, 'Une politisation croissante', *Rapport d'information déposé par la délégation de l'Assemblée nationale pour l'Union européenne sur l'Office européen de lutte anti-fraud*, p. 21.

unleashing of a wide range of – largely unchecked – powers against individuals who happen to be involved in these cases.

The lack of clarity as to the extent of OLAF's powers and their potential effects on investigated individuals has persisted in the equivocal case law of the EU judiciary in the field. The reluctance of the court to accept that OLAF actions themselves had a direct impact on the investigated individual in the heavily criticised *Tillack* ruling[127] has been reversed in *Franchet and Byk*,[128] where the Court of First Instance found, in examining the conduct of the internal investigation, that OLAF had violated Article 4 of Decision 1999/396 on the right to inform the interested party and the rights of the defendants in the context of the transmission of the dossiers to the national authorities;[129] Article 11 of Regulation 1073/1999 in not informing the OLAF Supervisory Committee of the transmission of the dossiers to national authorities;[130] and, with regard to information leaks concerning one of the dossiers,[131] the principle of the presumption of innocence.[132] However, the confirmation by the EU Civil Service Tribunal that OLAF's decision to forward information to national judicial authorities under Article 10(2) of Regulation No. 1073/1999 did constitute an act adversely affecting a person[133] was overturned on appeal.[134] The limits to the legal framework of OLAF and their effect on fundamental rights may be addressed as part of the general debate on the future establishment of a European public prosecutor's office; a legal basis for which is provided by the Lisbon Treaty.[135]

Implementation limits

The limits to EU legislative action in the field of corruption have a significant impact on the implementation of EU anti-corruption law. Sovereignty concerns over the impact of EU criminal law on national

[127] Case T-193/04 *Tillack* v. *Commission* ECR [2006] II-3995. For details see Mitsilegas, *EU Criminal Law*, ch. 4.
[128] Case T-48/05 *Franchet and Byk* v. *Commission* ECR [2008] II-01585, reported in French.
[129] *Franchet and Byk*, para. 152.
[130] *Franchet and Byk*, paras 164 and 166.
[131] *Franchet and Byk*, para. 206.
[132] *Franchet and Byk*, para. 217.
[133] Joined Cases F-5/05 and F-7/05, *Violetti and Schmit*, judgment, 28 April 2009, nyr.
[134] Case T-261/09P *Commission* v. *Violetti and Schmit*, judgment, 20 May 2010.
[135] Article 86 TFEU. For an overview of the various scenarios with regard to the nature and powers of the European Public Prosecutor see S. White, 'EU Anti-Fraud Enforcement: Overcoming Obstacles', *Journal of Financial Crime*, 17 (2010), 81–99.

criminal justice systems meant that third-pillar law was not subject to the ordinary mechanisms of enforcement of Community law, in particular, the institution of infringement proceedings by the Commission against Member States that did not implement, or implemented only partially or incorrectly, EU law. In the field of the criminal law on corruption, the lack of 'teeth' in the legislation was combined with the lack of political will by Member States to implement the relevant EU standards and the difficulties that Member States encountered in transposing the measures. This has been the case in particular with regard to the criminalisation of private sector corruption. According to the first Commission Implementation Report on the Framework Decision to combat corruption in the private sector,[136] Article 2 (on criminalisation) proved to be highly problematic for most of the twenty Member States that submitted reports to the Commission, with only two 'full' transpositions of the provision. In its second Implementation Report, published in 2011,[137] the Commission noted that the implementation of Article 2 of the 2003 Framework Decision (on the criminalisation of corruption in the private sector) had proved to be 'highly problematic' for Member States, with only nine Member States deemed to have transposed the provision correctly. The Commission noted that Member States found it particularly difficult to capture the full meaning of the phrases 'directly or through an intermediary' and 'a person who in any capacity directs or works' in their national legislation.[138] As the Commission sums up in its recent corruption Communication, the second Implementation Report shows that several Member States have still not transposed the most detailed provisions on criminalisation of all elements of active and passive bribery.[139] According to the Lisbon Treaty, the Commission will assume its full monitoring powers with regard to third-pillar law five years after the entry into force of the Lisbon Treaty.[140] It remains to be seen whether these powers will be used in practice and whether the threat of infringement proceedings will make a difference with regard to the implementation of the criminal law on corruption by Member States; in particular, in

[136] COM (2007) 328 final, Brussels, 18 June 2007.

[137] *Report from the Commission to the European Parliament and the Council based on Article 9 of Council Framework Decision 2003/568/JHA of 22 July 2003 on Combating Corruption in the Private Sector*, COM (2011) 309 final, Brussels, 6 June 2011.

[138] COM (2011) 309 final, p. 2. [139] COM (2011) 308 final, p. 9.

[140] Protocol No. 36 on Transitional Provisions, Article 10(1)–(3).

the light of the growing emphasis on 'soft monitoring' of implementation instead of the development of 'hard law' standards on corruption.

Coherence limits

The reluctance to legislate further and implement existing EU anti-corruption law sits at odds with the growing activism of the European Union in using and promoting anti-corruption standards at the international level. Such activism is reflected in a threefold manner by: attempting to influence the content of international law on corruption; requiring that both Member States and candidate countries implement international standards in addition to the relevant EU standards; and prioritising compliance with anti-corruption law in the context of the relations of the European Union with candidate countries and neighbours. In this context, there is a growing interdependence between international law (in particular, with regard to the evolution of monitoring mechanisms to ensure compliance) and EU law. The emphasis on international, rather than EU, law on corruption may lead to accusations of the European Union applying 'double standards': candidate countries and neighbours are required to comply with standards that EU Member States are reluctant to implement; moreover, the EU *acquis* (which EU Member States are reluctant to implement) is being exported to international fora via the negotiating activism of the EU. This may also be seen as an effort by the European Union to compensate for the limits in its internal law by promoting standards in international law which will then have to be implemented by its Member States.[141]

The emphasis on the need to implement international anti-corruption standards was already evident in the 2003 Commission Communication *On a Comprehensive EU Policy against Corruption*[142] – published before the accession of ten new Member States to the European Union in 2004. One of the key principles brought forward by the Commission was that 'current and future EU Members shall fully align with the EU *acquis* and ratify and implement all main international anti-corruption instruments they are party to (UN, Council of Europe and OECD

[141] For this trend with regard to EU criminal law more generally, see V. Mitsilegas, 'The EU and the Implementation of International Norms in Criminal Matters', M. Cremona, J. Monar and S. Poli (eds), *The External Dimension of the Area of Freedom, Security and Justice* (Brussels: Peter Lang, 2011), College of Europe Studies No. 13, pp. 239–72.

[142] COM (2003) 317 final, Brussels, 28 May 2003.

Conventions)'.[143] The Commission also calls upon 'those Member States which have not yet ratified the Criminal and/or Civil Law Convention on Corruption of the Council of Europe or which have not joined GRECO [the evaluation mechanism established at Council of Europe level], to do so without any further delay'.[144] This reflects a strategy by which Member States can remedy shortcomings in internal Community/EU law by ratifying international standards (some of which the European Union has negotiated) and, perhaps more importantly, undertaking to apply peer review mechanisms established by international fora. This strategy has been confirmed by recent moves to ensure the participation of the EU as such in GRECO. [145] Monitoring compliance of candidate countries with anti-corruption standards remains high on the Commission's agenda. According to the recent Commission Communication on enlargement strategy:[146]

> The important experience gained working with the enlargement countries has contributed to the development of the EU's own approach to fighting corruption, across all policy areas, internal as well as external. While the Commission is setting up a corruption monitoring mechanism for the Member States, it will continue to give high priority to the monitoring of anti-corruption policies in the enlargement countries, with an emphasis on results and sustainability, from the early stages of accession preparations. The Commission will also promote close coordination between international donors to ensure an optimal use of resources.[147]

The above initiatives confirm the growing interdependence between internal and external EU anti-corruption policy. In the light of the limits to internal EU action against corruption, the European Union is increasingly using international fora in order to ensure compliance with anti-corruption standards (by being inspired by, but also using, monitoring mechanisms established by international organisations), and in order to develop a global anti-corruption level playing field reflecting EU policy choices (which will in turn be useful in the context of the enlargement of the European Union and the development of the European Neighbourhood Policy).

[143] COM (2003) 317 final, Principle 2. [144] COM (2003) 317 final, p. 8.

[145] *Report from the Commission to the Council on the Modalities of European Union Participation in the Council of Europe Group of States against Corruption (GRECO)*, COM (2011) 307 final, Brussels, 6 June 2011.

[146] COM (2011) 666 final. [147] COM (2011) 666 final, p. 5.

Perhaps the best example of EU action towards influencing the creation of a global level playing field in anti-corruption law is the negotiation of the 2003 UN Convention against Corruption.[148] In spite of the limits of EU competence in the field and the fact that negotiations took place before the entry into force of the Lisbon Treaty, in the era of the pillars, the European Union demonstrated a clear political will to exert influence in the negotiations on the UN Convention. In this light, legal solutions were found to ensure the optimal participation of the European Union in negotiations. The Council Decision on behalf of the European Community on the conclusion of the United Nations Convention against Corruption[149] confirms that the Community's accession to the Convention involved a plethora of legal aspects, ranging from provisions on free movement and the internal market, to development cooperation and provisions related to the functioning of the EU institutions.[150] Similarly, the Declaration annexed to the Decision establishes Community competence for a range of issues, including the prevention of corruption, the proper functioning of the internal market and development cooperation. This is a wide range of quite disparate fields, where Community action has not necessarily taken the form of legally binding instruments. Moreover, the criminal (third-pillar) law aspects of the Convention were negotiated on the basis of a series of Common Positions aimed at ensuring joined up action by the EU Member States.[151]

With regard to criminal law, an examination of the final text of the Convention demonstrates that the EU negotiating objectives were largely attained. The Convention requires state parties to criminalise three types of conduct: bribery of national public officials;[152] bribery of foreign public officials and officials of public international organisations;[153] and

[148] For an overview of the Convention, see P. Webb, 'The United Nations Convention against Corruption: Global Achievement or Missed Opportunity?', *Journal of International Economic Law*, 8 (2005), 191–229.

[149] OJ 2008 No. L287/1, 29 October 2008.

[150] The legal bases of the Decision were: Articles 47(2) (free movement/right of establishment); 57(2) (free movement of capital); 95 (internal market); 107(5) (monetary policy, ESCB); 179 (development cooperation); 181a (economic, financial and technical cooperation with third countries); 190(5) (European Parliament); 195(4) (ombudsman); 199 (European Parliament rules of procedure); 207(3) (Council rules of procedure); 218(2) (Commission rules of procedure); 279 (Council financial regulations); 280 (fraud against EC financial interests); and 283 (staff regulations of officials of the EC Treaty).

[151] For further details, see V. Mitsilegas, 'The European Union and the Globalisation of Criminal Law', *Cambridge Yearbook of European Legal Studies*, 12 (2009/10), 337–407.

[152] Article 15. [153] Article 16.

embezzlement, misappropriation or other diversion of property by a public official.[154] The latter is not currently covered by EU criminal law, whereas the European Union has legislated on the criminalisation of corruption of national and Community officials. The criminalisation of bribery of national public officials in the UN Convention is worded in very similar terms to the relevant EU instruments on corruption.[155] The UN Convention also criminalises a series of further corruption-related offences (trading in influence,[156] abuse of functions,[157] illicit enrichment,[158] bribery in the private sector,[159] embezzlement of property[160]); however, criminalisation here is not compulsory for state parties, which need only *consider* going down that route. This wording seems to address EU concerns about the criminalisation of illicit enrichment – criminalisation which would in any case be subject to the state parties' constitutions and the fundamental principles of their legal system.[161]

The inclusion in the Convention of the criminalisation of bribery in the private sector represents a partial victory for the European Union. It is reported that extending the Convention to cover the private sector was one of the most contentious issues during the negotiations, with the EU calling for criminalisation and the United States resisting it.[162] The result was a compromise, whereby the Convention includes the criminalisation of private sector corruption in very similar terms to the relevant EU 2003 Framework Decision, but such criminalisation falls within the discretion of state parties to the Convention.[163] It appears thus that the European Union has managed to support a far-reaching and comprehensive international legal framework on corruption, while exporting some of its key internal policy choices and maintaining its autonomy with regard to other criminalisation options not currently covered by EU law. Compliance with this international legal framework will, in turn, form a key element in the EU's relations with candidate countries and neighbours alike.

[154] Article 17.
[155] The EU instruments refer, of course, to 'corruption', whereas the UN Convention refers to 'bribery'.
[156] Article 18. [157] Article 19. [158] Article 20. [159] Article 21. [160] Article 22.
[161] Similarly, the Convention provisions on judicial cooperation in criminal matters appear to address EU concerns, as they are drafted in very general terms.
[162] Webb, 'The United Nations Convention against Corruption', pp. 213–14.
[163] On the regulation of this issue in the United Kingdom, see Sullivan, Chapter 1, this volume.

Conclusion

The European Union has adopted a number of anti-corruption measures based on an extensive interpretation of the threat posed by corruption. The fight against corruption at EU level has been deemed necessary to protect EU objectives and policies ranging from the protection of the EU budget and the internal market, to facilitating judicial cooperation in criminal matters and safeguarding the rule of law. This diversity of objectives has also led to diversity in the legislative standards adopted. The core EU anti-corruption legislation in place consists of third-pillar instruments criminalising corruption in the public and private sectors, with this criminalisation approach supplemented by measures linking corruption with money laundering (corruption being treated as a money laundering predicate offence) and measures bringing forward anti-corruption considerations in public procurement law (corruption convictions being exclusion criteria for the award of public contracts). Anti-corruption considerations become relevant also in the context of judicial cooperation in criminal matters in particular via mutual recognition (with dual criminality for corruption being abolished) as well as with regard to institutional stability and judicial independence, in the context of the relations of the European Union with candidate countries for membership and its neighbours.

While EU intervention in this context has been diffuse, it has also been fragmented and, on a number of occasions, limited. The limits of EU action in the field can be partly explained by the fact that EU intervention is only contingent upon the extent of powers which have been conferred to it by Member States. Limits to EU competence do not allow the adoption of EU law in a number of areas linked to anti-corruption measures. The reluctance of Member States to cede sovereignty in criminal matters has further led to the adoption of criminal law instruments on corruption which do not encourage full implementation by Member States. However, EU constitutional law in the field has changed considerably after the entry into force of the Lisbon Treaty. The fact that EU institutions (or Member States) appear reluctant to use the legal bases offered by Article 83(1) or 83(2) TFEU to consolidate and clarify the existing old and fragmented EU criminal law on corruption betrays a lack of political will to intervene via hard, binding law in the field. The adoption of post-Lisbon criminal law on corruption would enhance the enforcement powers of the European Commission in a clear and speedy manner and highlight the need for Member States to implement fully the relevant EU *acquis*. Instead, there is an emphasis on the establishment of softer anti-corruption monitoring mechanisms culminating in an EU Anti-Corruption Report. The added value of such an exercise is that it may cover areas which fall outside EU legislative competence on corruption (such as rule of law issues, including the independence of the judiciary in Member States). Whether such a Report will act as leverage or as a limit to the development of further EU standards and to the implementation of anti-corruption law remains to be seen.

Limited EU ambition to legislate internally is coupled with a growing focus on the external dimension of anti-corruption policy. Anti-corruption measures are linked to rule of law measures in the context of the enlargement of the European Union and the European Neighbourhood Policy. The European Union is active in influencing international law in the field and requiring both its members and candidates and neighbours to comply with these standards. The European Union is also inspired by international law compliance mechanisms and is in the process of acceding itself to the GRECO compliance mechanism established within the framework of the Council of Europe. This will enhance the EU's regional anti-corruption efforts and may provide an added layer of evaluation to the anti-corruption efforts of EU institutions. However, the efficiency of EU external action against anti-corruption is questionable if this is not accompanied by a comprehensive internal EU anti-corruption framework.

7

Deterring bribery: law, regulation and the export trade

JEREMY HORDER

> "We've got to have rules and obey them. After all, we're not savages. We're English, and the English are best at everything."
>
> (William Golding, *Lord of the Flies*, ch. 2)

The Bribery Act 2010 ('the 2010 Act') deserves critical attention by virtue of at least three of its key features. There is the wide-reaching new offence of failing to prevent bribery (section 7(1)), the collapsing of the distinction between public and private sector bribery (sections 1–5), and the wide extraterritorial application of the law (section 12). These features will form part of the background to the discussion here. My concern will be the impact these changes will have on UK businesses[1] that trade – often through subsidiary companies or agents – overseas. My specific focus will be the impact of the new law on the arms trade, where more research and data are available to assist the analysis, and respecting which the greatest controversy concerning overseas trade has arisen.[2] In exploring this concern, I will consider whether the 2010 Act, which seeks to punish and deter bribery (and the failure to prevent it) through the ordinary criminal law, needs further buttressing in the form of regulatory intervention to reduce the risks that bribery (or the failure to prevent it) will be committed. I suggest that we have much to learn from the dominance of regulatory

[1] I will, for simplicity's sake, for the most part speak of 'UK' businesses or public officials, and of 'UK' law and the 'UK' Parliament, rather than seeking to distinguish when it would be more appropriate to use terms such as 'companies doing business in the UK', 'British businesses' or 'the law of England and Wales', and so forth. This will entail some inaccuracies in the text.

[2] A controversy centred not only on the risk of bribery and corruption in the activities of private firms, but also on the activities of public officials whose job it is to assist those companies when trading overseas: R. Neild, *Public Corruption: The Dark Side of Social Evolution* (London: Anthem Press, 2002), 139–40.

law in the governance of export control. The 'prophylactic' character of regulatory legal intervention in that field provides an important example of what could, and should, be done to further the goal of bribery prevention, especially in relation to export trade itself. The absence of such a regulatory infrastructure symbolises a broader failing. The 2010 Act, whatever its legal merits, has not been adequately supported by an unequivocal policy commitment to harness the energies of UK officials at all levels, at home and abroad, in the service of anti-corruption when facilitating the advancement of commerce.

Law and regulation: towards a truly modern law of bribery

Criminal law and (corporate) compliance: a familiar story

In relatively recent times, a familiar story in criminal law enforcement against companies runs along these lines.[3] Prosecutors seeking to deter and punish wrongful conduct in certain areas find that they have at their disposal only out-dated or poorly drafted criminal laws, often providing only inappropriate or inflexible penalties. These laws in themselves, together with the high standard of proof they carry, and the costs and delay involved in invoking them, manage at one and the same time both to provide obstacles to successful prosecution in anything other than the clearest cases, and to inspire little or no respect among those liable to prosecution.[4] The result has been under-enforcement, and very substantial reliance on negotiation to secure compliance, although that is a strategy notorious either for the dubious compromises it involves or for its ineffectiveness against serial offenders accustomed to evading the law.[5] In some areas of commercial activity, the remedy for this defect has been the creation or use of expert bodies to enforce more specialised forms of regulatory criminal law, and sometimes also new forms of civil penalty drawn up (and then used) in consultation with the relevant industry. Together, these can provide a more effective and respected system of enforcement, the more so when they buttress codes of conduct.[6]

[3] For an analysis, see Law Commission, 'Criminal Liability in Regulatory Contexts', Law Com. CP No. 195, 2010, paras. 3.52–3.96, and App. A.

[4] Law Commission, 'Criminal Liability in Regulatory Contexts'.

[5] J. Black, 'A Review of Enforcement Techniques', in Law Commission, 'Criminal Liability in Regulatory Contexts', Law Com. CP No. 195 2010, App. A; K. Hawkins, *Law as a Last Resort* (Oxford University Press, 2003).

[6] See Law Commission, 'Criminal Liability in Regulatory Contexts', paras 3.83–3.102.

The emerging ideal is that the criminal law, pursued through the traditional route of prosecution in the Magistrates' or Crown Court, is reserved for the most serious wrongdoing or for persistent flouting of the law.[7] Less serious wrongdoing and, most particularly, the accidental or careless creation of a threat thereof, is dealt with through specialised criminal offences or civil penalties in the form of fines, restrictions on a licence, expulsion from a licensing regime, or cancelling of or suspension from membership of a trade association.[8] An example is the approach now taken to employers employing people with no right to work in the United Kingdom.[9] Alongside an older strict liability criminal offence,[10] a new and more serious criminal offence targeted at deliberate wrongdoers has been created.[11] Its function is not so much to support the strict liability offence, as to support a newer system of civil penalties administered by an expert body, the UK Border Agency.[12] Such penalties involve (in a basic form) a fixed fine for each person illegally employed, and 'naming and shaming' in the Border Agency's annual reports.[13] How should one view the development of the law of bribery against this general background?

In important ways, the picture appears to fit well in terms of how problems arose under the old law. Until the coming into force of the 2010 Act, England and Wales were governed by an out of date set of laws that resulted in only a tiny number of prosecutions each year: only one or two convictions for public sector bribery, and around ten convictions annually for (largely) private sector bribery.[14] Even after the outdated domestic legislation was extended in 2001 to cover, for the first time, bribery of foreign public officials, prosecutions remained at a low level relative to the number conducted by countries with a comparable share of international trade.[15] The new law certainly improves the quality of the prosecutor's toolkit, and – insofar as this improvement becomes common knowledge – that may do something to improve international

7 Law Commission, 'Criminal Liability in Regulatory Contexts', paras 3.137–3.138.
8 Law Commission, 'Criminal Liability in Regulatory Contexts', paras 3.137–3.139.
9 See the discussion in Law Commission, 'Criminal Liability in Regulatory Contexts', paras 3.72–3.82.
10 Under the Asylum and Immigration Act 1996, s. 8.
11 Immigration, Asylum and Nationality Act 2006, s. 21.
12 Immigration, Asylum and Nationality Act 2006, s. 15.
13 See www.ukba.homeoffice.gov.uk/sitecontent/documents/employersandsponsors/listemployerspenalties.
14 See, Law Commission, 'Reforming Bribery', Law Com. CP 185, 2007, para. 2.30.
15 See text at n. 3, above.

business confidence in the UK's anti-corruption strategy.[16] However, some of the problems of a simple 'criminal law-led strategy'[17] to tackle bribery are going to plague the new law just as much as they plagued the old law. For example, the need for proof to the criminal standard of bribes paid, for the purposes of a prosecution for failing to prevent bribery under section 7, may involve very considerable delay and cost, perhaps especially in relation to the discovery of documents (if any exist), but also in relation to the costs of extradition proceedings (if available), the use (often of dubious value) of covert human intelligence sources, and the need to cooperate or collaborate with other investigating jurisdictions (including the jurisdiction where the recipient was based) having very different legal traditions and standards. In that regard, the Serious Fraud Office (SFO) faces an all too familiar dilemma. Is it better to husband precious resources, so that they can be devoted to the biggest cases posing perhaps the greatest legal, evidential and cross-border challenges, but with the risk that excessive delay or failure will bring the SFO into disrepute? Alternatively, should resources be spread more thinly and criminal prosecution focused on less high-profile cases with better prospects for success (where, for whatever reason, other prosecution authorities cannot or will not act)?

These problems are far from fatal, and may seem exaggerated in the rudimentary form in which they have just been presented. However, they throw into relief some crucial advantages of a 'regulatory' as opposed to a 'criminal offence-led' strategy, in some (if not all) contexts.[18] A 'criminal offence-led' strategy, as the name implies, relies on the deterrent effect of the ordinary criminal process to reduce the incidence of unacceptable risk posed or harm done in a given context. Such a strategy may not necessarily be 'second best', simply because criminal proceedings are expensive to invoke, may involve considerable delay, and require high standards of proof that may be difficult to meet. In some – perhaps many – contexts, sporadic criminal law enforcement may be preferred to regulatory intervention, even if the former is a less effective deterrent to rule-breaking, because it is feared that the cure – the imposition of

[16] On which see the text at n. 4, above.

[17] For the term, 'criminal offence-led strategy', and a critical analysis of its utility in tackling certain kinds of problem, see Law Commission, 'Criminal Liability in Regulatory Contexts', Part 2.

[18] For this contrast, see Law Commission, 'Criminal Liability in Regulatory Contexts', Part 2.

regulatory burdens – will turn out to be worse than the disease, insofar as it threatens people's willingness to engage in the relevant activity at all.[19] Where it is appropriately deployed, a regulatory strategy will typically have a number of distinctive features. Four important ones are these. First, such a strategy will usually be focused primarily on prevention and minimising risk, or on changing future behaviour plans systematically, and will probably much more rarely involve punishment purely for just deserts' sake.[20] Secondly (a related point), a regulatory prosecution strategy is likely to be focused on unacceptably risky practices in themselves, meaning that proof of harm done in consequence will often be significant only insofar as it highlights unacceptable risk-taking. Thirdly, a regulatory strategy may involve giving priority to the use of specialised context-specific criminal offences, or – or additionally – a flexible range of civil penalties that avoid the need for costly and lengthy criminal court proceedings.[21] Finally, a regulatory strategy will usually involve enforcement carried out by an expert body or bodies, familiar with patterns and kinds of offending as well as with the appropriateness of particular sanctions.[22]

Two questions in relation to the development of a regulatory strategy to counter bribery, alongside the new criminal offences, will be addressed here. First, to what extent does the criminal law, including the 2010 Act, already flirt with some element of a regulatory strategy for dealing with bribery? Secondly, is there a sufficiently strong analogy between bribery and other kinds of corporate wrongdoing dealt with through a mixture of traditional criminal offence-led and regulatory strategies to make the case for a partly regulatory approach to bribery compelling?

[19] See, in this context, the Law Commission's analysis of the law's 'criminal offence-led' strategy for dealing with cyclists: Law Commission, 'Criminal Liability in Regulatory Contexts', Part 2. The threat posed by cyclists is one of low risk of relatively trivial harm. By contrast, the prospect that having to obtain a licence to cycle, or the like, will deter many people from cycling at all is very real; hence, the absence of regulatory oversight, and the reliance on sporadic law enforcement to secure a tolerable degree of compliance with the rules of the road.

[20] For a subtle analysis of this point, illustrating how retributive thinking has recently come to intrude on regulatory ideals in the road safety context, see S. Cunningham, 'Punishing Drivers Who Kill: Putting Road Safety First?', *Legal Studies*, 27 (2007), 288–311.

[21] Although that is not uncontroversial, see R. M. White, 'Civil Penalties: Oxymoron, Chimera and Stealth Sanction', *Law Quarterly Review*, 126 (2010), 593–606.

[22] See Law Commission, 'Criminal Liability in Regulatory Contexts', Part 2.

Beyond make-do-and-mend: in search of regulatory impact

Turning to the first question, the Law Commission recommended an offence of failing to prevent bribery by someone acting (in a loose sense) on its behalf, with a defence that a company or partnership had adequate procedures in place to prevent such wrongdoing.[23] In making that recommendation, the Law Commission regarded this offence as having some regulatory dimension to it. The Commission remarked:

> The new criminal offence that we are recommending is not regulatory in nature ... However, the new offence does have a regulatory dimension to it in that the defence – proof that the company had adequate procedures designed to prevent bribery being committed on its behalf – is concerned with measuring the adequacy of 'internal standards' ... that might otherwise be disregarded. We regard this inclusion of a regulatory element as a positive virtue, but so also is the fact that the offence is in itself an ordinary criminal offence.[24]

The regulatory element was regarded as virtuous, in that it might encourage companies to take prophylactic measures (central to any regulatory scheme) to minimise risks, such as introducing or improving anti-bribery policies and procedures appropriate to the size and nature of the company. This view was in accord with the government's reaction to criticism by a House of Commons Select Committee that it had done too little to address the risk of bribery involved in granting export licences in relation to contracts to export defence equipment and the like (considered further below).[25] In response, the Secretary of State for Justice published a UK Foreign bribery strategy, in which it was said that there was a commitment to:

> establish a clear legal, *regulatory and policy* framework for action against foreign bribery. Law reform through the new Bribery Bill will be the keystone of this approach but the strategy also reinforces links to the wider international anti-corruption agenda – reflecting our commitment to focus on the causal drivers of foreign bribery and deepen our collaboration with international partners.[26]

However, probably motivated by fear that the reform of bribery law would become tarred by broader criticisms of excessive bureaucratic

[23] Law Commission, 'Reforming Bribery'.
[24] Law Commission, 'Reforming Bribery', paras 6.19–6.20.
[25] Security of Arms Export Control: First Joint Report (2007/8) of the Committee on Arms Export Controls (2008 HC 254), paras 115–117.
[26] Ministry of Justice, 'UK Foreign Bribery Strategy', Cm 7791 (2010) (added emphasis).

intervention to shape corporate participation in the market place, in introducing the legislation the government sought to make clear that its strategy was criminal offence-led and not regulatory. In the Impact Assessment that accompanied the consultation on guidance concerning what may count as 'adequate procedures' to prevent bribery, for the purposes of the offence in section 7, the Ministry of Justice said that the guidance would be concerned with broad principles of relevance, 'if [commercial organisations] are to avoid prosecution'.[27] The Ministry went on to add, 'there is no regulatory framework to monitor compliance'.[28] So, there was consequently 'no requirement on commercial organisations to adopt anti-bribery procedures'.[29] There is, then, to be no analogy with the approach to, say, corporate manslaughter, where the stigmatic criminal offence under the Corporate Manslaughter and Corporate Homicide Act 2007, focused on harm done, is underpinned by an already existing regulatory strategy centred on prevention and backed by specialised offences under the Health and Safety at Work Act 1974. This resolutely pure, criminal offence-led strategy (backed by a discriminating prosecution policy) for bribery would normally be appropriate only where the incentives to engage in valuable activities of the relevant kind – in this instance, commercial trading overseas – will not be strong enough if there are regulatory hurdles of any significant kind that must be surmounted to engage in that activity lawfully.[30] However, there is little or no evidence that people are deterred from participating – indeed, they may actually be encouraged to participate – in UK-based national and international markets by a moderate degree of regulation.[31] As far as a regulatory approach to deterring bribery is concerned, there is, quite simply, no evidence that, to use the government formula when considering legal intervention, 'the proposed intervention itself [will or may create] a further set of disproportionate costs and distortions'.[32] On the

[27] Ministry of Justice, 'Guidance about Commercial Organisations Preventing Bribery' (section 9 of the Bribery Act 2010)', Impact Assessment No. MOJ008, 2 August 2010, p. 5.

[28] Ministry of Justice, 'Guidance about Commercial Organisations Preventing Bribery'.

[29] Ministry of Justice, 'Guidance about Commercial Organisations Preventing Bribery'.

[30] See, in this respect, the Law Commission's analysis of a criminal offence-led, as opposed to a regulatory, strategy towards cycling, as opposed to driving and car ownership: Law Commission, 'Criminal Liability in Regulatory Contexts', paras 2.10–2.20.

[31] See the discussion in J. Kitching, 'Better Regulation and the Small Enterprise', in S. Weatherill (ed.), *Better Regulation* (Oxford: Hart, 2007), pp. 155–73, at 156–8.

[32] Ministry of Justice, 'Guidance about Commercial Organisations'.

contrary, there is every reason to think that a regulatory approach is required, alongside modernised general offences, because, using the same government formula, 'there are strong enough failures in the way markets operate … [and] there are strong enough failures in existing government interventions (e.g., waste generated by misdirected rules)'.[33] The government's economic justification for modernising the criminal law hinged on the law's capacity to avoid:

> A position where all businesses pay bribes in the course of competing for contracts, and in particular compete on the basis of who can pay the highest bribe. If all businesses, including overseas competitors, were to offer the highest bribes they can, the cycle of corruption would be perpetuated … The ideal position is for markets to operate efficiently and for UK businesses to compete without making additional payments.[34]

Increasingly commonly, it is the function of more formal (self-) regulatory strategies to play a role in securing compliance with sufficiently high standards on an adequately wide scale, in pursuit of ideal market conditions for exchange.[35] A sophisticated range of expert-led interventionist strategies now exists to further such goals in a range of contexts.[36]

In purporting to reject such a strategy for bribery and corruption, very revealing in policy terms was the Secretary of State for Justice's claim that the offences under the 2010 Act are aimed at, 'making life difficult for the mavericks responsible for corruption, not unduly burdening the vast majority of decent, law-abiding firms'.[37] There is, of course, an important question begged here about what kind or degree of legal burdens will be 'undue'; but of equal significance is the fact that, if the 2010 Act is principally aimed at 'mavericks', then this puts the failure to prevent bribery offence in section 7 in tension with that aim. To begin with, the

[33] Ministry of Justice, 'Guidance about Commercial Organisations'. On the importance of regulation as a means of preventing market failure, see S. Weatherill (ed.), 'The Challenge of Better Regulation', *Better Regulation* (Oxford: Hart, 2007), pp. 1–18.

[34] Ministry of Justice, 'Guidance about Commercial Organisations'.

[35] For example, such a strategy is pursued through the expert work of Trading Standards officials, the Competition Commission and the Financial Services Authority.

[36] See the Regulatory Enforcement and Sanctions Act 2008 and, for an example, the brief analysis of the role of Trading Standards authorities in Law Commission, 'Criminal Liability in Regulatory Contexts', paras 3.89–3.96. See also the discussion of export controls in the text at n. 69, below.

[37] Ministry of Justice, *The Bribery Act 2010: Guidance about Procedures which Relevant Commercial Organisations can put into Place to Prevent Persons Associated with Them from Bribing* (London: Ministry of Justice, 2011), p. 2.

section 7 offence is one of strict liability, apt to catch failures to prevent bribery by mavericks and non-mavericks alike. Moreover, the official guidance now available on the 'adequate procedures' defence (presumably, aimed principally at the non-mavericks) contains just the kind of detail that one would expect in a regulator's handbook or code. So, in illustrating the 'six principles'[38] that should inform anti-bribery procedures, the overwhelming impression given is of a need for 'hands on' preventative (regulatory) impact, even though the language itself is permissive in character. For example, in a case study to demonstrate the need for adequate communication and training (Principle 5), the Guidance suggests that when dealing with a commercial agent (K) in a foreign country where there is a high risk of bribery, a firm (J) 'could consider':

> Making employees of J engaged in bidding for business fully aware of J's anti-bribery statement [and] code of conduct ... Including suitable contractual terms on bribery prevention measures in the agreement between J and K ... Supplementing the information, where appropriate, with specially prepared training to J's staff involved with the foreign country.[39]

For the government itself to be suggesting prophylactic measures at this level of detail, while at the same maintaining that firms are perfectly free to avoid taking any notice whatsoever of the measures, creates a tension between an officially endorsed criminal offence-led strategy and a 'shadow' regulatory strategy. Mavericks will largely ignore 'bureaucratic red tape' of this kind, and are likely to be deterred only by a real prospect of criminal prosecution and punishment: at the heart of a criminal offence-led strategy. By contrast, only the conscientious will take the 'red tape' seriously, undermining the claim that the guidance is not principally (or at all) aimed at, 'unduly burdening the vast majority of decent, law-abiding firms'.[40]

What is more, the SFO, although hitherto thwarted in its attempts to strike legally binding plea bargains,[41] is already behaving in an important sense

[38] 'Proportionate procedures', 'top-level commitment', 'risk assessment', 'due diligence', 'communication', 'monitoring and review'.

[39] Ministry of Justice, *The Bribery Act 2010: Guidance*, p. 49.

[40] See n. 39, above.

[41] See *R.* v. *Innospec Ltd* [2010] EW Misc 7, 26 March 2010, available at: www.judiciary.gov.uk/media/judgments/2010/r-v-bae-systems-plc (sentencing remarks of Thomas LJ). However, see now the plans of the Ministry of Justice and Attorney General for deferred prosecution agreements to tackle economic crime, available at: www.attorneygeneral.gov.uk/NewsCentre/Pages/Newtoolto tackleeconomiccrime.aspx.

as if it were a regulatory authority. For example, in one case it rewarded self-reporting (confession) by an offender by showing itself willing to facilitate the improvement of compliance programmes agreed as a part of sentence:

> The company [Mabey & Johnson] having agreed that it would be subject to financial penalties to be assessed by the Court, will pay reparations and will submit its internal compliance programme to an SFO approved independent monitor.[42]

In legal policy terms, we appear to be in no-man's land, stuck with a purportedly criminal offence-led strategy whose specifics nonetheless draw heavily on practices common to a regulatory strategy. That position may be *made* to work (scholars can always tell you why something that may work perfectly well in practice does not work in theory), but it is an opportunity missed to develop a context-sensitive and coherent regulatory strategy to prevent bribery and corruption.

That brings me to the second question bearing on the case for a regulatory strategy to deal with bribery. As I indicated earlier, the risk of wrongdoing in many areas of corporate and commercial activity is now confronted through a mixture of traditional criminal offences (such as theft and fraud), more specialised criminal offences, and sometimes also civil penalties: in essence, a regulatory strategy. The question is whether activities liable to carry a risk of bribery and corruption are so different in nature or context that they are not appropriately subjected to the same treatment. I argue that they are not so different. To begin with, it is already the case that prosecutors and regulatory authorities have been adopting a make-do-and-mend approach towards the absence of a regulatory strategy to deal with instances of bribery where the costs of, and risk of failure in, a criminal prosecution for bribery itself have been too high. Prosecutors and regulators have used specialised regulatory offences, or civil penalties, concerned with risky accounting malpractice to deal with instances of corruption where use of the pre-2010 Act law would have been impossible or inappropriate:

(1) In January 2009, the Financial Services Authority (FSA) fined the insurer AON £5.25 million for failing to take reasonable care to establish and maintain effective systems and controls to counter

[42] Available at: www.sfo.gov.uk/press-room/latest-press-releases/press-releases-2009/mabey – johnson-ltd-sentencing-.aspx.

the risks of bribery and corruption associated with making payments to overseas firms and individuals. AON had made what were described as 'suspicious' payments of US$7 million to overseas firms and individuals who were assisting AON to win business. AON cooperated with the FSA and agreed the settlement. The case followed proactive steps taken by the FSA in 2007, in which it sent out an industry-wide letter to commercial insurance intermediaries reminding them of their regulatory obligations in relation to the risks of bribery and corruption.[43]

(2) In 2010, British Aerospace Defence Systems (BAE Systems) was convicted under section 221(5) of the Companies Act 1985, in respect of failures to keep proper accounting records to show and explain certain payments that it had made. These payments, to a covert adviser, related to a contract to supply a radar defence system in Tanzania at Dar-es-Salaam airport. To cover the activities of its covert advisers on confidential matters, the company set up a BVI-based company, Red Diamond Trading Company. Red Diamond Trading made a secret agreement with a covert adviser to pay, to a Panamanian company controlled by the adviser, up to just over 30 per cent of the contract price, although publicly the adviser was set to receive only 1 per cent of the contract price. No auditor inspecting BAE Systems' accounts would have discovered these arrangements. The agent was paid over US$12 million. The company was fined £500,000, but also agreed to make a payment of £29.5 million to Tanzania in the form of ex gratia compensation.[44]

Whether or not these individual cases could have been successfully prosecuted as bribery cases, it is certainly one of the major aims of the 2010 Act, and in particular of the section 7 offence of failing to prevent bribery, to target egregious cases of this type. Convictions under section 7 would enable the nature and amount of harm actually done to be better reflected through both criminal conviction and sentence; but this is not my present concern. More significant, in the present context, is that the alternatives to prosecution employed in these cases stemmed from legislation that was not primarily intended to deal with bribery and corruption. Quite simply, there is no set of specialised offences or civil

[43] See www.fsa.gov.uk/pages/Library/Communication/PR/2009/004.shtml.

[44] For the relevant links, see www.sfo.gov.uk/press-room/latest-press-releases/press-releases-2010/bae-fined-in-tanzania-defence-contract-case.aspx.

penalties – putting aside the general offences of assistance and encouragement[45] – dealing with conduct posing an unacceptable risk of bribery.[46]

I have already alluded to the contrast, in this respect, with corporate manslaughter.[47] Shoring up this offence there is a long-standing regime of specialised criminal offences relating to health and safety, whose prosecution is in the hands of an expert regulatory authority (the Health and Safety Executive) that also issues guidance on, among other things, good practice in particular industries.[48] Moving beyond that example, set against the background of the serious offences created by the Fraud Act 2006, there are a very large number of specialised regulatory criminal laws and civil penalties to deal with fraud, dishonesty, misrepresentation and wrongful failure to provide information in a wide variety of industries.[49] More broadly, in relation to the provision of financial services, the FSA exists as a specialised body to provide regulatory oversight of the financial sector in the interest of the consumer.[50] The FSA has the power to impose civil penalties on those who have engaged in misconduct, and this power can be used in pursuit of one of its four statutory objectives: 'fighting financial crime'.[51] A very significant proportion of such specialised regulatory offences and civil penalties deal with unacceptably risky conduct, rather than with harm done. The primary concern (admittedly also true, albeit more controversially, of the Fraud Act 2006), is the giving of false or misleading information, the concealment of important information, the maintenance of poor accounting practices and similar conduct of the 'ticking time bomb' variety: the conduct has not as yet caused harm, but creates an unacceptable risk that such harm may be done.

Closer to the present theme (but still in the shadow of the Fraud Act 2006), there is now an expert authority, the Independent Parliamentary Standards Authority, charged with devising a code of conduct to

[45] See Serious Crime Act 2007, Part 2.

[46] In some contexts, potentially corrupt conduct may be dealt with by specialised fraud offences: see, e.g., the offences in the Insolvency Act 1986, ss. 206–210.

[47] See text following n. 29, above.

[48] See www.hse.gov.uk/business/index.htm.

[49] See Law Commission, 'Criminal Liability in Regulatory Contexts', paras 3.123–3.128, 4.62–4.81. See also the enormous number of specialised finance-related offences set out in J. Richardson (ed.), *Archbold: Criminal Pleading, Evidence and Practice 2010* (London: Sweet & Maxwell, 2009), ch. 30 ('Commerce, financial markets and insolvency').

[50] See also Monteith, Chapter 9, this volume.

[51] The FSA was set up under the Financial Services and Markets Act 2000, to pursue the 'regulatory objectives' of 'market confidence', 'financial stability', 'the protection of consumers' and 'the reduction of financial crime' (s. 2).

eliminate what has hitherto been the participation of MPs in borderline corrupt practices in making expense claims.[52] The Authority can investigate possible breaches of the code, which is backed up with a specialised regulatory offence of making a claim, knowing it is supported by false or misleading information.[53] What kind of regulatory offences or civil penalties would be appropriate if the 2010 Act were to be embedded, at least in some sectors of commerce, in a more regulatory strategy?

It is noticeable that the US Federal anti-bribery statute, the Foreign Corrupt Practices Act 1977, contains a linked set of criminal and civil provisions.[54] First, there is the main bribery offence (of a kind now found in section 6 of the 2010 Act). Secondly, there are accounting provisions – aimed at issuers of securities – that require the maintenance of accurate corporate books and records and internal company controls to prevent misuse of corporate funds, especially for the purpose of bribery. Admittedly, there is no exact equivalent of the section 7 offence (failure to prevent bribery) in the 1977 Act. However, very broadly speaking, under US law companies are held strictly liable for the corrupt actions of their employees (if not their agents).[55] That diminishes, albeit without eliminating, the significance of the extra reach provided by the section 7 offence. Additionally, it is important to note that the prosecuting authority, the Department of Justice, has at its disposal civil penalties that can be imposed when the offender has acted 'corruptly' (additional proof of 'wilfulness' is required for criminal conviction).[56] This is something with no equivalent in the 2010 Act, given the avowedly criminal offence-led

[52] The Independent Parliamentary Standards Authority was set up under the Parliamentary Standards Act 2009.

[53] Parliamentary Standards Act 2009, s. 10. Perhaps predictably, the regulatory offence covers ground already covered by the Fraud Act 2006 (or by an attempt to commit an offence under that Act), but with a maximum sentence of only one year's imprisonment, as compared with ten years under the Fraud Act 2006. Further, the regulatory offence is narrower in scope, requiring (unlike the Fraud Act 2006) knowledge of the false or misleading nature of the information supporting the claim. I know of no other regulated group so favoured by the narrowness of the fault requirement in the only regulatory offence applicable to it.

[54] For an appreciative evaluation of the FCPA 1977, see now N. Cropp, 'The Bribery Act 2010: A Comparison with the Foreign Corrupt Practices Act: Nuance v. Nous', *Criminal Law Review*, 2 (2011), 122–40.

[55] See, e.g., the general discussion in H. Lowell Brown, 'Vicarious Criminal Liability of Corporations for the Acts of their Employees and Agents', *Loyola Law Review*, 41 (1995), 279–327; see also the discussion in Cropp, 'The Bribery Act 2010'.

[56] See the discussion by Cropp, 'The Bribery Act 2010', p. 128.

nature of its strategy.[57] Even with such a strategy solely in mind, though, some consideration might have been given to turning the civil offence created by the FSA – failing to take reasonable care to establish and maintain effective systems and controls to counter the risks of bribery and corruption[58] – into a more general regulatory criminal offence under the 2010 Act.[59] Building on that possibility, it would have been possible to introduce such an offence, but make its application limited to particular kinds of transaction through the use of secondary legislation. Examples are transactions governed by the Export Control Act 2002 ('the 2002 Act'), such as defence contracts, consideration of which helps us to contrast the criminal offence-led strategy of the 2010 Act with the regulatory approach of the 2002 Act.[60]

A regulatory strategy to deter bribery: the case of the arms industry

The US Department of Commerce has suggested that something like 50 per cent of all bribery allegations in the late 1990s were in the defence sector, in spite of the fact that this sector accounts for only 1 per cent of world trade.[61] In 2006, Britain was ranked second in the world in terms of its expenditure on military equipment (US$61,925 million), behind only the United States (US$546,018 million). BAE Systems – the fourth largest defence manufacturer in the world in 2005 – is dependent for 79 per cent of its income on defence contracts. About 60 per cent of the global arms trade is accounted for by developing countries, where the risk

57 Under the 1977 Act, settlements with offenders almost always include an agreement whereby an independent monitor is retained by the offending firm for a number of years. In the interests of compliance, the monitor has the power to obtain documents, and to recommend reform of the firm's practices, and hence its culture. Such agreements are virtually unheard of in the United Kingdom, although the SFO's settlement with Mabey & Johnson (referred to at n. 42, above) is a version of this.

58 See text at n. 43, above.

59 The Joint Committee on the draft Bribery Bill opposed the introduction of regulatory civil penalties, seemingly on the assumption that they would be taking the place of, rather than (as suggested here) supplementing criminal legislation, available at: www.publications.parliament.uk/pa/jt200809/jtselect/jtbribe/115/11508.htm#a16, paras 88–90.

60 See further, Z. Yihdego and A. Savage, 'The Arms Export Regime: Progress and Challenges', *Public Law*, Autumn (2008), 546–65.

61 US Department of Commerce Trade Promotion Coordinating Committee Report (March 2010), cited by the Committee on Arms Export Controls, 'Scrutiny of Arms Export Controls (2010): UK Strategic Export Controls Annual Report 2008, Quarterly Reports for 2009, Licensing Policy and Review of Export Control Legislation' (2010 HC 202), para. 108.

of bribery and corruption is also much higher than in the developed world.[62] It is obvious that very considerable risks are present for both the firms in question and the state when firms export military hardware and equipment. For example, such goods may end up being used against civilians, or against combatants from the exporting state itself or from its allies.[63] Such risks also exist in relation to the export of material of use in manufacturing weapons of mass destruction or devices commonly associated with torture; and the risks extend to the provision of certain kinds of service rather than goods, such as 'know-how' or technical assistance in relation to the use of the items just mentioned. For these reasons, certain kinds of technology transfer or expert assistance, along with the export (and import) of items of the relevant type – and of certain 'dual use' items that may have legitimate or illegitimate uses – are governed by the 2002 Act. There is no space to say much about it here, but the 2002 Act is an unusual piece of legislation from a criminal lawyer's point of view.

The 2002 Act is almost entirely 'permissive', granting powers to the Secretary of State to introduce, through secondary legislation, regulatory controls over exports and the provision of services of certain kinds (such as those just mentioned), and to create criminal offences in the same manner for breaches of the controls.[64] Consider, by way of example, the criminal law-creating activities of the Department for Business, Innovation and Skills (BIS) in 2008, under the 2002 Act. In 2008, BIS created no less than thirty-one criminal offences by Order under the 2002 Act. These offences are targeted at conduct that, more or less directly or indirectly, unjustifiably increases the risk that wrongful harm may be done. In this context, an example of conduct prohibited because it more directly increases the risk of wrongful harm being done is the prohibition involved in providing Burma with financial assistance related to military activities.[65] Given the directness of the increase in risk involved in such

[62] Stockholm International Peace Research Institute Yearbook, *Armaments, Disarmament and International Security* (Oxford University Press, 2001), p. 326.

[63] For example, the Dassault-Breguet Super Étendard carrier-borne strike fighter, although designated for the French navy, was first used in combat by Argentina against British forces. Fourteen such aircraft had been purchased by Argentina in 1980, *after* an arms embargo imposed by the United States in the light of the political situation in Argentina, which meant that spare parts for Argentina's US-made planes became unavailable. Twenty members of the crew of HMS *Sheffield* were killed in an Argentine attack employing one of these fighters on 4 May 1982.

[64] On the regulatory nature of such offences, see text following n. 47, above.

[65] Export Control (Burma) Order No. 2008/1098.

conduct, the conduct will not be licensed by the UK Government in any circumstances. Other offences are targeted at more indirect ways in which risks of wrongful harm being done may unjustifiably be increased (a common example is failing to ensure one's vehicle has a valid MOT certificate).[66] In this context, prohibitions on indirectly risk-enhancing conduct can be found in rules and regulations governing the conditions on which one is entitled to engage in primary activities governed by Orders issued under the 2002 Act. An example is making a false statement or furnishing a document or information which to an applicant's knowledge is false in a material particular (*ex hypothesi*, in order to obtain an export licence).[67] Another example is failing to comply with any of the requirements or conditions to which a licence is subject.[68] Under the main piece of secondary legislation in this field, the Export Control Order 2008, we can see prohibitions on directly risk-enhancing conduct (paragraph (4), below) and more indirectly risk-enhancing conduct (paragraphs (6) and (7), below) placed together, as part of a coherent hierarchy of offences:

> 35 … (4) Subject to paragraph (8), a person knowingly concerned in an activity prohibited or restricted by Article 3(1), 4(1), 4(2), 4(3) or 21(1) of the dual-use Regulation with intent to evade the relevant prohibition or restriction commits an offence and may be arrested.
>
> (5) A person guilty of an offence under paragraph (4) shall be liable: …
>
> (b) on conviction on indictment to a fine or to imprisonment for a term not exceeding ten years, or to both.
>
> (6) A person who fails to comply with Article 9(1) (provision of relevant information for licence applications) of the dual-use Regulation commits an offence and shall be liable on summary conviction to a fine not exceeding level 3 on the standard scale and any licence which may have been granted in connection with the application shall be void as from the time it was granted.
>
> (7) A person who fails to comply with Article 16 (record-keeping), 21(5) (records of exportation and transfer of listed items within the customs territory) or 21(7) (requirement in relation to commercial documents for exportation and transfer of listed items within the customs territory) of the dual-use Regulation commits an offence and shall be liable on summary conviction to a fine not exceeding level 3 on the standard scale.

[66] This example can explained more casuistically. It is a kind of 'secondary' prohibition, a prohibition on risk-enhancing conduct whose unjustifiability needs to be understood in relation to a 'primary' prohibition: in this case, the offence (and the offences related to it) of dangerous driving.

[67] Export Control Order No. 2008/3231.

[68] Export Control Order No. 2008/3231.

Consistent with the regulatory nature of the export control strategy, there is a specialist agency, the Export Control Organisation,[69] responsible for taking prophylactic steps to avoid breaches of the legislation, through (for example) compliance visits to companies registered for export licences. Where breaches of export control legislation are suspected, they may be investigated by a specialist arm of Her Majesty's Revenue and Customs (HMRC), on whose behalf a prosecution may be taken by the Crown Prosecution Service (CPS).[70] Typically, there are also between 50 and 100 instances annually in which HMRC seizes goods subject to export control that appear to be intended for export without a valid licence.[71] The Committee on Arms Export Controls has also advocated the introduction of civil penalties to buttress the regulatory criminal law.[72]

This background is of relevance here because there is a close association between defence (and associated) contracting, and the payment of bribes. Bribes may be paid to obtain or keep contracts. However, bribes may also be paid to secure evasion of rules meant to govern how, when, on what terms and so on, such contracts are entered into. A simple example of the latter would be a secret payment to an official to issue a licence to a firm to export military hardware, even though the exporter has not met the conditions for the issue of such a licence. A more complex example would be a secret payment by a UK firm to an end-user of military equipment authorised by the UK Government (say, a stable democracy), whereby the authorised end-user agrees to allow an unauthorised end-user (say, a state illegally occupying another state's territory) to purchase that equipment from the authorised end-user if they wish to do so. The close connection between bribery and defence contracting[73] has led respected organisations such as Transparency International, as well as the UK's Committee on Arms Export Controls,[74] to

[69] See www.bis.gov.uk/exportcontrol.

[70] See www.berr.gov.uk/policies/export-control-organisation/eco-press-prosecutions.

[71] 'Security of Arms Export Control: First Joint Report (2007/8) of the Committee on Arms Export Controls' (2008 HC 254), para. 49.

[72] Committee on Arms Export Controls, 'Scrutiny of Arms Export Controls', (2009 HC 178), paras 81–85.

[73] Recently noted by the Committee on Arms Export Controls, 'Scrutiny of Arms Export Controls (2011): UK Strategic Export Controls Annual Report 2009, Quarterly Reports for 2010, licensing policy and review of export control legislation – Committee on Arms Export Controls' (2011 HC 686), paras 108–116.

[74] See n. 25, above, at para. 115; C. Courtney, 'Corruption in the Official Arms Trade', in Transparency International (UK), Policy Research Paper No. 001 (London: Transparency International, 2002).

recommend the introduction of (in effect) a more regulatory strategy to combat bribery in this field. The UK Committee recommended extending the remit of the Export Control Organisation to include prophylactic measures to prevent bribery and corruption in its processing of applications for export licences:[75]

> the creation of a requirement for those seeking export licences to produce a declaration that the export contract has not been obtained through bribery or corruption; the revocation of licences where an exporter had been convicted of corruption; and the amendment of the National Export Licensing Criteria to make conviction for corruption by an exporter grounds for refusing an export licence.[76]

For its part, in 2002, Transparency International made recommendations along similar lines:

> Recommendation 2: export licensing should be strictly conditional on presentation by exporting countries of rigorous contract-specific no-bribery warranties. These should be reinforced by evidence that companies have in place sufficient internal compliance systems capable of detecting corruption-risk and preventing the payment of bribes. Exclusion from export licences should be used as a sanction against companies or brokers found to have paid bribes …
>
> Recommendation 7: Prior scrutiny of individual licences should be undertaken by a Parliamentary Committee of both Houses to ensure that sales conform with the UK Consolidated Criteria. This Committee should consider the potential for corruption in the procurement process in the importing country in its advice to the government on whether to award the licence.[77]

The 'reinforcing' measures in Recommendation 2 look very much like the substance of the guidance now issued to firms on what should be taken into account in determining whether 'adequate procedures' were in place to avoid bribery being committed on a firm's behalf.[78] There is, though, a strong argument that such prophylactic regulatory measures should be mandatory in this sector of the economy, not merely advisory in all sectors (as they now are). In other words, it should not be left to the general prohibitions in the 2010 Act to deter and prevent bribery by incentivising only (potential) perpetrators. The strong association between defence contracting and the risk of corruption should

[75] See n. 25 above, at para. 117. [76] HC (2007/8) 254, paras. 112–117.
[77] Courtney, 'Corruption in the Official Arms Trade', p. 6. [78] See n. 38, above.

additionally be regarded as a reason to give officials and experts working in export control powers to develop a proactive regulatory strategy, to reduce the risk of perpetration by focusing on 'at risk' companies and risky practices.

Regrettably, that is not to be government policy in the near future. The official response of the Business, Innovation and Skills Minister, Mr Mark Prisk MP, to the proposal that the risk of corruption should be added specifically as a reason to refuse an export licence was to say:

> I don't think it's something we would be minded to support, and I doubt whether it would be successful. I think on the whole we've got to distinguish here between dealing with the risks of an unacceptable use or an illegal use, and how a contract is secured, and they're actually two distinct things, so I think we shouldn't confuse in law those two different elements.[79]

What all this shows is that the UK's commitment to an anti-corruption policy is not fully worked through, and is in effect half-hearted. The UK Government has adopted a criminal offence-led strategy without explaining why a (prophylactic) regulatory strategy, common to UK policy both in combating fraud and – to use my special focus – in reducing irresponsible exporting, is not also a necessary element in tackling bribery, if that is to be done in a fully committed way. Naturally, many will share the government's fears about the burdensomeness of increased regulatory impact in general. Acknowledging that, the government has nonetheless failed to explain why a regulatory strategy to address bribery should not be implemented sectorally. There is an extremely strong case for making the guidance on adequate anti-corruption procedures mandatory in some industries, even if it is only advisory for other industries, if the United Kingdom, as a world leader in arms export, is to be taken seriously as a force in anti-corruption policy across the world.

Conclusion

The criminal offence-led strategy for bribery has brought some improvements in the law, but government commitment to anti-corruption policy remains half-hearted. The strategy is unlikely to work as effectively as it might have done had it been supplemented by a regulatory strategy

[79] Cited by the Committee on Arms Export Controls, n. 73, above, para. 114.

aimed at reducing the risks of bribery being committed. That regulatory strategy could, in the first instance, have been targeted at sectors of industry, and practices such as commission payments, prone to bribery and corruption. Ironically, the scheme recently introduced under the Parliamentary Standards Act 2009 to deter misuse, and govern the use, of expense claims by MPs provides a rudimentary model.

PART III

Ill-gotten gains: the challenge of prosecution, enforcement and asset recovery

8

Bribery and the changing pattern of criminal prosecution

PETER ALLDRIDGE

Issues

In order for prosecutions to succeed under the Bribery Act 2010, something needs to be done about the prosecution process. This chapter will deal with the introduction, contemporaneously with the Bribery Act 2010, of means of proceeding against defendants that differ radically from the 'traditional' prosecution conviction/sentence model of criminal justice. It will concentrate upon self-reporting, negotiation of pleas, deferred prosecution agreements and multilateral transnational agreements. It will consider the recent (almost) challenges to the BAE Systems settlement, the cases of *Innospec* and *Dougall*, and more generally the policy of the Serious Fraud Office (SFO) and its successor organisations in this area, and the proposal for the use of deferred prosecution agreements to deal with some types of corporate criminality.

The relationship between, on the one hand, bribery and, on the other, agreements not to prosecute, or agreements not to press for the imposition of the fullest rigour of the law, places a range of problems in particularly vivid relief. There is no clearer case of bribery, whatever the age of the laws and whatever the jurisdiction, than that of paying someone not to prosecute the briber for an offence he or she is alleged to have committed. If a person is able to pay to avoid criminal liability then he or she is not really subject to the criminal law at all. Generality is one of the characteristics of criminal law. One of the clearest indicators of a corrupt society is that it is possible to flex economic muscle so as to avoid the consequences of breaking the law. The fundamental principle is clear and does not admit of shades of grey. Allowing people to pay to avoid criminal proceedings very clearly undermines the rule of law, which requires impartial application of clear rules to everybody. A rule whose effects can be avoided by bribing the appropriate person is a rule whose generality is compromised.

And yet we live in the real world. The costs and cumbersome nature of highly adversarial jury trial make it very difficult to operate it as an everyday mode of adjudication for financial crime.[1] It is better that some adverse consequence be visited upon someone who bribes than none. All systems of criminal justice have arrangements for dealing with cases in which some kind of agreement has been made between the prosecutor and the accused. Plea bargaining has long been a feature of criminal justice.[2] These agreements may be informal or even covert, or may be public and endorsed by the courts. Typically, the less they are approved formally, the more they will happen informally or covertly. One such arrangement that has always been publicised by courts in England and Wales, to the point where there is no need for it to be mentioned in individual cases, is the sentencing discount following a guilty plea.[3] There may be specific arrangements to deal with particular offences, particular locations for offences or particular defendants.

In general, discussion of agreements to avoid full criminal trials puts in question the roles both of the prosecutor and the judge in arriving at and in sanctioning such arrangements. More specifically in this context, it raises questions as to what extent and in what ways bribery is different, in particular, if performed by a corporation, out of the country or in circumstances such that the prosecution comes from two or more jurisdictions. Considerable fluidity has been brought to both roles by the perceived exigencies of the prosecution of frauds and other economic crimes.

The traditional adversarial model holds that the role of the prosecutor begins when the role of the investigating police officer is, if not over, then at least advanced to such a point that charges are preferred. The traditional view of the judge in the adversarial system is that she or he assumes jurisdiction over the case when the trial begins, and then

[1] A. W. Alschuler,'Mediation with a Mugger: The Shortage of Adjudicative Services and the Need for a Two-Tier System in Civil Cases', *Harvard Law Review*, 99 (1986),1808–59.

[2] *Pace* A. W. Alschuler, 'Plea Bargaining and its History', *Columbia Law Review*, 79 (1979), 1–43; J. Baldwin and M. McConville, *Negotiated Justice* (Oxford University Press, 1977); C. Brants, 'Consensual Criminal Procedures: Plea and Confession Bargaining and Abbreviated Procedures to Simplify Criminal Procedure', *Electronic Journal of Comparative Law*, 11(1) (2007), available at: www.ejcl.org/111/article111-6.pdf; M. Boll, *Plea Bargaining and Agreement in the Criminal Process* (Hamburg: Diplomica Verlag, 2009).

[3] This remains a matter of judicial discretion, not law, but an offender who pleads guilty may expect some credit in the form of a discount in sentence. Section 144 of the Criminal Justice Act 2003 does not confer a statutory right to a discount, which remains a matter for the court's discretion.

operates only in a reactive role, responding to the respective petitions of prosecution and defence. The fact that this model was found to be inadequate in the case of serious economic crimes led to the establishment of the SFO.[4] The roles of investigation and prosecution are in many respects combined. The introduction of more active case management by the judge, at an earlier stage in the proceedings,[5] moves the judge's entry into the proceedings earlier in time and makes the role a more active one.[6] The overlap between the periods during which the investigator, the prosecutor and the judge represent the state in its continuing interaction with the accused is an important focus. This chapter will consider the role of prosecutors first, but it must always be borne in mind that the freedom of action of prosecutors is constrained by what judges will accept.

In addition to the 'usual' problems in the prosecution of financial crime, there are two major overlapping problems to be resolved in bribery prosecutions. The first is that the alleged offenders will frequently be corporations. There is a view that offenders are offenders are offenders, that serious crime is undifferentiated by the nature of the crime involved, that any attempt to represent any form of corporate offending as appropriate to treatment in another way is to dilute the message of the criminal law, and is unfair to burglars and others who are subject to its rigours. On that account, the most important part of any response to white-collar crime ought to be to minimise the differences between the way in which it, on the one hand, and 'regular crime', on the other, are treated. Ever since Sutherland drew attention to it, much has been made of the differential treatment of 'white-collar' from 'regular' criminality.[7] The concern has been that in important respects, at every juncture in the system of criminal justice, white-collar crimes are treated differently (and usually less seriously) than other 'regular' crimes. This is an entirely legitimate concern. Furthermore, if there is a perceived need to bring corporate offending within the criminal law then it should be recognised that the range of sentencing options currently on offer by English law is disappointingly narrow. Financial penalties are the only realistic option.

4 Criminal Justice Act 1987, ss. 1 *et seq.*
5 Criminal Procedure Rules 2011 (SI 2011 No. 1709).
6 R. Julian, 'Judicial Perspectives in Serious Fraud Cases: The Present Status of and Problems Posed by Case Management Practices, Jury Selection Rules, Juror Expertise, Plea Bargaining and Choice of Mode of Trial', *Criminal Law Review*, October (2008), 764–82.
7 E. Sutherland, *White Collar Crime* (New York: Dryden Press, 1949).

The 'identification doctrine' in English law makes the conviction of a company dependent upon establishing that there was a single person, high up within the organisation, who could him- or herself be convicted of the crime.[8] It has followed that the history of the view that crime is crime is crime when applied to corporate prosecutions through the prism of the identification doctrine has been that prosecutions against companies face significant and frequently insuperable obstacles.

The second major and increasing problem is that prosecutions operate on an international basis. Authorities in more than one jurisdiction legitimately aspire to prosecute. The reconciliation of these countervailing claims is partly a matter of the power of the respective parties, but there are also questions about the charges to be brought in each jurisdiction, the evidence available in each and so on. This is a particularly sensitive matter when the United States is involved. The United States has pursued far more vigorously than other countries a policy involving the imposition of extraterritorial liability. It is also an enormously powerful country, and in any conflict of interest between a US prosecutor and one from the United Kingdom, must be seen against that background.

The major solution which has been offered to these obstacles is to make some sort of deal with the defendant. There are various possibilities on offer. They include a range of types of plea bargain, whether or not achieved by means of a system of self-report, whether or not including civil recovery orders, whether or not involving international agreements to which more than one jurisdiction's prosecutor is party, and – the latest wrinkle – deferred plea agreements. Each of these solutions will involve some variation of the traditional roles both of judge and prosecutor, which will now be considered.

Role of the prosecutor

The SFO is the lead agency in England and Wales for investigating (jointly with the police in some cases) and prosecuting cases of overseas corruption. The Crown Prosecution Service (CPS) also prosecutes bribery offences investigated by the police, committed either overseas or in England and Wales.

The establishment of the SFO crossed the theoretical disjunction, historically more honoured in the breach than in the observance,

[8] *Tesco Supermarkets Ltd* v. *Nattrass* [1972] AC 153 (HL). A recent example of the application of this doctrine is *R.* v. *St Regis Paper Co. Ltd* [2011] EWCA Crim 2527.

between investigation and prosecution.[9] First, a single body has been introduced that is charged both with investigation and prosecution,[10] a body that has the power to question after charge.[11] Secondly, the introduction of pre-trial case management by the trial judge has blurred the formerly separate roles of judge and prosecutor. The developments to be considered are driven by the SFO and especially, during his tenure as director, by Richard Alderman.

In a case of bribery the prosecutor may need to secure consent to prosecute. In England and Wales, proceedings for offences under the Bribery Act 2010 require the personal consent of the relevant director (Director of Public Prosecutions or the Director of the Serious Fraud Office).[12] This is a significant and uncontroversial change from the previous arrangements, under which the consent of the Attorney General was required.[13] The relevant director must give personal consent to a prosecution.[14] Prosecutors should follow any relevant internal procedures when submitting cases for consideration.

Beyond that, what should they do? Thomas LJ set out the duties of a prosecutor in *Innospec*.[15] He or she:

(a) Must, in accordance with the relevant Attorney General's guidelines, including those applicable in US–UK cases,[16] exercise his discretion as to the charges to be preferred.
(b) May, subject to the provisions of the consolidated Criminal Practice Directions,[17] indicate his acceptance of a plea.
(c) May also discuss a basis of plea and agree it, subject to the principles set in [in the relevant guidance].[18] These paragraphs … make it clear that the court is not bound by any agreement and must

9 See n. 47, below.
10 This was precisely a reversal of the quasi-constitutional shift involved in the establishment by the Prosecution of Offences Act 1985 of the CPS.
11 *R.* v. *Director of Serious Fraud Office, ex parte Smith* [1993] AC 1.
12 Bribery Act 2010, s. 10.
13 Prevention of Corruption Act 1906, s. 2(1). The role of the Attorney General in bribery prosecutions was a continual source of friction between the UK Government and the OECD, vastly exacerbated by the *Al-Yamamah* case.
14 Bribery Act 2010, s. 10.
15 *R.* v. *Innospec Ltd* [2010] EW Misc 7, [2010] CLR 665, para. 25.
16 Below, pp. 000–000.
17 Code for Crown Prosecutors (CCP), available at: www.cps.gov.uk/publications/code_for_crown_prosecutors/decision.html, IV 45.5–45.9.
18 See at: www.justice.gov.uk/criminal/procrules_fin/contents/practice_direction/part4.htm#id6178240.

consider itself whether evidence is called to establish the basis on which it is to sentence.

(d) In cases involving serious fraud, may also enter a plea agreement in accordance with the [relevant] procedure.[19] This was originally part of the Practice Direction introduced in May 2009 after consultation and was published at the same time as the AG's guidance on plea discussions in cases of *serious or* complex fraud.[20] The provisions make it quite clear that the judge must be provided with full details so that she or he can understand the facts of the case and the history of the plea discussions. This is to enable a judge to make an assessment of whether the plea agreement is fair and in the interests of justice and to decide the appropriate sentence.

(e) Upon conviction, sentencing submissions should not include a specific sentence or agreed range, other than the ranges set out in the Sentencing Guidelines of authorities.

The first three paragraphs apply, in principle, to all offences. Paragraph (d) is crucial to what follows. Paragraph (e) raises general issues which have particular sensitivity in England and Wales, where the exercise of discretion by a judge is generally regarded as being one of the indicators of an independent judiciary. These issues come under stress in the particular context of transnational agreements.

A prosecutor considering a case of bribery, particularly of overseas bribery involving large sums, will not lack for advice. The applicable guidance consists of one or more of the following:

(1) the Code for Crown Prosecutors, and in particular;
(2) Guidance of the Attorney General on Plea Discussions;[21]
(3) Guidance upon Corporate Prosecutions;[22]
(4) Guidance on the approach of the SFO to overseas corruption offences;[23]

[19] Set out in CCP, IV 45.16–45.28.

[20] D. Watson, 'The Attorney General's Guidelines on Plea Bargaining in Serious Fraud: Obtaining Guilty Pleas Fairly?', *Journal of Criminal Law*, 74 (2010), 77–90.

[21] Available at: www.attorneygeneral.gov.uk/Publications/Documents/AG's%20Guidelines%20on%20Plea%20Discussions%20in%20Cases%20of%20Serious%20or%20Complex%20Fraud.pdf.

[22] Available at: www.sfo.gov.uk/media/65228/com1%20joint%20guidance%20on%20corporate%20prosecutions%20for%20publication%20v1.pdf.

[23] See Serious Fraud Office, *Approach of the SFO to Dealing with Overseas Corruption* (London: Serious Fraud Office, 2009).

(5) Guidance on Prosecutions under the Bribery Act;[24] and
(6) Guidance for Handling Criminal Cases with Concurrent Jurisdiction between the United Kingdom and the United States of America.[25]

The layers of guidance indicate strongly the overlapping sources of complexity in these decisions. An approach that states baldly that serious crime is serious crime and should be treated the same, irrespective of location, type, whether the perpetrator is or is not a corporation, and which is not sensitive to these nuances, is unlikely to be adequate. If it were, there would be no reason for special rules governing the matters in question. The chapter will consider the prosecutorial and judicial roles in bribery prosecutions generally, and then turn to the additional layers of complexity that can be added, and their implications.

The general CCP question: bribery and the 'two-stage test'

As with any other criminal offences, prosecutors must make their decisions in accordance with the Code for Crown Prosecutors. The test has two stages:[26] (i) the evidential stage, frequently described by reference to a probability of conviction in excess of 50 per cent; and (ii) the 'public interest' stage, involving a decision whether the public interest requires that a prosecution be brought. The evidential stage must be considered before the public interest stage. The enquiry then is as to what, beyond the general considerations applicable to all offences, might be especially appropriate to, or have special significance in, bribery.

The general approach to bribery prosecutions follows from the maximum sentence that has been allocated by Parliament.[27] Bribery is a

[24] Available at: www.sfo.gov.uk/media/167348/bribery%20act%20joint%20prosecution%20guidance.pdf.

[25] C. Warbrick and K. Brookson-Morris, 'Conflicts of Criminal Jurisdiction', *International and Comparative Law Quarterly*, 56 (2007), 659–66. See *R (On the Application of Ahsan)* v. *Director of Public Prosecutions, Ahsan* v. *Government of the United States of America and another, Tajik* v. *Government of the United States of America and another* [2008] EWHC 666 (Admin).

[26] This remains controversial: see, e.g., J. Rogers, 'Restructuring the Exercise of Prosecutorial Discretion in England', *Oxford Journal of Legal Studies*, 26 (2006), 775–803. Much recent discussion arose from the decision in *Purdy* that the DPP could issue guidance on the circumstances under which prosecutions would be brought. See, e.g., K. Greasley, 'R (Purdy) v. DPP and the Case for Wilful Blindness', *Oxford Journal of Legal Studies*, 30 (2010), 301–26; J. Finnis, 'Invoking the Principle of Legality against the Rule of Law', *New Zealand Law Review*, (2010), 601–16.

[27] Ten years; Bribery Act 2010, s. 11.

serious offence. There is an inherent public interest in bribery being prosecuted in order to give practical effect to Parliament's criminalisation of such behaviour.[28] The relevant Crown Prosecutors' Code guidance specific to bribery prosecutions states:

> A case which does not pass the evidential stage must not proceed, no matter how serious or sensitive it may be and no matter how powerful the public interest arguments.[29] A prosecution will then usually take place unless the prosecutor is sure that there are public interest factors militating against prosecution which outweigh those tending in favour.

Assessing the public interest is not simply a matter of adding up the number of factors on each side and seeing which side has the greater number. The absence of a factor does not necessarily mean that it should be taken as a factor tending in the opposite direction. Each case must be considered on its own facts and merits in accordance with the Code.

The Code sets out some public interest considerations common to the offences under sections 1, 2, 6 and 7. Factors arguing in favour of prosecution in bribery cases include the following: a conviction for bribery is likely to attract a significant sentence;[30] offences will often be premeditated and may include an element of corruption of the person bribed;[31] offences may be committed in order to facilitate more serious offending (Code 4.16i); and that those involved in bribery may be in positions of authority or trust and take advantage of that position.[32] Factors tending against prosecution include that the court is likely to impose only a nominal penalty;[33] that the harm can be described as minor and was the result of a single incident;[34] and that there has been a genuinely proactive approach involving self-reporting and any remedial action that has already been taken.[35]

In order to comply with the OECD Convention on Combating Bribery of Foreign Public Officials in International Business Transactions, the Bribery Act 2010 put in place a specific offence dealing with bribery of foreign public officials.[36] There are particular factors affecting the

[28] Code for Crown Prosecutors.
[29] This has been a problem elsewhere, where there are public interest arguments for a prosecution but weak evidence.
[30] Code 4.16a. On sentencing for bribery see *R.* v. *Dougall* [2011] 1 Cr App R (S) 37; *R.* v. *Messent* [2011] EWCA Crim 644.
[31] Code 4.16e and k. [32] Code 4.16n. [33] Code 4.17a [34] Code 4.17e
[35] Additional factor (a) in the Guidance on Corporate Prosecutions. And see below, p. 241.
[36] Bribery Act 2010, s. 6.

overseas public official (section 6) offence. As concerns the public interest test, it is clear that prevention of bribery of foreign public officials is a significant policy aspect of the Act. When considering the public interest stage, the factors tending in favour of and against prosecution referred to in respect of 'active bribery' (the section 1 offence) are likely to be relevant. A prosecution will usually take place unless the prosecutor is sure that there are public interest factors tending against prosecution which outweigh those tending in favour.

The Convention itself excludes one set of considerations from the decision whether or not to prosecute. It provides that:

> Investigation and prosecution of the bribery of a foreign public official … shall not be influenced by considerations of national economic interest, the potential effect upon relations with another State or the identity of the natural or legal persons involved.

In the *Corner House* case,[37] the House of Lords skirted consideration of Article 5, but ultimately did not have to decide upon its effect in English law. The case arose from the decision of the then Director of the SFO, Robert Wardle, to end the investigation which was being conducted into the Al-Yamamah arms deal. The House held that Wardle's decision was prompted by a threat to the security of the United Kingdom – that lives on the streets of Britain would be endangered as a consequence of the threatened withdrawal of cooperation in anti-terrorist intelligence by the Saudi government.[38] The then Attorney General (Lord Goldsmith QC) defended the decision to end the Al-Yamamah enquiry in a short Parliamentary statement:

> The Director of the Serious Fraud Office has decided to discontinue the investigation into the affairs of BAE Systems plc as far as they relate to the Al Yamamah defence contract. This decision has been taken following representations that have been made both to the Attorney General and the Director concerning the need to safeguard national and international security. It has been necessary to balance the need to maintain the rule of

[37] *R. (On the Application of Corner House Research and Others)* v. *Director of the Serious Fraud Office* [2008] UKHL 60, [2009] 1 AC 756. See J. R. Spencer, 'Fiat justicia, ruatque concordia cum Arabe?', *Cambridge Law Journal*, 67 (2008), 456–8; S. Williams, 'The BAE/Saudi Al-Yamamah Contracts: Implications in Law and Public Procurement', *International & Comparative Law Quarterly*, 57 (2008), 200–9.

[38] *R. (On the Application of Corner House Research)* v. *Director of the Serious Fraud Office* [2008] EWHC 1354 (Admin), at para. 28.

> law against the wider public interest. No weight has been given to commercial interests or to the national economic interest.[39]

The director based his contention that the ending of the enquiry was consistent with the Convention, in particular to Article 5, on a belief that it permitted him to take account of threats to human life as a public interest consideration. But he also gave evidence that he would have made the same decision even if he had believed, which he did not, that it was incompatible with Article 5 of the Convention. The House upheld the legality of his decision, but deprecated the situation in which he had been placed.

Public interest considerations which *are* applicable to the section 6 offence (the offence of bribing officials overseas) include the consideration that prevention of bribery of foreign public officials is a significant policy aspect of the Act. The United Kingdom had been severely criticised by the OECD for its failure successfully to prosecute in any overseas bribery cases prior to *Balfour Beatty*,[40] and still recognises that there is much to be done.

Following upon the considerations common to all bribery offences, a prosecution will usually take place unless the prosecutor is sure that there are public interest factors tending against prosecution which outweigh those tending in favour. Specific factors tending in favour of a prosecution in a section 6 case include that large or repeated payments are more likely to attract a significant sentence;[41] that facilitation payments[42] that are planned for or accepted as part of a standard way of conducting business may indicate the offence was premeditated;[43] that payments may indicate an element of active corruption of the official in the way the offence was committed.[44]

Factors tending against prosecution include the case where a commercial organisation has a clear and appropriate policy setting out procedures an individual should follow if facilitation payments are requested and these have not been correctly followed; that a single small payment was made likely to result in only a nominal penalty;[45] that the payment(s)

[39] *Hansard*, HL, Debates, cols 1711–12, 14 December 2006.

[40] D. Leigh and R. Evans, 'Balfour Beatty Agrees to pay £2.25m over Allegations of Bribery in Egypt', *The Guardian*, 7 October 2008.

[41] Code for Crown Prosecutors, para. 4.16a.

[42] 'Facilitation payments' are small payments to allow a small part of a large transaction to continue unhindered: to get the perishable goods out of the dock, to secure official approval of some sort and so on.

[43] Code 4.16e. [44] Code 4.16k. [45] Code 4.17a.

came to light as a result of a genuinely proactive approach involving self-reporting and remedial action (additional factor (a) in the Guidance on Corporate Prosecutions); that (in the case of facilitation payments) a commercial organisation has a clear and appropriate policy setting out procedures an individual should follow if facilitation payments are requested and these have been correctly followed; and that the payer was in a vulnerable position arising from the circumstances in which the payment was demanded.

The factors tending in favour of and against prosecution referred to above in respect of section 1 may be equally applicable to the section 7 offence. The additional factors in the Guidance on Corporate Prosecutions will also be particularly relevant in determining whether or not it is in the public interest to prosecute.

The role of the judge

There are two significant aspects to the role of the judge which bear upon the issues in point. First, there is the handling of the case prior to hearing; and, secondly, the participation or endorsement by the judge of plea agreements of some sort.

Case management

The classical model of the adversarial process[46] has two boundaries: the point of charge as that point at which the relationship between the state and the defendant moves from one of investigation to one of accusation; and the beginning of the trial marks the point at which the matter moves from accusation to adjudication.[47] Active case management has been introduced over recent years in England and Wales, and is most clearly embedded in Part 3 of the Criminal Procedure Rules 2011.[48] The idea is to reduce the time that trials will take by identifying in advance significant considerations, and eliminating irrelevant ones, and bringing the parties to agreement on any issues in respect of which that is able to be

46 J. L. Langbein, *The Origins of Adversary Criminal Trial* (Oxford University Press, 2003), M. Damaska, *The Faces of Justice and State Authority* (New Haven, CT: Yale University Press, 1986), J. Jackson, M. Langer and P. Tillers (eds), *Crime, Procedure and Evidence in a Comparative and International Context* (Oxford: Hart, 2008).

47 E. Luna and M. Wade, 'Prosecutorial Power: A Transnational Symposium: Prosecutors as Judges', *Washington & Lee Law Review*, 67 (2010), 1413–532.

48 Criminal Procedure Rules 2011 (SI 2011 No. 1709) (L. 15).

achieved. This chapter will not deal more fully with it, save to note that this sort of departure from the traditional model has in general been regarded, particularly in financial crime cases, as a success, and the further emphasis on it in the 2011 Rules should yield fruit.

The Criminal Procedure Rules 2011 set down the rules governing plea and case management hearing in the Crown Court.[49] They now specifically require the judge to be active and to exercise the powers conferred on him or her by giving any direction appropriate to the needs of that case as early as possible. A practical consideration is that, whereas the Rules allow another judge (other than the trial judge) to be appointed as case manager,[50] it is the view of professionals in the field that the management is best achieved by the same judge.

For present purposes, plea bargains are more important than case management. The idea that the judge holds a reactive, umpireal role, acting only in response to the parties is deeply ingrained in English criminal justice, and, more broadly, in the adversarial model of adjudication. Moreover the exercise of discretion by a judge in sentencing is generally regarded in England and Wales as being one of the indicators of an independent judiciary, and it is jealously guarded.[51] Judges in England and Wales object on this ground to the imposition by Parliament of mandatory sentences.[52] The reasons for the reluctance to adopt more enthusiastically a system like that which operates in the United States are well known. Briefly, if plea bargaining is permitted, it is argued, the criminal might get undeserved leniency, might be deprived of procedural rights and the innocent might be convicted.

If bribery cases (and other cases of financial crime) are to be dealt with by making agreements with suspected criminals, then either the judge must make offers as a part of the process of case management or of other pre-trial negotiations, or the prosecutors must be able to make offers that judges will recognise. The history of the treatment of these sort of discussions involves, however, a considerable degree of denial. There does appear to have been something recognisable as a plea bargain even

[49] Criminal Procedure Rules 2011 (SI 2011 No. 1709), paras 3.1 *et seq*.

[50] Criminal Procedure Rules 2011 (SI 2011 No. 1709), para 3.4(2).

[51] But see, e.g., A. Ashworth, *Sentencing and Criminal Justice*, 5th edn (Cambridge University Press, 2010), pp. 51–4.

[52] T. Jones and T. Newburn, 'Three Strikes and You're Out: Exploring Symbol and Substance in American and British Crime Control Politics', *British Journal of Criminology*, 46 (2006), 781–802.

in the eighteenth century,[53] yet for many years the courts roundly denied its existence.[54] In one of the ground-breaking socio-legal studies in England, Baldwin and McConville showed that events around Crown Court trials were explicable only by the inference that some kind of covert deals were being struck.[55] While this study had a tremendous effect upon the legal academy, the effect upon the courts was less striking. *R.* v. *Turner*,[56] as underlined and applied in subsequent cases, save in the most exceptional circumstances, effectively prohibited the judge from giving any indication of sentence in advance of a guilty plea by the defendant. The Royal Commission on Criminal Justice noted wistfully that:

> A significant number of those who now plead guilty at the last minute would be more ready to declare their hand at an earlier stage if they were given a reliable early indication of the maximum sentence that they would face if found guilty.[57]

Sir Robin Auld's review of the criminal courts discussed advance indications of sentence. It concluded that subject to a number of specified safeguards, a defendant, through his advocate, should be able to request to be informed of, and the judge should be entitled formally to indicate, the maximum sentence in the event of a plea of guilty at that stage and the possible sentence on conviction following a trial.[58] Auld believed that the ability of the judge to give an indication to a defendant who wished to know the maximum sentence she or he faced would 'enable the guilty defendant and those advising him to evaluate the judge's indication and

[53] B. P. Smith, 'Plea Bargaining and the Eclipse of the Jury', *Annual Review of Law and Social Science*, 1 (2005), 131–49.

[54] For example, *R.* v. *Wise* [1979] RTR 57: 'If a judge enters into a blatant plea-bargain, his fitness to sit as a judge on the criminal law Bench is called into question', *per* Lord Widgery CJ, at p. 59C–D; *R.* v. *Grice* (1978) 66 Cr App R 167: 'We find it quite astonishing that any recorder should characterise what he is doing as "plea bargaining". But even more so when it clearly was "plea bargaining"', *per* Roskill LJ, at p. 308.

[55] Baldwin and McConville, *Negotiated Justice*. See P. A. Thomas, 'Plea Bargaining in England and Wales', *Journal of Criminal Law and Criminology*, 69 (1978), 170–8; for a contemporary reaction, see M. McConville, J. Hodgson, L. Bridges and A. Pavlovic, *Standing Accused* (Oxford University Press, 1994), pp. 189–98.

[56] *R.* v. *Turner* [1970] 2 QB 321.

[57] W. Runciman (chair), *Report of the Royal Commission on Criminal Justice*, Cm. 2263 (London: The Stationery Office, 1993), paras 41–58. See also M. McConville, 'Plea Bargaining: Ethics and Politics', *Journal of Law and Society*, 25 (1998), 562–87.

[58] R. Auld, *Review of the Criminal Courts of England and Wales* (Auld Report) (London: The Stationery Office, 2001), pp. 434–44.

assess the advantage or otherwise of proceeding with a plea'.[59] It would clearly be in the interests of all that the defendant be able to undertake a comparison between the sentence on a plea of guilty and a possible sentence on conviction:

> He knows, and will in any event, be advised by his lawyer that a plea of guilty can attract a lesser sentence and broadly what the possible outcomes are, depending on his plea. So what possible additional pressure, unacceptable or otherwise, can there be in the judge, whom he has requested to tell him where he stands, indicating more precisely the alternatives?[60]

As noted by Auld, one aspect of the criminal justice system in England and Wales that has always been inconsistent with the idea that pleas should be uninfluenced by considerations as to what their outcome might be is the sentencing discount. Judicial precedent created the one-third discount for guilty pleas, which was incorporated into criminal law later.[61]

Some departure from the 'no bargains' rule is now permitted by statute. Under the 'plea before venue system', the accused is entitled to request an indication of sentence, in particular, whether 'a custodial sentence or non-custodial sentence would be more likely to be imposed if he were to be tried summarily … and to plead guilty. The court is entitled, but not obliged, to respond to such a request.'[62] That is, there is no longer any absolute prohibition against an advance indication of sentence.[63] In cartel offences in which the enforcement authority is the Office of Fair Trading (OFT) bargains of some sorts have been permitted.[64] The question is not

59 See at p. 000.

60 See Ashworth, *Sentencing and Criminal Justice*, p. 172. Sentencing Advisory Panel (now Council), *Reduction in Sentence for a Guilty Plea: Definitive Guideline* (London: Sentencing Advisory Council, 2007).

61 Criminal Justice and Public Order Act 1994, s. 48, Criminal Justice Act 2003, s. 144.

62 Criminal Procedure and Investigations Act 1996: venue being significant because of the differing sentencing powers of the Magistrates' and Crown Court.

63 In Schedule 3 of the Criminal Justice Act 2003, dealing with the allocation of cases triable either way, and sending cases to the Crown Court, para. 6, substituting s. 20 of the Magistrates' Court Act 1980, addresses the procedure where summary trial appears to be more suitable.

64 J. Lawrence, M. O'Kane, S. Rab and J. Nakhwal, 'Hardcore Bargains: What could Plea Bargaining Offer in UK Criminal Cartel Cases?', *Company Lawyer*, 7 (2008), 17–42. Office of Fair Trading, *The Cartel Offence: Guidance on the Issue of No-Action Letters by Individuals, OFT 513* (April 2003), available at: www.oft.gov.uk/shared_oft/business_leaflets/enterprise_act/oft513.pdf.

whether an absolute bar should be maintained, but whether and how deal-making might properly be extended to bribery offences.

Following the guidance published in December 2004 by the Sentencing Guidelines Council[65] in *Goodyear*,[66] adopting the procedure in *Attorney General's Reference (No. 1 of 2004)* and *Simpson*,[67] a five-judge Court of Appeal, presided over by the Lord Chief Justice, was convened to consider whether the *Turner* rule of practice should be modified, and if so, to what extent. It laid down new guidelines[68] which state that, normally speaking, an indication of sentence should not be given until the basis of the plea has been agreed or the judge has concluded that he or she can properly deal with the case without the need for a trial of the issue. The plea and case management hearing in the Crown Court now specifically requires the judge to seek and be given, first, on whether the defendant has in fact been advised about the credit to be obtained for a guilty plea, and, secondly, what steps had been taken to see whether the case might be resolved without a trial.[69]

There are several techniques of 'negotiated diversion'. The idea is obvious: to avoid costly and time-consuming opportunities for adversarial conflict. This recommendation and subsequent legislation placed it on a more formal footing.[70] Subject to those imposed by the judges,[71] the main constraints upon the prosecutor in making deals with defendants are set out in the *Attorney General's Guidelines on the Acceptance of Pleas*.[72] This requires, among other things, attention to transparency, the basis of plea, attention to the interests of victims and to mitigating factors.

This chapter started by considering the reasons why deal-making might not be appropriate in the case of bribery. Why might deals be particularly appropriate in bribery cases?[73] There is nothing particularly to differentiate it from other types of financial crime, but financial crime

65 Sentencing Guidelines Council, *On the Reduction in Sentence for Guilty Plea* (London: Sentencing Guidelines Secretariat, December 2004).

66 *R.* v. *Goodyear (Karl)* [2005] EWCA Crim 888.

67 *Attorney General's Reference (No. 1 of 2004)* [2004] 1 WLR 2111, *R.* v. *Simpson* [2004] QB 118.

68 See Julian, 'Judicial Perspectives'; Auld Report, paras 55–80.

69 *R.* v. *Goodyear (Karl)* [2005] EWCA Crim 888, para. 46.

70 Criminal Justice and Public Order Act 1994, s. 48.

71 See p. 237, below.

72 Available at: http://www.attorneygeneral.gov.uk/Publications/Pages/AttorneyGenerals-Guidelines.aspx.

73 R. Tyler, 'Lord Goldsmith Urges Plea Bargaining in Bribery Cases', *Daily Telegraph*, 13 September 2011.

in general is an area in which successful prosecutions are difficult and the length of the trial involves substantial risk of an acquittal (with its attendant bad publicity) and expense.[74] The complicating features, which are not unique to bribery prosecutions, but which are as typical to them as to some other forms of financial crime, are the corporate element and the international aspect. In any corporate case the possibility of a deal is attractive where the management has changed since the offence was committed, or can in some other way distance itself from the offence.

A false start? 'Global settlements' and the overseas element

Greater emphasis upon making deals with defendants is also consistent with the possibility of developing 'global settlements' in criminal matters.[75] Traditional doctrine holds that a criminal matter is something to be resolved between an individual or corporate defendant and a sovereign state. This doctrine has had difficulty adapting to the realities in a globalisation, including policing, arrests, evidence gathering and prosecutions that cross borders. *R.* v. *Whittle*[76] tested the waters in the Court of Appeal. The defendants negotiated simultaneous plea bargains for offences prosecuted by the US Department of Justice and the UK Office of Fair Trading. The agreement was that they were to be sentenced in the United States, returned to the United Kingdom, and then plead guilty to offences in England. They would return to serve the US sentences only if they were to receive sentences in the United Kingdom that were shorter than those imposed in the United States. Without expressing a concluded view, the Court of Appeal was not happy to have constraints imposed upon it, and upon counsel arguing before it and other UK courts, by a US prosecutor.

The Court noted that 'part of the agreement [with the US Department of Justice] was that each applicant would … not seek from the UK Court

[74] Roskill, Lord E., *Fraud Trials Committee Report* (the 'Roskill Report') (London: The Stationery Office 1986) (HL 471), gave us the SFO with its special investigative powers, and the Criminal Justice Act 2003, s. 43 gave a power to operate without a jury, but these provisions were never brought into force, and a subsequent attempt to bring them in failed. See R. Wright, 'Why (Some) Fraud Prosecutions Fail', *Journal of Financial Crime*, 13 (2006), 177–82.

[75] See B. L. Garrett, 'Globalized Corporate Prosecutions', *Virginia Law Review*, 97 (2011), 1776–876.

[76] *R.* v. *Whittle* [2008] EWCA Crim 2560 – *the Marine Hoses Cartel.*

a sentence of imprisonment less than that provided for by the agreement'. Giving the judgment of the Court, Hallett LJ said:

> As we have already indicated, we are not in a position to judge the full strength of that argument and its consequences in this case because of the way the submissions have been constrained by the considerations to which we have referred. All we can say is that had the submissions not been so constrained, we may well have been persuaded to reduce the sentences further than we have been invited to do.

The Court thus reduced the sentence to match the terms of imprisonment imposed in the United States, but by clear implication expressed the view that this may still have been a more severe sentence than might, but for the constraints of the US plea agreement, otherwise have been in the Court's sights.[77]

The attitude of the courts in England and Wales is currently shaped by two decisions – *BAE* and *Innospec*. The SFO commenced an investigation into BAE Systems plc in 2004. The investigation, which was prompted by allegations received concerning a defence contract with Saudi Arabia, ultimately also included contracts between BAE and a number of other countries (including the Czech Republic, Romania and South Africa). The SFO investigation relating to Saudi Arabia was discontinued in December 2006.[78] A contract for the supply of a radar defence system for Dar-es-Salaam International Airport was agreed in 1999 between British Aerospace Defence Systems Ltd and the Government of Tanzania. The value of the contract was US$39.97 million. BAE's practice was to engage advisers to help with its marketing. These advisers were either classified by BAE as 'overt' (i.e., they operated openly as BAE's in-country representatives), or 'covert'. The latter operated in circumstances where there was a perceived need for confidentiality. In order to maximise confidentiality with regard to its use of covert advisers and the making of payments to them, BAE set up Red Diamond Trading Company, a shell company incorporated in the British Virgin Islands.

In Tanzania a local businessman, Vithlani, was recruited at an early stage (initially by Siemens) to advise BAE on its negotiations with the government on the radar contract. Shortly before the contract was signed two new adviser arrangements with Vithlani were concluded. One was

[77] *R.* v. *Whittle* [2008] EWCA Crim 2560, para. 31.

[78] *R. (On the Application of Corner House Research and Others)* v. *Director of the Serious Fraud Office* [2008] UKHL 60, at para. 22.

made between Red Diamond and a Vithlani-controlled Panama-incorporated company, Envers Trading Corporation. This was a 'covert' arrangement where the fee for Vithlani's services was to be not more than 30.025 per cent of the radar contract price. The other arrangement was 'overt' and was for services direct to BAE by a Vithlani-controlled business. It did not involve Red Diamond and the fee was 1 per cent of the radar contract value.

Between January 2000 and December 2005 around US$12.4 million was paid to Vithlani's two companies. BAE has accepted that there was a high probability that part of this sum would be used to favour it in the contract negotiations. The payments were not subject to proper and adequate scrutiny or review. Furthermore, it was not possible for any person auditing the accounts to investigate and determine whether the payments were properly accounted for or were lawful. BAE conducted negotiations with the US Department of Justice in relation to contracts with Saudi Arabia and Central and Eastern Europe, and with the SFO in relation to the Tanzania contract. On 5 February 2010, it was announced on the SFO website that BAE had reached settlements with the UK and US authorities and agreed to pay fines totalling US$400 million (approximately £250 million) to settle the long-running corruption allegations concerning the Tanzanian air traffic control system. BAE Systems plc admitted that it had failed to keep adequate accounting records in relation to a defence contract for the supply of an air traffic control system to the Government of Tanzania.[79] The settlement with the SFO related to the Tanzania contract whereby BAE agreed to pay an ex gratia payment for the benefit of the people of Tanzania of £30 million, less any fine imposed by the Crown Court. Additionally, BAE was to be ordered to pay £225,000 costs to the SFO.

When the case came for trial,[80] in sentencing BAE, HHJ Bean took the view that BAE had concealed from the auditor and ultimately the public the fact that they were making payments to Vithlani, the overwhelming preponderance via offshore companies, and that they were giving him wide powers to make such payments to such people as he thought fit in order to secure the radar contract for BAE, but in such circumstances that BAE did not need and did not want to know the details. He therefore questioned whether the charge under section 221 of the Companies Act 1985 (which deals with the maintenance of accounting records) was an

[79] Companies Act 1985, s. 221. [80] *R. v. BAE Systems plc* [2010] EW Misc 16.

appropriate one. The danger of this charge, which did not, for example, carry debarment from procurement tendering,[81] was that it may have appeared to have understated the extent of the defendant's culpability. The judge also took into account in sentencing BAE that, following the report of Lord Woolf,[82] the group had committed itself to a process of change and also that it would be making a payment for the benefit of the people of Tanzania of £30 million less the fine. He said that the people of Tanzania were the real victims, and he decided in these circumstances to impose a fine of £500,000.

An attempt was made to restrain the trend towards global settlements, in which the Guidance for Handling Criminal Cases with Concurrent Jurisdiction between the United Kingdom and the United States of America[83] is a significant milestone, was made in the judgment of Thomas LJ in *Innospec.*[84] In this case an agreement had been arrived at between the SFO and the defendants whereby a series of guilty pleas, fines, confiscation orders and civil recovery orders were to be presented to a judge, in effect, for ratification. Thomas LJ was very firm both in rejecting such a restricted view of the role of the judge and in refusing to differentiate between types of serious crime:

> It is of the greatest public interest that the serious criminality of any, including companies, who engage in the corruption of foreign governments, is made patent for all to see by the imposition of criminal and not civil sanctions. It would be inconsistent with basic principles of justice for the criminality of corporations to be glossed over by a civil as opposed to a criminal sanction.[85]

Of the sentencing role of the judge in general, in what is rapidly becoming a *locus classicus*, Thomas LJ said:

> the imposition of a sentence is a matter for the judiciary … It is in the public interest, particularly in relation to the crime of corruption, that although, in accordance with the Practice Direction, there may be discussion and agreement as to the basis of plea, the court must rigorously scrutinise in open court in the interests of transparency

[81] Under EU Directive 2004/18/EC, Art. 45.

[82] Woolf Committee, *Business Ethics, Global Companies and the Defence Industry: Ethical Business Conduct in BAE Systems Plc*, May 2008, available at: http://ir.baesystems.com/investors/storage/woolf_report_2008.pdf.

[83] Available at: www.cps.gov.uk/legal/h_to_k/jurisdiction/#Concurrent.

[84] *R.* v. *Innospec Ltd* [2010] EW Misc 7, [2010] CLR 665. See also *R.* v. *Dougall* [2010] EWCA Crim 1048.

[85] *R.* v. *Innospec Ltd* [2010] EW Misc 7, para. 36.

> and good governance the basis of that plea and to see whether it reflects the public interest.[86]

Evidently, neither judge took at all kindly to being treated by prosecutors as little more than a rubber stamp. Much was made at the time of *Innospec* and *BAE Systems* about the force with which the judges expressed their concerns about the use of bargains of the nature in question. At that time it was written that, to all intents and purposes, the possibility of global settlements had been ended, particularly by Thomas LJ.[87] *E pur si mouve.* If the view of Thomas LJ prevails and global settlements are ruled out, nothing will change. It will continue to be difficult to achieve results in court against corporate offenders. The management of bribery prosecutions was claimed to be one of the reasons that the SFO retained its independence.[88]

Plea agreements

Most of Thomas LJ's objections to the way in which the SFO had conducted *Innospec* speak to whether there should be plea agreements at all. The international aspect adds no further insuperable difficulties. If it is possible at all to proceed along *Innospec* lines, save with appropriate attenuations, then there is no clear reason why these agreements cannot be reached internationally. One possibility that remains, therefore, would be the reinstatement, with appropriate limitations and checks of the sorts of practices that were used in *Innospec.*

Notwithstanding *Innospec*, we can expect to see greater use of deal-making with corporate defendants, and for those deals to include civil recovery,[89] but deal-making should not take place unconstrained. Thomas LJ in *Innospec* and HHJ Bean in *BAE Systems* each consented

[86] *R.* v. *Innospec Ltd* [2010] EW Misc 7, para. 27.

[87] DLA Piper, 'Judge Signals Death Knell for Global Settlements', available at: www.dlapiperrapidresponse.com/export/sites/rapid-response-old/bulletins/pdfs/2010_Judge_-Signals_Death_Knell_for_Global_Settlements.pdf.

[88] N. Kochan, 'SFO Targets Big Fish for Bribery Act Prosecutions', available at: www.kochan.co.uk/articles/bribery/bigfish.htm.

[89] The Consolidated Criminal Practice Direction, s. IV.45 and the decision of the Court of Appeal in *R.* v. *Underwood* [2004] EWCA Crim 2256 establish that whether or not pleas have been agreed, the judge is not bound by any such agreement, and that any view formed by the prosecution on a proposed basis of plea is deemed to be conditional of the judge's acceptance of the basis of plea. *R* v. *BAE Systems plc* [2010] EW Misc 16 is an application of this principle.

to the deal that had been struck between prosecutor and defendant, but neither was happy about it. If this practice of negotiation is to continue or increase a series of issues will need to be addressed. The first is the general one of the appropriate role of the judge in sentencing. Even though it bears many of the hallmarks of an executive function, judicial discretion in sentencing is maintained to be one of the stigmata of the independent judicial role, and it is one of which judges in England and Wales are fiercely protective.

Secondly, proper attention needs to be given to the basis for plea. Thomas LJ in *Innospec* and HHJ Bean in *BAE Systems* were both critical of the factual basis upon which the agreements constrained them to pass sentence. Most obviously, HHJ Bean had to sentence on the section 221 charge rather than on a bribery charge, which was wholly artificial, and seemed, in the light of the evidence, to offend the general considerations of transparency and publicity. It would be unacceptable for defendants to be able to buy their way out of adverse publicity or convictions of offences of an appropriate gravity to the conduct in question. In *BAE Systems* the charge was a technical/regulatory one of failing to keep proper accounts, whereas the evidence seemed to point very strongly to an offence of bribery. The judge eventually allowed the case to proceed to sentence on this basis, but made it clear that there may be cases in which the charges were so inappropriate that the judge ought not to let the case proceed. Likewise, in *BAE*, the judge, quite correctly,[90] criticised the fact that the wording of the SFO press release, to be published at the time of the announcement of the settlement, had formed part of the deal. This was a matter of particular concern to the OECD.[91]

The third matter is the penalty on 'offer'. The incentive for pleading guilty should be a reduced sentence and not, at least in the first instance, a civil recovery order. When civil recovery orders were introduced they were a fall-back mechanism to deal with cases where criminal proceedings could not successfully be brought. Now this sequential relationship has been changed to one in which civil recovery can supplement or provide an alternative to criminal proceedings. The calculation is more complex, and the possibility of the power of money operating to prevent adverse publicity and the other effects of convictions is a clear one to

[90] *R* v. *BAE Systems plc* [2010] EW Misc 16, para. 13.

[91] Specifically mentioned in the 2012 report on the 2011 site visit. OECD, *United Kingdom: Phase 3 Report on Implementing the OECD Anti-Bribery Convention in the United Kingdom* (Paris: OECD, 2012).

which regard must be had. The existence of civil recovery as a mechanism threatens the power of the judge to give effect to the denunciatory role of the criminal law, because in principle it makes the matter a civil one, and as long as it is civil it is susceptible to agreement between civil parties.[92]

Finally, it should be noted that double jeopardy does not provide a problem. The defences of *autrefois convict* or *acquit* are not available when the conviction has been obtained in another jurisdiction.[93]

To encompass the international dimension, the additional feature that must be addressed is that international dealing should not be permitted to extend to overseas prosecutors dictating the criminal justice policy of the United Kingdom, any more than overseas diplomats. Mechanisms must be in place which are reliable and transparent for determining priorities between countries asserting jurisdiction. Global pleas agreements can work only if plea agreements work, but, notwithstanding *Innospec*, we can expect to see greater use of deal-making with corporate defendants, and for those deals to include civil recovery, but deal-making should not take place unconstrained.

Self-reporting and section 7

The significance of the SFO's preference for deal-making is heightened by the introduction, particularly in the case of bribery and corporate fraud, of incentives for self-reporting.[94] A subset of the development in respect of plea agreements, but one that can develop only with wider recognition of such agreements, is the increased use of self-reporting. Self-reporting has for some time occupied the attention of economists dealing with law.[95] From time to time people walk into police stations to turn themselves in. On the SFO website is an invitation to do very much the same thing, virtually.[96] This is proactive deal-making – deal-making even before the authorities are aware that the crime has, or may have been, committed. It invites the corporation to make a clean breast of previous wrongdoing. No one is 'just' going to self-report. It is particularly attractive for a company wishing to draw a line under the wrongdoing of a

[92] Albeit in accordance with the guidance. [93] *Brannigan* v. *Davison* [1997] AC 238.

[94] See www.sfo.gov.uk/victims/corporate-victims/should-i-self-report-directly-to-the-sfo-.aspx.

[95] For an alternative view see M. F. Weismann, 'The Foreign Corrupt Practices Act: The Failure of the Self-Regulatory Model of Corporate Governance in the Global Business Environment', *Journal of Business Ethics*, 88 (2009), 615–61.

[96] Self-reporting corruption, see www.sfo.gov.uk/bribery–corruption.aspx.

previous management. There is far more chance of this sort of declaration being made by someone who does not him- or herself face sanctions, and this will be the case where there has been a change of management within a corporate offender. The new management will not face prosecution, and has every reason to want to eliminate any risk arising from the past events coming to light. The twenty-first century has seen a growth in third-party policing,[97] and self-reporting can be regarded as a subset of this phenomenon.

The guidance for prosecutors when dealing with alleged corporate offenders[98] contains 'additional public interest factors against prosecution' which include the following: 'a genuinely proactive approach adopted by the corporate management team when the offending is brought to their notice, involving self-reporting and remedial actions, including the compensation of victims'; 'the existence of a genuinely proactive and effective corporate compliance programme'; and that 'the availability of civil or regulatory remedies that are likely to be effective and more proportionate'. It is noted that appropriate alternatives to prosecution may include civil recovery orders combined with a range of agreed regulatory measures. Negotiated civil recovery is particularly attractive to a corporate entity because of the opportunity the negotiation offers to control the publicity that is given and to avoid any other automatic consequences of criminal conviction.[99]

If a self-reporting regime is to work, it must be within a juridical framework that takes due notice of the public interest in seeing justice being done against the need for consistency of approach, so that corporate offenders can assess with a degree of certainty the outcome of the criminal process. The things to which regard must be had include the following:

> Is the board of the corporate genuinely committed to resolving the issue and moving to a better corporate culture?
>
> Is the corporate prepared to work with us on the scope and handling of any additional investigation we consider to be necessary?
>
> At the end of the investigation (and assuming acknowledgement of a problem) will the corporate be prepared to discuss resolution of the issue on the basis, for example, of restitution through civil recovery, a

97 L. G. Mazerolle and J. Ransley, *Third Party Policing* (Cambridge University Press, 2001).

98 Available at: http://www.sfo.gov.uk/about-us/our-policies-and-publications/guidance-on-corporate-prosecutions.aspx.

99 Making the terms of the consequential press release was in accordance with the SFO's, *Approach of the SFO to Dealing with Overseas Corruption*, but was strongly criticised by Thomas LJ in *Innospec.*

> programme of training and culture change, appropriate action where necessary against individuals and, at least in some cases, external monitoring in a proportionate manner?
>
> Does the corporate understand that any resolution must satisfy the public interest and must be transparent? This will almost invariably involve a public statement although the terms of this will be discussed and agreed by the corporate and us.
>
> Will the corporate want us, where possible, to work with regulators and criminal enforcement authorities, both in the UK and abroad, in order to reach a global settlement?[100]

Part of the fallout from the al-Yamamah affair was an emphasis upon greater efforts within corporate governance to bring the wrongdoing to the attention of the authorities. Lord Woolf, the former Lord Chief Justice, was employed by BAE Systems to look into the way in which the company's corporate governance could be improved to prevent the recurrence of the sorts of difficulties to which it had been subject.[101] There has been increasing recognition that the criminal law can provide only part of a strategy towards the reduction in levels of corruption.

Before the 2010 Act, it was impossible to defend the record of English law and English prosecutors in furnishing 'effective proportionate and dissuasive sanctions'.[102] It would not have been sufficient simply to enact sections 1 and 6, even with the extended jurisdictional provisions of the Act.[103] In order to comply with the Convention, the offence under section 7 of the Bribery Act was structured as it was to place pressure on companies to self-police. Under section 7 of the Bribery Act 2010 there is a defence for the corporate offender of having in place adequate measures. The Act does not compel the introduction of adequate measures, but provides a strong incentive. It also provides very helpful guidance as to the sort of things that might amount to adequate procedures.[104] The conduct of these procedures may well involve self-reports. It should be possible, within a framework incentivising self-reports, for sentencing guidance to be generated that does not fall foul of a revised *Innospec*.

[100] SFO, *Approach of the SFO to Dealing with Overseas Corruption*, para. 4.

[101] Woolf Committee, *Business Ethics, Global Companies and the Defence Industry*.

[102] OECD Convention on the Bribery of Foreign Public Officials in International Business Transactions (Paris, 1997).

[103] Bribery Act 2010, s. 12; J. Horder, 'On Her Majesty's Commercial Service: Bribery, Public Officials and the UK Intelligence Services', *Modern Law Review*, 74 (2011), 911–31.

[104] Ministry of Justice, *The Bribery Act 2010: Guidance about Procedures which Relevant Commercial Organisations can put into Place to Prevent Persons Associated with Them from Bribing* (London: Ministry of Justice, 2011).

Civil recovery

Civil recovery is the procedure whereby property in the hands of a person (not necessarily the original criminal) is pursued in a civil action. The original basis upon which civil recovery was established was that this use was an alternative to criminal prosecution, to be used after the possibility of prosecution had been ruled out. It was a fall back, or longstop. This may have been one of the reasons for the failure of the Assets Recovery Agency (ARA).[105] The agency had been established to pursue civil recovery claims in cases in which a decision had been made not to prosecute. It was abolished abruptly in 2007 following the publication of a report by Grant Shapps MP, which established that in the first four years of its existence the ARA had not been able to acquire enough money to cover its own costs.[106] The proceedings may now be brought by a range of officials, in this case, most significantly for these purposes, the Director of the Serious Fraud Office.

As first introduced, civil recovery was not intended to be an alternative to criminal proceedings where conviction and a subsequent confiscation order were available. During the parliamentary stages of the Proceeds of Crime Act 2002, a clear hierarchy seems to have been contemplated in the approach the ARA was to take to someone suspected of being in possession of the proceeds of crime. First preference was for criminal prosecution, followed by civil recovery, then, if appropriate, for the invocation of the tax jurisdiction.[107]

Statutes do not usually assert one policy rather than another to be the preferred one. They usually implement the preferred policy. However, the Proceeds of Crime Act 2002 states that directors who have responsibility for civil recovery proceedings must exercise their functions under this Act in the way which it considers is best calculated to contribute to the reduction of crime, and in doing so must have regard to guidance from the relevant minister, and that the guidance must indicate that the reduction of crime is in general best secured by means of criminal

[105] The agency was established by the Proceeds of Crime Act 2002.

[106] G. Shapps, *Report into the Underperformance of the Assets Recovery Agency* (London: Shapps, 2006), available at: www.shapps.com/reports/AssetsRecoveryAgency-underperformance.pdf; www.shapps.com/AssetsRecoveryAgency-underperformance.pdf

[107] P. Alldridge, *Money Laundering Law* (Oxford: Hart, 2003), pp. 246 *et seq*. At the time the legislation was enacted, the Irish Criminal Assets Bureau, which in some respects provided the model for the ARA, was raising more money from the exercise of its tax than its recovery jurisdiction.

investigations and criminal proceedings.[108] The requirement for guidance on these lines is, therefore, striking. It is possible to imagine a conference of penologists coming together to discuss whether or not it is indeed correct to say that, 'the reduction of crime is in general best secured by means of criminal investigations and criminal proceedings'. In the field of acquisitive crime it seems that if reduction of crime is really 'in general' secured at all well by means of criminal investigations and criminal proceedings, the Proceeds of Crime Act 2002 would have been unlikely to have been brought forward in the first place. Attempts to deal with crime by 'following the money trail' are a clear result of the failure of criminal investigations and criminal proceedings to secure the reduction of crime.[109] A note of caution should therefore be heard. Nonetheless, a code of practice was put in place for the ARA, which was superseded by a second,[110] which encouraged memoranda of understanding between law enforcement bodies but did not change the priorities.[111]

Civil recovery actions originally concentrated upon a range of cases in which prosecution followed by the imposition of confiscation orders is not available, and others in which they are difficult to obtain. There are two major sets of cases where civil recovery is the preferred option. The first is where criminal prosecution followed by a confiscation order is not feasible at all. The principal ones are as follows:[112]

(i) Where the person in question is dead.[113] No criminal proceedings can be brought where the defendant is dead, so confiscation orders are not available.[114]

[108] Proceeds of Crime Act 2002, s. 2A. See also *SOCA* v. *Agidi* [2011] EWHC 175 (QB), paras 130 *et seq.*

[109] This provision was probably written not to be litigated. Note that the statute says 'best' not 'most effectively' or 'most efficiently' secured. That is, the criterion is 'goodness'.

[110] Available at: www.assetsrecovery.gov.uk/downloads/SOSrevisedguidanceFeb2005.pdf. See also the statement by Caroline Flint, *Hansard*, HC, Deb, cols 90–91 WS, 10 February 2005.

[111] Such memoranda were put in place. See www.assetsrecovery.gov.uk.

[112] See also A. Kennedy, 'Civil Recovery Proceedings under the Proceeds of Crime Act 2002: The Experience so Far', *Journal of Money Laundering Control*, 9 (2006), 245–64.

[113] For example, *R. (On the Application of Director of Assets Recovery Agency)* v. *Cecilia Obialo* [2006] EWHC 2876.

[114] See also *R.* v. *Kearley (No. 2)* [1994] 2 AC 414. It follows from this that no Article 6.2 or 6.3 argument against the use of civil recovery will arise in such circumstances. 'It is a fundamental rule of criminal law that criminal liability does not survive the person who has committed the criminal act. Inheritance of the guilt of the dead is not compatible

(ii) Where there is insufficient admissible evidence to secure a criminal conviction, and criminal proceedings are not brought. The prosecutor must take a view as to the prospects of success before instituting proceedings.[115] Cases in which there is some, but not overwhelming, evidence might not be brought before the criminal courts. Either because of the differing rules of admissibility,[116] or the difference in the burden of proof, it may still be possible to prove on the balance of probabilities in a civil action that the property is the proceeds of criminal conduct.

(iii) Where a prosecution is brought, on the basis that it has a prospect of success such as to satisfy the guidance for the CPS,[117] but in fact the defendant is acquitted, either because of the differing rules of admissibility or the difference in the burden of proof, or error by the prosecutor, or because of any of the other reasons for which juries acquit, it may still be possible to prove on the balance of probabilities in a civil action that the property is the proceeds of criminal conduct.

(iv) Where the property is, but the defendant is not, and is unlikely to be brought, within the jurisdiction. In this case it will not be possible to prosecute, but there will be legal mechanisms available to freeze and subsequently to seize the property.[118]

(v) Where there is insufficient evidence admissible at a confiscation hearing to link the proceeds to the crime.[119]

(vi) Where an English court would not have jurisdiction over the crime.

These cases were always thought of as clear ones for civil recovery. After the ARA was abolished and the Asset Recovery Incentive Scheme, under which 50 per cent is paid to the agencies responsible for investigation (18.75 per cent), prosecution (18.75 per cent), and

with the standards of criminal justice in a society governed by the rule of law.' *A.P., M.P. and T.P.* v. *Switzerland* (1998) 26 EHRR 541, para. 48.

115 CPS Prosecution Guidelines, available at: www.cps.gov.uk/publications/docs/code2004 english.pdf.

116 Though the hearsay and bad character provisions of the Criminal Justice Act 2003 have reduced the differences in this regard, there are still significant differences in the rules of evidence.

117 CPS Prosecution Guidelines.

118 Kennedy, 'Civil Recovery Proceedings', also mentions the case where the ownership of the property is uncertain.

119 This is unlikely to happen. The strict rules of criminal evidence do not apply in a confiscation hearing (*R.* v. *Silcock & Levin* [2004] EWCA Crim 408, [2004] 2 Cr App R (S) 323) and the standard of proof is the civil one (Proceeds of Crime Act 2002, s. 6(7)).

enforcement (12.5 per cent) of the offences in question, was in place,[120] a significant shift occurred. Additions were made to the categories of cases against which civil recovery was to be deployed. New guidance was issued by the Home Secretary and the Attorney General in 2009,[121] which rehearsed the appropriateness of the use of prosecution, but shifted emphasis by giving far greater attention to the use of civil recovery where prosecution would be a plausible option – that is, to the use of civil recovery not because prosecution is not possible, but because it is not thought to present the best possible outcome. This gives rise to a second group of cases where conviction might be feasible, but civil recovery is now considered a better option. Those cases are as follows:

(i) Using non-conviction-based powers better meets an urgent need to take action to prevent or stop offending which is causing immediate harm to the public, even though this might limit the availability of evidence for a future prosecution.
(ii) It is not practicable to investigate all those with a peripheral involvement in the criminality, and a strategic approach must be taken in order to achieve a manageable and successful prosecution.
(iii) Civil recovery represents a better deployment of resources to target someone with significant property which cannot be explained by legitimate income.
(iv) The offender is being prosecuted in another jurisdiction and is expected to receive a sentence that reflects the totality of the offending, so the public interest does not require a prosecution in this country.[122]

In these cases criminal prosecution and conviction are no longer thought to be the most appropriate ways by which the State should proceed because there are other, more financially advantageous, avenues available, and negotiated settlements offer greater probability of a return. The SFO has been criticised for its low conviction rate in contested trials, and it has been suggested that the length and complexity of financial crime

[120] Asset Recovery Incentive Scheme 2010–11.
[121] Attorney General's Guidance under Proceeds of Crime Act 2002, s 2A, November 2009, available at: www.attorneygeneral.gov.uk/Publications/Pages/AttorneyGeneralissuedguidancetoprosecutingbodiesontheirassetrecoverypowersunder.aspx.
[122] Attorney General's Guidance under Proceeds of Crime Act 2002, s 2A.

trials is a contributory factor to this low rate.[123] It is happy to avoid long and complex trials if it can, and is consequently not averse to making deals. The possibility of some sort of bargain has long been recognised by the common law[124] and now has statutory expression.[125] Part of the consolidated Practice Direction for Prosecutors deals with guilty pleas and discussions prior to them.[126]

The shift from regarding civil recovery as a fall back, consequent upon the failure of an attempt to prosecute, to its being one of the primary weapons in the armoury of the prosecutor arose out of the failure of the ARA. The use of civil recovery raises most clearly the relationship between the use of criminal justice (prosecution, conviction and sentence) and other approaches to acquisitive crime. To what extent is the use of alternatives to prosecution and conviction in the area of acquisitive crime justified?

A prosecutor will consequently now assess a bribery case with one of the possible outcomes being civil recovery as an alternative to or as part of any settlement that is reached. Whether the prosecutor is proceeding with a view to securing a plea agreement on its own or a plea agreement plus a civil recovery order, or a settlement in lieu of a civil recovery order, then full consideration needs to be made of the effects. In particular, since the civil recovery component of the settlement will be, in essence, a private one, then, in principle, everything, including the publicity, is negotiable.

Civil recovery orders are not, strictly speaking, part of a sentence for crime, and, so far as they are used, the agency responsible for their being put in place will have incentives to reach a settlement.[127] In cases of large

123 Wright, 'Why (Some) Fraud Prosecutions Fail'. It is not yet clear what will follow from David Green's succession in March 2012 of Richard Alderman as the Director of the SFO.

124 *R.* v. *Turner* [1970] 2 QB 321; *R.* v. *Goodyear (Karl)* [2005] EWCA Crim 888. In *McKinnon* v. *Government of the USA and another* [2007] EWHC 762 (Admin), the court expressed 'a degree of distaste' for the way in which plea negotiations had taken place, but said that these 'cultural reservations' were not such that extradition should not take place, but on appeal Lord Brown was far more accepting (difference between United States and England and Wales 'not so stark as it seems'): *McKinnon* v. *Government of the United States* [2008] UKHL 59, para. 34).

125 Plea agreements with a 'cooperating defendant' under s. 73 of the Serious Organised Crime and Police Act 2005.

126 Available at: www.justice.gov.uk/criminal/procrules_fin/contents/practice_direction/part4.htm#id6178240.

127 See p. 127, below

companies, the defendant is better resourced and has better legal advice available than would a normal defendant, but that should not be a reason not to deal. It may be that financial detriments become business expenses. Thomas LJ is correct to emphasise the problems in setting off the financial element of the agreement against any loss of opprobrium, but if corporate criminal liability is defensible at all it is no more or less of a problem here than elsewhere. This is something that needs to be considered very closely, in the light of the increasing use of civil recovery orders both in this area and in financial crime more generally.[128]

The deferred prosecution agreement proposal

At the time of writing (May 2012) the possible introduction of deferred plea agreements is under consideration.[129] A formal consultation has been promised. The Attorney General said that:

> Deferred prosecution agreements (DPAs) are an established part of the United States response to corporate crime. DPAs encourage companies to self-report wrongdoing and discuss with the Department of Justice (DOJ) the possibility of an outcome which does not necessarily result in a criminal conviction. The United States Principles of Federal Prosecution of Business Organisations gives guidance to prosecutors on the factors to consider when contemplating such a course of action and include the nature and seriousness of the offence, whether there was disclosure of wrongdoing and a willingness to cooperate, and consideration of collateral consequences. If a DPA is negotiated between the parties then it will typically be predicated upon the filing at court of the agreement and 'charging document' and, if the court agrees, the prosecution may be deferred for a specified period of usually 2 or 3 years subject to compliance with the terms of the agreement including payment of a substantial fine. These terms have included requirements to improve governance structures, reimburse victims, pay large sums in civil penalties, and the appointment of an independent monitor (at the company's expense) to review the effectiveness of any compliance programme.
>
> And since in many cases UK prosecutors will be working with their counterparts in the United States, the biggest financial market in the world, we need to ensure that we have arrangements in place that can cater for trans-jurisdictional matters, the effective gathering of evidence

128 Serious Fraud Office, 'Shareholder Agrees Civil Recovery by SFO in Mabey & Johnson', Serious Fraud Office press release, 13 January 2012, available at: www.sfo.gov.uk/press-room/latest-press-releases/press-releases-2012/shareholder-agrees-civil-recovery-by-sfo-in-mabey–johnson.aspx.

129 See https://consult.justice.gov.uk/digital-communications/deferred-prosecution-agreements.

> from abroad, and the issues of forum-shopping and double jeopardy. A crucial question for any comparable UK process would be the degree of judicial oversight and the mechanism for achieving that. However, if the UK can learn from the US experience and avoid some of the pitfalls the Americans have encountered then deferred prosecution agreements may offer a new way for the UK to deal with corporate crime in appropriate cases.

The idea is to encourage companies that have done wrong to self-report their bad behaviour. In exchange for the deferral of a prosecution, the company would agree with the prosecuting authority, the SFO, to pay a penalty and to other appropriate sanctions, such as compensation for victims or independent corporate monitoring. In some ways it could be regarded as a corporate ASBO. Various admissions would be made by the company in the deferred prosecution agreement (DPA), but, provided the company complied with the terms of the agreement, after a predetermined period the prosecution would be dropped. However, if the company were to breach the agreement, the prosecutor could revive the criminal proceedings and would be able to rely on admissions made in the DPA. While the Office of the Attorney General has confirmed that this is still policy, the proposal and its status have yet to be made public.

Conclusion

It is necessary to recognise the significance of the United States.[130] The SFO may have been using *Innospec* to draw attention to difficulties it faced, or it may be that the offer of cooperation and encouragement by the United States to pursue a joint settlement led to talk about the exact level of fine that ought to be imposed. In any event, the court took the opportunity to remind defendants and state agencies, in no uncertain terms, that sentencing takes place in court and is not agreed beforehand; there are important constitutional reasons for that. Certainly in cases of bribery and corruption, it would be deeply unattractive for the defendant to try and reach a favourable outcome with a state body in private and without the scrutiny of a court hearing.

[130] R. A. Kagan, 'Globalization and Legal Change: The "Americanization" of European Law?', *Regulation & Governance*, 1 (2007), 99–120; M. Ryznar and S. Korkor, 'Anti-Bribery Legislation in the United States and United Kingdom: A Comparative Analysis of Scope and Sentencing', *Missouri Law Review*, 76 (2011), 415–53; J. N. Djilani, 'The British Importation of American Corporate Compliance', *Brooklyn Law Review*, 76 (2010), 303–41.

More importantly, it is necessary to recognise the value of deal-making with defendants. If done against a framework of appropriate constraints, it can provide a worthwhile and defensible alternative to the unpredictability of trial. We should be exploring those constraints, not ruling the possibilities out from the outset.

9

Bribery and corruption: the UK framework for enforcement

CHARLIE MONTEITH

The UK framework for the enforcement of bribery and corruption laws has a bewildering tapestry of different agencies, investigators, prosecutors, intelligence gatherers, and government and non-government agencies and offices. In part, this has been caused by the difficulty in pinning down and defining bribery and corruption, but it also has a great deal to do with the multilayered approach to the investigation of crime and the different policy requirements involved.[1] However, I will be concentrating on the main enforcers on the Bribery Act 2010 ('the 2010 Act') in England and Wales, and in particular on the Serious Fraud Office (SFO),[2] in relation to overseas bribery. This is because there is a UK obligation to deal effectively with the bribery of foreign officials contained in the 1997 OECD Convention on Combating Bribery of Foreign Public Officials in International Business Transactions. The Convention helped to create an enforcement focus for overseas bribery of foreign public officials (albeit within a UK anti-corruption context), but the equivalent is lacking for domestic bribery.

Records of historical investigation and prosecution of bribery have proved hard to come by for a number of reasons, not least because there was no branded bribery offence until the advent of the 2010 Act. More confusion is caused through the general practice of subsuming bribery within general anti-corruption enforcement, which makes the gathering

[1] In 2004, for a manual on disclosure, I stopped counting when I reached over 900 different local and national government and non-government departments and agencies that conducted criminal investigations.

[2] I ought to confess straight away that, at the SFO, I was formerly Head of Assurance and policy lead on the Fraud and Bribery Acts. In the interests of some balance, before that for many years I worked for the Crown Prosecution Service. I have had practical working experience of all the other main agencies mentioned.

of branded bribery information difficult. A comprehensive approach to corruption (including enforcement) is now route-mapped in the United Nations Convention against Corruption (UNCAC).[3] In 2010, the United Kingdom agreed to subject itself to a pilot review evaluation of compliance with UNCAC, which is on-going.[4]

Defining corruption and bribery

As the government tries to give lead roles to particular investigatory agencies or departments in this context, it would help to try to define what is meant by 'corruption and bribery', as the definition helps to inform such choices. We must also consider 'fraud' as it has a close overlap with corruption and bribery. In drafting new laws everyone – not just enforcers – seeks some clarity of definition. 'Fraud' and 'corruption' have this in common: it is an impossible task. Legislators around the world have struggled to come up with satisfactory definitions; we in the United Kingdom are no different. The history of judicial attempts to bring clarity to fraud and corruption makes for a less than illuminating read. In fact, neither can be satisfactorily defined, which is why the Law Commission created an Advisory Group on the reform of bribery legislation, leading up to the 2010 Act.[5] Both fraud and corruption are chameleon-like creatures, capable of disappearing like water through one's fingers. The best approach is not to try to define them at all, but to treat them like a virus or complex disease that shows itself through its most common symptoms: abuse of position and false representation for fraud, and bribery for corruption.

That leaves the problem of distinguishing fraud from corruption. Very simply, corruption (and bribery) usually involves two persons: the corrupter and the corrupted (the briber and the bribed); whereas a fraud can be committed by one person acting alone. For corruption and bribery, it takes two to tango; whereas fraud is a dance one can do on one's own. For both there is usually an abuse of position, but the briber seeks to

[3] The United Kingdom signed the United Nations Convention against Corruption (UNCAC) on 9 December 2003 and ratified it on 14 February 2006. See Daniel and Maton, Chapter 11, this volume.

[4] Other relevant international instruments include the Council of Europe Criminal Law Convention on Corruption, Strasbourg, 27 January 1999, STE No. 173; the Criminal Justice (International Co-operation) Act 1990 (Enforcement of Overseas Forfeiture Orders) (Scotland) Order 2005; and the Proceeds of Crime Act 2002 (External Requests and Orders) Order 2005.

[5] In force since 1 July 2011.

abuse someone else's position through offering an advantage or benefit. Of course, through seeking to abuse someone else's position, the briber may also be abusing a position that he or she holds in relation to another financial interest, and may therefore also commit an offence under section 4 of the Fraud Act 2006 ('the 2006 Act'). The same may be true of those who accept the bribe. There are close links between the 'improper performance' sought under the 2010 Act offences and abuse of position under section 4 of the 2006 Act. It is important to distinguish such positions under the 2010 Act. The anticipated abuse under the 2010 Act became an intended breach of an expectation that a particular function or activity would be performed with trust, impartiality or good faith (which need not involve a fiduciary relationship). However, the functions and activities were limited to business or employment roles.

One similarity that has been overlooked is contained in section 14 of the 2010 Act. Section 14 is the section dealing with the offence of 'consenting and conniving' at bribery. There has been much talk about this 'new' offence in the 2010 Act. In fact, there is nothing 'new' about this offence, which merely replicates a similar offence in the 2006 Act, which in turn merely replicated a similar offence under the Theft Act 1968. However, I can recall no case where there has been a successful prosecution based upon acts of consenting and conniving in relation to which direct knowledge or intent is not required, only awareness that the specified offending is going on and turning a blind eye to it.

Directing minds

One area that remains unchanged is the criminal liability of legal persons, which still requires an individual representing the 'directing mind' of the company to commit a Bribery or Fraud Act offence. Proving it has been problematic for enforcers in the United Kingdom. Commercial bribery usually takes place in far off places via far off persons at the end of a long corporate chain. A board policy of ignorance about whether there is bribery or not has proved to be the lowest and safest risk.

But one of the great ironies about having adequate procedures to prevent bribery is that, by definition, there is a requirement for boardroom participation, and, ideally a compliance officer reporting to the board. The chief compliance officer (CCO) will (or should) be representing the 'directing mind'. Moreover, as the role requires reporting to the board over any 'bribery incidents', UK boardroom members will be unable to say they lacked knowledge or awareness if another 'bribery incident' were to occur again. Unless they act robustly to stop it happening again, their act of omission may amount to assisting or encouraging bribery.[6] Even if they did not believe it would happen again, there is another gateway to criminality via the potential complicity of the CCO. If he or she fails to act, board members may be liable under the consent and connive provision, if they are found to have turned a blind eye to what was going on.

The players in overseas corruption

The lead enforcer for bribery of overseas officials is the SFO, but cross-agency collaboration is essential in the majority of cases of corruption and bribery. The SFO maintains the national Anti-Corruption Register of all overseas corruption allegations, and manages the allocation of cases. There is a strategic corruption group chaired by the Serious Organised Crime Agency (SOCA) comprising the Foreign and Commonwealth Office (FCO), the Department for International Development (DFID), the SFO, the City of London Police Overseas Anti-Corruption Unit (OACU), City of London Police (CoLP), the Metropolitan Police, the Financial Services Authority (FSA), the Ministry of Defence and the Exports Credits Guarantee Department. This group oversees investigatory activity and provides a steer for areas of particular concern. The investigative skills and local knowledge of the police assist the SFO's financial expertise and legal capacity. There is also a tactical group comprising representatives of SFO, SOCA (terrorist funding team), the police and the FSA which meets to share intelligence, discuss areas of common interest and to identify areas for possible targeting.

Under a Memorandum of Understanding, all allegations are reported to SFO with the intention of making the current status of every allegation of overseas corruption available to all signatories from one source.

The Serious Fraud Office

The SFO was created under the Criminal Justice Act 1987 ('the 1987 Act), in response to the findings of the Roskill Report.[7] The report recommended that a new, multidisciplinary organisation be set up with responsibility for the detection, investigation and prosecution of serious

[6] Serious Crime Act 2007, s. 45.

[7] Lord Roskill, *Fraud Trials Committee Report* (London: The Stationery Office, 1986) (HL 471).

fraud cases in the United Kingdom. Since its inauguration, the SFO has investigated and prosecuted some of the biggest cases of fraud and corruption in British history.

The SFO can itself launch an inquiry without a referral if there is reason to believe that a serious or complex fraud has been committed. To that end, fraud includes corruption and bribery. The key criteria for accepting a case are whether the investigation should be in the hands of those responsible for the prosecution; whether the SFO's unique powers are required; if there is a need for international assistance; where significant reputational damage is at stake; or where the monies at risk are at least £1 million. (In foreign bribery cases, this figure is applied to the size of a contract obtained through bribery, not just the amount of the bribe.) Where an allegation does not appear likely to meet the discretionary SFO criteria for investigation, the SFO will, where appropriate, send the case directly to the OACU, who will then use the CPS to prosecute cases.

No complaint is required if an investigation is to be opened. A press article is not sufficient on its own to open an investigation, but it can lead to the opening of an investigation. Once the SFO Intelligence Unit sees or receives notice of a press article, steps are taken to verify the nature of the allegation. Once it is substantiated, it is general practice to open a vetting/preliminary investigation file. Preliminary enquiries are then undertaken to ascertain whether there are reasonable grounds to believe that an offence has been committed and whether it is appropriate to begin a formal enquiry. These steps would include contact with an overseas authority, for intelligence and under formal mutual legal assistance (MLA) requests.

Under section 2 of the 1987 Act, the SFO director may issue a written notice requiring a person under investigation or any other person to provide any relevant information or documents. Failure to comply with a notice without reasonable excuse is an offence, and may also result in the issuance of a search warrant. Section 2 powers were extended in 2007 to the vetting stage in foreign bribery cases. When deciding whether to formally open a foreign bribery investigation, the SFO director may gather additional information via section 2 notices if he or she considers it expedient to do so. Thus, the SFO has significantly greater power than the police to obtain documents in foreign bribery cases.[8]

[8] The police operate under the constraints of s. 9 of the Police and Criminal Evidence Act 1984.

The United Kingdom accepts requests for assistance from overseas criminal courts or tribunals, overseas prosecutors or any other overseas authority that makes requests for assistance in criminal cases. For the period 2007–2010 the SFO accepted nearly 150 new requests for assistance involving over 100 countries. The work of international assistance done by the SFO has largely been unheralded, but it is of huge importance because a lot of this assistance has a UK connection or nexus. It is also one of the main contributors to the SFO having a worldwide reputation for excellence with other law enforcement agencies.

Richard Alderman's term as director from 2008 to 2012 saw the main thrust of the SFO's approach (called 'Outreach') changing in order to reach out to business, to listen to their concerns and to do something about them. To work with business, in other words, not against it, has meant the SFO placing a huge emphasis on raising awareness, and on education, persuasion, and, ultimately, prevention. The SFO seeks to help and support ethical corporates who are determined to have an anti-corruption culture in their organisations. The SFO can advise them on their approach to an anti-corruption culture, and on their internal procedures, and it can discuss issues concerning their business. The SFO recognises that ethical businesses will sometimes run into difficulties when, despite their best intentions, they find that corruption has taken place. Alderman has rightly said that it is the role of the SFO to try to find satisfactory, sensible and commercial solutions to problems with corruption, so that an ethical corporate can put the past behind it and move on. This is the SFO's approach to self-reporting cases of corruption. The SFO published details concerning corporate self-referrals on their website in 2008. There is a strong indicator that 'ethical businesses running into difficulties' will not be prosecuted.

The other aspect to the approach is to come down very vigorously on those corporates who continue to behave corruptly, and who see such behaviour as enabling them to gain a business benefit. When I left in January 2011, there were around fifteen ongoing bribery investigations within a designated corruption division, each allocated to an interdisciplinary team of investigators, lawyers, accountants and IT specialists. This interdisciplinary approach has been a both key strength and a key factor that marks the SFO out from other enforcers. The common focus for bribery investigations over the last ten years has been the extractive industries, construction, armaments, government procurement, aid-funded programmes and pharmaceuticals.

Until 2008, there were no successful prosecutions of corporates for overseas bribery. However, since 2008, over £100 million has been recovered by the SFO, of which two-thirds were proceeds of crime (civil recovery orders) or ex gratia payments. Notable outcomes (which all pre-date the 2010 Act) include:

- Macmillan Publishers: civil recovery order £11.264 million (July 2011);
- De Puy: civil recovery order £4.8 million (April 2011);
- M. W. Kellogg: £7 million civil recovery order (February 2011);
- Charles Forsyth, twenty-one months' imprisonment; David Mabey, eight months; Richard Gledhill (cooperating accomplice) eight months, suspended/disqualification from directorship (February 2011);
- BAE Systems plc: £500,000 fine/£29.28 million compensation (December 2010);
- Julian Messent: twenty-one months' imprisonment/£100,000 compensation (October 2010);
- Robert Dougall: twelve-month suspended sentence (April 2010);
- Innospec Ltd: global settlement with SEC/US$12.7 million fine (March 2010);
- Amec: £4.9 million civil recovery order (October 2009);
- Mabey & Johnson Ltd: £6.6 million fine (September 2008);
- Balfour Beatty plc: £2.25 million civil recovery order (October 2008).

The M. W. Kellogg case concerned an innocent company that was about to be paid tainted dividends by a US company. Civil recovery orders (which the SFO could use only from April 2008) are applicable to any property that has been obtained by unlawful conduct anywhere in the world. So far, SFO orders have concerned property that is, or is about to be, in the United Kingdom, and UK incorporated companies.[9] While there are undoubted practical difficulties in obtaining such an order against property and persons outside the United Kingdom, the message for investors is to beware where they place their investments, and to try to ensure that there are appropriate anti-corruption measures in place.

Financial Services Authority

The Financial Services Authority (FSA) is (or was) an independent non-governmental body with statutory powers under the Financial Services

[9] On civil recovery orders, see further Alldridge, Chapter 8, this volume.

and Markets Act 2000 ('the 2000 Act'). It is a company limited by guarantee and financed by the financial services industry. At the time of writing, government policy appeared to be split over whether to transfer its main functions in relation to the 2000 Act to the Bank of England and create a Consumer Protection Agency.

The key objectives of the FSA (which will remain for some body) are:

- market confidence: maintaining confidence in the financial system;
- public awareness: promoting public understanding of the financial system;
- consumer protection: securing the appropriate degree of protection for consumers;
- reducing financial crime: reducing the extent to which it is possible for a business to be used with financially criminal intent.

The SFO engages with the FSA Enforcement regularly on cases that have been referred to the FSA and which may also involve bribery. This requires both organisations to agree a course of action to ensure that cases are dealt with in the most appropriate way by the most appropriate body. Both agencies regularly exchange information and intelligence.

Through its developed investigatory techniques, advanced powers and enhanced cooperation with overseas agencies, the FSA has access to a significant variety and volume of information. The FSA uses a transaction monitoring system ('Sabre') to identify and monitor unusual financial transactions and identify cases of potential market abuse. Following such investigations, a decision is made on whether there has been a breach of FSA rules and/or principles, and if so, whether to take a regulatory or criminal path to prosecution. The two dominant criminal charges of 'insider dealing' and 'misleading the market' are laid out in the Market Abuse Directive (MAD), under section 118(7) of the 2000 Act. However, civil or criminal action is not an inevitable consequence of an FSA investigation, and in recent years approximately half of the FSA's cases have been concluded without the use of its coercive powers. Private warnings have been deemed sufficient outcomes in a number of cases.[10]

Bribery allegations have been dealt with under Principle 3, 'Management and Control' in the FSA *Handbook of Principles for Businesses*: a firm must organise and control its affairs effectively. It is worth looking in more detail at the FSA's approach to regulating bribery-related issues.

[10] On the regulatory approach to bribery in the United Kingdom, see Horder, Chapter 7, this volume.

On 8 January 2009, the FSA fined Aon Ltd £5.25 million for failing to take reasonable care to establish and maintain effective systems and controls to counter the risks of bribery and corruption associated with making payments to overseas firms and individuals. Margaret Cole, FSA Director of Enforcement, said:

> It sends a clear message to the UK financial services industry that it is completely unacceptable for firms to conduct business overseas without having in place appropriate anti-bribery and corruption systems and controls … The involvement of UK financial institutions in corrupt or potentially corrupt practices overseas undermines the integrity of the UK financial services sector. The FSA has an important role to play in the steps being taken by the UK to combat overseas bribery and corruption. We have worked closely with other law enforcement agencies in this case and will continue to take robust action focused on firms' systems and controls in this area.[11]

Aon Ltd cooperated fully with the FSA and agreed to settle at an early stage of the FSA's investigation. The firm qualified for a 30 per cent discount under the FSA's settlement discount scheme.

In 2010, the FSA fined Willis Ltd £6.895 million for failings in its anti-bribery and anti-corruption systems and controls. These failings had created an unacceptable risk that payments made by Willis Ltd to overseas third parties could be used for corrupt purposes. The FSA investigation found that, up until August 2008, Willis Ltd had been guilty of a number of failings: it had failed to ensure that it established and recorded an adequate commercial rationale to support its payments to overseas third parties; it had not ensured that adequate due diligence was carried out on overseas third parties to evaluate the risk involved in doing business with them; and it had not adequately reviewed its relationships on a regular basis to confirm whether it was still necessary and appropriate for Willis Ltd to continue with the relationship. These failures contributed to a weak control environment surrounding payments to overseas third parties, and gave rise to an unacceptable risk that these payments could be used for corrupt purposes, including the payment of bribes.[12]

[11] See www.fsa.gov.uk/pages/Library/Communication/PR/2009/004.shtml.

[12] In May 2010, the FSA published the results of its useful thematic review into the adequacy of the systems and controls in place at a number of commercial insurance intermediary firms for preventing illicit payments and inducements particularly through the use of overseas third parties, available at: www.fsa.gov.uk/pubs/anti_bribery.pdf.

City of London Police

The City of London Police has 'lead force' status for economic crime, including corruption. This is run through its Economic Crime Department, which consists of 144 officers. The department has considerable expertise in dealing with fraud and is regarded as the police centre of excellence for economic crime. It has an Overseas Anti-Corruption Unit (CoLP, OACU). At present, the unit works exclusively on foreign bribery cases except in emergencies, that is, to save life and limb. It supports all foreign bribery investigations conducted by the SFO except those assigned to the Ministry of Defence Police (MoDP). It also conducts investigations of foreign bribery cases that the SFO has declined to investigate. The OACU has approximately twenty officers. The unit is funded by the DFID and the Department for Business Innovation and Skills (BIS). The jurisdiction of the CoLP was expanded from southeast England to the whole of England and Wales in 2008. This greatly expanded the OACU's territorial competence and largely eliminated the need to rely on local police in foreign bribery cases.

CoLP conducted the investigation leading to the first UK prosecution of a foreign bribery offence, which the CPS prosecuted in August 2008. The managing director of a UK-based company was found guilty of making corrupt payments to foreign officials, and a Ugandan Government official who received the payment was arrested in London and also convicted.[13]

Serious and Organised Crime Agency/National Crime Agency

The Serious Organised Crime Agency (SOCA) is an executive non-departmental intelligence-led agency with law enforcement powers and harm reduction responsibilities including corruption, due to be replaced by the National Crime Agency (NCA). On the creation of this new agency, in 2011 Theresa May said:

> For too long we have lacked a strong, collaborative national response in the fight for criminal justice, with a fragmented approach to policy, prevention and investigation. It is time for a fresh start. By creating a powerful new body of operational crime fighters – the National Crime Agency (NCA) – we will confront the serious and organised criminality that threatens the safety and security of the UK … The NCA will work in

[13] *R.* v. *Tobiasen & Tumukunde*, unreported, 2008.

> partnership with the police, law enforcement agencies, businesses and the public to ensure those who commit serious and organised crime are tracked down, pursued, brought to justice and their ill-gotten gains are stripped away.[14]

The NCA will answer to the Home Secretary and will be made up of four distinct crime teams: Organised Crime, Border Policing, Economic Crime and the Child Exploitation and Online Protection Centre. It will employ investigators, enforcement officers, intelligence analysts and technical, financial and operational specialists. Subject to the passing of the necessary legislation, the NCA is expected to be operational by December 2013.

Crown Prosecution Service

The Crown Prosecution Service (CPS) is a prosecuting agency independent of government that does no investigating itself. Generally, the police via the designated CoLP or a regional police force will seek advice on prosecutions or, where necessary, on Civil Recovery Orders under Part 5 of the Proceeds of Crime Act 2002. The Ministry of Defence (MoD) or the Department for Innovation, Business and Skills may also seek similar input from the CPS into their investigations. The CPS has no designated central unit dealing with bribery. Bribery with an element of serious public corruption will usually be dealt with by the Serious Crime and Counter Terrorism Division. Bribery with an element of serious fraud will probably be dealt with by the CPS Fraud Division. Any bribery case outside these will be dealt with by complex casework units in local areas. No other CPS area unit is permitted to deal with offences under the 2010 Act.

The CPS prosecuted the first case under the Bribery Act against a court clerk, who received three years' imprisonment for accepting a bribe.[15] He also received six years' imprisonment for misconduct in public office.

The Ministry of Defence

The Ministry of Defence Police investigate foreign bribery cases involving MoD employees or defence contracts to which the MoD is a party. As

[14] See www.homeoffice.gov.uk/crime/nca.

[15] *R.* v. *Munir Patel*, unreported, 18 November 2011.

such, it supported the SFO in the Al Yamamah case.[16] Foreign bribery investigations are conducted by the MoDP's Economic Crime Unit and are funded from the existing MoD budget.

Metropolitan Police

A Proceeds-of-Crime Team within the Metropolitan Police ('the Met') investigates and recovers money laundered through the UK financial system by politically exposed persons. The unit provides useful information to foreign bribery investigations. The SFO may also ask SOCA to perform tasks that can be done more effectively or efficiently by a central agency, or where SOCA has competencies or knowledge not widely available elsewhere. The Met, with the CPS, have done considerable good work in investigating an ex-governor of Nigeria, James Ibori,[17] and his family for money laundering and fraud.

Resourcing

The difference in funding for the SFO and the FSA is now marked. The SFO's budget will shrink from just over £50 million in 2009 to just under £30 million by 2014. Moreover, the SFO no longer has access to Treasury-sponsored separate budgeting for 'blockbuster' cases. The separate budgeting had been a tradition of the SFO for a number of years up until 2009 (despite the unusual nature of the financial arrangement). Separate budgeting gave flexibility, and gave the SFO the appetite to take on huge, voluminous cases, the cost of investigating and prosecuting which its normal budget could not withstand. For example, the Oil for Food investigations[18] were all initially funded via this route in 2006 at an average of around an extra £10 million per year until 2010. By 2014 the budget will have nearly halved in real terms. In the same period, FSA enforcement has seen an increase of 50 per cent, so that by 2010 it had, for the first time, a bigger budget than the SFO.

[16] See www.sfo.gov.uk/press-room/latest-press-releases/press-releases-2008/baesaudi-defence-contract-house-of-lords-ruling-on-the-discontinued-investigation.aspx.

[17] Convicted in the United Kingdom in February 2012 for money laundering and conspiracy to defraud. For a more detailed discussion, see Chapter 11.

[18] See www.sfo.gov.uk/press-room/latest-press-releases/press-releases-2011/united-nations-sanctions-breaker-jailed.aspx.

Absence of sentencing guidelines

Although the maximum sentence for bribery increased from seven to ten years as a result of the 2010 Act, we still await sentencing guidelines. The absence of a clear, comprehensive frame work is a major deterrent to companies to contemplating admitting to any wrongdoing, because they do not know what the level of fines are likely to be. We await Sentencing Council guidelines for bribery with bated breath, but there is a need for proper corporate sentencing guidelines.

Plea discussions

Plea negotiation has actually been a long-established feature of the criminal justice system; indeed, without it there would not be the high percentage (over 60 per cent) of guilty pleas that we currently have. A comparable percentage is lacking in corruption and bribery cases. When I first arrived at the SFO, the guilty plea rate was around half the national average. Suspects generally know that they can claim up to a third off any sentence for an early guilty plea, plus another third depending on the level of cooperation and help provided. A difference of two to three years in prison may make a difference, but it is unlikely to matter that much. Staying out of prison altogether is much more of an incentive that will influence lesser offenders more. For companies the problem is more acute, because no one knows at what level the fine should be pitched. There can be no navigation through uncharted waters. Companies and their advisers therefore have no idea what discounts or incentives might lead to, although the biggest incentive is not to be prosecuted, which is where self-reporting might prove advantageous.

The potential for deferred prosecution agreements (DPA), if legal in the United Kingdom, faces similar problems. I see another issue on DPAs concerning the degree of culpability to which the company is prepared to admit. In the United States, this can be a grey area and has been subject of judicial criticism recently. It also begs an interesting question: if the company has to admit to offending to get a DPA, what exactly is being deferred: the full extent of their culpability? What are they being sentenced for?

The prosecution of legal persons is an issue that few other countries have to deal with because, outside the United Kingdom and United States, corporate criminal offending is largely dealt with by administrative fine. In non-US/UK jurisdictions, there is never the fear of the nuclear option: mandatory debarment upon conviction.[19] This raises the question of whether we should be prosecuting companies at all. What is the point when they can be fined and debarred through an administrative process without need of a conviction? Their reputation will still take a hit. What to do with corporate offending that is too serious to deal with through a regulatory, administrative process is the issue.

Global implications

On a more positive note, interest has been shown by international corporates in compliance with the 2010 Act. One could see that those carrying on business in the United Kingdom might have a vested interest in having adequate procedures to prevent bribery, as (in effect) required under the 2010 Act. What has been really encouraging and exciting is the number of corporates who do not carry on business in the United Kingdom, but who are developing adequate procedures. This is not just because the adequate procedures are a gold standard of corporate anti-bribery measures. It is also because: (a) the companies are finding that their values are suffering a negative impact unless they have adequate procedures; and (b) they are finding it more costly to trade, to do business, to carry out transactions – with higher insurance banking and transactional costs – because such higher costs are associated with those that lack anti-corruption procedures.

When I first started attending OECD meetings in 2005 there were fifty global investigations into bribery. Now, there are nearly 400, involving the enforcement agencies of over forty countries. There is routine sharing of intelligence and information across the globe. Investigation priorities are usually determined on a practical basis: the country where the evidence lies is usually best placed to lead an investigation, but much still depends upon the capacity and resources of each country's enforcing agency. Moreover, I wonder if the potential availability of millions, especially where proceeds of crime are concerned, might not prove a dysfunctional factor. It will be interesting to see different enforcers' assessments on civil recovery or its equivalent (if available).

19 Directive 2004/18/EC, OJ 2004 No. L134, 30 April 2004, Art. 45, although there is increasing use of discretionary debarment. See the World Bank and Macmillan, available at: www.sfo.gov.uk/press-room/latest-press-releases/press-releases-2011/action-on-macmillan-publishers-limited.aspx.

As civil recovery requires no prosecution, *ne bis in idem* or double jeopardy does not apply, and while the UK enforcer might recognise public interest or equitable justice, other enforcers might not. So far, the SFO has secured civil recovery orders against UK incorporated companies where the proceeds lie in the United Kingdom. However, where overseas jurisdictions are concerned, practical difficulties may determine that the country where the unlawful conduct has taken place takes precedence in that respect: and it may simply refuse to cooperate where the enforcer needs to show that unlawful conduct in the United Kingdom is of a similar type. This will impact on global settlements, which will remain difficult to achieve.[20] In future, I suspect corporations will frequently have to deal with at least three different enforcers from three different countries: the United States, the United Kingdom and the country where the bribe occurs.

Conclusion

Some have expressed surprise that there have as yet been no prosecutions or settlements under the 2010 Act. It is not surprising. The average length of an SFO investigation is at least eighteen months. Moreover, for the 2006 Act section 7 offence of failing to prevent bribery, I do not expect many enforcement challenges to the adequacy of procedures, unless they are plainly or woefully inadequate or missing altogether. The relevant company will probably just have to hand over the guilty individuals, together with any proceeds of crime, pay a regulatory fine (if applicable) and adjust its procedures accordingly. There may be a focus on non-UK companies. However, extracting relevant evidence from a non-UK company with few assets in the United Kingdom will prove challenging. Although there is a very good UK government strategy for overseas corruption, one is lacking for UK domestic corruption. It may well be that such a strategy is impossible until the make-up of the various enforcement agencies is more certain. This could be an instance in which a tail-wagging-the-dog policy can surely lead the way.

The practical difficulties of joining regulators with prosecutors are likely to be the factor that ends the possibility of an Economic Crime

[20] To date, the *Innospec* case remains the only truly global settlement case with US and UK enforcers and courts trying to work together: see www.sfo.gov.uk/press-room/latest-press-releases/press-releases-2010/innospec-limited-prosecuted-for-corruption-by-the-sfo.aspx.

Agency, not least on the grounds of cost. The emergence of the NCA and the threat to swallow up the SFO is a risk: is the NCA old wine (SOCA) in new bottles? I would not want to see the SFO disappear into the NCA, because there is a danger that the investigation of bribery will be given a much lower priority, and the separation of the investigatory and prosecutorial functions may also have an adverse impact on law enforcement.

The appointment of a new director of the SFO in April 2012, Sir David Green, appears to express some confidence in the future of the SFO. Far more problematic for the SFO is the chronic lack of funding, amounting to a 40 per cent reduction in real terms. For all the good work that has been done in the last three years (with the United Kingdom shooting up to second place in the OECD enforcement table), it would be a shame if the 2010 Act's excellent framework could not be properly tested due to lack of resources.

10

Prosecuting bribery in Hong Kong's human rights environment

SIMON N. M. YOUNG*

Introduction

Hong Kong was one of the earliest common law jurisdictions to enact comprehensive modern bribery laws.[1] For this reason alone, it was surprising that the Law Commission's reports on bribery did not refer to the Hong Kong experience. The omission is likely explained by aspects of Hong Kong's bribery laws, which the Law Commission refrained from adopting, such as the agent–principal paradigm and separation of public and private bribery.[2] This chapter will not try to defend a superior Hong Kong approach to substantive law. Instead, it will focus on enforcing bribery laws, a topic which was not given special attention in the Bribery Act 2010. Hong Kong has close to forty years of experience in enforcing anti-corruption laws, including two decades of enforcement in a human rights environment with an entrenched bill of rights, robust independent judiciary and increasingly open society.

Established in 1974, Hong Kong's Independent Commission Against Corruption (ICAC) is regarded as one of the world's most successful anti-corruption agencies.[3] It cured the serious ills of public corruption

* I thank Bryan Chan for his research assistance and Michael Blanchflower and Allan Bell for their comments on an earlier draft

[1] The relevant history of these laws is described in I. McWalters, *Bribery and Corruption Law in Hong Kong*, 2nd edn (Hong Kong: LexisNexis, 2010), pp. 19–34.

[2] See Prevention of Bribery Ordinance (Cap. 201), originally Ord. 102 of 1970, in force 14 May 1971; B. Downey, 'Combating Corruption: The Hong Kong Solution', *Hong Kong Law Journal*, 6 (1976), 27–66.

[3] See Independent Commission Against Corruption Ordinance (Cap. 204), originally Ord. 7 of 1974, in force 15 February 1974. On the achievements of the ICAC, see McWalters, *Bribery and Corruption Law in Hong Kong*, pp. 76–133; J. S. T. Quah, *Curbing Corruption in Asia: A Comparative Study of Six Countries* (Singapore: Eastern Universities Press, 2003), pp. 129–49; A. Neoh, 'An Impartial and Uncorrupted Civil Service: Hong Kong's

that had plagued Hong Kong society for decades up to the early 1980s.[4] It is seen as a leader in interdicting corruption in the private sector. Its greatest impact has probably come from its far-reaching educational and prevention work, giving it a ubiquitous presence in the community from kindergarten classrooms to prime-time television to corporate boardrooms.[5] As part of the 1997 resumption of sovereignty, it was given a special protected status in Hong Kong's constitution, the Basic Law.[6]

In recent years, however, it has been experiencing a growing public confidence crisis. Its officers were found by courts to have violated fundamental rights of residents. With graphic scenes of police officers surrounding the ICAC building, several ICAC officers were arrested and charged with attempting to pervert the course of justice. The courts have become more critical of ICAC operations and practices, and the public has questioned whether the level of corruption today still justifies the scale of ICAC's size and annual budget. There were also concerns over how the agency was to fill a growing number of vacancies in senior posts.

The confidence crisis is largely explained by the socio-political changes that have taken place in Hong Kong since 1997. As Hong Kong moves towards greater democratic self-government, its people have become more critical of their government and insistent on greater openness, accountability and integrity in government officials. With the vibrant culture of free expression protected, public protest has become commonplace. The judiciary's strong approach to constitutional review has also made people more rights conscious, and in turn increasingly more rights demanding. The human rights culture that developed in Hong Kong runs counter to many of the elements that made the ICAC effective in its glorious past. This chapter argues that in order to regain the public's

Fight Against Corruption in the Past 34 Years', in C. Forsyth, M. Elliott, S. Jhaveri, A. Scully-Hill and M. Ramsden (eds), *Effective Judicial Review: A Cornerstone of Good Governance* (Oxford University Press, 2010), pp. 217–242; B. de Speville, 'Anticorruption Commissions: The "The Hong Kong Model" Revisited', *Asia-Pacific Review*, 17 (2010), 47–71.

[4] See E. Tu, *Colonial Hong Kong in the Eyes of Elsie Tu* (Hong Kong University Press, 2003), pp. 119–20.

[5] See Donald's discussion of some of these initiatives in Chapter 3 of this volume; T. Kwok, 'Formulating an Effective Anti-Corruption Strategy: The Experience of Hong Kong ICAC', in UNAFEI, *Annual Report for 2005 and Resource Material Series No. 69* (Tokyo: UNAFEI, 2006), pp. 196–201.

[6] Article 57 of the Basic Law provides as follows: 'A Commission Against Corruption shall be established in the Hong Kong Special Administrative Region. It shall function independently and be accountable to the Chief Executive.'

confidence and overcome the current crisis, the ICAC needs to re-examine its current approach to operational work in the light of current societal values and expectations. It needs to inculcate and promote a human rights culture in its operational work and insist upon the highest standards of integrity among its staff. After all, the ICAC Code of Ethics requires officers at all times to 'uphold the good name of the Commission', 'adhere to the principles of integrity and fair play' and 'respect the rights under the law of all people'.[7] The chapter begins with an examination of the current crisis of confidence.

Crisis of confidence

The past decade has seen an escalating amount of critical media coverage of the ICAC and its operations. In 2002, there were stories reporting on the criticism by the Hong Kong police of the premature arrest of Sin Kam Wah, a senior vice officer later convicted of misconduct in public office for receiving sex from prostitutes.[8] Next, there were the continuous reports over several years of court decisions and judges criticising individual ICAC officers for their tactics and misconduct. The cumulative effect of these criticisms is reflected in recent news stories. With headlines such as 'Clean up your act, lawmakers warn', 'ICAC's questionable acts under fire for years', 'ICAC committed five blunders and close to collapse', criticisms are being made of the institution itself.[9] While overall public support for the ICAC appears to be high,[10] there is a growing sense of distrust with the means by which the ICAC carries out its work and a perception that its operational capacity is weakening.

[7] See ICAC Code of Ethics, available at: www.icac.org.hk/en/about_icac/mp/index.html.

[8] M. Joanilho, 'Police Blast ICAC over Arrests', *South China Morning Post*, 20 May 2002, p. 1; *Sin Kam Wah* v. *HKSAR* (2005) 8 HKCFAR 192.

[9] M. Wong, 'ICAC's Questionable Acts under Fire for Years', *South China Morning Post*, 20 November 2010, p. 2; C. Lee and N. Wong, 'Clean up Your Act, Lawmakers Warn', *The Standard*, 29 June 2010; H. Kei, 'CCB Rushed into the Headquarters to Arrest Three; ICAC Committed Five Blunders and Close to Collapse', *Hong Kong Economic Journal*, 20 November 2010, p. 10.

[10] See, e.g., ICAC's Annual Survey data, available at: www.icac.org.hk/en/useful_information/sd/sd/index.html. In 2010, 97.1 per cent of those surveyed believed the ICAC deserved their support, see ICAC Community Relations Department, *ICAC Annual Survey 2010 Executive Summary*, Table C, available at: sc.icac.org.hk/TuniS/www.icac.org.hk/en/useful_information/sd/sd/index.html

Using illegitimate means to achieve ends

The ICAC is known not only as an aggressive and uncompromising law enforcement body, but also one whose officers are over-zealous and prepared to use unlawful or improper means to achieve their ends.

Invading privacy

The perception is strongest in relation to their covert operations, which take place without the usual degree of public scrutiny of government action. The 2006 judicial review case of *Leung Kwok Hung* v. *Chief Executive* exposed the unconstitutionality of past covert operations interfering with privacy rights of individuals.[11] The case held that the statutory power to intercept private telecommunications, exercised by the chief executive on the sole ground of 'public interest', violated the constitutional principle of legal certainty.[12] It also held that all other forms of covert surveillance had no legal basis; an executive order of the chief executive, being only an administrative measure, did not have the quality of prescribed law capable of restricting a fundamental right.[13] A new legislative scheme was necessary if law enforcement was to continue its covert activities. The court, however, suspended its remedial orders to give the government six months to enact the legislative scheme, during which time covert operations could continue without being in breach of the judicial orders.[14]

The result in *Leung Kwok Hung* was not a surprise to the government. In December 1996, the Law Reform Commission of Hong Kong reported that the chief executive's interception power was in violation of the Hong Kong Bill of Rights and recommended reform to ensure greater protection against interferences with privacy.[15] Before the handover on 1 July 1997, legislators passed an interception law to introduce a scheme of prior judicial authorisation for wiretapping, but the government,

[11] *Leung Kwok Hung* v. *Chief Executive of HKSAR* [2006] HKEC 239 (CFI), aff'd [2006] HKEC 816 (CA). Privacy rights are protected by Arts 29 and 30 of the Basic Law and Art. 14 of the Hong Kong Bill of Rights, being Part II of the Hong Kong Bill of Rights Ordinance (Cap. 383).

[12] *Leung Kwok Hung* v. *Chief Executive of HKSAR* [2006] HKEC 239 (CFI), 126–127.

[13] *Leung Kwok Hung* v. *Chief Executive of HKSAR* [2006] HKEC 239 (CFI), 151. See also S. N. M. Young, 'The Executive Order on Covert Surveillance: Legality Undercover?', *Hong Kong Law Journal*, 35 (2005), 265–76.

[14] *Koo Sze Yiu* v. *Chief Executive of HKSAR* (2006) 9 HKCFAR 441.

[15] Law Reform Commission of Hong Kong, *Report on Privacy: Regulating the Interception of Communications* (December 1996), p. 39.

particularly law enforcement agencies, resisted bringing this law into force.[16] Then the government worked at a slow pace in coming up with an alternative proposal.[17] Only after the Court of Final Appeal (CFA) affirmed the six-month deadline in 2006 did the reform process accelerate and a new surveillance law materialise.[18]

The Interception of Communications and Surveillance Ordinance came into force on 9 August 2006.[19] The Ordinance prohibits interception or surveillance by government agents unless authorised under the legislation, typically by authorisation of a panel judge, or an authorising officer of high seniority in cases of less intrusive surveillance.[20] It established the office of Commissioner of Interception of Communications and Surveillance, held by a former Court of Appeal judge, Justice Woo Kwok-hing, since 2006.[21] The Commissioner's annual reports disclose the number of fresh and renewed authorisation applications issued annually: 1,785 (2007); 1,924 (2008); 1989 (2009); 1,490 (2010).[22] The vast majority of authorisations were for interception rather than other forms of surveillance. Such figures were never made public in the past.[23] They indicate the extensive degree of privacy intrusions by law enforcement both before and after the statutory scheme.[24]

[16] See Interception of Communications Ordinance (Cap. 532), originally Ord. 109 of 1997, passed on 27 June 1997 and history described in *Leung Kwok Hung* v. *Chief Executive of HKSAR* [2006] HKEC 239 (CFI), 27–32.

[17] See Security Bureau, 'Review on Interception of Communication', paper for Legislative Council (LegCo) Panel on Security, LC Paper No. CB(2)1873/03-04(04) (Hong Kong Legislative Council, March 2004).

[18] The Law Reform Commission of Hong Kong also published a report on covert surveillance in the six-month suspension period, see *Privacy: The Regulation of Covert Surveillance* (March 2006).

[19] Interception of Communications and Surveillance Ordinance (Cap. 589), originally Ord. 20 of 2006 (ICSO).

[20] Interception of Communications and Surveillance Ordinance, ss. 4–24.

[21] Interception of Communications and Surveillance Ordinance, s. 39.

[22] Partial year data from the Annual Report 2006 not included. See Annual Summaries and Reports accessible on the website of the Secretariat, Commissioner on Interception of Communications and Surveillance at: www.info.gov.hk/info/sciocs/eng. Figures taken from ch. 3 of the 2007–2010 Annual Summaries.

[23] See N. H. Wah, 'Remedies Against Telephone Tapping by the Government', *Hong Kong Law Journal*, 33 (2003), 543–66.

[24] See the comparison with usage in New Zealand and Canada in the Hong Kong Bar Association's submission to LegCo, 'Comments of the Bar Association on the Interception of Communication and Surveillance Ordinance (Cap. 589)', LC Paper No. CB(2)529/11-12(01), (Hong Kong Legislative Council, 9 September 2011), pp. 61–9.

More critically, the annual reports also revealed many instances of ICAC and other law enforcement officers acting in breach of the Ordinance.[25] The detailed reports narrate attempts by the ICAC and others to avoid or minimise scrutiny by the Commissioner or panel judges. Law enforcement argued that panel judges did not have the power to revoke an authorisation even where there were legal privilege concerns;[26] that the Commissioner had no power to listen to the intercepted product;[27] and that officers were required to destroy the recordings and other materials, even when specifically asked by the Commissioner to retain them.[28] To further frustrate, the Commissioner found that materials when provided were so heavily sanitised as to prevent proper oversight.[29] In a 2011 interview, Justice Woo attributed the lack of cooperation to a history of non-regulation:

> They were not very willing to cooperate, yet dared not to not cooperate. Although I have the authority to ask questions, I felt they did not give me complete answers. I guess it was because they were not under regulation in the past. They were unhappy coming under regulation when the law came into being. They were also unhappy for having to do a lot of corrective work when I pointed out their irregularities.[30]

Violating legal professional privilege

The Commissioner's annual reports also document many instances of unauthorised recording of privileged communication by the ICAC.[31] This may reflect a previous cavalier attitude towards confidential lawyer–client communication, a right specifically protected under the Basic Law.[32] The interference with privilege in the *Wong Hung Ki* case

25 See, e.g., J. But, 'Head of Snooping Watchdog Hits Out at Law Enforcers', *South China Morning Post*, 8 December 2009, p. 3; 'Phone Tapping Mistakes Must Not be Glossed Over', *Sing Tao Daily*, 3 December 2009, p. F7; ICAC, 'Information Paper by the ICAC in Response to Issues Raised in the Report', paper for LegCo Panel on Security, LC Paper No. CB(2)467/09-10(01), (Hong Kong: ICAC, 4 December 2009).

26 See Annual Report 2007, paras [5.15]–[5.28], [10.27].

27 See Annual Report 2007, paras [5.88]–[5.90]; Annual Report 2008, paras [5.20]–[5.35]; Annual Report 2009, paras [5.77]–[5.79]; Annual Report 2010, para. [1.4].

28 See Annual Report 2007, paras [5.45]–[5.48], [5.53]–[5.58], [5.71], [5.91]–[5.97], [10.24], [10.27]–[10.29]; Annual Report 2010, paras [5.13]–[5.18], [5.67], [8.8].

29 See Annual Report 2007, paras [4.22]–[4.24], [12.7].

30 J. Li, 'A Mission to Protect', *China Daily (Peak View)*, 29 July 2011, available at http://pub.chinadailyapac.com/peakview/figures/201201/103.html.

31 See generally ch. 5 of the 2007–2010 Annual Reports, n. 22, above.

32 Article 35 of the Basic Law provides that 'Hong Kong residents shall have the right to confidential legal advice'.

was especially alarming.[33] ICAC knowingly arranged an informant to record a privileged communication between a defendant and his two solicitors in a public restaurant in November 2002. Five days later, the ICAC officers listened to the privileged conversation with the informant who used the recording to prepare a detailed witness statement. In accordance with policy, the recordings were destroyed and not to be used as evidence.

In 2011, the Court of Appeal found the deliberate breaches of the right to confidential legal advice so egregious as to amount to an abuse of process requiring the charges against all the defendants to be permanently stayed.[34] Even the charges of those defendants who were not present at the meeting were stayed because they could no longer have a fair trial without disclosure of the destroyed intercepted communication, which could have materially aided their cross-examination of the informant.[35] Justice Stock made the following critical comments:

> The evidence in this case displayed on the part of the ICAC officers who took the key decisions, particularly the decision to listen to the recorded conversation, either a cavalier approach to privileged communications or a failure to appreciate the nature and importance of the principle. It matters not which it was, for if it was the latter, it is a failure on a fundamental issue which cannot be countenanced in the case of a law enforcement authority operating in a society governed by the rule of law.[36]

The affront to the rule of law was such that in respect of one of the co-defendants who had pled guilty to the charges, the Court of Appeal set aside the guilty plea and entered a stay of proceedings.[37]

Witness coaching

ICAC practices in relation to prosecution witnesses have given rise to significant public concerns in recent years. As witnesses rarely come forward on their own in corruption cases, the ICAC has strategies to induce individuals to betray co-conspirators and become witnesses, usually with the promise of immunity from prosecution. Having divided

[33] *HKSAR* v. *Wong Hung Ki* [2011] 1 HKLRD 183 (CA).
[34] *HKSAR* v. *Wong Hung Ki* [2011] 1 HKLRD 183 (CA).
[35] *HKSAR* v. *Wong Hung Ki* [2011] 1 HKLRD 183 (CA), at para. [95].
[36] *HKSAR* v. *Wong Hung Ki* [2011] 1 HKLRD 183 (CA), at para. [94].
[37] *HKSAR* v. *Shum Chiu* [2011] 2 HKLRD 746 (CA).

their loyalties and concerned that they may later recant, investigators take steps to ensure that they testify consistently with their statements. This involves what is euphemistically known as the ICAC's memory refreshing exercises. Such exercises involve multiple meetings during which the witness' statement is repeatedly read back to the witness, who is trained to memorise his or her evidence. The courts have condemned these practices and held that they should stop.[38] In *HKSAR* v. *Tse Tat Fung*, the Court of Appeal held that:

> what they must not do is go further and put words into the witness's mouth or subvert his true recollection with another version of events, whether by repetitive reading of the statement to the witness or by otherwise 'influencing' the witness so as to attempt to ensure the witness will, in evidence, simply regurgitate the contents of his statement. That is 'coaching'.[39]

The Court concluded that it was improper for the ICAC officer in this case to summarise back to the witness his statement during the course of the twenty-three hours of memory refreshing exercises done over fifteen meetings in 2007.[40]

What exactly happens at these memory refreshing sessions is rarely made known. Mr Cheung Ching-ho secretly recorded some of his meetings with the ICAC and later made them public when he was prosecuted, having decided not to cooperate with them. Cheung's recordings provide a rare glimpse into ICAC tactics in witness preparation. It was alleged that the ICAC officers in late 2009 coached Cheung on what to say in court and incited him to lie in his testimony.[41] Although the trial judge in Cheung's trial was not prepared to permanently stay his charges, he found the ICAC officers had dealt with Cheung 'in a way that was entirely unacceptable'.[42] In November 2010, around forty police officers surrounded the ICAC offices while the three ICAC officers involved in

[38] See, e.g., *HKSAR* v. *Lee Wing Kan* [2007] 3 HKC 368, at para. [67] (CA); leave to CFA refused, *Lee Wing Kan* v. *HKSAR* FAMC 28/2007, 18 September 2007, CFAAC, at para. [8].

[39] *HKSAR* v. *Tse Tat Fung*, unreported, CACC 167/2008, 13 May 2010 (CA), at para. [82].

[40] *HKSAR* v. *Tse Tat Fung*, CACC 167/2008, at para. [84].

[41] A. Chiu, 'ICAC Officers in Court for Coaching False Evidence', *South China Morning Post*, 16 March 2011, p. 4; D. Lee, 'Secret Tapes Aired in ICAC Trial', *South China Morning Post*, 3 February 2012, p. C1.

[42] M. Ng, 'Judge Decries ICAC Officers' Coaching of Witness', *South China Morning Post*, 6 May 2011.

Cheung's case were arrested.[43] The dramatic raid was front-page material in most Hong Kong newspapers, and it was said that the unprecedented action would 'deepen the long-standing tension between the two forces'.[44] The three ICAC officers were later charged and prosecuted for perverting the course of justice and misconduct in public office.[45]

It was also a secret recording by a prospective witness (Hung) that led to ICAC officer Lau Wing Tim's conviction for perjury. Lau's denial in cross-examination of threatening or inducing Hung to give a statement was unmistakably rebutted when the recording was played. In convicting Lau of perjury in April 2003, the trial judge found the effort to 'induce, threaten and mislead Hung with the aim of convincing him to divulge information' was 'grossly improper'.[46]

Material non-disclosure

The systematic practice by the ICAC of destroying records of intercepted communications has frustrated not only the Commissioner, but also defendants and their legal representatives who argue that the destroying of the records amounts to a breach of the duty of disclosure.[47] In some cases where the materiality of the destroyed records is more than merely speculative, courts have found in favour of the defence.[48]

In 2006, the conviction of a senior housing official in a serious bribery case was quashed after it was revealed that the ICAC officer, who obtained the defendant Chan Kau Tai's confession statements, failed to disclose his conviction for drink-driving and related disciplinary record.[49] The Court of Appeal found the non-disclosure significant because the information could have been used to undermine the officer's credibility, which was challenged during the *voir dire* to determine the admissibility of Chan's statements. The public followed the case closely as Chan was the father of a well-known local star and musician. The public

43 P. Tsang and C. Lo, 'Police Raid ICAC, Arrest Three Graft-Busters', *South China Morning Post*, 20 November 2010.

44 Tsang and Lo, 'Police Raid ICAC'.

45 Lee, 'Secret Tapes'. Convicted in April 2012, they received jail sentences from 18 to 30 months.

46 *HKSAR* v. *Lau Wai Tim*, unreported, CACC 152/2003, 4 Mar 2004 (CA), at para. [8].

47 Only the prosecution owes a duty of disclosure to the defence, but investigating agencies have a duty to disclose to the prosecution, see *HKSAR* v. *Lee Ming Tee* (2003) 6 HKCFAR 336, at paras [168], [179].

48 *HKSAR* v. *Wong Hung Ki* [2011] 1 HKLRD 183 (CA), at para. [95], but cf. *HKSAR* v. *Ying Jim Ming Jimmy*, unreported, HCMA432/2009, 6 May 2010 (CFI), at paras [48]–[49].

49 *HKSAR* v. *Chan Kau Tai* [2006]1 HKLRD 400 (CA), at paras [44]–[50].

wondered how a serving ICAC officer could have a criminal record and why the record was not disclosed before the 2003 trial, when previous cases, including a 2000 CFA decision, had stressed the importance of disclosing the criminal records of prosecution witnesses.[50]

Failed prosecutions

Several recent failed high profile prosecutions have shaken public confidence in the ICAC and the lawyers who advise them. The most notorious of the recent cases was the one against criminal barrister, Kevin Egan, and solicitor, Andrew Lam. Egan, Lam and two other defendants (Mandy Chiu and Derek Wong) were charged with conspiracy to pervert the course of justice in relation to an ICAC investigation into Semtech International Holdings.[51] In July 2009, Derek Wong, Chairman of Semtech, and his secretary, Becky Wong, were arrested. Derek Wong was released on bail on 11 July, while Ms Wong remained with the ICAC and would later enter their witness protection programme. In the week following Derek Wong's release, the defendants and others tried to access Ms Wong by, *inter alia*, bringing a *habeas corpus* application on the ground that she was being held against her will. The judge dismissed the application, finding that Ms Wong was not unlawfully detained. The conspiracy charge was based on the theory that the defendants wanted to reach Ms Wong to persuade her not to cooperate with the ICAC thereby having the effect of impeding the ICAC investigation and subsequent prosecution.

Lam, Chiu and Wong were convicted of the conspiracy; Egan was acquitted, but convicted of two counts of attempting to disclose to a journalist the identity of a participant in the witness protection programme. Chiu was also convicted of attempted perjury in her affirmation supporting the *habeas corpus* application. In the Court of Appeal, all the convictions were upheld with the exception of Egan's attempted disclosure offences. On further appeal by Lam, Chiu and the prosecution to the CFA, all convictions were quashed and acquittals upheld. In meticulous detail, the Court found that there was insufficient evidence to prove that Lam and Chiu had the specific intention of perverting the course of justice.[52] The Court was especially critical of the credibility of an ICAC

[50] *Ching Kwok Yin* v. *HKSAR* (2000) 3 HKCFAR 387.
[51] *HKSAR* v. *Egan* (2010) 13 HKCFAR 314.
[52] *HKSAR* v. *Egan* (2010) 13 HKCFAR 314, at paras [211], [238]–[242], [265].

paid witness (Aaron Nattrass), who claimed he had heard Lam make incriminating statements at a dinner party.[53] Egan's acquittal was upheld because the trial judge had given insufficient reasons in coming to findings on whether Ms Wong's identity as a protected witness was disclosed to the journalist and whether Egan believed she was a protected witness.[54] Following the acquittals, views circulated that the proceedings against Egan and Lam were motivated by revenge, as both defence lawyers had been a thorn in the side of the ICAC for many years.[55] However, Justice Litton in the CFA, writing for himself, found that the 'ICAC officers acted with total propriety in this case'.[56]

The second notable failed prosecution was the *Shanghai Land* case involving senior lawyers, bank officials and accountants who were accused of conspiracy to defraud and other offences.[57] The case alleged a conspiracy to assist a dishonest Shanghai businessman to acquire control of a Hong Kong publicly listed company using false statements to give the impression of compliance with the Stock Exchange's Listing Rules and the Securities and Futures Commission's Takeover Code. As in the Egan case, when finally decided by the CFA, all defendants were acquitted of all charges. Another similarity was the Court's criticism of a prosecution witness (Angela Gong) who testified under partial immunity. She was described as a 'tainted witness with a self-interest to serve and an axe to grind' and whose testimony 'had to be approached with great caution'.[58]

These were not the only occasions on which the CFA acquitted defendants prosecuted with the assistance of tainted ICAC witnesses. In 2000, the CFA acquitted Wong Pui Sham, a former superintendent of the customs and excise department.[59] The person (Siu) who allegedly gave the bribe to Wong testified for the prosecution under immunity. Siu was described as 'a dishonest businessman [who] told a quite different story on arrest from that contained in his later statements … and from his evidence at trial. He had previous convictions for dishonesty'.[60] The Court of Appeal had doubts about Siu's evidence and set aside the

[53] *HKSAR* v. *Egan* (2010) 13 HKCFAR 314, at paras [193]–[210].
[54] *HKSAR* v. *Egan* (2010) 13 HKCFAR 314, at paras [386]–[393].
[55] Lee and Wong, 'Clean Up Your Act'.
[56] *HKSAR* v. *Egan* (2010) 13 HKCFAR 314, at para. [330].
[57] *Vivien Fan* v. *HKSAR*, unreported, FACC 6/2010, 15 July 2011 (CFA).
[58] *Vivien Fan* v. *HKSAR* FACC 6/2010, at para. [71].
[59] *Wong Pui Sham* v. *HKSAR* (2000) 3 HKCFAR 449.
[60] *Wong Pui Sham* v. *HKSAR* (2000) 3 HKCFAR 449, at para. [22].

convictions for two of the three offences charged; the CFA held that since the third conviction was also dependent on Siu's credibility the conviction also had to be set aside.[61]

Another difficult case was Stephen Chan, who was then the general manager of TVB, Television Broadcasts Limited.[62] Chan and two others were charged with several counts of conspiracy to accept an advantage and conspiracy to defraud.[63] It was alleged that Chan had received undisclosed payments for hosting a Chinese New Year shopping mall event produced by TVB and for organising a book-signing event attended by TVB stars, with little or no payment, at the request of Chan. In September 2011, the District Court acquitted the defendants of all charges.[64] It was found that Chan was not an 'agent' of TVB when he 'performed' at the mall event, performing being outside the duties of a general manager. And it was not proven that TVB was unaware that Chan would receive payment for such performance. As for the book-signing event, it was not proven that Chan knew of the full payment arrangements between the companies involved, nor could it be proven that TVB had a policy to decide when its actors could appear in events of this kind. This case highlights a possible limitation of the agent–principal paradigm used to define private corruption in Hong Kong. The result also made people question whether at the outset the case for corruption or fraud was sufficiently strong enough to proceed.

Perceived weakening in operations

The failed prosecutions, including the ones lost due to officer misconduct, are a possible indication of a weakening in the operational arm of the ICAC. There are a number of other indicators that suggest weakening and raise questions about future operations. First, there was the story of Raymond Yuen's arrest and later departure from ICAC

61 *Wong Pui Sham* v. *HKSAR* (2000) 3 HKCFAR 449, at paras [46]–[52].

62 A. Nip and A. Chiu, 'TVB's Chan Cleared of Graft Charges', *South China Morning Post*, 3 September 2011, p. 1.

63 ICAC Press Release, 'TV Senior Executives and Company Director Charged for Alleged Corruption and Fraud', 16 September 2010, available at: www.icac.org.hk/en/news_and_events/pr2/index_uid_1058.html.

64 G. Jiaxue, 'Stephen Chan Found Not Guilty of Corruption Charges', *China Daily*, Hong Kong Edition, 3 September 2011, p. 1. But the prosecution's appeal was allowed in November 2012, and the case was returned to the District Court.

in April 2011.[65] Yuen was in charge of the ICAC's public sector corruption group and described as a 'rising star'.[66] He was never charged with an offence and news reports said only that he was arrested on suspicion of corruption. Unlike previous high profile sackings accompanied with some public airing of the underlying reasons, such as in the cases of Alex Tsui in 1993[67] and Yu Chee Yin in 1999,[68] the public was left to speculate whether the non-disclosure of the reasons for Yuen's arrest and departure was done only to prevent the release of information that might damage the reputation of the ICAC. While every law enforcement agency has officers who transgress the law, with the ICAC, however, there is a high public expectation that its officers will respect the law and act according to the highest standards of integrity. Whenever their officers are dismissed, disciplined or prosecuted, significant public attention is paid to such events and questions are asked as to why and how the officer's impugned conduct arose.[69]

There were many news reports in 2011 of staff shortages (particularly senior investigators) in the operations department and raising concerns about how and when available positions would be filled.[70] Many staff members who joined in the late 1970s shortly after ICAC's establishment were beginning to reach the mandatory retirement age of sixty. Some recent departures were due to senior staff migration to the Independent Police Complaints Council,[71] which was given a statutory footing in 2009.[72]

[65] S. Cheung, 'Was Top ICAC Man Sacked, Then Charged?', *South China Morning Post*, 30 July 2011, p. C1.

[66] P. Tsang and N. Fraser, 'Rising Star of ICAC Arrested in Graft Probe', *South China Morning Post*, 30 April 2011, p. 1; N. Fraser, 'Top ICAC Investigator Released on Bail', *South China Morning Post*, 1 May 2011, p. 1.

[67] See LegCo hearings described in S. S. H. Lo, 'Independent Commission Against Corruption', in D. H. McMillen and M. Si-wai (eds), *The Other Hong Kong Report 1994* (Hong Kong: Chinese University Press, 1994), pp. 27–36.

[68] See judicial review proceedings reported in *Yu Chee Yin* v. *Commissioner of ICAC* [2001] 2 HKC 91 (CFI); [2001] 4 HKC 532 (CFI).

[69] Such as the cases of theft involving two ICAC officers, see J. Man, '"Bullied" ICAC Worker Sentenced for Stealing from her Supervisor', *South China Morning Post*, 3 September 2009, p. C3; 'ICAC Investigator Who Stole Wine Ordered to do Community Service', *South China Morning Post*, 12 January 2010, p. C3.

[70] S. Cheung, 'ICAC Plugs Holes Amid Shortage of Investigators', *South China Morning Post*, 20 November 2011, p. A3; 'Setting Precedent for Establishing a Retirement Heaven', *The Sun*, 21 November 2011, p. A12; P. Tsang, 'Single-tender Contract by ICAC under Scrutiny', *South China Morning Post*, 19 March 2011, p. C1.

[71] Cheung, 'ICAC Plugs Holes'.

[72] Independent Police Complaints Council Ordinance (Cap. 604), in force 1 June 2009.

The previous ICAC Commissioner, whose extension in 2009 raised public concerns about transparency,[73] stepped down in 2012 when the new chief executive came into office.[74] The head of the operations department, Daniel Li, retired in 2012, and was replaced by a retired ICAC director.[75]

Finally, there was the view, expressed colourfully by columnist Jake van der Kamp, that having brought bribery and corruption much under control since the 1970s, the ICAC was now resigned to pursuing minor or worthless cases in order to justify its existence and significant annual budget.[76] Van der Kamp writes: 'The ICAC, as it is behaving now with its minnow fishing in pools far distant from the one to which it was sent, is past its sell-by date and ought at a minimum to be scaled back to less than half its present size'.[77] The ICAC's press information office responded to the article by noting the ICAC's 'statutory duty to investigate all pursuable corruption allegations' and pointing to their annual surveys 'which show that the community's tolerance for corruption is extremely low'.[78]

Reasons for the crisis

There is no single reason that can explain the current crisis of confidence within the ICAC. It is the product of the evolving sentiments of the public and their expectations of governmental officials after 1997. Such sentiments themselves have been shaped by the realities of the legal and political order set down in the Basic Law. Much has been written about Hong Kong's socio-political changes since the handover, and several characteristics of those changes relevant to the present inquiry can be sketched. The sum of the characteristics and their contributing factors will be described here as Hong Kong's 'human rights environment',

[73] P. Tsang and E. Wu, 'Tsang Criticized in Row over Secret Deal for ICAC Chief', *South China Morning Post*, 11 September 2009, p. 3.

[74] S. Cheung, C. Lee and E. Tsang, 'Conflict of Interest Rules ICAC Chief Out of Tsang Probe', *South China Morning Post*, 1 March 2012, p. C1.

[75] Cheung, Lee and Tsang, 'Conflict of Interest Rules ICAC Chief Out of Tsang Probe'.

[76] J. van der Kamp, 'Graft-busters go from Hooking Big Fish to Catching Minnows', *Sunday Morning Post*, 20 November 2011, p. 16.

[77] Kamp, 'Graft-busters go from Hooking Big Fish to Catching Minnows'.

[78] V. Chan, 'Committed to Investigating Corruption, Wherever it Lurks', *South China Morning Post*, 25 November 2011, p. 20.

reflecting the values and principles of a liberal and open society committed to the protection of fundamental human rights.

An important characteristic of this human rights environment is the public's willingness to make outward demands of the government. It is manifested vividly in the frequent and now famous Hong Kong public demonstrations, which once reached a boiling point in 2003 when half a million people marched against proposed national security law legislation.[79] Demands express themselves also in high profile judicial review challenges, often brought by ordinary people against governmental decisions and policies. The frequency of such cases led notable figures, including the former and current chief justices, to discourage judicial review as a means for solving social, economic and political problems.[80]

A related characteristic is the public's expectation of high standards of integrity and accountability from politicians and civil servants. These expectations became readily apparent during the campaigning for the 2012 chief executive (CE) election. What began as credibility attacks involving accusations of adultery, having an illegal basement and conflict of interest against the two leading candidates[81] eventually spilled over to the CE in office, Donald Tsang, who was found to have received benefits from wealthy friends in the form of a private yacht, private jet trips and renovations to a luxury Shenzhen penthouse suite where he planned to reside upon retirement in 2012. Tsang admitted that there was a 'gap' between the current rules and 'the expectations of our people',[82] then explained to the civil service that he was not applying a different integrity standard for himself,[83] and eventually apologised to the public in an unprecedented ninety-minute question and answer session in the legislature.[84]

[79] See essays in J. Y. S. Chen (ed.), *The July 1 Protest Rally: Interpreting a Historic Event* (City University of Hong Kong Press, 2005).

[80] See Press Release, 'CJ's Speech at Ceremonial Opening of the Legal Year 2010', 11 January 2010; Press Release, 'CJ's Speech at Ceremonial Opening of the Legal Year 2011', 10 January 2011, both available at: www.info.gov.hk.

[81] See 'The Rigging Unravels: China Faces Unpalatable Choices for Hong Kong's Next Chief Executive', *The Economist*, 3 March 2012; S. Pepper, 'Small-circle Campaigns, Big-circle Implications', China Elections and Governance Blog, 21 March 2012, available at: chinaelectionsblog.net.

[82] Press Release, 'CE Provides Detailed Information in Response to Recent Media Reports about Him', 26 February 2012, available at: news.gov.hk.

[83] Press Release, 'CE Writes to the Members of the Civil Service', 28 February 2012, available at: news.gov.hk.

[84] A. Lo, 'A Long Way to Fall', South *China Morning Post*, 2 March 2012, p. 4; E. Luk, 'I Solemnly Apologize', *The Standard*, 2 March 2012, p. 2.

He established an ad hoc committee, chaired by the former chief justice, to review the existing rules on conflicts of interest for the CE and political appointees. When the ICAC began investigating Tsang, the Commissioner, Timothy Tong, was quick to withdraw from the investigation for having ties with the developer of the Shenzhen penthouse.[85] These recent events, which happened within a very short period of time, confirmed the public expectation that its highest political leaders should be subject to the same law as everyone else and held to account to the public in an open and fair way.

Many factors contribute to the visible demands and expectations of the public. First, Hong Kong's long-standing free press ensures the wide and speedy dissemination of any news critical of public figures and authority.[86] Courts have remained independent and active in protecting rights and keeping government in check. Of all the branches of the political system, the courts have earned the greatest degree of respect and confidence from the people.[87] The CFA's public law jurisprudence has served to build and reinforce strong societal values that recognise the importance of the rule of law and respect for human rights, which is said to 'lie at the heart of Hong Kong's separate system'.[88] People have become more rights conscious and more likely to frame their demands using rights language and arguments.[89]

The recurring governance problems since 1997 are another contributing factor. In the absence of democratic institutions through which to vent its demands, the public literally take to the streets and use other media-seeking channels to air their demands and dissatisfaction with government.[90] As referenda are illegal, public opinion polls have acquired importance and are watched closely both in and outside Hong Kong, although poll results have not always been received well by those in power.[91]

[85] Cheung, Lee and Tsang, 'Conflict of Interest Rules ICAC Chief Out of Tsang Probe'.

[86] See J. M. Chan and F. L. F. Lee, 'Mass Media and Public Opinion', in L. Wai-man, P. L-t. Lui, W. Wong and Ian Holliday (eds), *Contemporary Hong Kong Politics: Governance in the Post-1997 Era* (Hong Kong University Press, 2007[1]), pp. 155–75.

[87] See, e.g., Rule of Law Indicators data from the University of Hong Kong's Public Opinion Programme, available at: http://hkupop.hku.hk/english/popexpress/index.html.

[88] *Ng Ka Ling* v. *Director of Immigration* (1999) 2 HKCFAR 4, at para. [29].

[89] See J. Chan, 'Basic Law and Constitutional Review: The First Decade', *Hong Kong Law Journal*, 37 (2007), 405–47, at 434–47.

[90] See L. Wai-man and I. L. K. Tong, 'Civil Society and NGOs', in L. Wai-man, P. L-t. Lui, W. Wong and I. Holliday (eds), *Contemporary Hong Kong Politics: Governance in the Post-1997 Era* (Hong Kong University Press, 2007), pp. 135–51.

[91] See the controversies surrounding Robert Chung's Public Opinion Programme, C. J. Petersen, 'Preserving Academic Freedom in Hong Kong: Lessons from the "Robert

The legislature under the Basic Law has a weak policy-making role; but its oversight role is strong and has become one of the main vehicles by which the public tries to make the government accountable.[92] Finally, and perhaps most importantly, the outward public demands can oftentimes work, first, to get the attention of the Hong Kong and Chinese governments and, secondly, to instigate change in government policy or decisions. Such was the case with the withdrawal of the national security bill,[93] the withdrawal of the proposal to abolish by-elections,[94] the resignations of ministers and other officials including the first CE, and so on.

The human rights environment helps to explain the past decade of negative media reports about ICAC operations. Several ICAC officials have also noted these societal changes. Anna Wu, a former chair of the ICAC's Operations Review Committee, thought that the policy of appointing civil servants as ICAC commissioners should be reviewed as 'the political landscape in Hong Kong has changed dramatically in recent years and the community is becoming more and more demanding on issues of accountability and transparency'.[95] In December 2011, the ICAC Head of Operations, Daniel Li wrote, 'our investigators continued to face higher challenges arising from the increased complexity of cases, prolonged investigations and trials and, most challenging of all, the changing and evermore transparent and publicly accountable environment in which we have to conduct our investigations'.[96]

What made the ICAC so effective in its early years was its use of a two-pronged strategy of secrecy and betrayal.[97] Its widespread use of wiretaps and covert surveillance was done with little or no scrutiny; the public, including the legislature, could find out little about their methods, as

Chung Affair",' *Hong Kong Law Journal*, 30 (2000), 165–76; S. Pepper, 'Free Political Expression … But Towards What End?', China Elections and Governance Blog, 6 February 2012, available at: chinaelectionsblog.net.

92 M. Ngok, *Political Development in Hong Kong: State, Political Society, and Civil Society* (Hong Kong University Press, 2007), pp. 127–31.

93 See C. J. Petersen, 'Hong Kong's Spring of Discontent', in F. Hualing, C. J. Petersen and S. N. M. Young (eds), *National Security and Fundamental Freedoms: Hong Kong's Article 23 Under Scrutiny* (Hong Kong University Press, 2005), pp. 13–62.

94 See P. Chau and S. N. M. Young, 'Abolishing By-elections to Fill Vacancies in the Legislative Council', *Hong Kong Law Journal*, 41 (2011), 601–9.

95 A. Wu, 'Hong Kong's Fight Against Corruption Has Lessons for Others', *Hong Kong Journal*, Spring (2006), at 2, available: at www.hkjournal.org/archive/2006_spring/wu.html.

96 D. Li, 'Letter from Hong Kong', *U.K. I.C.A.C. Association Newsletter*, Issue 4/11 (December 2011).

97 See McWalters, *Bribery and Corruption Law in Hong Kong*, p. 120.

broad public interest immunity was claimed. Wiretaps were invariably destroyed rather than used as evidence at trial; the intelligence from the wiretaps led to the discovery of derivative evidence that could be and was indeed used in court. To obtain further evidence the ICAC induced accomplices to betray one another. Breaking the circle of trust among conspirators required the use of promises of immunity, witness protection and other benefits.[98] Like covert surveillance, these practices, including those of witness preparation, went largely unregulated with only minimal oversight by prosecutors.

In the human rights environment, however, the ICAC's two-pronged strategy has been increasingly frustrated. Litigants, including public interest litigants like legislator Leung Kwok-hung, are more likely to bring judicial review challenges, or defend criminal charges, on human rights grounds. The courts' critical approach and changes in the law have resulted in new requirements of transparency and legitimacy in the means and methods used by ICAC to fight corruption. All covert surveillance and wiretapping must now be authorised under a statutory scheme overseen by a commissioner and a group of panel judges. Courts look more closely at the credibility of immunity witnesses and practices used to 'prepare' them for trial because 'there is a minimum below which the danger of wrongful conviction is not adequately guarded against'.[99]

While the CFA has been critical, its approach has been balanced and not hostile or condemnatory. Indeed, the Court has been supportive of the ICAC's work in carefully chosen statements made in its judgments. For example, in *Secretary for Justice* v. *Lam Tat Ming*, the CFA recognised a court's power to exclude evidence obtained by undercover agents who substantively interrogate defendants and violate their right of silence.[100] At the same time, Li CJ made the following statement recognising the importance of and need for undercover operations:

> The law recognises that the use of undercover operations is an essential weapon in the armoury of the law enforcement agencies; particularly their use when the criminal activities are ongoing, but also their use after crimes are completed to obtain evidence to bring the criminal to book.

[98] Other benefits include allowing the witness to keep ill-gotten gains, and not investigating the witness' family and friends. See *HKSAR* v. *Tse Tat Fung*, CACC 167/2008, at para. [97]; *Peter Gerardus van Weerdenburg* v. *HKSAR*, unreported, FACC 9/2010, 27 July 2011 (CFA), at para. [40].

[99] *Peter Gerardus van Weerdenburg* v. *HKSAR*, FACC 9/2010, at para. [14] *per* Bokhary PJ.

[100] *Secretary for Justice* v. *Lam Tat Ming* (2000) 3 HKCFAR 168.

> The use of undercover operations plays an important part in society's struggle to combat crime especially serious crime, whether it be corruption, trafficking in dangerous drugs or terrorism. But the success and indeed viability of such undercover operations depend upon the concealment of the true identity of the law enforcement officer in order to establish the appropriate relationship with the alleged wrongdoers. They therefore unavoidably involve elements of subterfuge, deceit and trickery. The law accepts that law enforcement agencies may find it necessary to resort to tactics of that kind.[101]

In a case concerning the ICAC's powers to obtain evidence from non-suspects, the CFA recognised a more robust role for the court to scrutinise *ex parte* applications, but was also mindful of the need for such powers especially in the context of cross-border crime. Li CJ's opening paragraphs of his judgment are symbolic of the Court's balanced approach, which aims both to protect rights and support the governmental objective:

> Corruption is an evil which cannot be tolerated. For the purpose of combating corruption, special powers of investigation have been conferred by statute on the Independent Commission Against Corruption (the ICAC). These powers are necessary as crimes of corruption are inherently difficult to investigate and prove. But as their exercise intrudes into the privacy of citizens, the statutory scheme provides that they are exercisable only after judicial authorization has been obtained. In this way, the scheme seeks to balance the public interest in fighting corruption and the public interest in the protection of the individual. A judicial safeguard is thus introduced between the citizen and the state. The need for independent scrutiny by the courts provides protection for the citizen against the unjustified use of the special investigatory powers.[102]

In a third example, the Court considered the offence of failing to comply with a notice to furnish information to the ICAC, and found that imposition of a legal burden on the defendant to prove a reasonable excuse for non-compliance was an unjustified derogation on the presumption of innocence under the Basic Law.[103] Instead of striking down the offence, the Court left it intact, but read down the provision to impose only an evidential burden on the defendant. Ribeiro PJ stated that such a remedial outcome 'would accord with the intent, which may properly be attributed to the legislature, of arming the ICAC with

[101] *Secretary for Justice* v. *Lam Tat Ming*, 2000) 3 HKCFAR 168, at paras [180]–[181].
[102] *P* v. *Commissioner of ICAC* (2007) 10 HKCFAR 293, at paras [1]–[2].
[103] *HKSAR* v. *Ng Po On* (2008) 11 HKCFAR 91.

appropriate investigative powers, backed by criminal sanctions, in a manner compatible with the Basic Law and the Bill of Rights'.[104]

Regaining public confidence

A former ICAC Commissioner once wrote that: 'The community's trust is the foundation of its support for the fight against corruption, a crucial matter since strong community support is the key to success.'[105] If this is true, then the current public distrust with the operational methods of the ICAC cannot be ignored or dismissed and must be addressed thoroughly. A public relations exercise by the community relations department, though important and necessary, is not the full answer. There has to be comprehensive change in both thinking and practices within the ICAC itself, and also with their legal advisers within the Department of Justice (DoJ). Some suggestions for implementation and further discussion are provided below.

Changing practices and attitudes

Justice Woo identified three reasons for why officers were not complying with the new surveillance law: (1) ignorance; (2) couldn't care less attitudes; (3) being recalcitrant.[106] He thought the answer was education, but only if the officers were genuinely willing to learn and change:

> Ignorance can be cured by learning. The other two likely reasons relate to attitude which could only be changed by education with the necessary heart to accept. As a starting point, the person concerned must have willingness to learn, or else the task of the educator would be rendered almost impossible. The crucial thing to learn is respect for the law and for the rule of law ... Once they appreciate the importance of respect for the law and rule of law, I have little doubt that their attitude will change.[107]

So training is important, but there needs to be more than a few one-off training seminars, which the ICAC has held with Woo J, the Director of Public Prosecutions and others.[108] There needs to be regular human rights education that informs all officers (not only new recruits) of the

[104] *HKSAR* v. *Ng Po On* (2008) 11 HKCFAR 91, at para. [77].
[105] de Speville, 'Anticorruption Commissions', p. 58.
[106] Annual Report 2007, at para. [12.11]. [107] Annual Report 2007, at para. [12.12].
[108] See, e.g., ICAC Press Release, 'Mr Justice Woo Shares with Graft Busters Insight into ICSO', 4 November 2009; *ICAC Operation Department Review 2009*, p. 68.

ever-expanding body of relevant local and overseas human rights jurisprudence. At a minimum, courses on privacy rights, the right to silence, the right to legal representation, legal professional privilege, proper use of informants, proper witness preparation, miscarriages of justice and wrongful convictions, duty of disclosure, right to a fair trial, and the offence of perverting the course of justice should be made available and mandatory in some cases. This is the first step in building a human rights culture within the ICAC. There were signs of a human rights culture in the ICAC during the early 1990s when a major attempt was made to review and reform anti-corruption practices and laws to comply with the Hong Kong Bill of Rights.[109] That same spirit needs to be rekindled.

To effect systemic attitudinal change in a large institution, there needs to be clear and repeated direction from the top. The message should not appear to pit human rights as an adversary to law enforcement, nor should it appear as only paying lip service to human rights. Instead, the balanced approach as reflected in the CFA's jurisprudence should be adopted. The message should be that human rights and the rule of law are part of the core values of Hong Kong society, that their requirements must be known to officers and be complied with fully at all times and that to do so is entirely compatible with the achievement of law enforcement aims and objectives.

Previous ICAC commissioners conveyed this message. In a 1992 seminar, Peter Allan spoke of the need for ICAC to comply with the Bill of Rights:

> In the early days when the Bill of Rights was touted, some used to describe the ICAC as not wanting this 'bill of wrongs'. There was a suggestion – which did not get very far – that the ICAC might actually be exempted from the operation of the Bill of Rights. That, I may say, is not a view to which I subscribe … There is no one more concerned than I to ensure the compatibility of our legislation with the Bill of Rights. The possible difference is that I would like to have my legislation compatible with the Bill of Rights, but nonetheless preserve all the powers which I have and which I believe are necessary.[110]

[109] P. Allan, 'Independent Commission Against Corruption', in G. E. Edwards and A. C. Byrnes (eds), *Hong Kong's Bill of Rights: The First Year* (Faculty of Law, University of Hong Kong, 1993), pp. 18–19; B. de Speville, 'Law Enforcement and the Independent Commission Against Corruption', in W. Fong, A. Byrnes and G. E. Edwards (eds), *Hong Kong's Bill of Rights: Two Years On* (Faculty of Law, University of Hong Kong, 1994), pp. 14–15.

[110] Allan, 'Independent Commission Against Corruption'.

In the following year, Bertrand de Speville expressed the view that compatibility did not diminish operational efficiency.[111] He also described how the Bill of Rights had formed 'part of the essential reference tools of the working investigator', that Commission-wide briefings on the Bill were held regularly, lectures on the Bill were included in both induction and refresher courses, and there was a regular Commission bulletin published and circulated throughout the operations department concerning Bill of Rights decisions and their implications.[112] For the current commissioner in 2009 to speak of a 'paradigm shift' brought about by the new surveillance law is a telling sign that the Bill of Rights culture that previous commissioners had worked to develop had somehow been lost in the 1997 transition.[113]

To reinforce a human rights culture and the highest standards of integrity there need to be appropriate process and sanctions for those who transgress human rights norms and rules of law. It must be transparent and the public should be told promptly when such sanctions are applied, annual reporting being insufficient.[114] Where judges criticise individual officers for improper or illegal behaviour that surely is a sign that the matter must be dealt with quite severely in disciplinary terms. The ICAC must be seen to be taking these types of transgression seriously if the public's trust in their methods is to be restored. The detailed standards of conduct expected of ICAC officers should be made a public document to enable assessment of the appropriateness of the standards and compliance in individual cases.[115]

Critical role of the Department of Justice

Without the benefit of having in-house counsel, the ICAC relies exclusively on counsel in the DoJ for its legal advice. Thus, the role of DoJ counsel, including counsel prosecuting on fiat, is crucial to ensuring the

[111] de Speville, 'Law Enforcement'.
[112] de Speville, 'Law Enforcement'.
[113] ICAC Press Release, 'Mr Justice Woo Shares with Graft Busters Insight into ICSO', 4 November 2009.
[114] See ICAC Annual Reports, available at: www.icac.org.hk/en/about_icac/p/icacar/index.html; and ICAC Complaints Committee's Annual Reports, available on Chief Secretary of Administration's website at: www.admwing.gov.hk/eng/links/icac.htm.
[115] Cf. the twenty-three-page *ICAC Code of Conduct* for New South Wales, available at: www.icac.nsw.gov.au/about-the-icac/independence-accountability/code-of-conduct.

quality and integrity of ICAC prosecutions.[116] DoJ counsel also play a critical role in advising officers against taking investigative steps that are improper and run the risk of prosecutorial failure or miscarriage of justice. Many of the failures and judicial criticisms mentioned earlier in this chapter could have been avoided if DoJ counsel played a more proactive and vigilant role in case preparation and screening. For example, the non-disclosure in *Chan Kau Tai* was avoidable, and the unreliable witnesses used in the *Andrew Lam* and *Shanghai Land* prosecutions should probably have been dropped. Though it is always easier to be critical after the fact, the point is not to blame but to highlight the important gate-keeping role of the Prosecutions Division of the DoJ.

The recent ICAC cases have highlighted two important prosecutorial issues that require immediate review and reform. The first issue is the use of unreliable or unsavoury witnesses in trials. The DoJ has a published policy on granting immunity from prosecution, but not a policy on the use of potentially unreliable witnesses, whether they have been granted immunity or not.[117] Unsavoury characters will fabricate seemingly helpful prosecution evidence in order to receive advantages other than immunity, such as financial/economic benefits, credit in the form of future sentencing discounts,[118] or simply notoriety. Given the risks of wrongful conviction associated with using unsavoury informants,[119] a general policy that sets the limits on the use of such witnesses is needed. The entire practice of granting immunity from prosecution also needs to be reviewed. The practice is unregulated by law and there is a perception that immunities are conferred too frequently and without sufficient circumspection.[120] Another issue for review is the scope and extent of benefits conferred on immunity witnesses, including the controversial benefit of allowing such witnesses to keep their ill-gotten gains.

[116] See H. S. Chan and J. Lo, 'Hong Kong Facing China: Administrative Competence of the ICAC and Fundamental Rights of Public Employees', *Asian Journal of Public Administration*, 13 (1991), 39–66, at 56.

[117] Prosecutions Division, *The Statement of Prosecution Policy and Practice: Code for Prosecutors* (Hong Kong: Department of Justice, 2009), paras [19.1]–[19.6].

[118] Those who assist the authorities can receive up to a 50 per cent reduction in sentence in their own matters, see *Z* v. *HKSAR* (2007) 10 HKCFAR 183.

[119] See generally, K. Roach, 'Unreliable Evidence and Wrongful Convictions: The Case for Excluding Tainted Identification Evidence and Jailhouse and Coerced Confessions', *Criminal Law Quarterly*, 52 (2007), 210–36; G. Botting, *Wrongful Conviction in Canadian Law* (Markham, Ontario: LexisNexis, 2010).

[120] Cf. Serious Organised Crime and Police Act 2005 (UK), ss. 71–75.

The second issue concerns the long-standing practice of prosecutorial non-involvement in witness interviews and preparation. It was based on English practice, but in 2008 the practice changed and prosecutors in England and Wales began conducting pre-trial witness interviews.[121] When the Director of Public Prosecutions mooted the idea in the Legislative Council of following this change in Hong Kong, it was met with resistance by legislators who were concerned about possible witness coaching by prosecutors.[122] The recent ICAC cases show that witness training and coaching is already practised. Having prosecutors, who are officers of the court bound by strict codes of professional conduct, assume responsibility over witness preparation can only enhance the integrity of that process. The misguided view about prosecutors expressed at the 2008 meeting must be revisited again, informed now by the repeated judicial criticisms of law enforcement manipulation of witness' evidence.

Better survey data

Notwithstanding the positive image projected by the annual survey data, those in charge of the ICAC should maintain a healthy scepticism and genuinely enquire into what problems may exist within the institution. The ICAC survey data available on the website appears to have been compiled primarily to inform an 'education strategy' and not to obtain feedback on its operational work.[123] Only four main questions were asked about the work of the ICAC in the 2010 survey: effectiveness of the ICAC's anti-corruption work; support for the ICAC; aspects of work the ICAC should strengthen; and target groups for which the ICAC should strengthen prevention and education work.[124] This was a major change from previous surveys, which had asked many more questions about public perception of the ICAC's performance and confidence in the ICAC.[125] An entire section on the public perception of the ICAC's powers and accountability was

[121] Prosecutions Division, DoJ, 'Information Paper on Pre-trial Interviewing of Witnesses by Prosecutors', paper for LegCo Panel on Administration of Justice and Legal Services, LC Paper No. CB(2)2327/07-08(05) (Hong Kong: Department of Justice, June 2008).

[122] LegCo Panel on Administration of Justice and Legal Services, Minutes of meeting held on 23 June 2008, LC Paper No. CB(2)2826/07-08, pp. 30–46.

[123] See the Objectives of the ICAC Annual Survey on the ICAC website, available at: www.icac.org.hk/en/useful_information/sd/sd/index.html.

[124] Annual Survey 2010, pp. 11–13.

[125] ICAC Community Relations Department, *ICAC Annual Survey 2009 Executive Summary*, pp. viii–xi.

dropped from the 2010 survey.[126] One wonders whether this section was removed because the 2009 survey showed a sharp decline in the percentage of people who believed that the ICAC had not abused their powers (57 per cent down from 77 per cent in 2008), and threefold increase of those who were unsure (32 per cent from 9 per cent in 2008).[127]

The question of whether the ICAC deserves support was designed to elicit a high positive response rate and not designed to canvass views on what aspects of the ICAC's work may or may not deserve support. Naturally more than 97 per cent answered in the affirmative.[128] On the effectiveness question, a change in the 2010 survey question and set answers gave the impression that the data was being manipulated to give a more favourable impression. Prior to 2010, respondents were asked to choose from five-point scale set of answers (i.e., very effective, effective, average, ineffective, very ineffective).[129] From 2007 to 2009, approximately 24 per cent of respondents believed the effectiveness of the ICAC's work was 'average', and the percentage of those who thought the work was very effective/effective decreased from 74 per cent to 68 per cent.[130] In the 2010 survey, only a four-point scale was used (i.e., very effective, quite effective, not quite effective, very ineffective).[131] The survey suddenly showed that 87 per cent of respondents believed that the ICAC's work was either 'very effective' or 'quite effective'.[132] This was an artificially inflated figure that masked the segment of the population that had previously thought the effectiveness of the work was only average.

The recent changes to the survey design can only leave the impression that the annual survey exercise is not meant to obtain feedback to improve service delivery or performance, but to obtain results that can give a positive image of the ICAC. As such, the surveys cease to be a true measure of 'progress' and 'trust in the ICAC'.[133]

Conclusion

The story of the ICAC and human rights is unique in many ways. Its first fifteen glorious years saw the ICAC flex its extraordinary powers to eradicate rampant corruption in the territory. Then it was confronted

[126] *ICAC Annual Survey 2009 Executive Summary*, pp. xii–xiii.
[127] *ICAC Annual Survey 2009 Executive Summary*, Table D.
[128] Annual Survey 2010, Table C.
[129] See, e.g., Annual Survey 2009, Table C.
[130] Annual Survey 2009, Table C.
[131] Annual Survey 2010, Table C.
[132] Annual Survey 2010, Table C.
[133] de Speville, 'Anticorruption Commissions', p. 60.

with two periods of human rights impact. The first came in 1991 with the introduction of the Bill of Rights. Successive commissioners were responsive, and the Commission continued to achieve its law enforcement aims while accommodating the dictates of new human rights norms. The second came in 1997 and, though the impact was more gradual, it hit harder in some areas, particularly in covert work, and more time was needed for officers to cope with the new standards of procedural fairness, openness and accountability. The chapter holds out the hope that once the current crisis of confidence is acknowledged and understood, public confidence in the ICAC can be readily restored if the suggestions outlined above are followed.

The United Kingdom may tell a different story as its Bribery Act was born into a thriving human rights environment after ten years of a Human Rights Act. But the intrinsic difficulties of investigating corruption and bribery offences are such that inevitably some officers will see rights to privacy, legal representation and silence as impediments to investigative work. As the Hong Kong experience has shown, prosecuting bribery in a human rights environment is rife with challenges for both investigators and prosecutors. The Serious Fraud Office's approach of engaging companies and using alternatives to prosecution appears to be wise and measured.[134] But constant vigilance and proactive processes will be needed as both senior officials and individual officers will be under enormous pressure to show that the Bribery Act is not only a beautifully drafted piece of legislation.

[134] R. Alderman, 'The Bribery Act 2010: The SFO's Approach and International Compliance', speech hosted by McGrigors, UK, 9 February 2011, available at: www.sfo.gov.uk/about-us/our-views/director's-speeches/speeches-2011.

11

Is the UNCAC an effective deterrent to grand corruption?

TIM DANIEL AND JAMES MATON

Introduction

This chapter is about corruption on a grand scale, as encountered in a number of well-publicised cases. All predate the UK's Bribery Act 2010 ('the 2010 Act'), and concentrate on efforts to thwart the perpetrators or to recover the proceeds of the corruption which took place. Time will tell how effective the 2010 Act will be in helping to curb corruption on the scale practised in these examples; although bribery was certainly present in many of the cases, large-scale embezzlement, or theft of public funds, was also a recurrent feature. Consideration is given in the chapter to whether the United Nations Convention against Corruption (UNCAC) can assist in bringing this 'kleptocracy' to justice. In reading this chapter it should be borne in mind that the World Bank, in the Preface to its *Asset Recovery Handbook*,[1] published at the beginning of 2011 as part of its Stolen Assets Recovery (StAR) initiative, stated that an estimated US $20–40 billion is siphoned out of developing countries each year: to date only US$5 billion has been recovered, and probably half of that is accounted for by the Abacha case, referred to below.

The chapter will also touch on the growing evidence that governments in states where there is a history of grand corruption continue to actively collude in corrupt practices and to take steps which thwart the aims and objectives of UNCAC, despite having ratified the Convention and claiming to implement its provisions.[2]

[1] Available at: www.unodc.org/documents/corruption/Publications/StAR/StAR_Publication_-_Asset_Recovery_Handbook.pdf.

[2] A detailed study entitled *Can UNCAC Address Grand Corruption?*, a political economy analysis based on studies of Bangladesh, Kenya and Indonesia, was published in November 2011 by U4 Anti-Corruption Centre Resource Centre, available at: www.U4.no.

The implementation of the UNCAC

On 28 October 2011, the final day of the Fourth Conference of States Parties (COSP 4) to the United Nations Convention against Corruption (UNCAC), Russia, backed by China and Iran among others, moved a Resolution on the role of the UNCAC Implementation Working Group (IWG).[3] The effect of the Resolution was to exclude civil society from the deliberations of the IWG, a move which not only flies in the face of the letter and spirit of the Convention, but is also contrary to an opinion previously expressed by the UN's own legal adviser.[4] Reuters had this to say about the Resolution:

> Marrakesh, Morocco, October 28: Campaigners on Friday accused governments at a major U.N. conference on corruption of excluding civil society from fully participating in reviewing how states are doing in enforcing the world's biggest anti-graft convention.
>
> More than 150 countries have ratified the U.N. Convention against Corruption (UNCAC), and the results of a review into how 26 of them are doing in implementing the treaty were discussed at the week-long conference in the Moroccan city of Marrakesh.
>
> Campaigners and experts say the review process is shrouded in secrecy, while the lack of a mechanism to 'name and shame' the countries doing least to fight sleaze raises question marks over UNCAC's impact.
>
> Civil society organisations attending the talks campaigned hard to be allowed to attend discussions by the convention's main review body – the Implementation Review Group (IRG), which assesses whether governments are living up to their obligations under the convention.
>
> But the conference ended without a commitment to broaden access for civil society, which campaigners say is all the more surprising after recent popular uprisings of the Arab Spring.
>
> UNCAC explicitly recognises that anti-corruption efforts must go hand-in-hand with transparency and civil society participation, but some governments, said by sources to include Russia, China, Algeria, Cuba and Ecuador, reject this notion.[5]

[3] COPC Resolution No. 4/4 on International Cooperation in Asset Recovery CAC/COSP/2011/L.5/Rev.2, available at: www.unodc.org/unodc/en/treaties/CAC/CAC-COSP-session4-resolutions.html.

[4] United Nations, Implementation Review Group of the UN Convention Against Corruption, 2010, UN docs CAC/COSP/IRG/2010/9, available at: www.unodc.org/documents/treaties/UNCAC/WorkingGroups/ImplementationReviewGroup/29Nov-1Dec2010/V1056031e.pdf.

[5] Filed by Astrid Zweynert of Reuters, available at: www.trust.org/trustlaw/news/secrecy-undermines-un-anti-graft-talks-activists.

The next COSP, in 2013, will be held in Panama, and the one after that will be hosted by Russia itself. When the issue of peer review was discussed at COSP 3 in Doha, four nations were strongly against introducing it: Russia, China, Iran and Egypt. Within little more than a year, the Arab Spring had dawned, and Egypt's president had been toppled amid widespread allegations of corruption and nepotism. Tunisia and Libya have experienced the same fate. The leaders in all three countries were toppled by uprisings backed by civil society. As the Reuters article states, the passing of the Resolution is all the more surprising in light of the recent Arab Spring events.

However, there does exist recognition at the COSP that the issues arising in the context of asset recovery are fundamental to the working of the Convention. At COSP 3 and again at COSP 4 resolutions were passed, the wording of which go to the heart of the problems which arise in the implementation of Chapter V, the section of the UNCAC which deals with asset recovery. Iran, on behalf of the so-called Group of 77,[6] and China tabled a resolution which had, in the first instance, been tabled by Egypt. The resolution was passed,[7] and specifically noted in the preamble:

> the efforts made by all States parties in tracing, freezing and recovering their stolen assets, in particular those States parties in the Middle East and North Africa, taking into consideration recent developments in those States in fighting corruption, and the efforts of and willingness expressed by the international community to assist them in the recovery of those assets in order to preserve stability and sustainable development.

However, the Resolution goes on to encapsulate many of the difficulties which states encounter when they look to their fellow states for assistance in the recovery of stolen assets. It calls on states to take a proactive approach to mutual legal assistance requests, and make spontaneous disclosures of information on stolen assets. It emphasises the importance of states 'doing their homework' in their own jurisdictions before launching requests, and of implementing fully the anti-money laundering provisions, including the taking of steps that 'help to establish the linkage between assets and offences under the Convention'. A very full account of the types of difficulties states encounter is contained in the World Bank's StAR initiative, *Barriers to Asset Recovery*.[8] The volume is intended to 'guide policy makers in their efforts to ensure necessary

[6] Consisting of developing states. [7] Resolution 4/4 CAC/COSP/2011/L.5/Rev.2.
[8] Available at: www1.worldbank.org/finance/star_site/publications/barriers.html.

resources and the development of a plan, policy or strategy aimed at eradicating the barriers to asset recovery'. In addition, 'actions to be taken by the G20, international organisations, financial institutions, developmental agencies and civil society' are proposed.

Yet, according to World Bank estimates, despite all this high-level input, billions of dollars are illicitly transferred between jurisdictions each year – mainly from developing to developed countries. The assets are never returned, and the perpetrators all too easily escape justice. This chapter will look at some historic examples of grand corruption and the impunity enjoyed by the kleptocrats who practise it. When states which are the victims of corruption fail to take action on behalf of their citizens the legal steps taken by certain non-state actors (NSAs) are also considered.

The chapter will also look at action that can and should be taken by governments of non-victim states, whose banking systems are frequently the recipients of corrupt monies, and who are in a position to render valuable assistance to the victim states, but who still fall down on their obligations. The regulatory authorities in the United Kingdom and Switzerland both recently carried out in-depth assessments of the effectiveness of their anti-money laundering regimes as applied in particular to the handling of politically exposed persons (PEPs). Both referred in their reports to the seminal case of Abacha, and both found shortcomings in present bank practices, despite the lessons that the Abacha case taught. The background and history of the UNCAC is also closely intertwined with Abacha, and the chapter commences with a brief study of corruption in Nigeria and the Abacha case.

Corruption in Nigeria and the Abacha case

Nigeria is often cited as an example of a state in which corruption, both petty and grand, is endemic. General Sani Abacha was only the last in a long line of military rulers who seized power in more or less violent coups over the years following Nigeria's independence in 1960. Nigeria joined the Organisation of Petroleum Exporting Countries (OPEC) in 1971, and soon found its oil revenues increasing substantially following the hike in oil prices effected by OPEC in the early 1970s. This led directly to the arrival of the notorious 'cement armada'. By the beginning of 1976, there were over 400 vessels waiting to discharge cement at Lagos, the main port. As Lagos could handle only one cement vessel a week, this was the equivalent of eight years' worth of vessels stretching over the horizon. Nigeria cancelled all the cement supply contracts which had been placed by the Ministry of Defence in the hope of building military barracks around the country. In the litigation that followed, Nigeria claimed sovereign immunity, but this was rejected by the Court of Appeal.[9] The UK Parliament passed the State Immunity Act in 1978, largely as a direct result of the Nigerian situation, which at one time threatened to provoke a crisis in the secondary banking market as so much money was riding on the cement letters of credit in London. Nigeria had to pay out millions of dollars to contractors.[10] There was little doubt that large-scale corruption was involved in the placing of the original contracts,[11] but there was scant interest at the Ministry of Justice in pursuing the perpetrators: there was far more money to be made from settling the claims on terms advantageous to the negotiators.

Sani Abacha is generally held up to be the most notorious example of a corrupt Nigerian dictator. However, during the eight years that his predecessor (General Ibrahim Babangida) was in office, US$12 billion of oil revenues were said to be unaccounted for.[12] Babangida is still active behind the scenes in Nigerian politics, and is often mentioned as a backer of political candidates, but no action has ever been taken against him. Indeed, it was only with the demise of Abacha[13] that Nigeria finally set out to attempt to recover some of what had been looted. Four-and-a-half years of mis-rule finally came to an end in June 1998.[14]

The Abacha case was to prove a landmark in the history of the worldwide fight against corruption. 'Enough is enough' has become a

[9] *Trendtex Trading Corp* v. *Central Bank of Nigeria* [1977] QB 529.

[10] Nigeria's total liability under the contracts, including demurrage payments to the ship-owners whose vessels waited in the Lagos roads, would have been of the order of US$1 billion – a great deal of money in the 1970s.

[11] A Commission of Enquiry headed by Mr Justice Belgore was set up by the Nigerian Government, but its findings were thought to be too sensitive to publish at the time. A brief description of some of the fraud that took place is contained in B. Conway, *The Piracy Business* (London: Hamlyn, 1981), pp. 49–50.

[12] M. Peel, *A Swamp Full of Dollars* (London: I. B. Taurus, 2009), p. 116.

[13] In suitably lurid circumstances, see 'General Sani Abacha (Adapted from Naiwu Osahon's book, *The Viper's Den*)', *The Nigerian Voice*, 28 October 2010.

[14] By a curious coincidence, that was also the month in which President Suharto, the long-standing (thirty years) ruler of Indonesia was overthrown in a popular uprising. There were many parallels between Indonesia and Nigeria: both had discovered oil soon after achieving independence in the 1960s, and both had suffered forty years of mis-rule at the hands of dictators who were as greedy as they were cruel. However, as will be seen below, there are significant differences in the successes achieved in attempting to recover the assets stolen by them.

common cry among anti-corruption campaigners around the world.[15] The world itself, through the auspices of the United Nations, finally came to feel the same way. Under Resolution No. 55/61 of 4 December 2000 the General Assembly, spurred on by Abacha revelations,[16] decided to establish an Ad Hoc Committee for the Negotiation of an Effective International Legal Instrument Against Corruption, building on the work of the Ad Hoc Intergovernmental Working Group on the Problem of Corrupt Practices,[17] as it was felt that the UN Convention against Transnational Organised Crime[18] (The Palermo Convention, or UNTOC) had only a limited impact.

The sessions of the Ad Hoc Committee took place between 21 January 2002 and 1 October 2003, against the backdrop of Nigeria's fight to recover the Abacha loot. There had been previous high-profile asset recovery exercises against former heads of state, most notably ex-President Marcos of the Philippines,[19] but it was the Abacha case which really caught international public attention. This was probably due to a number of factors, most notably the summary execution by the Abacha regime of the poet and human rights activist, Ken Saro-Wiwa, on 10 November 1995, hours after the Commonwealth Heads of Government Meeting had opened in New Zealand. This resulted in Nigeria's suspension from the Commonwealth. Commonwealth suspensions have an immediate impact across fifty-four sovereign states dedicated in principle, and increasingly in practice, to upholding the rule of law:[20] together those states represent over 1.6 billion people around the world.

[15] It was the slogan adopted on billboards by Nigeria's Economic and Financial Crimes Commission after its incorporation in 2003.

[16] See, e.g., address by President Obasanjo to the UN General Assembly calling for an international convention to repatriate Africa's illicitly appropriated wealth, September 1999, available at: www.un.org/ga/54/president/brief/br09_23.htm.

[17] Established following UNGA Resolution No. 3514 (XXX), 15 December 1975.

[18] It came into force 29 September 2003.

[19] 'In 1986, the Republic of the Philippines filed a request for mutual assistance with the Swiss authorities in connection with the repatriation of Marcos deposits in Swiss banks. Twelve years elapsed before these deposits were transferred to escrow accounts in the Philippine National Bank (PNB) and another six years passed before the concerned US $624 million were transferred to the Philippine Treasury, following a Philippine Supreme Court decision ordering the forfeiture of the Marcos Swiss deposits in July 2003.' See World Bank, *Stolen Asset Recovery (StAR) Initiative: Challenges, Opportunities, and Action Plan* (Washington, DC: World Bank, 2007).

[20] See, for example, The Commonwealth (Latimer House) Principles on the Three Branches of Government: Commonwealth Secretariat: www.thecommonwealth.org.

The second highly significant factor was the effort put in train by Nigeria's new democratically elected leader, Olusegun Obasanjo[21] to recover the Abacha loot. Within four months of being elected, Obasanjo approached the authorities in Switzerland with a request for assistance in locating Abacha-held accounts. The results were spectacular. Within a very short space of time a Swiss Government decree went out to all 11,000 financial institutions in Switzerland requiring them to report any account suspected of harbouring Abacha funds. The timing was, in one sense, impeccable: Switzerland was reeling from a series of hugely damaging revelations concerning monies in accounts still held in Swiss banks by victims of the Holocaust: funds which had played no little part in the post-war enrichment of those banks. Smarting from those revelations and from the enormous damage done to Switzerland's reputation worldwide, the government was only too keen to be seen to be helping Nigeria in this high-profile case.

Switzerland thus became the spearhead for a worldwide asset recovery exercise, which is ongoing today, but already ranks as the most successful such exercise that the world has seen. Estimates as to the total value of the assets stolen during the four-and-a-half years that Abacha was in power vary between about US$3 and US$5 billion. To date, about US$2.3 billion has been recovered, but further sums, probably totalling as much as US$1 billion,[22] are frozen, and will one day, it is to be hoped, be returned to Nigeria.

The Abacha case taught a number of lessons which are fundamental to successful asset recovery:

- First, there is no substitute for an in-depth and thorough enquiry being carried out in the first instance by the domestic authorities in the victim country. Such an enquiry should preferably be carried out by a body with coercive powers. In the Abacha case, Nigeria set up a Special Investigation Panel (SIP), headed by its Assistant Commissioner of Police. The SIP uncovered much valuable information subsequently

[21] Previously second-in-command to General Gowon during the Biafran War, he had returned Nigeria to a brief period of civilian rule in 1979.

[22] According to figures given by the Geneva lawyer, Enrico Monfrini, to *Financial Times* legal correspondent, Michael Peel, there was US$300 million in Jersey, US$300 million in Liechtenstein, US$350 million in Luxembourg and US$60 million in the Bahamas: Peel, *A Swamp Full of Dollars*. Peel's chapter entitled 'The Discerning Gentlemen' gives an extensive account both of the Abacha saga, and of Governor Alamieyeseigha's activities (see below).

used in requests for mutual legal assistance (MLA). It also indicated to requested countries that Nigeria was taking proper steps to investigate the crimes of the Abacha family 'at home'.

- The MLA requests, which were made to a number of countries, produced many and varied responses, by no means all of which were helpful to Nigeria. For example, it took the Home Office, the designated central authority for receipt of such requests in the United Kingdom, some four years to transmit the requested information to Nigeria. They were twice subjected to judicial review applications brought before the UK courts by the Abacha family,[23] and numerous technical objections to the request were raised by Home Office lawyers in the early stages. Similar difficulties were raised in other jurisdictions, and that is why, to this day, there are monies still trapped in jurisdictions such as Luxembourg, Liechtenstein and even the United States.
- Even in cooperative jurisdictions, such as Switzerland and the Channel Island of Jersey, it was possible for the Abacha family to mount numerous challenges, both in those jurisdictions and in Nigeria. The Abachas seemingly always continued to command almost unlimited funds to pay for the best legal representation in fighting these cases.[24]
- In Switzerland it was possible to make use of the so-called *partie civile* procedure, under which the victim of the alleged crime is able to join the criminal proceedings as the party which has suffered the damage. This gives the victim, in this case the state of Nigeria, the opportunity to play an active part in the proceedings. In the Abacha case, Nigeria's participation was instrumental in persuading the court that the Abacha family were members of a criminal organisation. Once such a finding is made by the court, the burden of proof shifts to the accused to demonstrate that the provenance of the funds is legitimate. The Abachas were totally unable to discharge that burden. As a result, judgment[25] for a sum in excess of US$ 0.5 billion was given in favour of Nigeria, the largest single recovery in the case to date. This took six years to achieve.

[23] See *R (On the application of Abacha)* v. *Secretary of State for the Home Department (No. 2)* [2001] EWHC Admin 787.

[24] £50 million was initially frozen in the United Kingdom: that sum has now dwindled to £20 million as the result of numerous draw-downs for legal costs in jurisdictions around the world. The UK courts have acceded to these requests in the absence of conclusive evidence from Nigeria linking the frozen sums with specific acts of corruption.

[25] Swiss Federal Court Decision, 1A.215/2004/col, 7 February 2005.

- In the United Kingdom, Nigeria's request did spark an investigation by the Financial Services Authority (FSA). In March 2001, the FSA reported in a press release[26] that some US$1.3 billion of Abacha monies had passed through banks in the City of London on their way to banks in, among other places, Switzerland, Luxembourg and Liechtenstein. The FSA investigation identified forty-two personal and corporate account relationships linked to Abacha family members and close associates in the United Kingdom. These accounts were held at twenty-three banks, which included UK banks and branches of banks from both inside and outside the European Union. The investigation found that fifteen of the banks had significant control weaknesses. It also found that eight of those banks had corrected the weaknesses since the accounts were opened through strengthening their anti-money laundering controls. The FSA did not say what, if anything, the other seven banks did, and it was not prepared to divulge to Nigeria the names of the banks concerned, on confidentiality grounds.
- Repatriation to Nigeria of the monies recovered in Switzerland was an issue for the Swiss Government, and became a major issue with civil society. It was not difficult to understand why. In the Marcos case, Switzerland recovered US$624 million. The monies were paid into an escrow account at the National Bank of the Philippines, to which the Philippine and Swiss governments were joint signatories. Switzerland did not authorise release of the monies until there was a final judgment in the Philippine courts, and it was satisfied that a democratically elected government was in place which was untainted by corruption: that took eighteen years.[27] In the case of Nigeria, Switzerland at first tried to tie release of the monies to the deportation of about 400 Nigerians it wished to deport back to Nigeria. The suggestion was dismissed out of hand by President Obasanjo. The Swiss then asked for certain assurances from Nigeria concerning the use to which the money would be put on being returned to Nigeria. Those assurances were given by the president and his tough-talking Minister of Finance, Ngozi Okonjo-Iweala.[28] The monies were to be devoted to expenditure

[26] Press Release, FSA/PN/029/2001, 8 March 2001, available at: www.fsa.gov.uk/Pages/Library/Communication/PR/2001/029.shtml.

[27] See n. 19, above.

[28] She became Managing Director of the World Bank, and was then persuaded by Nigeria's President Goodluck Jonathan to return to Nigeria as a super-minister for finance and the economy: presidency of the World Bank is also a possibility.

by the ministries of Education, Health and Local Government on projects which would be of direct benefit to the Nigerian people. In a last-minute accommodation with civil society representatives, the World Bank was appointed trustee to see that the returned monies were so used.[29]

- During the whole history of the Abacha recovery effort there has been a sufficient display of political will by the victim state government to drive the process forward. That will has ebbed and flowed as successive governments have taken office, but, on the whole, it has been maintained, and the Nigerian state has played its part. Where there have been failings, these have often been at the domestic level, and particularly where prosecution of members of the Abacha family at home and the obtaining of judgments in Nigerian courts have been concerned.
- Dark deeds and attempted settlement: Mohammed Abacha, the eldest surviving son,[30] was initially jailed after the death of his father for alleged involvement in the murder of the wife of the winner of the 1993 elections,[31] but when he was released from prison in 2002, it was stated he had been jailed on embezzlement charges.[32] Obasanjo tried to get him to agree to an amnesty, under which the family would have kept US$100 million in return for handing over all remaining assets, estimated at about US$1.5 billion. The deal was controversial at the time, and Mohammed refused to sign. He then proceeded to head up the resistance to Nigeria's recovery efforts, presumably calculating that he

[29] The World Bank has produced a detailed report on the use to which the monies were put, available at: http://siteresources.worldbank.org/INTNIGERIA/Resources/Abacha_Funds_Monitoring_1221.pdf, but there has been some scepticism among civil society in Nigeria concerning the content of this report. In September 2011, the Socio-Economic Rights and Accountability Project (SERAP) issued a Freedom of Information Request addressed to the Accountant General requesting an account of the spending of recovered assets, available at: www.serap-nigeria.org/news-update/foi-serap-wants-accountant-general-to-disclose-spending-on-recovered-stolen-assets.

[30] The eldest, Ibrahim, was killed in an air crash in Nigeria in January 1995. The manner of his death gave rise to much speculation: see, e.g., S. Oduyela, 'A Chronicle of Unresolved Murder Cases in Nigeria', *Nigeriaworld*, 16 August 2003.

[31] BBC News, 14 October 1999, available at: http://news.bbc.co.uk/1/hi/world/africa/474854.stm. He was accused of having ordered the assassination of Kudirat Abiola, the senior wife of the 1993 election winner, M. K. O. Abiola, who was arrested by Babangida, and imprisoned by Abacha, who deposed Babangida in a coup immediately after the elections. Abiola died in prison four weeks after Abacha died, having almost certainly been poisoned in State House.

[32] BBC News, 24 September 2002, available at: http://news.bbc.co.uk/1/hi/world/africa/2278292.stm.

could better the deal offered by Obasanjo. No deals were on offer from Obasanjo's successor, Umaru Yar'Adua. Abacha had had his elder brother, Major General Shehu Yar'Adua, murdered by lethal injection.[33] Obasanjo had also been imprisoned with Yar'Adua, and had narrowly escaped the same fate by feigning illness.[34]

- The role of the judiciary: at least two Nigerian judgments handed down during the recovery process were almost certainly obtained by corrupt means. It was claimed in the judicial review proceedings in the United Kingdom challenging the Home Secretary's decision to assist Nigeria[35] that a judgment had been given in Nigeria to the effect that a request for MLA was unconstitutional under the Nigerian Constitution.[36] Most recently, in 2009, the Liechtenstein Examining Magistrate wished to examine Mohammed Abacha in Nigeria in connection with the US$US 300 million still held in Liechtenstein. She was given permission to travel to Nigeria for that purpose, and did so. Before she was able to see him, however, she was served with a Nigerian court order forbidding her to proceed, almost certainly on the grounds that such an interview would be 'an infringement of Nigeria's sovereignty', and 'against the rule of law'.[37] The Abacha family are contesting Nigeria's claim to the $300 million: a judgment from the Supreme Court in Liechtenstein was expected in 2012.

Nigeria ratified the UNCAC in 2004. It is instructive to relate some of the points made above by reference, where appropriate, to Articles in the Convention[38] in order to observe at firsthand what 'barriers' to asset recovery have been thrown up in Nigeria's case: reference will also be made to some of the barriers which have been thrown up in other jurisdictions.

33 Said by some to have been anthrax – as reported to the author by a close friend of the Yar'Adua family doctor.

34 See n. 30, above. 35 See n. 23, above.

36 A similar argument was used more successfully in Kenya in one of the *Anglo-Leasing* cases; see further below.

37 These were two of the Attorney General's standard responses to any request for assistance on corruption matters. According to Liechtenstein's Dr Robert Wallner, Head of the Liechtenstein Public Prosecutor's Office (PPO), the judgment was obtained on an application by Nigeria's Attorney General Michael Aondoakaa, as to whom, see further below.

38 Accounts of the Abacha case, and the Alamieyeseigha case referred to below, are also given in C. Nicholls, T. Daniel, A. Bacarese and J. Hatchard, *Corruption and Misuse of Public Office*, 2nd edn (Oxford University Press, 2011).

Investigation, prosecution and anti-corruption commissions

There are a number of Articles in UNCAC that are relevant to investigation, prosecution and anti-corruption commissions. Article 36 deals with specialised law enforcement authorities, encouraging states parties to set up bodies with specialised expertise within existing structures of police, prosecution and courts. As far as Nigeria was concerned, the setting up of the SIP could be seen as a forerunner to the Economic and Financial Crimes Commission (EFCC), set up by Obasanjo in 2004 during his second term in office (2003–2007). The EFCC was in fact a second body in Nigeria charged with investigating corruption. There already existed the Independent Corrupt Practices and other Related Offences Commission (ICPC), which had also been formed by President Obasanjo in 2000. The ICPC investigates corruption in civil/public service. The EFCC has a much wider remit, and the power to bring prosecutions independently of the Attorney General, the Director of Public Prosecutions and the state prosecution service.

Under its first chairman, Nuhu Ribadu, a legally trained former Deputy Police Commissioner, the EFCC rapidly became a force to be reckoned with. Ribadu started by arresting his old boss, Nigeria's Police Commissioner. A number of other high-profile arrests followed, but the EFCC was prevented from pursuing some of its highest profile potential targets by a clause in the Nigerian Constitution which grants immunity from both criminal and civil suit to state governors. The thirty-six governors are, between them, undoubtedly the biggest bestowers of patronage within the Federation, and, before he left office, Ribadu claimed that he had sufficient evidence to prosecute thirty-one of them. It was not long before political opponents of Obasanjo were claiming that the EFCC was being used for political ends in order to bring down opponents of the government. This is a common accusation made against successful anti-corruption commissions; similar accusations have been made in a number of countries, including Indonesia, Kenya and Zambia, when charges were brought against senior politicians.

It is common to see the effectiveness of anti-corruption commissions being neutralised by their governments. In Commonwealth countries, this is often effected through the office of the Attorney General.[39] In Nigeria, under President Yar'Adua, who succeeded Obasanjo, but did not live to complete his term of office having been a sick man even when

[39] See further below for an example of this happening in Kenya.

elected, the Attorney General, Michael Aondoakaa, effectively neutralised the work of the EFCC. When Aondoakaa assumed office, Ribadu was demoted and sidelined, as were all his most effective lieutenants. Thereafter, the EFCC concentrated on going after 'smaller fry', leaving the 'big fish' to swim freely. Ribadu's replacement was a senior policewoman, Farida Waziri. She was dismissed on 23 November 2011. According to the BBC report on her dismissal, the EFCC has prosecuted thirty politicians since its formation, of whom only four have been convicted and none are now in prison.[40]

However, even in the face of the most determined attempts by the Attorney General to thwart prosecutions, he turned out to be powerless to stop them all, particularly when foreign jurisdictions became involved. The most striking example of this has been the action taken in the United Kingdom against James Ibori.[41] Ibori was the Governor of Delta State, one of Nigeria's richest oil-producing states. He was also a major contributor to the campaign to get the ailing Yar'Adua elected. Aondoakaa used to be Ibori's personal lawyer; he was also the personal lawyer to a number of other high-profile backers of Yar'Adua. He had previously run his own law firm in Benue, one of Nigeria's smallest states: like many such firms in Nigeria, it was effectively a one-man operation. Further examples of barriers erected by this small-time lawyer turned Attorney General are cited in the section on MLA in Nigeria, below.[42]

Mutual legal assistance

The whole of Chapter IV of the UNCAC is devoted to international cooperation. The need for, and the desire to achieve, a high level of assistance between states was one of the driving forces behind the negotiation of the Convention. Article 43 deals with several of the important features of such cooperation, which is stated to be mandatory. It includes the use of treaties and conventions to facilitate evidence-gathering, and addresses specific issues such as dual criminality, and

40 See www.bbc.co.uk/news/world-africa-15855916.

41 See below. See also, H. O. Yusef, 'The Rule of Law and the Politics of Anti-Corruption Campaigns in a Post-Authoritarian State: the Case of Nigeria', *King's Law Journal*, 22 (2011), 57–83.

42 A heavily ironic characterisation of Aondoakaa's approach to the law was written in September 2009 by M. Adega, 'The Attorney General has Gone Mad Again', available at: http://saharareporters.com/article/michael-aondoakaa-attorney-general-has-gone-mad-again.

the importance of having a central authority to deal with requests for assistance. Article 46 builds on the general provisions of Article 43, and focuses on the provision of mutual legal assistance, which is at the heart of the Convention.

Mutual legal assistance as applied in Nigeria

In the wake of Abacha, and further high-profile Nigerian governor cases, the Metropolitan Police (the Met) was in 2006/7 funded by the Department for International Development (DFID) to set up a specialist unit of six officers, the Proceeds of Corruption Unit (PCU), to keep a specific watch on politically exposed persons (PEPs). This unit has been highly successful, but its biggest catch to date has undoubtedly been Ibori. The Met first started investigating him and his circle in 2005, as a result of suspicions over an engineering company controlled by him which supplied houseboats for Shell and Chevron oil workers to live on. It was quite plain that on a governor's salary[43] Ibori could not have been acquiring assets on the scale that he apparently was. Ibori stands accused of having stolen nearly US$300 million from Delta State, but, according to leaked Wikileaks cables, the sum may be nearer US$3.4 billion, stolen during the seven years he was in office.[44]

As with many such people, Ibori had not been without his helpers. In rapid succession his sister, wife, mistress and lawyer were all arrested in the United Kingdom on money-laundering charges, tried and jailed.[45] Ibori himself, seeing what had happened to Governor Alamieyeseigha,[46] steered clear of the jurisdiction. The PCU had enlisted the assistance of the EFCC. That help was at first given freely for the purposes of prosecuting his accomplices, the investigation having commenced shortly before Yar'Adua came to power. Thus, the EFCC's assistance was, to

[43] Currently, the basic salary recommended by the Revenue Mobilisation Allocation and Fiscal Commission (RMAFC) of Nigeria for the President himself is only Naira 3.5 million, which converts to US$28,000 pa at a rate of Naira 125 = $1 See at: www.africanmanager.com/site_eng/articles/11629.html. Ibori's salary was less than US $25,000 pa: see BBC report at n. 51, below.

[44] Source: Sahara Reporters, available at: http://saharareporters.com/news-page/london-money-laundering-trial-james-ibori-victor-attah-love-ojakovo-henry-imashekka-and-da. Sahara reporters are hard-hitting, New York-based, purveyors of (usually accurate) inside information on corruption in Nigeria.

[45] Sahara Reporters, n. 44, above, and at: http://saharareporters.com/news-page/breaking-news-london-money-laundering-trial-theresa-ibori-sentenced-5-years.

[46] See below.

begin with, given by leave of Obasanjo's Attorney General, Bayo Ojo SAN – the Attorney General being Nigeria's central authority for MLA purposes.

When Aondoakaa came on the scene, one of the first things he attempted to do was to halt the trial at Southwark Crown Court by writing directly to Ibori's London lawyers stating he had never been charged with any criminal activity in Nigeria, and should not therefore be the subject of legal proceedings in London.[47] They were, he claimed, an infringement of Nigeria's sovereignty, and 'against the rule of law in Nigeria'. Nigeria was a country, he claimed, perfectly well able to prosecute its criminals itself, and he proceeded to bring 135 charges against Ibori in Nigeria, purportedly placing him under house arrest.

Aondoakaa also stated that any evidence before the court which had been provided by the EFCC was in contravention of the express orders of the central authority (viz himself), and should be returned forthwith. It was not returned, and a careful exercise was carried out to determine exactly what evidence had been provided before he came on the scene, and after. As it turned out, there was sufficient pre-Yar'Adua evidence to secure the conviction of Ibori's associates. According to Sahara Reporters, there was an active policy on the part of Aondoakaa[48] to disrupt all attempts to prosecute Nigeria's governors and senior politicians. This policy allegedly had the support of Yar'Adua himself.[49] The very first step taken by Nigeria's new president, Goodluck Jonathan, on assuming (at that stage only temporary) office in 2010 was to dismiss Aondoakaa. He was also stripped of his SAN status (Senior Advocate of Nigeria: equivalent to Queen's Counsel in the United Kingdom).[50]

[47] The letter appears in the report by Sahara Reporters (n. 45, above), at: http://saharareporters.com/report/exclusive-attorney-general-michael-aondoakaas-letter-iboris-lawyer.

[48] According to a Wikileaks cable sent to Washington in May 2009, Aondoakaa refused to discuss with the United Kingdom the return of 400 prisoners to Nigeria unless the Crown Prosecution Service dropped their prosecution of Ibori. (There are currently 1,000 Nigerian-origin prisoners in the United Kingdom, costing the UK taxpayer £40 million pa.). See at: http://saharareporters.com/news-page/wikileaks-cables-how-former-agf-michael-aondoakaa-pressured-uk-drop-charges-against-james.

[49] See at: http://saharareporters.com/news-page/nigeria%E2%80%99s-attorney-general-michael-aondoaka-destroys-cases-against-corrupt-former-governor.

[50] Nigeria's Legal Practitioners Privileges Committee (LPPC) said it concluded that Aondoakaa deserved to be stripped of the title of Senior Advocate of Nigeria, in view of the judgment delivered by a Federal High Court sitting in Calabar on 1 June 2010, which it said not only categorically branded him unfit to hold the office of the AGF or any public office in Nigeria, but equally declared him as persona non-grata for offences relating to corruption, see at: http://allafrica.com/stories/201012070222.html.

The charges against Ibori in Nigeria were later dropped, but shortly afterwards Yar'Adua died. Ibori's time was effectively up, and he fled the country, seeking refuge in Dubai, a well-known haven for the politically corrupt. No one had ever been extradited from there on corruption charges, but, again, things were about to take a change for the worse for Mr Ibori. Instead of Nigeria applying for his extradition, it was the UK authorities who applied. Ibori was duly extradited, despite appealing, and reportedly attempting to commit a crime in Dubai in order to be placed under arrest there. Perhaps Dubai calculated that a cooling in diplomatic relations with the United Kingdom was not worth the trouble when set against the fate of one Nigerian ex-governor. Dubai may also have wanted to raise its status in the West by being seen as a cooperative state. On 27 February 2012, the opening day of his trial in London, Ibori changed his plea to guilty on ten counts of money laundering and conspiracy to defraud.[51] He was sentenced on 17 April 2012 to thirteen years' imprisonment following the trial of his accomplice, Elias Preko, a Ghanaian, formerly at Goldman Sachs, who set up offshore trusts and opened bank accounts for him in Guernsey.[52] Ibori's guilty plea avoided a long trial, during the course of which his dealings with Nigeria's ruling party, the People's Democratic Party (PDP), would no doubt have played a large part: in the view of many, Ibori was on course to become Nigeria's president.[53]

The investigating Metropolitan police officer is on record as saying that a confiscation order will now be sought,[54] and an application will no doubt be made on behalf of either Delta State or the Federal Government, or both, for compensation.[55] It is to be hoped that such an application will be successful. The sums involved are likely to be large; not as large as in the Abacha case, but significant. Careful thought is therefore being given by the DFID and others as to how repatriation of these monies can be handled in such a way as to satisfy not only the applicants, but also civil society in Nigeria. Earlier this year, freedom of information legislation was passed, and Nigerian civil society is not proving slow to take full advantage of it.[56]

[51] See at: www.bbc.co.uk/news/world-africa-17181056.

[52] 'Banker Helped Corrupt Nigerian Steal Millions', *Daily Telegraph*, 14 March 2012.

[53] See at: www.bbc.co.uk/news/world-africa-17184075.

[54] See comments of DI Paul Whatmore in the BBC report, at n. 53, above.

[55] For more information and photographs of some of Ibori's UK assets, see at: www.dailymail.co.uk/news/article-2107280/Nigerian-state-governor-funded-international-playboy-lifestyle-50million-fraud-rose-humble-roots-working-London-DIY-store.html.

[56] See, e.g., the SERAP website at: www.serap-nigeria, n. 29, above.

> The best check on arbitrariness, mistakes and corruption is transparency, which allows thousands of citizens to act as monitors of public interest. There must be transparency as regards such organisations so that citizens can make an informed choice about them.[57]

As far as UNCAC is concerned, the Ibori case is instructive in a number of ways:

- the setting up of a crack police unit in the United Kingdom dedicated to identifying and prosecuting PEPs has proved its worth;
- MLA is a valid concept only between cooperating states, whatever the Convention may say;
- firm action taken by a requested state in the face of a total collapse of political will in the requesting state can still be very effective;
- anti-money laundering laws can be instrumental in bringing the beneficiaries of corruption to justice, whether or not those laws were UNCAC-inspired;[58]
- extradition laws can be used more effectively on occasion by requested rather than by requesting states;[59]
- the role of civil society, in the form of the press, and in particular that of the offshore-based Sahara Reporters, in bringing about the demise of a corrupt attorney general, was notable.

Apart, possibly, from the setting up of the PCU at the Met, none of the steps taken could be attributed directly to the UNCAC, but, at the same time, the UNCAC has had the effect of raising international awareness of the evils of corruption, and moved the fight against it up the political agenda, so that governments are devoting more resource to it. This has been particularly marked in the United Kingdom, with the appointment of an international anti-corruption champion (the Minister of Justice), the passing of the 2010 Act and the publication of the UK

57 Attributed to Mahatma Gandhi: a passage recently quoted by an Indian NGO, available at: http://profit.ndtv.com/news/show/disclose-audit-reports-of-cooperative-banks-cic-to-rbi-186239?cp.

58 The Ibori prosecutions took place under ss. 327 and 328 of the Proceeds of Crime Act 2002, s. 1(1) of the Criminal Law Act 1977 and s. 93C(1) of the Criminal Justice Act 1988. For a full list of the charges, see at: http://saharareporters.com/news-page/london-money-laundering-trial-james-ibori-victor-attah-love-ojakovo-henry-imashekka-and-da.

59 This was shown to be the case with Abacha: Switzerland successfully extradited the youngest Abacha son, Abba, from Germany to stand trial in Switzerland; the threat of extradition both by Switzerland and by Jersey against Mohammed Abacha's right-hand man, Bagudu, extracted a US$180 million settlement from him, to Nigeria's benefit.

Foreign Bribery Strategy paper.[60] Again, civil society has played an important role – particularly Transparency International UK, which has monitored and contributed to developments at every step. However, it should also be recognised that much of this activity has been more the result of pressure from the OECD Anti-Bribery Working Group than specifically of UNCAC implementation. Nevertheless, the UK response, while not perfect,[61] is at least happening: not every state can make a similar claim.

Mutual legal assistance in other jurisdictions

Examples of delay and flagrant disregard of MLA provisions in the Nigerian context have been given above. It is a matter for serious concern that countries seeking assistance are still encountering severe problems. Evidence of this was given at the COSP 4 in Marrakesh, Morocco, by Egypt, Tunisia and Algeria: Libya was not officially represented, but representatives from civil society who were present expressed similar concerns. At the beginning of this chapter the concerns of civil society regarding monitoring of the ongoing implementation of the UNCAC, particularly in the light of the events of the Arab Spring were mentioned. People fought and died to shed the rule of corrupt tyrants; there is now a real danger that their achievements will be frustrated as they try to enlist support from other states to recover what has been stolen from them.

Egypt, in particular, was scathing about the varied nature of the responses it is receiving to its MLA requests: these range from countries which are exceedingly helpful, to those which put up barriers, to those which do not deign to respond at all. The most common responses take the form of a barrage of counter questions, seemingly put for the requested state to satisfy itself that Egypt is not on some kind of 'fishing expedition'. Drawing that line may in some cases be difficult, but the reality may be that the requesting state has genuinely scarce knowledge concerning the location and ownership of assets. This is particularly likely to be the case where 'offshore' jurisdictions are used and complex trust arrangements are set up deliberately to disguise beneficial ownership. There were several calls at the COSP for states to follow the example

[60] See at: www.official-documents.gov.uk/document/cm77/7791/7791.pdf.

[61] See, in particular, the still-existing shortcomings in enforcement of anti-money laundering regulations mentioned below.

of Brazil, where beneficial ownership of financial instruments, including bank accounts, must be disclosed.[62]

There may, of course, be genuine difficulties for requested states when the status and legitimacy of an interim regime is in question following a revolution, but in such cases it may be that one option for the requested state is to commence its own proceedings for recovery of the assets. This is reportedly the case with the United Kingdom, which, as in the Nigerian cases mentioned above, has started its own money-laundering proceedings on the basis of additional information supplied by Egypt, but apparently without informing the Egyptian authorities of the details.[63] Elections were due to be held in Egypt in December 2011, but, at the time of writing, it is clear that the situation in Egypt is still highly volatile, and it is possible that the UK authorities wish to see what happens, and who is finally returned to power, before divulging further information. The situation may be viewed as not being different in substance from the issues which may arise on repatriation of funds alluded to above.

Other types of difficulty that may arise are frequently associated with the nature and form of the request. The UNODC has placed online a 'request writer' tool, designed to assist states with formulating acceptable requests. However, there is probably no substitute, particularly in difficult cases, for assistance being given to the requesting state by the requested state. Switzerland has sent a team from its federal authority to Tunisia to assist with formulation of requests, which action appears already to have borne fruit, as the Swiss state is now in a position to assist Tunisia.[64] There has been a general expectation among the public, particularly in the affected Arab states, that, once the tyrants are toppled, recovery of assets and their repatriation will follow swiftly. The Abacha experience indicates a different expectation. The Algerian representative at the COSP said in plenary that states should expect the process to take between five and twenty years. This is a chilling measure of the failings of the present MLA regime. It remains to be seen whether the exhortatory tone of the Asset Recovery Resolution passed at COSP 4 (above) will

[62] For detailed information, see at: www.clearstream.com/ci/dispatch/en/cicbinary/CICDownloads/Clearstream/Market_Reference/ICSD/Brazil/mpe_brl.pdf/mpe_brl.pdf?yawlang=en.

[63] According to conversations with the representatives of the Egyptian delegation at COSP 4.

[64] Swissinfo.ch, 'Tunisian Request Marks a Major Step', 12 October 2011, available at: http://m.swissinfo.ch/eng/politics/Tunisian_legal_aid_request_marks_major_step.html?cid=31335162.

make a difference. However, as far as Switzerland is concerned, states where there is a complete breakdown of the country's legal system may, paradoxically, be in a better position to receive positive assistance from the Swiss authorities, particularly as far as the freezing of assets is concerned. This is the result of the implementation of the so-called 'Duvalier law'.[65]

Money laundering

Article 14 of UNCAC requires states to set up a comprehensive domestic regulatory and supervisory regime for banks and non-bank financial institutions to combat money laundering. Article 23 requires states to criminalise money laundering and envisages inclusion of predicate offences committed both within and outside the jurisdiction. At the heart of the anti-money laundering (AML) regime lies the requirement for customer due diligence to be carried out when banks and financial institutions take on new clients. Where the new client is a PEP, enhanced due diligence is required. As mentioned above, in 2001, the UK's FSA carried out an investigation into banks in the City of London which had been involved in laundering Abacha monies. It might have been hoped that the 'strengthening of money laundering controls' which was supposed to have resulted from that investigation would have led to a general tightening up of AML requirements, and that more stringent regulation and supervision might have followed from what was generally recognised to have been a salutary warning, both for the financial services sector and the FSA.

Yet, within just four years of the Abacha experience, another Nigerian state governor, Diepreye Alamieyeseigha of Bayelsa State, was able to deposit millions of pounds with, among others, Barclays, HSBC and the Royal Bank of Scotland in London with seemingly no questions asked. With the monies, Alamieyeseigha was able to purchase a number of expensive properties in desirable locations in London and, again, no questions were asked.[66] In September 2005, Alamieyeseigha travelled to London. By this time, one of the banks had thought to file a Suspicious

[65] As to which, see further below.

[66] The Money Laundering Regulations 2007 which cover the business of estate agents did not come into force until 15 December 2007. They implement the EU's Third Anti-Money Laundering Directive. The Alamieyeseigha case underlined the need for such regulations to be put in place.

Transaction Report (STR) with the UK authorities. Acting on this information, the newly formed specialist Proceeds of Corruption Unit at the Met arrested Alamieyeseigha as he came through Heathrow. He was taken back to his flat in West London and a search was carried out. In his bedroom £1 million in cash was found, placed in drawers and cupboards. The police mounted a watch on the property. Two days later, Alamieyeseigha's wife was seen, apparently returning from a shopping trip. In her shopping bags were a further £200,000 in cash. Alamieyeseigha was bailed in the sum of £1.3 million, paid into court, which was put up by a close (Nigerian) associate of his. Despite this, Alamieyeseigha left the country through Heathrow just two months after his arrest.[67]

At about the same time, another Nigerian governor, Joseph Dariye of Plateau State, was arrested in London and charged with money-laundering offences. For quite some time after it became less fashionable for Nigerian governors to visit London: a major blow to them, their wives and families. Ibori stayed away, but his retinue were unable, it seems, to avoid the temptations of shopping in London, with disastrous consequences for them, as has been seen. Both Alamieyeseigha and Dariye had to be pursued through the civil courts in the end (Dariye also jumped bail), having escaped the jurisdiction. Both were in fact prosecuted in Nigeria, but this was in the days before President Yar'Adua and his attorney general came on the scene. A total of some £20 million was recouped from Alamieyeseigha and returned to Nigeria. Most of this money was raised by selling the London properties, and a valuable ($US 1 million) waterfront property in Cape Town, as well as confiscating the contents of bank accounts in Cyprus, Denmark and the Bahamas: further monies are in the course of being recovered in the United States. In the case of Dariye, two civil actions were initiated in London, the first of which recovered property worth £395,000, and the second £5.7 million from accounts he held in London.[68]

These events did not go unnoticed by civil society in the United Kingdom, even if the authorities, in the shape of the FSA, seemingly continued to slumber. In 2009, the NGO Global Witness published a

[67] The bail monies were forfeited, and, as a result of a further investigation, Alamieyeseigha's surety was found to have been involved in mortgage fraud, for which he was prosecuted and convicted, and had his London property confiscated.

[68] Information from the Basel International Centre for Asset Recovery (ICAR), available at: www.assetrecovery.org/kc/node/44186379-8580-11dd-81c3-399112e3d573.0;jsessionid=2A8E1F5BC621512F7F0348AFBCF35DE7.

hard-hitting account of international money laundering by high-profile PEPs.[69] This was followed by 'International Thief Thief: How British Banks are Complicit in Nigeria Corruption',[70] the title taken from a well-known protest song by Fela Kuti,[71] the iconic Nigerian singer much in vogue in the 1970s when Nigeria's military dictators were getting under way with their high-profile graft. In this second publication, Global Witness give detailed accounts of both the Alamieyeseigha and Dariye cases.

In June 2011, the FSA, perhaps stirred into action not so much by the publication of the Global Witness accounts of these cases as by the perceived threat to their ability to investigate financial crime as an independent body,[72] finally commissioned an in-depth study of money-laundering compliance by the UK's banks and financial institutions.[73] What they discovered they professed to find deeply shocking. Under their conclusions they stated:

> Our main conclusion is that around three quarters of banks in our sample, including the majority of major banks, are not always managing high-risk customers and PEP relationships effectively and must do more to ensure they are not used for money laundering. Despite changes in the legal and regulatory framework a number of the weaknesses identified during this review are the same as, or similar to, those identified in the FSA report of March 2001 covering how banks in the UK handled accounts linked to the former Nigerian military leader, General Sani Abacha. We are concerned there has been insufficient improvement in banks' AML systems and controls during this period.

The conclusions continued:

> Serious weaknesses identified in banks' systems and controls, as well as indications that some banks are willing to enter into very high-risk business relationships without adequate controls when there are potentially large profits to be made, means that it is likely that some banks are handling the proceeds of corruption or other financial crime.

69 Global Witness, 'Undue Diligence: Banks Helping the Poor to get Poorer', October 2010, www.undue-diligence.org.

70 Global Witness, 'International Thief Thief: How British Banks are Complicit in Nigeria Corruption', October 2010, available at: www.globalwitness.org/sites/default/files/pdfs/international_thief_thief_final.pdf.

71 Subsequently revived in the late 2000s in the hit West End and Broadway musical *Fela*.

72 See, e.g., at: http://citywire.co.uk/new-model-adviser/fsa-could-lose-financial-crime-mandate/a488914.

73 See www.fsa.gov.uk/pubs/other/aml_final_report.pdf.

More precisely, what the FSA found, having visited a number of leading banks and interviewed their Money Laundering Reporting Officers (MLROs) and Customer Relationship Managers (RMs) was that, far too often, the perceived risk presented by PEPs was downgraded quite deliberately in order to enable the banks to accept large, wealth-generating deposits from them. A particularly damning conclusion was that:

> Three quarters of the banks in our sample failed to take adequate measures to establish the legitimacy of the source of wealth and source of funds to be used in the business relationship.

The Report includes case studies, and in case after case the profit motive appears to have dominated decisions, unless there was perceived to be a real danger of substantial reputational risk through exposure in the media. A similar exercise was recently conducted by the Swiss Financial Market Supervisory Authority (FINMA).[74] The report refers to 'a ruling issued on 30 August 2000 in connection with the Abacha case'. While the majority of banks were found to be compliant with their AMLA obligations, FINMA had cause to 'intervene by way of administrative proceedings against four banks'.

The report is unusual in making specific reference to the events of the Arab Spring, giving chapter and verse on the freezing of Tunisian (19 January 2011), Egyptian (11 February 2011) and Libyan (24 February 2011) assets. The Federal Department of Foreign Affairs (FDFA) froze CHF 60 million Tunisian, CHF 410 million Egyptian, and CHF 360 million Libyan funds held in Swiss banks. The report goes on to state that few figures have been published internationally regarding asset seizure, noting that such information is available only from media reports, but states that in excess of US$35 billion have been frozen worldwide: US$30 billion in the United States, US$2 billion in Canada and US$3.2 billion in the United Kingdom. It also states that assets had been paid into Swiss banks not only from banks in Tunisia, Egypt and Libya, but also from banks in France, the United States, the United Kingdom and Italy: an implicit condemnation of failings in the anti-money laundering regimes in all those jurisdictions.[75]

74 FINMA, 'Due Diligence Obligations of Swiss Banks when Handling Assets of "Politically Exposed Persons": An Investigation by FINMA', 10 November 2011, available at: www.finma.ch.

75 FINMA, 'Due Diligence Obligations of Swiss Banks', pp. 4, 5.

Political will, or the lack of it

'It takes two to tango' is a phrase frequently used in a bribery context, but, as has been seen, it is equally apt when it comes to mutuality in assistance requests. There are examples of states which request assistance, but fail to produce evidence of any will to prosecute at home. The other, more egregious, situation is where the government of a victim state fails to take any action whatsoever to recover assets which are known to be the proceeds of corruption. Examples of the first type of situation are Indonesia and Kenya; examples of the second are the Democratic Republic of Congo (DRC), Haiti, Equatorial Guinea, Gabon and the Congo Republic (Congo Brazzaville).

The UNCAC is, unsurprisingly, posited on the underlying notion that states which have suffered from corruption and the looting of state assets will want to get them back. Yet the fact is that the last thing an endemically corrupt regime will be disposed to do is to take action which may expose its leaders to the possibilities of prosecution and confiscation of their ill-gotten wealth. Their peoples may suffer, their children may die as the result of failure to provide infrastructure, fresh water, vaccination and mosquito nets, and their parents may be expected to survive on US$1 a day, but greed and the acquisition of needless wealth becomes, in all too many states, an all-consuming passion which brooks no interference from without.

Indonesia

With regard to the non-prosecution at home issue there are basically two barriers. One is fear, the other is political intrigue, and very often, a combination of both. In the case of Indonesia, fear is undoubtedly a factor. Tommy Suharto, the favoured son of the deposed, late president, reached new heights of kleptocratic behaviour with his love of fast cars when he purchased not a Lamborghini, but the Lamborghini company itself. The shares were held through an offshore BVI company, Garnet Investments, part of his Humpus Group. When Suharto was deposed, *Time* magazine ran a detailed article which calculated that the Suharto family had diverted US$70 billion for its own use during the thirty years that Suharto was in power. By the time he was deposed it was estimated that there were probably US$30 billion in corruptly acquired assets held at home and abroad. Shortly after his father was deposed, Tommy disposed of his Lamborghini shareholding, banking €35 million in an account with BNP Banque Paribas (as it then was) in Guernsey. When (and only when) he decided to withdraw that money from the bank, BNP filed an STR with Guernsey's FIS (Financial Intelligence Service). The FIS ordered BNP not to pay the money out. Tommy sued BNP in Guernsey, not only for the proceeds of sale, but also for the losses incurred by the bank on its investment of the money. At this point Guernsey informed the Indonesian Government of what was happening, and asked if the government wished to intervene in the Guernsey proceedings and itself lay claim to these monies. This, the Indonesian Government did.

When Indonesia's intervention came before the Guernsey court, the judge asked what action Indonesia was taking to prosecute and recover assets from Tommy at home in Indonesia. Not an unreasonable question to ask, considering the scale of corruption by the Suharto family, and Tommy in particular, being alleged. The answer was that no action was being taken. Action had been taken in the past, and Tommy had been found guilty of corruption and convicted. Two weeks later the judge in that case was shot through the head, and Tommy was charged with having ordered his murder. Tommy was again found guilty, and served a short prison sentence. Notwithstanding these events, the Guernsey judge sought some kind of evidence that the purchase of Lamborghini had been made with the proceeds of corruption and that this fund in Guernsey was not the sole focus of Indonesia's recovery efforts. Indonesia then commenced a series of civil proceedings in Jakarta against Tommy which were designed to demonstrate that he owed money to the Indonesian state as the result of his corrupt transactions. One by one those actions failed, perhaps because, in Indonesia, it is possible to hire the services of a 'markuse',[76] a fixer who will obtain the judgment you want.

Guernsey's Appeal Court ultimately ordered that the money be paid out to Tommy, and leave to appeal to the Privy Council was refused. At this point Guernsey's FIS again intervened and itself imposed a freezing order on the monies. Tommy requested a judicial review of this action, which at first instance was granted, but overturned on appeal.[77] This time, the Appeal Court effectively said that Tommy must explain where the money to purchase Lamborghini came from: something which, arguably, he should have been asked in the first place. Tommy sought

[76] See N. Onoshi, 'In Indonesia Middlemen Mold the Outcome of Justice', *New York Times*, 19 December 2009, available at: www.nytimes.com/2009/12/20/world/asia/20indo.html.

[77] *The Chief Officer, Customs and Excise, Immigration and Nationality Service* v. *Garnet Investments Ltd*, Guernsey Court of Appeal (File No. 432), 6 July 2011.

leave to appeal to the Privy Council; it was refused. The Guernsey Court of Appeal pointed out that it was still open to Tommy to proceed with his action against BNP, and that this was the forum best suited to determining the issues. As things stand, it is not quite a reversal of the burden of proof, because the bank will still have to justify its refusal to pay out under Tommy's mandate with it, but, on the other hand, it might be said that a continued refusal is justified in circumstances where, as Clare Montgomery QC, sitting as an Appeal Judge, said:

> It is of the essence of anti-money laundering methods to seek to maintain a system whereby funds are properly traceable in order to seek to defeat the mischief which is facilitated where all the links cannot be traced or all the underlying transactions verified.[78]

As she went on to say:

> The transaction for the purchase of the Lamborghini shares by Mr Hutomo [Tommy] must have been a singular event, and it would be surprising if Mr Hutomo, still in the prime of life, would not remember such an acquisition at the very may-morn of youth.[79]

The circumstances of this case highlight the single greatest difficulty prosecutors in common law countries face: the linking of the proceeds of corruption with specific corrupt acts. As has been seen above, this was dealt with in the Abacha case in Switzerland by having the Abachas declared a criminal organisation, thus reversing the burden of proof there. One possible route to easing the burden of proof problem would be to utilise the illicit enrichment provision, Article 20 of the Convention, which has been done by Hong Kong,[80] but with mixed results.[81]

Again, however, the appetite of the Indonesian Government for pursuing the case against Tommy may be called into question. At no time has it engaged the KPK (Corruption Eradication Commission), a body

[78] *The Chief Officer, Customs and Excise, Immigration and Nationality Service* v. *Garnet Investments Ltd*, Guernsey Court of Appeal, at para. 106.

[79] *The Chief Officer, Customs and Excise, Immigration and Nationality Service* v. *Garnet Investments Ltd*, Guernsey Court of Appeal, at para. 105.

[80] A useful discussion of the law appears in D. Wilsher, 'Inexplicable Wealth and Illicit Enrichment of Public Officials: A Model Draft that Respects Human Rights in Corruption Cases', *Crime, Law & Social Change*, 45 (2006), 27–53.

[81] An exhaustive report on the legal implications of criminalising illicit enrichment by Dr Guillermo Jorge, *The Romanian Legal Framework on Illicit Enrichment*, was published by the American Bar Association Central European and Eurasian Law Initiative (ABA/CEELI) in July 2007.

which has a 100 per cent record of success in the cases that it has pursued in the Jakarta anti-corruption court. It has instead preferred to leave matters in the hands of the Attorney General's Office, where greater political influence can be exerted. A recent attempt was made by the Indonesian legislature to remove some of the KPK's most powerful investigative tools, which does not bode well for the future effectiveness of the Commission.[82]

Kenya

With Kenya there is a situation connected with the notorious *Anglo-Leasing* affair[83] in which MLA has been requested from both Switzerland and the United Kingdom. Twelve of the eighteen Anglo-Leasing contracts were placed in 2001 while President Moi was in power. Six were placed after the election of President Kibaki in 2003. In 2007, a determined effort was made in the Kenyan Parliament to have any enquiries into matters which took place before 2003 declared time-barred: this would have included the equally notorious *Goldenberg* affair, and the majority of the Anglo-Leasing contracts. The Bill was passed by Parliament, but President Kibaki withheld his signature to it. In 2008, a decision was handed down in the High Court in Nairobi declaring MLA requests made by the Kenya Anti-Corruption Commission (KACC) *ultra vires*.[84] The case arose as the result of an action brought by one of the Anglo-Leasing contractors in Geneva suing on the balance due under its contract. Seeking evidence of corruption in placing the contract, a raid was made on the offices of the shell company contractor situated in Geneva. Computers and papers were seized. The Nairobi action was brought within twenty-four hours.

Following the court ruling,[85] Kenya's Attorney General, Amos Wako, placed an absolute ban on MLA being either given or received by the KACC. The High Court judgment was overturned,[86] but more than two-and-a-half years were lost. Wako, who during a record twenty years in

[82] See 'Lawmakers Not Helping End Corruption, Says ICW', *Jakarta Post*, 28 October 2008, available at: www.thejakartapost.com/news/2011/10/28/lawmakers-not-helping-end-corruption-says-icw.html.

[83] See M. Wrong, *It's Our Turn to Eat: The Story of a Kenyan Whistleblower* (London: Fourth Estate, 2009).

[84] In the High Court of Kenya at Nairobi, Misc Civil Application No. 695, 2007.

[85] Which has been said by members of KACC staff to have been purchased for £3,000.

[86] In the Court of Appeal at Nairobi, Civil Appeal No. 194 of 2008.

office had failed to bring a single prosecution against a prominent politician despite Kenya having been the subject of two major corruption scandals (Goldenberg and Anglo-Leasing) during that time, was issued with a travel ban by the United States in 2009. It was said that Wako, 'obstructed the reform process, failed to end the cycle of impunity and has been an obstacle in the fight against corruption'.[87] He also failed to bring any prosecutions against the perpetrators of the post-election violence in 2007: the individuals concerned are now the subject of proceedings before the International Criminal Court in the Hague.

Both the last two directors of the KACC have had to step down in controversial circumstances. Aaron Ringera, appointed as a result of his purge of the Kenyan judiciary, was not re-appointed, despite the backing of the president; the most recent director, Professor P. L. O. Lumumba, was dismissed in August 2011. In both cases suspicions were voiced that the dismissals were the result of the Commission closing in on leading figures, but neither was able to make significant progress in prosecuting high-level corruption. It is to be hoped that the agency, renamed the Ethics and Anti-Corruption Commission under the terms of the new Constitution,[88] will have a greater impact in the future.

Victim states that fail to take action

Haiti

With regard to victim states which fail to take necessary action, two have involved monies held in Switzerland. The first involved Haiti, systematically looted by the notorious Duvalier family. After long and tortuous litigation in the Swiss courts it was found that monies were due under a trust to 'Baby Doc' Duvalier. No claim was made to those monies by Haiti and they were about to be returned to Baby Doc. On the day after that judgment was given Haiti suffered its most devastating earthquake. The Swiss Parliament intervened and stopped the money from being remitted. Shortly afterwards they passed the so-called 'Duvalier law',[89] which permits Switzerland to freeze assets when it believes that the rule

[87] See http://news.bbc.co.uk/1/hi/8343088.stm.

[88] A short history of anti-corruption agencies in Kenya can be found at: www.kacc.go.ke/default.asp?pageid=2.

[89] See at: www.swissinfo.ch/eng/politics/Duvalier_Law_enters_into_force.html?cid=29395684.

of law has broken down in a victim country, with the result that no request is, or can be, made for assistance. The value of this law is already in evidence in Switzerland's treatment of Libyan assets.[90]

Zaire/Democratic Republic of Congo

Some of the most egregious examples of the flaunting of impunity are to be found in Africa, particularly sub-Saharan Africa, where the names of kleptocratic heads of state have become bywords for corruption. In Michaela Wrong's, *In the Footsteps of Mr Kurz*,[91] the eponymous Mr Kurz, the central figure in Joseph Conrad's allegorical novella, *The Heart of Darkness*, becomes a metaphor for Mobutu Sese Seko, Zaire's president for thirty-two years until he died in 1997. During the years he was in power it is estimated that Mobutu mis-spent US$12 billion building vainglorious palaces deep in the jungle and securing political support at home from his so-called 'mouvanciers'.[92] The monies he got through were mostly provided by the World Bank, who were warned at an early stage that they would never see repayment of their 'loans', but at that time the word 'corruption' was not even allowed to be mentioned within the World Bank.

Many believed that he had left enormous sums in his Swiss bank accounts which would be repatriated to Zaire. In fact, there was only US$6 million, which was frozen by the Swiss authorities. Yet even that comparatively paltry sum was not repatriated to what had by then become the Democratic Republic of Congo (DRC), because no request was forthcoming from the government of Joseph Kabila, only from Mobutu's grandchildren. Professor Mark Pieth, who has for twenty years headed the OECD's Working Group on Bribery, tried in

[90] See Swissinfo.ch, 'Swiss Primed to Hand Over Libyan Assets', 26 October 2010, available at: http://m.swissinfo.ch/eng/specials/the_arab_spring/Swiss_primed_to_hand_over_Libyan_assets.html?cid=30971506.

[91] M. Wrong, *In the Footsteps of Mr Kurz* (London: Fourth Estate, 2000).

[92] 'Mouvancier' is a term used by the DRC diaspora to describe businessmen and former politicians of Mobutu's day: the bourgeoisie of which he was himself a member. Many ex-DRC mouvanciers now reside in the wealthy suburb of Sandton in Johannesburg, SA. G. K. Kamuangu, 'Language, Immigration and Ethnicity: The Choice of Language in DRC Immigrant Families', unpublished PhD thesis, University of the Witwatersrand, Johannesburg, 2006, available at: http://wiredspace.wits.ac.za/bitstream/handle/10539/4715/Thesis.pdf.

vain through the Swiss courts to prevent the return of the monies to Mobutu's family.[93]

The Mobutu story encapsulates a key failing in the UNCAC. Article 57 deals with return and disposal of assets. It contains innovative, and even mandatory, provisions, but gives states discretion to make their own arrangements between themselves on a case-by-case basis. The Article clearly envisages that victim states will want assets returned. In the case of the DRC, the assets could not be returned because there was no request forthcoming from the government.

Fundamental weakness of the UNCAC

This outcome highlights the fundamental weakness of the UNCAC. It is a Convention to which states are parties, based on the fundamental assumption that states will take action when their citizens are the victims of grand corruption. This is simply not the case: it is like expecting a burglar to hand himself in to the police after committing a crime, with the further requirement that he should hand over his swag. It does not happen. The police have to be called in to investigate, but, in the case of a state looted by its autocratic leader, that will not happen either. The difference between the burglary example and state looting is in the classification of the victims. The burgled citizen can go to the police; the citizens of the looted nation have nowhere to turn, at least under the UNCAC. The underlying premise on which the UNCAC is built is that the victim state will take action: absent the state being willing to take such action, to whom does the citizen turn? What possibilities does the non-state actor have?

This question has formed the basis of a recent study by the Basel Institute on Governance.[94] The study was the outcome of a meeting held at the Institute in September 2010. The participants were drawn from NGOs involved in anti-corruption work, academia and the private sector, as represented by the banking and insurance industries, lawyers and accountants in private practice, and the media. As such, they represented a credible grouping to fall under the definition of non-state actors.

[93] See, e.g., K. O. Ori, 'Swiss Court Approves African Kleptocracy: Mobutu's Loot to go to his Family', *Afrik News*, 15 July 2009, available at: www.afrik-news.com/article15923.html.

[94] D. Thelesklaf and P. G. Pereira, *Non-State Actors in Asset Recovery* (Bern: Peter Lang, 2011).

The continuing resistance of states to the activities of NSAs is well illustrated by the article cited at the beginning of the chapter. The study highlights ways in which NSAs can help to facilitate the asset recovery process through their intimate knowledge of the societies in which they live, but such facilitation mainly takes the form of assisting state action, giving it greater credibility and transparency. Only one contribution[95] deals with the possibility of the citizen taking action to recover assets where the state fails to take such action. This possibility has been translated into the action which is described in the next section.

Civil society action against leaders of victim states

The final three cases all involve long-serving dictators in west Africa. In 2007, Antoine Dulin and Jean Merckaert from the Catholic Committee against Hunger and for Development (CCFD), a French NGO, published a report entitled (in translation) *Stolen Assets: Dictators' Wealth and Western Connivance*, which contained estimates of amounts of assets stolen from developing countries located in the West. Based on this report, the French NGO Sherpa[96] decided to start its own investigation, and discovered that a number of African heads of state and their relatives owned properties in France, particularly in Paris. The following account is adapted from a Briefing Note which Sherpa produced after the initial hearings.[97]

Complaint No. 1

In March 2007, Sherpa, together with two other French NGOs,[98] filed a complaint with the French Public Prosecutor against the ruling families of Angola, Burkina Faso, Congo, Equatorial Guinea and Gabon alleging that they owned millions of euros worth of properties in France, the value of which was not consistent with their published official salaries. The complaint was based on the specific offence of

[95] Maud Perdriel-Vaissiere, Managing Director of the Paris-based NGO Sherpa, 'How to Turn Article 51 into Reality', in D. Thelesklaf and P. G. Pereira, *Non-State Actors in Asset Recovery* (Bern: Peter Lang, 2011).

[96] See at: www.asso-sherpa.org.

[97] An account of the case is at: www.asso-sherpa.org/nos-programmes/ffid/campagne-ra/bma.

[98] Survie and the Federation of the Congolese Diaspora.

handling stolen assets, which is prohibited under Articles 321-1[99] and 432-15[100] of the French Code pénal. According to these Articles, retention of illegally acquired assets on French territory is an offence. Given the vast quantity of real estate apparently held by or on behalf of these heads of state and their close associates, the complainants argued that these properties could not possibly have been acquired on their official salaries, but were far more likely to represent the proceeds of stolen public assets.

Police investigation

In June 2007, a police investigation was launched in response to the complaint. It confirmed most of the allegations and uncovered further tens of millions of euros-worth of luxury properties and cars, as well as hundreds of bank accounts belonging to the heads of state, their family members and close associates. It was apparent that the sources of funding were highly questionable: for example, Edith Bongo, wife of the Gabonese president, had acquired a Daimler-Chrysler which was paid for by direct transfers from the Gabonese public treasury. The investigation also highlighted the role played by intermediaries such as banks and other agencies, and established the complicity of a large number of individuals.

Despite those findings, the investigation was closed down in November 2007 after the Public Prosecutor ruled that the crimes were 'insufficiently characterised'. Sherpa then decided to try to lodge a criminal complaint coupled with a civil party (*partie civile*[101]) petition,

[99] Article 321-1: Receiving is the concealment, retention or transfer of a thing, or acting as an intermediary in its transfer, knowing that that thing was obtained by a felony or misdemeanour. Receiving is also the act of knowingly benefiting in any manner from the product of a felony or misdemeanour. Receiving is punished by five years' imprisonment and a fine of €375,000.

[100] Article 432-15: The destruction, misappropriation or purloining of a document or security, of private or public funds, papers, documents or securities representing such funds, or of any other object entrusted to him, committed by a person holding public authority or discharging a public service mission, a public accountant, a public depositary or any of his subordinates, is punished by ten years' imprisonment and a fine of €150,000.

[101] Under civil law, the party which has suffered loss can join criminal proceedings as a *partie civile*, as Nigeria did in the Swiss criminal proceedings against Abacha. The *partie civile* then plays a full part in the proceedings, and is entitled to see all the evidence obtained in the criminal proceedings, but is restricted in the uses to which that evidence can then be put.

the only option open to it in order to get an inquiry launched.[102] Sherpa therefore asked the French chapter of Transparency International to join them.[103] TI France eventually accepted, after ensuring that such an action was compliant with TI policy.

Complaint No. 2

Thus, on 9 July 2008, TI France, together with individual Congolese and Gabonese citizens, lodged a further complaint with the Public Prosecutor. This complaint was in all respects identical to the one filed by Sherpa sixteen months before. The sole objective was to enable TI France and the Gabonese and Congolese citizens to lodge a criminal complaint coupled with a *partie civile* application in order to come before an investigating judge.[104] Predictably, the Public Prosecutor announced, on September 3 2008, that he would not pursue the case.

Complaint with civil party petition

On 2 December 2008, the case was filed by TI France and Gregory Ngbwa Mintsa, a Gabonese citizen, both represented by M William Bourdon, Attorney-at-law and President of Sherpa. The immediate objective was to get an investigating judge appointed in order to extend the scope of the initial police investigation.

Before assessing the merits of the case, the judge had to rule on the standing of TI France and the Gabonese taxpayer to lodge the complaint. After months of argument between Sherpa and the Public Prosecutor, the Dean of investigating judges ruled that the case lodged by TI France and Mr Mintsa in December 2008 was admissible. This was a landmark

102 An enquiry led by an investigating judge is much more intrusive than the police investigation requested by the Public Prosecutor. The investigating judge has greater powers to establish the truth (forensic experts, telephone tapping, etc.).

103 As an organisation dedicated to fighting corruption, TI France was more likely to be an admissible party in the case than any other NGO.

104 According to Art. 85 of the French Criminal Code of Procedure (Code de procédure pénale): 'Any person claiming to have suffered harm from a felony or a misdemeanor may petition to become a civil party by filing a complaint with the competent investigating judge in accordance with the provisions of Articles 52 and 706-42.' However, the civil party petition is admissible only provided that the plaintiff proves that either the Public Prosecutor let him know, following a complaint lodged before him or a police investigation, that he will not initiate proceedings, or a three-month period has passed since the complaint before was lodged before the judge.

decision. For the first time in France, collective legal action taken by an organisation dedicated to fighting corruption was permitted to represent the victims of corruption in a civil action in order to be able to advance the facts directly affecting their collective interests.[105] In the event, Mr Mintsa had to stand down because of intensifying threats both against his person and against his family. The Public Prosecutor appealed the Dean's decision to the Paris Court of Appeal, which ruled against TI France and Sherpa. They duly appealed to the Cour de Cassation, the highest court in France, which reversed the decision of the Court of Appeal and ordered that a judicial investigation be opened. In the event, two high calibre judges were appointed, and the investigation continues.

The next public development was dramatic. Teodoro Obiang has been in power in Equatorial Guinea since 1979. The great majority of the 500,000 population live on less than US$2 per day, but per capita income should be in excess of US$30,000 thanks to the country's relatively small population and massive oil income, derived mainly from the huge offshore Zafiro (Saphire) field, operated by ExxonMobil. The majority of the population live in the capital Malabo, on Bioko, a large island offshore Cameroon. There are virtually no paved roads in the capital, yet Teodoro Nguema Obiang, Obiang's eldest son and heir apparent, who is currently Forestry Minister, hit the headlines in June 2011. A large car transporter had been stopped outside his apartment in the wealthy Avenue Foch in Paris, loaded with a selection of Maseratis, Ferraris, Porsches, two Bugatti Veyrons and a Silver Cloud Rolls Royce, all of which are now held by the French Prosecutor.[106]

Proceedings in the United States

More bad luck came Obiang Jr's way at the end of October 2011 with the announcement by the US Department of Justice (DoJ) that they were going to freeze US$70 million of his assets, plus his US$30 million mansion at Malibu Beach, California, and US$2 million worth of Michael Jackson memorabilia.[107] It is to be hoped that this long overdue action by the authorities in the United States will be the precursor of further action, both against the Obiangs and against Omar Bongo Jr, who was the

[105] As had happened in the Swiss Abacha proceedings.

[106] Pictures of the cars appear on: www.gtspirit.com/2011/09/29/11-supercars-of-teodoro-obiang-nguema-mbasogo-seized-by-french-police.

[107] See at: www.bbc.co.uk/news/world-africa-15464988.

subject of a case study carried out by Senator Carl Levin, Chairman of the US Senate Subcommittee on Investigations published in 2010.[108] So far as is known, no action has yet been taken against Bongo: perhaps the Obiang case will provide the necessary precedent.

Notwithstanding these actions against the Obiang family, the Executive Board of UNESCO on 18 March 2012 in a deeply split decision voted in favour of setting up a US$3 million Award for Research into Life Sciences donated by President Obiang. The Board has fourteen African state members, all of whom voted in favour. Civil society organisations have recorded their outrage at this apparent betrayal of the principles and objectives of UNESCO.[109]

The African Commission on Human and People's Rights

The Open Society Justice Initiative, together with the Spanish human rights organisation, Asociación Pro Derechos Humanos de España (APDHE), and EG Justice, a US-based rights organisation, filed a complaint with the African Commission on Human and People's Rights arguing that the diversion of oil wealth that has taken place in Equatorial Guinea violates the African Charter on Human and People's Rights.[110] The Commission is understood still to be considering the complaint.

Pioneering actions

These are the first, and leading, examples of civil society taking the initiative before courts in an effort to recover assets where victim states remain moribund. It is to be hoped that these actions will generate further cases in other jurisdictions where high value assets are held overseas by notoriously corrupt politicians and officials. There is no obvious route for such action to be taken in common law countries, but close attention is being paid to the Indian model of public interest litigation, which may provide helpful precedents in the future.

[108] US Senate, Permanent Subcommittee on Investigations, *Keeping Foreign Corruption out of the United States*, February 2010, available at: www.financialtaskforce.org/wp-content/uploads/2010/02/Levin-report-on-US-facilitators-of-Africa-corruption-FOREIGN-CORRUPTION-REPORT-FINAL-as-of-2–210.pdf.

[109] See at: www.hrw.org/news/2012/03/09/unesco-disappointing-vote-obiang-prize.

[110] For more information, visit: www.soros.org/initiatives/justice/litigation/equatorialguinea.

BIBLIOGRAPHY

Aghion, P. *et al.*, 'The Unequal Effects of Liberalization: Evidence from Dismantling the Licence Raj in India', *CEPR*, 22 December 2005, available at: www.cepr.org/meets/wkcn/2/2360/papers/Burgess.pdf.

Al-Sadig, A., 'The Effects of Corruption on FDI Flow', *Cato Journal* 29(2) (2009), 267.

Alderman, R., 'The Bribery Act 2010: The SFO's Approach and International Compliance', speech hosted by McGrigors, UK, 9 February 2011, available at: www.sfo.gov.uk/about-us/our-views/director's-speeches/speeches-2011.

Allan, P., 'Independent Commission Against Corruption', in G. E. Edwards and A. C. Byrnes (eds), *Hong Kong's Bill of Rights: The First Year* (Faculty of Law, University of Hong Kong, 1993), pp. 18–19.

Alldridge, P., *Money Laundering Law* (Oxford: Hart, 2003).

'Reforming Bribery: Law Commission Consultation Paper 185(1) Bribery Reform and the Law Commission – Again', *Criminal Law Review*, 9 (2008), 671–89.

'The Law Relating to Free Lunches', *Company Lawyer*, 23 (2002), 264–73.

Allen, C. K., *Legal Duties and Other Essays in Jurisprudence* (Oxford: Clarendon Press, 1931).

Alschuler, A. W., 'Mediation with a Mugger: The Shortage of Adjudicative Services and the Need for a Two-Tier System in Civil Cases', *Harvard Law Review*, 99 (1986), 1808–59.

'Plea Bargaining and its History', *Columbia Law Review*, 79 (1979), 1–43.

Amin, M., 'Is there More Corruption in Larger Countries? Evidence Using Firm-level Data', September 2011, available at: works.bepress.com.

Anderson, L., 'Demystifying the Arab Spring', in *The New Arab Revolt*, Foreign Affairs/CFR eBook, May/June 2011.

Ansley, J. J. *et al.*, 'Commercial Bribery and the New International Norms', *Bloomberg Law Reports* (October 2009), available at: http://works.bepress.com/cgi/viewcontent.cgi?article=1005&context=don_berthiaume&sei-redir=1#search=%22travel%20act%20bribery%22.

Antolisei, F., 'Manuale di diritto penale', in L. Conti (ed.), *Parte speciale*, vol. II (Milan: Giuffrè, 2003).

Argandona, A., 'The 1996 ICC Report on Extortion and Bribery in International Business Transactions', *Business Ethics: A European Review*, 6 (1997), 134–46.

Ashworth, A., *Principles of Criminal Law*, 4th edn (Oxford University Press, 2003).

Sentencing and Criminal Justice, 5th edn (Cambridge University Press, 2010).

Asian Development Bank (ADB), *Anticorruption and Integrity* (Manila: Asian Development Bank, 2007).

Assemblée nationale (France), *Rapport d'information déposé par la délégation de l'Assemblée nationale pour l'Union européenne sur l'Office européen de lutte anti-fraude (OLAF)*, No. 1533, 8 April 2004, pp. 9–10.

Auld, R., *Review of the Criminal Courts of England and Wales* (London: The Stationery Office, 2001).

Baldwin, J. and McConville, M., *Negotiated Justice* (Oxford University Press, 1977).

Bank Information Centre, 'World Bank Accused of Tolerating Corruption in Kenya', 3 April 2008, available at: www.bicusa.org/en/Article.3717.aspx.

'Banker Helped Corrupt Nigerian Steal Millions', *Daily Telegraph*, 14 March 2012.

Benussi, C., 'Art. 319', in G. Marinucci and E. Dolcini (eds), *Codice penale commentato* (Milan: Giuffrè, 2006).

Black, J., 'A Review of Enforcement Techniques', in Law Commission, 'Criminal Liability in Regulatory Contexts', Law Com. Consultation Paper No. 195 2010, App. A.

Boll, M., *Plea Bargaining and Agreement in the Criminal Process* (Hamburg: Diplomica Verlag, 2009).

Botting, G., *Wrongful Conviction in Canadian Law* (Markham, Ontario: Lexis-Nexis, 2010).

Bowen, H. R., *Social Responsibilities for the Businessman* (New York: Harper, 1953).

Bozhilova, D., 'Measuring Success and Failure of EU-Europeanization in the Eastern Enlargement: Judicial Reform in Bulgaria', *European Journal of Law Reform*, 9 (2007), 285–319.

Brants, C., 'Consensual Criminal Procedures: Plea and Confession Bargaining and Abbreviated Procedures to Simplify Criminal Procedure', *Electronic Journal of Comparative Law*, 11(1) (2007), available at: www.ejcl.org.

Breau S. and Carr, I., 'Humanitarian Aid, Human Rights and Corruption', in M. Odello and S. Cavandoli (eds), *Emerging Areas of Human Rights in the 21st Century* (New York: Routledge, 2011), pp. 149–75.

Brereton, M. and Temple, M., 'The New Public Service Ethos: An Ethical Environment for Governance', *Public Administration*, 77 (1999), 455–74.

Bricola, F., 'Tutela penale della pubblica amministrazione e principi costituzionali', *Temi* (1968).

Brown, G. D., 'Stealth Statute: Corruption, the Spending Power, and the Rise of 18 U.S.C. § 666', *Notre Dame Law Review*, 73 (1998), 247–314.

Burke, J., 'Indian Activist Anna Hazare Refuses to End Hunger Strike', *The Guardian*, 7 April 2011, available at: www.guardian.co.uk/world/2011/apr/07/anna-hazare-hunger-strike.

'Indian Activist Anna Hazare on Hunger Strike as MPs Debate Anti-Graft Bill', *The Guardian*, 27 December 2011, available at: www.guardian.co.uk/world/2011/dec/27/indian-anti-graft-hunger-strike.

But, J., 'Head of Snooping Watchdog Hits Out at Law Enforcers', *South China Morning Post*, 8 December 2009, p. 3.

Cahn, A. and Donald, D. C., *Comparative Company Law: Text and Cases on the Laws Governing Corporations in Germany, the UK and the USA* (Cambridge University Press, 2010).

Calo, Z. R., 'Empirical Desert and the Moral Economy of Punishment', *Arizona State Law Journal*, 42 (2011), 1123–40.

Carr, I., 'Corruption in Africa: Is the African Union Convention on Combating Corruption the Answer?', *Journal of Business Law*, March (2007), 111–36.

'Corruption, the Southern African Development Community Anti-corruption Protocol and the Principal–Agent–Client Model', *International Journal of Law in Context*, 5 (2009), 147–77.

'Fighting Corruption through Regional and International Conventions: A Satisfactory Solution?', *European Journal of Crime, Criminal Law and Criminal Justice*, 15 (2007), 121–53.

'The United Nations Convention on Corruption: Improving the Quality of Life of Millions in the World?', *Manchester Journal of International Economic Law*, 3 (2006), 3–44.

Carr, I. and Lewis, D., 'Combating Corruption through Employment Law and Whistleblower Protection', *Industrial Law Journal*, 39 (2010), 51–81.

Carr, I. and Outhwaite, D., 'Controlling Corruption through Corporate Social Responsibility and Corporate Governance: Theory and Practice', *Journal of Corporate Law Studies*, 11 (2011), 299–341.

Carroll, A. B., 'A Three-Dimensional Conceptual Model of Corporate Performance', *Academy of Management Review*, 4 (1979), 497–505.

Chalmers J. and Leverick, F., 'Fair Labelling in Criminal Law', *Modern Law Review*, 71 (2008), 217–46.

Chan, H. S. and Lo, J., 'Hong Kong Facing China: Administrative Competence of the ICAC and Fundamental Rights of Public Employees', *Asian Journal of Public Administration*, 13 (1991), 39–66.

Chan, J., 'Basic Law and Constitutional Review: The First Decade', *Hong Kong Law Journal*, 37 (2007), 405–47.

Chan, J. M. and Lee, F. L. F., 'Mass Media and Public Opinion', in L. Wai-man, P. L-t. Lui, W. Wong and Ian Holliday (eds), *Contemporary Hong Kong Politics: Governance in the Post-1997 Era* (Hong Kong University Press, 2007), pp. 155–75.

Chan, V., 'Committed to Investigating Corruption, Wherever it Lurks', *South China Morning Post*, 25 November 2011, p. 20.

Chau, P. and Young, S. N. M., 'Abolishing By-elections to Fill Vacancies in the Legislative Council', *Hong Kong Law Journal*, 41 (2011), 601–9.

Chen J. Y. S. (ed.), *The July 1 Protest Rally: Interpreting a Historic Event* (City University of Hong Kong Press, 2005).

Cheung, S., 'ICAC Plugs Holes Amid Shortage of Investigators', *South China Morning Post*, 20 November 2011, p. A3.

'Setting precedent for establishing a retirement heaven', *The Sun*, 21 November 2011, p. A12

'Was Top ICAC Man Sacked, Then Charged?', *South China Morning Post*, 30 July 2011, p. C1.

Cheung, S., Lee, C. and Tsang, E., 'Conflict of Interest Rules ICAC Chief Out of Tsang Probe', *South China Morning Post*, 1 March 2012, p. C1.

Chiu, A., 'ICAC Officers in Court for Coaching False Evidence', *South China Morning Post*, 16 March 2011, p. 4.

Coase, R. H., 'The Nature of the Firm', *Economica* (N.S.), 4 (1937), 386–405.

Collier, P., 'The Failure of Conditionality', in C. Gwin and J. M. Nelson (eds), *Perspectives on Aid and Development* (Washington, DC: Overseas Development Council, 1997), pp. 51–77.

Collier, P., Guillaumont, P., Guillaumont, S. and Gunning, J. W., 'Redesigning Conditionality', *World Development*, 25 (1997), 1399–407.

Conway, B., *The Piracy Business* (London: Hamlyn, 1981).

Courtney, C., 'Corruption in the Official Arms Trade', in Transparency International (UK), Policy Research Paper No. 001 (London: Transparency International, 2002).

Covolo, V., 'The Legal Framework of OLAF Investigations', *New Journal of European Criminal Law*, 2 (2011), 201–19.

Craig, P., 'The Fall and Renewal of the Commission: Accountability, Contract and Administrative Organisation', *European Law Journal*, 6 (2000), 98–116.

Cremer, G., *Corruption and Aid Development: Confronting the Challenges*, trans. Elisabeth Shüth (London: Lynne Reinner, 2008).

Cropp, N., 'The Bribery Act 2010: A Comparison with the Foreign Corrupt Practices Act: Nuance v. Nous', *Criminal Law Review*, 2 (2011), 122–40.

Cunningham, S., 'Punishing Drivers Who Kill: Putting Road Safety First?', *Legal Studies*, 27 (2007), 288–311.

Damaska, M., *The Faces of Justice and State Authority* (New Haven, CT: Yale University Press, 1986).

Darley, J. M. *et al.*, 'Community Standards for Defining Attempt: Inconsistencies with the Model Penal Code', *American Behavioral Scientist*, 39 (1996), 405–20.

Darroch, F., *The Lesotho Corruption Trials: A Case Study* (Berlin: Transparency International, 2003), available at: www.ipocafrica.org/index.php?option=com_content&view=article&id=71&Itemid=66.

Davigo, P. and Mannozzi, G., *La corruzione in Italia, percezione sociale e controllo penale* (Bari: Laterza, 2007).

Dimitrova, A. L., 'The New Member States of the EU in the Aftermath of Enlargement: Do New European Rules Remain Empty Shells?', *Journal of European Public Policy*, 17 (2010), 137–48.

Djilani, J. N., 'The British Importation of American Corporate Compliance', *Brooklyn Law Review*, 76 (2010), 303–41.

DLA Piper, 'Judge Signals Death Knell for Global Settlements', available at: www.dlapiperrapidresponse.com/export/sites/rapid-response-old/bulletins/pdfs/2010_Judge_Signals_Death_Knell_for_Global_Settlements.pdf.

Dobb, M., *Soviet Economic Development since 1917* (London: Routledge & Kegan Paul, 1948).

Donald, D. C., 'Some Observations on the Use of Structural and Remedial Measures in American and German Law after Sarbanes–Oxley', *German Law Journal*, 4 (2003), 127–35.

Downey, B., 'Combating Corruption: The Hong Kong Solution', *Hong Kong Law Journal*, 6 (1976), 27–66.

Duff, R. A., 'Perversions and Subversions of the Criminal Law', in R. A. Duff, L. Farmer, S. E. Marshall, M. Renzo and V. Tadros (eds), *The Boundaries of the Criminal Law* (Oxford: Hart, 2010).

Earle, B., 'The United States' Foreign Corrupt Practices Act and the OECD Anti-Bribery Recommendation: When Moral Suasion Won't Work, Try the Money Argument' (citing OTCA, Title V, Subtitle A, Part I, s. 5003(d), 102 Stat. 1424), *Dickinson Journal of International Law*, Winter (1996), 207–42.

Elkington, J., *Cannibals with Forks: The Triple Bottom Line of 21st-Century Business* (Hoboken, NJ: John Wiley, 1999).

Energy Probe Research Foundation, 'M12 Million Bribery Scam on Sole', 16 July 2010, available at: http://eprf.probeinternational.org/node/9016.

European Commission, Communication to the European Parliament and the Council, *Enlargement Strategy and Main Challenges 2011–2012*, COM (2011) 666 final, Brussels, 12 October 2011.

Communication to the European Parliament and the Council, *Taking Stock of the European Neighbourhood Policy*, COM (2010) 207, Brussels, 12 May 2010.

Communication to the European Parliament, the Council and the European Economic and Social Committee, *On a Comprehensive EU Policy against Corruption*, COM (2003) 317 final, Brussels, 28 May 2003.

Communication to the European Parliament, the Council and the European Economic and Social Committee, *Fighting Corruption in the EU*, COM (2011) 308 final, Brussels, 6 June 2011.

Communication to the European Parliament, the Council, the European Economic and Social Committee and the Committee of the Regions, *Delivering European Renewal*, COM (2011) 777 final, Brussels, 15 November 2011.

Green Paper on the Modernisation of EU Public Procurement Policy, *Towards a More Efficient European Procurement Market*, COM (2011) 15 final, Brussels, 27 January 2011.

Implementation of the European Neighbourhood Policy in 2009. Progress Report Ukraine, SEC (2010) 524, Brussels, 12 May 2010.

Joint Communication by the High Representative of the Union for Foreign Affairs and Security Policy and the European Commission, *A New Response to a Changing Neighbourhood*, COM (2011) 303, Brussels, 25 May 2011.

Joint Staff Working Paper, *Implementation of the European Neighbourhood Policy in 2010. Sector Progress Report*, SEC (2011) 645, Brussels, 25 May 2011.

Monitoring Report on the State of Preparedness for EU Membership of Bulgaria and Romania, COM (2006) 549 final, Brussels, 26 September 2006.

Report to the Council on the Modalities of European Union Participation in the Council of Europe Group of States against Corruption (GRECO), COM (2011) 307 final, Brussels, 6 June 2011.

Report to the Council based on Article 9 of the Council Framework Decision 2003/568/JHA of 22 July 2003 on Combating Corruption in the Private Sector, COM (2007) 328 final, Brussels, 18 June 2007.

Report to the European Parliament and the Council based on Article 9 of Council Framework Decision 2003/568/JHA of 22 July 2003 on Combating Corruption in the Private Sector, COM (2011) 309 final, Brussels, 6 June 2011.

Report to the European Parliament and the Council on the Management of EU Funds in Bulgaria, COM (2008) 496 final, Brussels, 23 July 2008.

Report to the European Parliament and the Council on Progress in Bulgaria under the Co-operation and Verification Mechanism, COM (2011) 459 final, Brussels, 20 July 2011.

Report to the European Parliament and the Council on Progress in Romania under the Co-operation and Verification Mechanism, COM (2011) 460 final, Brussels, 20 July 2010.

Second Report Implementation of the Convention on the Protection of the European Communities' Financial Interests and its Protocols, COM (2008) 77 final, Brussels, 14 February 2008.

European Council, *The Stockholm Programme: An Open and Secure Europe Serving and Protecting Citizens*, OJ (2010) No. C115, 4 May 2010.

Feinstein, A., *The Shadow World: Inside the Global Arms Trade* (London: Hamish Hamilton, 2011).

Fiandaca, G. and Musco, E., *Diritto penale, parte speciale, vol. I: delitti contro il patrimonio* (Bologna: Zanichelli, 2002).

Fiandaca, G., 'Esigenze e prospettive di riforma dei reati di corruzione e concussione', in *Riv. it. dir. e proc. pen.* 883 (2000).

FINMA, 'Due Diligence Obligations of Swiss Banks when Handling Assets of "Politically Exposed Persons": An Investigation by FINMA', 10 November 2011, available at: www.finma.ch.

Finnis, J., 'Invoking the Principle of Legality against the Rule of Law', *New Zealand Law Review*, (2010), 601–16.

Financial Services Authority (FSA), *Anti-Bribery and Corruption in Commercial Insurance Broking* (London: FSA, 2010).

Handbook of Principles for Businesses (London: FSA, 2012).

Fornasari, D., 'Delitti di corruzione', in A. Bondi, A. di Martino and G. Fornasari (eds), *Reati contro la pubblica amministrazione* (Turin: Giappichelli, 2004).

Forti, G. (ed.), *Il prezzo della tangente. La corruzione come sistema a dieci anni da "mani pulite"* (Milan: Vita e Pensiero, 2003).

Fraser, N., 'Top ICAC Investigator Released on Bail', *South China Morning Post*, 1 May 2011, p. 1.

Garrett, B. L., 'Globalized Corporate Prosecutions', *Virginia Law Review*, 97 (2011), 1776–876.

Georgakakis, D., 'La démission de la Commission européenne: scandale et tournant institutionnel (octobre 1998–mars 1999)', *Cultures et Conflits*, Nos 38–39 (2000), available at: www.conflicts.org.

Gevurtz, F. A., 'Commercial Bribery and the Sherman Act: The Case for Per Se Illegality', *University of Miami Law Review*, 42 (1987), 365–400.

Glenn, H. P., *Legal Traditions of the World: Sustainable Diversity in Law*, 4th edn (New York: Oxford University Press, 2010).

Global Compact Regional Learning Forum, 'Creating a Culture Intolerant of Fraud and Corruption in Total South Africa (PTY Ltd)', in *UNGC, Businesses Fighting Corruption: Experiences from Africa* (New York: UNGC, 2007), available at: www.unglobalcompact.org/docs/news_events/8.1/bfc_web.pdf.

Global Witness, 'International Thief Thief: How British Banks are Complicit in Nigeria Corruption', October 2010, available at: www.globalwitness.org/sites/default/files/pdfs/international_thief_thief_final.pdf.

'Undue Diligence: Banks Helping the Poor to get Poorer', October 2010, available at www.undue-diligence.org.

Goodstadt, L. F., *Uneasy Partners: The Conflict between Public Interest and Private Profit in Hong Kong* (Hong Kong University Press, 2010).

Greasley, K., 'R (Purdy) v. DPP and the Case for Wilful Blindness', *Oxford Journal of Legal Studies*, 30 (2010), 301–26.

Green, S. P., 'Broadening the Scope of Criminal Law Scholarship', *Criminal Justice Ethics*, 20 (2001), 55–62.

Lying, Cheating, and Stealing: A Moral Theory of White Collar Crime (Oxford University Press, 2006).

Thirteen Ways to Steal a Bicycle: Theft Law in the Information Age (Cambridge, MA: Harvard University Press, 2012).

Green, S. P. and Kugler, M. B., 'Public Perceptions of White Collar Crime Culpability: Bribery, Perjury, and Fraud', *Law and Contemporary Problems*, 75 (2012), 33–59.

Greenberg, T. S. *et al.*, *Politically Exposed Persons* (Washington, DC: World Bank, 2010).

Grosso, C. F., 'Corruzione', *Dig disc. pen.*, 3 (1989), 153.

'Dazione o promessa di denaro al pubblico ufficiale in ragione delle funzioni esercitate: corruzione punibile o fatto penalmente atipico?', *Foro it.*, 2 (1996).

Guerrini, R., *La responsabilità da reato degli enti, sanzioni e loro natura* (Milan: Giuffrè, 2006).

'The Crimes of Civil Servants against the Public Administration in Italy: Perspectives of Reform', *Studi Senesi* (1997).

Hale, R. L., 'Coercion and Distribution in a Supposedly Non-Coercive State', *Political Science Quarterly*, 38 (1923), 470–94.

Hastings, M., 'Current Affairs', *Sunday Times*, 30 October 2011, p. 46.

Hawkins, K., *Law as a Last Resort* (Oxford University Press, 2003).

Heidenheimer, A. J., Johnson, M. and LeVine, V. T. (eds), *Political Corruption: A Handbook* (New Brunswick, NJ: Transaction Publishers, 1989).

Heine, G., Huber, B. and Rose, T. O., *Private Commercial Bribery* (Freiburg: International Chamber of Commerce, 2003).

Hillion, Ch., 'The European Union is Dead. Long Live the European Union … A Commentary on the Treaty of Accession 2003', *European Law Review*, 29 (2004), 583–612.

Holliday, C., Schmidheiny, S. and Watts, P., *Walking the Talk: The Business Case for Sustainable Development* (Sheffield: Greenleaf, 2002).

Hong Kong Bar Association, 'Comments of the Bar Association on the Interception of Communication and Surveillance Ordinance (Cap. 589)', LC Paper No. CB(2)529/11-12(01) (Hong Kong Legislative Council, 9 September 2011).

Hong Kong Department of Justice, Prosecutions Division, 'Information Paper on Pre-trial Interviewing of Witnesses by Prosecutors', paper for LegCo Panel on Administration of Justice and Legal Services, LC Paper No. CB(2)2327/07-08(05), (Hong Kong: Department of Justice, June 2008).

The Statement of Prosecution Policy and Practice: Code for Prosecutors (Hong Kong: Department of Justice, 2009).

Hong Kong Legislative Council (LegCo) Panel on Administration of Justice and Legal Services, Minutes of meeting, LC Paper No. CB(2)2826/07-08 (Hong Kong Legislative Council, 23 June 2008).

Hong Kong Monetary Authority, *Half-Yearly Monetary and Financial Stability Report*, September 2011, available at: www.hkma.gov.hk.

Hong Kong SAR Information Services Department, *Hong Kong: The Facts* (2010), p. 2, available at: www.gov.hk/about/abouthk/factsheets/docs/icac.pdf.

Horan, S. and Johnsen, D. B., 'Does Soft Dollar Brokerage Benefit Portfolio Investors: Agency Problem or Solution?', *George Mason Law & Economics Research Paper No. 04-50*, March (2004), available at SSRN: http://ssrn.com/abstract=615281 or doi:10.2139/ssrn.615281.

Horder, J., 'Bribery as a Form of Criminal Wrongdoing', *Law Quarterly Review*, 127 (2010), 37–54.

'On Her Majesty's Commercial Service: Bribery, Public Officials and the UK Intelligence Services', *Modern Law Review*, 74 (2011), 911–31.

Hotchkiss, G., 'The Sleeping Dog Stirs: New Signs of Life in Efforts to End Corruption in International Business', *Journal of Public Policy and Marketing*, 17 (1998), 108–15.

Huang, Y., *Capitalism with Chinese Characteristics: Entrepreneurship and the State* (New York: Cambridge University Press, 2008).

Ilisu Dam Campaign, *2000: Balfour Beatty's Annus Horribilis* (Oxford: Ilisu Dam Campaign, 2000), available at: www.thecornerhouse.org.uk/sites/thecornerhouse.org.uk/files/balfour.pdf.

Independent Commission Against Corruption (ICAC), 'Information Paper by the ICAC in Response to Issues Raised in the Report', Paper for LegCo Panel on Security, LC Paper No. CB(2)467/09-10(01) (Hong Kong: ICAC, 4 December 2009).

'The Landmark Case: Godber's Downfall' (Hong Kong: ICAC, 2010, available at: www.icac.org.hk.

International Chamber of Commerce (ICC), *Guidelines on Whistleblowing*, 2008, available at: www.iccwbo.org/uploadedFiles/ICC%20Guidelines%20Whistleblowing%20%20as%20adopted%204_08(2).pdf.

Report on Extortion and Bribery in Business Transactions (Paris: ICC, 1977).

Iser, W., *Der Akt des Lesens: Theorie ästhetischer Wirkung*, 4th edn (Munich: Wilhelm Fink, 1994).

Jackson, J., Langer, M. and Tillers, P. (eds), *Crime, Procedure and Evidence in a Comparative and International Context* (Oxford: Hart, 2008).

Jensen, M. C. and Meckling, W. H., 'Theory of the Firm: Managerial Behavior, Agency Costs and Ownership Structure', *Journal of Financial Economics*, 3 (1976), 305–60.

Jiaxue, G., 'Stephen Chan Found Not Guilty of Corruption Charges', *China Daily*, Hong Kong Edition, 3 September 2011, p. 1.

Joanilho, M., 'Police Blast ICAC over Arrests', *South China Morning Post*, 20 May 2002, p. 1.

Jones, T. and Newburn, T., 'Three Strikes and You're Out: Exploring Symbol and Substance in American and British Crime Control Politics', *British Journal of Criminology*, 46 (2006), 781–802.

Jorge, G., *The Romanian Legal Framework on Illicit Enrichment* (Chicago, IL: ABA/CEELI, July 2007).

Judt, T., *Postwar: A History of Europe since 1945* (London: Heinemann, 2005).

Julian, R., 'Judicial Perspectives in Serious Fraud Cases: The Present Status of and Problems Posed by Case Management Practices, Jury Selection Rules, Juror Expertise, Plea Bargaining and Choice of Mode of Trial', *Criminal Law Review*, October (2008), 764–82.

Kagan, R. A., 'Globalization and Legal Change: The "Americanization" of European Law?', *Regulation & Governance*, 1 (2007), 99–120.

Kaiafa-Gbandi, M., 'The Penal Repression of Corruption in the Public and Private Sector' (in Greek), *Poinika Chronika* (2010), 3 *et seq.*

Kamp, J. van der, 'Graft-busters go from Hooking Big Fish to Catching Minnows', *Sunday Morning Post*, 20 November 2011, p. 16.

Kamuangu, G. K., 'Language, Immigration and Ethnicity: The Choice of Language in DRC Immigrant Families', unpublished PhD thesis, University of the Witwatersrand, Johannesburg, 2006, available at: http://wiredspace.wits.ac.za/bitstream/handle/10539/4715/Thesis.pdf.

Kaufmann, D. and Wei, S., 'Does "Grease Money" Speed Up the Wheels of Commerce?', NBER Working Paper No. 7093 (Cambridge, MA: NBER, 1999).

Kei, H., 'CCB Rushed into the Headquarters to Arrest Three; ICAC Committed Five Blunders and Close to Collapse', *Hong Kong Economic Journal*, 20 November 2010, p. 10.

Kennedy, A., 'Civil Recovery Proceedings under the Proceeds of Crime Act 2002: The Experience so Far', *Journal of Money Laundering Control*, 9 (2006), 245–64.

Kitching, J., 'Better Regulation and the Small Enterprise', in S. Weatherill (ed.), *Better Regulation* (Oxford: Hart, 2007), pp. 155–73.

Klitgaard, R., *Controlling Corruption* (Berkeley, CA: University of California Press, 1988).

Kochan, N. and Goodyear, R., *Corruption: The New Corporate Challenge* (London: Palgrave Macmillan, 2011).

Kolber, A. J., 'How to Improve Empirical Desert', *Brooklyn Law Review*, 75 (2009), 433–61.

Kraakman, R. *et al.*, *The Anatomy of Corporate Law: A Comparative and Functional Approach*, 2nd edn (New York: Oxford University Press, 2009).

Kwok, T., 'Formulating an Effective Anti-Corruption Strategy: The Experience of Hong Kong ICAC', in UNAFEI, *Annual Report for 2005 and Resource Material Series No. 69* (Tokyo: UNAFEI, 2006).

Langbein, J. L., *The Origins of Adversary Criminal Trial* (Oxford University Press, 2003).

Law Commission (UK), 'Legislating the Criminal Code: Corruption', Law Com. Consultation Paper No. 145, 1997.

Legislating the Criminal Code: Corruption, Law Com. No. 248 (London: The Stationery Office, 1998).

'Reforming Bribery', Law Com. Consultation Paper No. 185, 2007.

Reforming Bribery, Law Com. No. 313 (London: The Stationery Office, 2008).

Law Commission, 'Criminal Liability in Regulatory Contexts', Law Com. Consultation Paper No. 195, 2010.

Law Reform Commission of Hong Kong, *Privacy: The Regulation of Covert Surveillance* (Hong Kong, March 2006).

Report on Privacy: Regulating the Interception of Communications (Hong Kong, December 1996).

Lawrence, J., O'Kane, M., Rab, S. and Nakhwal, J., 'Hardcore Bargains: What could Plea Bargaining Offer in UK Criminal Cartel Cases?', *Company Lawyer*, 7 (2008), 17–42.

Lazowski, A., 'And Then They Were Twenty-Seven ... A Legal Appraisal of the Sixth Accession Treaty', *Common Market Law Review*, 44 (2007), 401–30.

Lee, C. and Wong, N., 'Clean Up Your Act, Lawmakers Warn', *The Standard*, 29 June 2010.

Lee, D., 'Secret Tapes Aired in ICAC Trial', *South China Morning Post*, 3 February 2012, p. C1.

Leff, N. H., 'Economic Development through Bureaucratic Corruption', *American Behavioral Scientist*, 8 (1964), 8–14.

Leigh, D. and Evans, R., 'Balfour Beatty Agrees to pay £2.25m over Allegations of Bribery in Egypt', *The Guardian*, 7 October 2008.

Levi, N., 'I delitti contro la pubblica amministrazione', in E. Florian (ed.), *Trattato di diritto penale* (Milan: Giuffrè, 1935).

Leys, C., 'What is the Problem about Corruption?', *Journal of Modern African Studies*, 3 (165), 215–30.

Li, D., 'Letter from Hong Kong', *U.K. I.C.A.C. Association Newsletter*, Issue 4/11 (December 2011).

Li, J., 'A Mission to Protect', *China Daily (Peak View)*, 29 July 2011, available at: http://pub.chinadailyapac.com/peakview/figures/201201/103.html.

Li, K-W., *The Hong Kong Economy: Recovery and Restructuring* (Singapore: McGraw-Hill, 2006).

Lo, A., 'A Long Way to Fall', *South China Morning Post*, 2 March 2012, p. 4.

Lo, S. S. H., 'Independent Commission Against Corruption', in D. H. McMillen and M. Si-wai (eds), *The Other Hong Kong Report 1994* (Hong Kong: Chinese University Press, 1994), pp. 27–36.

Longobardo, C., 'I progetti per uscire da "Tangentopoli"', *Riv. trim. dir. pen. econ.* (2000).

Lowell Brown, H., 'Vicarious Criminal Liability of Corporations for the Acts of their Employees and Agents', *Loyola Law Review*, 41 (1995), 279–327.

Lowenstein, D. H., 'Political Bribery and the Intermediate Theory of Politics', *UCLA Law Review*, 32 (1985), 784–850.

Luk, E., 'I Solemnly Apologize', *The Standard*, 2 March 2012, p. 2.

Luna, E. and Wade, M., 'Prosecutorial Power: A Transnational Symposium: Prosecutors as Judges', *Washington & Lee Law Review*, 67 (2010), 1413–532.

Luo, Y., 'The Changing Chinese Culture and Business Behavior: The Perspective of Intertwinement between Guanxi and Corruption', *International Business Review*, 17 (2008), 188–93.

Lynch, G. E., 'RICO: The Crime of Being a Criminal: Part I', *Columbia Law Review*, 87 (1987), 661–764.

Macey, J. R., *Corporate Governance: Promises Kept, Promises Broken* (Princeton University Press, 2008).

Maclagan, P. W., *Management and Morality* (London: Sage, 1998).

Madison, J., 'The Structure of the Government Must Furnish the Proper Checks and Balances Between the Different Departments', in A. Hamilton, J. Madison and J. Jay, *The Federalist Papers* (Kindle edn, 2011), No. 51, location 5451.

Maggiore, G., *Diritto penale*, vol. II (Bologna: Zanichelli, 1950).

Maitland, F. W. and Montague, F. C., *A Sketch of English Legal History* (Boston, MA: Adamant Media Corporation, 2001).

Man, J., '"Bullied" ICAC Worker Sentenced for Stealing from her Supervisor', *South China Morning Post*, 3 September 2009, p. C3.

'ICAC Investigator Who Stole Wine Ordered to do Community Service', *South China Morning Post*, 12 January 2010, p. C3.

Maris, M. and Singer, E., 'Foreign Corrupt Practices Act', *American Criminal Law Review*, 43 (2006), 575–601.

Mazerolle, L. G. and Ransley, J., *Third Party Policing* (Cambridge University Press, 2001).

McConville, M., 'Plea Bargaining: Ethics and Politics', *Journal of Law and Society*, 25 (1998), 562–87.

McConville, M., Hodgson, J., Bridges, L. and Pavlovic, A., *Standing Accused* (Oxford University Press, 1994).

McGregor, R., *The Party: The Secret World of China's Communist Rulers* (London: Allen Lane, 2010).

McWalters, I., *Bribery and Corruption Law in Hong Kong*, 2nd edn (Hong Kong: LexisNexis, 2010).

Mekay, E., 'Poorest Pay for World Bank Corruption: US Senator', *Common Dreams*, 14 May 2004, available at: www.commondreams.org/headlines04/0514-07.htm.

Milhaupt, C. and Pistor, K., *Law and Capitalism: What Corporate Crises Reveal About Legal Systems and Economic Development around the World* (University of Chicago Press, 2008).

Mills, D. and Weisberg, R., 'Corrupting the Harm Requirement in White Collar Crime', *Stanford Law Review*, 60 (2008), 1371–445 (citing J. Klick, 'Performance of Bond Pooling: An Efficiency Argument for Insurance Steering', unpublished manuscript, 2004).

Ministry of Justice, *The Bribery Act 2010: Guidance about Procedures which Relevant Commercial Organisations can put into Place to Prevent Persons Associated with Them from Bribing* (London: Ministry of Justice, 2011).

Mitsilegas, V., 'Corruption and the European Union', in U. Cassani and A. Héritier Lachat (eds), *Lutte contre la corruption internationale: The Never Ending Story* (Zurich: Schulthess, 2011), pp. 83–106.

EU Criminal Law (Oxford: Hart, 2009).

Money Laundering Counter-Measures in the European Union (London: Kluwer, 2003).

'The Constitutional Implications of Mutual Recognition in Criminal Matters in the EU', *Common Market Law Review*, 43 (2006), 1277–311.

'The EU and the Implementation of International Norms in Criminal Matters', in M. Cremona, J. Monar and S. Poli (eds), *The External Dimension of the Area of Freedom, Security and Justice* (Brussels: Peter Lang, 2011), College of Europe Studies No. 13, pp. 239–72.

'The European Union and the Globalisation of Criminal Law', *Cambridge Yearbook of European Legal Studies*, 12 (2009/10), 337–407.

Mitsilegas, V. and Gilmore, W., 'The EU Legislative Framework against Money Laundering and Terrorist Finance: A Critical Analysis in the Light of Evolving Global Standards', *International and Comparative Law Quarterly*, 56 (2007), 119–41.

Monari, S., 'Utilizzo di somme extrabilancio tra distrazione e appropriazione indebita (nota a Cass. pen. V, 21 gennaio 1998, Cusani)', *Giust pen.*, 3 (1999).

Mullen E. and Nadler, J., 'Moral Spillovers: The Effect of Moral Mandate Violations on Deviant Behavior,' *Journal of Experimental Social Psychology*, 44 (2008), 1239–45.

Munn, C., *Anglo-China: Chinese People and British Rule in Hong Kong, 1841–1880* (Hong Kong University Press, 2001).

Nadler, J., 'Flouting the Law', *Texas Law Review*, 83 (2005), 1399–441.

National White Collar Crime Center, *National Public Survey on White Collar Crime* (Fairmont, VA: National White Collar Crime Center, 2000).

Neild, R., *Public Corruption: The Dark Side of Social Evolution* (London: Anthem Press, 2002).

Neoh, A., 'An Impartial and Uncorrupted Civil Service: Hong Kong's Fight Against Corruption in the Past 34 Years', in C. Forsyth, M. Elliott, S. Jhaveri, A. Scully-Hill and M. Ramsden (eds), *Effective Judicial Review: A Cornerstone of Good Governance* (Oxford University Press, 2010).

Ng, M., 'Judge Decries ICAC Officers' Coaching of Witness', *South China Morning Post*, 6 May 2011.

Ngok, M., *Political Development in Hong Kong: State, Political Society, and Civil Society* (Hong Kong University Press, 2007).

Nicholls, C., Daniel, T., Bacarese, A. and Hatchard, J., *Corruption and Misuse of Public Office*, 2nd edn (Oxford University Press, 2011).

Nicola, A. di, 'Dieci anni di lotta alla corruzione in Italia: cosa non ha funzionato e cosa può ancora funzionare', in M. Barbagli (ed.), *Rapporto sulla criminalità in Italia* (Bologna: Zanichelli, 2003).

Nip, A. and Chiu, A., 'TVB's Chan Cleared of Graft Charges', *South China Morning Post*, 3 September 2011, p. 1.

Noonan, J. T., Jr, *Bribes: The Intellectual History of a Moral Idea* (Berkeley, CA: University of California Press, 1984).

North, D. C. and Thomas, R. P., *Rise of the Western World: A New Economic History* (Cambridge University Press, 1996).

Nuvolone, P., 'Norme penali e principi costituzionali', in P. Nuvolone (ed.), *Trent'anni di diritto e procedura penale*, vol. I (Padova: CEDAM, 1969).

Nye, J. S., 'Corruption and Political Development: A Cost–Benefit Analysis', in A. Heidenheimer (ed.), *Political Corruption: Readings in Comparative Analysis* (New York: Holt, Reinhart & Wilson, 1970), pp. 564–78.

Oduyela, S., 'A Chronicle of Unresolved Murder Cases in Nigeria', *Nigeriaworld*, 16 August 2003.

Office of Fair Trading, *The Cartel Offence: Guidance on the Issue of No-Action Letters by Individuals*, OFT 513 (London: OFT, April 2003), available at: www.oft.gov.uk/shared_oft/business_leaflets/enterprise_act/oft513.pdf.

Olson, K. W., *Watergate: The Presidential Scandal that Shook America* (Lawrence, KS: Kansas University Press, 2003).

Oman, C. P. and Arndt, C., *Measuring Governance, Policy Brief No. 39* (Paris: OECD Development Centre, 2010).

Onoshi, N., 'In Indonesia Middlemen Mold the Outcome of Justice', *New York Times*, 19 December 2009, available at: www.nytimes.com/2009/12/20/world/asia/20indo.html.

Organisation for Economic Cooperation and Development (OECD), *Guidelines for Multinational Enterprises*, available at: www.oecd.org.

United Kingdom: Phase 1 Report on the Application of the Convention on Combating Bribery of Foreign Officials in International Business Transactions and the 2009 Revised Recommendation on Combating Bribery in International Business Transactions (Paris: OECD, 2009).

United Kingdom: Phase 2 Report on the Application of the Convention on Combating Bribery of Foreign Public Officials in International Business Transactions and the 1997 Recommendation on Combating Bribery in International Business Transactions (Paris: OECD, 2005).

United Kingdom: Phase 2 Follow-up Report on the Implementation of the Phase 2 Recommendations (Paris: OECD, 2007).

United Kingdom: Phase 3 Report on Implementing the OECD Anti-Bribery Convention in the United Kingdom (Paris: OECD, 2012).

Ori, K. O., 'Swiss Court Approves African Kleptocracy: Mobutu's Loot to go to his Family', *Afrik News*, 15 July 2009, available at: www.afrik-news.com/article15923.html.

Pagliaro, A., *Principi di diritto penale, parte speciale, I delitti contro la pubblica amministrazione* (Milan: Giuffrè, 2000).

Palazzo, F., 'Corruzione: per una disciplina "integrata" ed efficace', *Dir. pen. proc.* (2011).

'La tutela penale della pubblica amministrazione e il rapporto tra politica e legalità', in S. Vinciguerra and F. Dassano (eds), *Scritti in onore di G. Marini* (Naples: ESI, 2010).

Pannain, R., *I delitti dei pubblici ufficiali contro la pubblica amministrazione* (Naples: Jovene, 1966).

Peaslee, A. J., *Constitutions of Nations*, vol. III (The Hague: Martinus Nijhoff, 1968).

Peel, M., *A Swamp Full of Dollars* (London: I. B. Taurus, 2009).

Peerenboom, R., *China's Long March Toward the Rule of Law* (New York: Cambridge University Press, 2002).

Pellissero, M., 'La nozione di atto d'ufficio nel delitto di corruzione tra prassi e teoria', in *Dir pen. proc.*, No. 8 (Milan: Ipsoa, 2000).

Pepper, S., 'Free Political Expression … But Towards What End?', China Elections and Governance Blog, 6 February 2012, available at: chinaelectionsblog.net.

'Small-circle Campaigns, Big-circle Implications', China Elections and Governance Blog, 21 March 2012, available at: chinaelectionsblog.net.

Perdriel-Vaissiere, M., 'How to Turn Article 51 into Reality', in D. Thelesklaf and P. G. Pereira, *Non-State Actors in Asset Recovery* (Bern: Peter Lang, 2011).

Petersen, C. J., 'Hong Kong's Spring of Discontent', in F. Hualing, C. J. Petersen and S. N. M. Young (eds), *National Security and Fundamental Freedoms: Hong Kong's Article 23 Under Scrutiny* (Hong Kong University Press, 2005), pp. 13–62.

'Preserving Academic Freedom in Hong Kong: Lessons from the "Robert Chung Affair"', *Hong Kong Law Journal*, 30 (2000), 165–76.

Phenal, J., 'India Journal: Companies Need to Ride the Anticorruption Wave', *The Wall Street Journal*, 13 September 2011, available at: http://blogs.wsj.com/indiarealtime/2011/09/13/india-journal-companies-need-to-ride-the-anticorruption-wave.

Pop, V., 'Dutch Insist on Anti-Corruption Measures in Border Row', *euobserver.com*, 14 December 2011, available at: http://euobserver.com/22/114629.

Posner, R., 'An Economic Theory of the Criminal Law', *Columbia Law Review*, 85 (1985), 1193–231.

Provis, C., 'Guanxi and Conflicts of Interest', *Journal of Business Ethics*, 79 (2007), 57–68.

Public Concern at Work (PCAW), *Where is Whistleblowing Now?* (London: PCAW, 2010).

Pujas, V., 'The European Anti-Fraud Office (OLAF): A European Policy to Fight against Economic and Financial Fraud?', *Journal of European Public Policy*, 10(2003), 778–97.

Quah, J. S. T., 'Combating Corruption in the Asia-Pacific Countries: What do We Know and What Needs to be Done', *International Public Management Review*, 10 (2009), 5–33.

Curbing Corruption in Asia: A Comparative Study of Six Countries (Singapore: Eastern Universities Press, 2003).

'Defying Institutional Failure: Learning from the Experiences of Anti-corruption Agencies in four Asian Countries', *Crime Law and Social Change*, 53 (2010), 23–54.

Rampioni, R., *Bene giuridico e delitti dei pubblici ufficiali contro la pubblica amministrazione* (Milan: Giuffrè, 1984).

Raphael, M., 'A Defining Problem for the 2010 Bribery Act', *The Guardian*, 2 February 2011, available at: www.guardian.co.uk/law/2011/feb/02/bribery-act-monty-raphael?INTCMP=SRCH.

Riccio, S., 'Corruzione', *Noviss Dig. It.*, vol. IV (Turin: UTET, 1959).

Richardson, J. (ed.), *Archbold: Criminal Pleading, Evidence and Practice 2010* (London: Sweet & Maxwell, 2009), ch. 30.

Roach, K., 'Unreliable Evidence and Wrongful Convictions: The Case for Excluding Tainted Identification Evidence and Jailhouse and Coerced Confessions', *Criminal Law Quarterly*, 52 (2007), 210–36.

Robbins, F., 'Why Corporate Social Responsibility should be Popularised but not Imposed', *Corporate Governance*, 8 (2008), 330–41.

Robinson, P. H. and Darley, J. M., 'Intuitions of Justice: Implications for Criminal Law and Justice Policy', *Southern California Law Review*, 81 (2007), 1–67.

Justice, Liability, and Blame: Community Views and the Criminal Law (Boulder, CO: Westview Press, 1995).

'Testing Competing Theories of Justification', *North Carolina Law Review*, 76 (1998), 1095–143.

Rogers, J., 'Restructuring the Exercise of Prosecutorial Discretion in England', *Oxford Journal of Legal Studies*, 26 (2006), 775–803.

Romano, M., *Comm. sist. c.p., I delitti contro la pubblica amministrazione* (Milan: Giuffrè, 2006).

Rose-Ackerman, S., *Corruption and Government: Causes, Consequences, and Reform* (New York: Cambridge University Press, 1999).

'The Economics of Corruption', *Journal of Public Economics*, 4 (1975), 187–203.

'The Political Economy of Corruption', in K. A. Elliott (ed.), *Corruption and the Global Economy* (Washington, DC: Institute for International Economics, 1997).

Roskill, Lord E., *Fraud Trials Committee Report* (the 'Roskill Report') (London: The Stationery Office, 1986) (HL 471).

Rossi, G., 'Per un'etica degli affari. Se le regole vengono trasgredite', *La Repubblica*, 18 June 2003.

Runciman, Viscount W. (chair), *Report of the Royal Commission on Criminal Justice*, Cm. 2263 (London: The Stationery Office, 1993).

Ryznar, M. and Korkor, S., 'Anti-Bribery Legislation in the United States and United Kingdom: A Comparative Analysis of Scope and Sentencing', *Missouri Law Review*, 76 (2011), 415–53.

Security Bureau, 'Review on Interception of Communication', paper for Legislative Council (LegCo) Panel on Security, LC Paper No. CB(2)1873/03-04(04) (Hong Kong Legislative Council, March 2004).

Segreto, A. and de Luca, G., *Delitti dei pubblici ufficiali contro la pubblica amministrazione* (Milan: Giuffrè, 1999).

Sentencing Advisory Panel, *Reduction in Sentence for a Guilty Plea: Definitive Guideline* (London: Sentencing Advisory Council, 2007).

Sentencing Guidelines Council, *On the Reduction in Sentence for Guilty Plea* (London: Sentencing Guidelines Secretariat, December 2004).

Serious Fraud Office (SFO), *Approach of the SFO to Dealing with Overseas Corruption* (London: SFO, 2009).

'Shareholder Agrees Civil Recovery by SFO in Mabey & Johnson', Serious Fraud Office press release, 13 January 2012, available at: www.sfo.gov.uk/press-room/latest-press-releases/press-releases-2012/shareholder-agrees-civil-recovery-by-sfo-in-mabey–johnson.aspx.

Shapps, G., *Report into the Underperformance of the Assets Recovery Agency* (London: Shapps, 2006), available at: www.shapps.com/reports/Assets RecoveryAgency-underperformance.pdf; www.shapps.com/AssetsRecovery Agency-underperformance.pdf.

Shelter Offshore, 'OECD Update on Offshore Tax Havens', 2011, available at: www.shelteroffshore.com/index.php/offshore/more/oecd-update-on-offshore-tax-havens.

Shleifer, A. and Vishny, R. W., 'Corruption', *Quarterly Journal of Economics*, 106 (1993), 599–618.

Shute, S., 'Knowledge and Belief in the Criminal Law', in S. Shute and A. Simester (eds), *Criminal Law: Doctrines of the General Part* (Oxford University Press, 2002).

Sibley C. G. and Duckitt, J., 'Big-Five Personality, Social Worldviews, and Ideological Attitudes: Further Tests of a Dual Process Cognitive–Motivational Model', *Journal of Social Psychology*, 149 (2009), 545–61.

Sigler, M., 'The Methodology of Desert', *Arizona State Law Journal*, 42 (2011), 1173–202.

Simons, K. W., 'The Relevance of Community Values to Just Deserts: Criminal Law, Punishment Rationales, and Democracy', *Hofstra Law Review*, 28 (2000), 635–66.

Skeel, D., *The New Financial Deal: Understanding the Dodd–Frank Act and its (Unintended) Consequences* (Hoboken, NJ: John Wiley, 2010).

Slobogin, C., 'Is Justice Just Us? Using Social Science to Inform Substantive Criminal Law', *Journal of Criminal Law & Criminology*, 87 (1996), 315–33.

Smith, B. P., 'Plea Bargaining and the Eclipse of the Jury', *Annual Review of Law and Social Science*, 1 (2005), 131–49.

Spalding, A. B., 'The Irony of International Business Law: US Progressivism, China's New Laissez-Faire, and their Impact in the Developing World', *UCLA Law Review*, 59 (2011), 354–413.

Spector, B., 'Business Responsibility in a Divided World: The Cold War Roots of Corporate Social Responsibility', *Enterprise and Society*, 9 (2008), 314–36.

Spencer, J. R., 'Fiat justicia, ruatque concordia cum Arabe?', *Cambridge Law Journal*, 67 (2008), 456–8.

Speville, B. de, 'Anticorruption Commissions: The "The Hong Kong Model" Revisited', *Asia-Pacific Review*, 17 (2010), 47–71.

'Law Enforcement and the Independent Commission Against Corruption', in W. Fong, A. Byrnes and G. E. Edwards (eds), *Hong Kong's Bill of Rights: Two Years On* (Faculty of Law, University of Hong Kong, 1994), pp. 14–15.

Stigliz, J. E., *Freefall: America, Free Markets, and the Sinking of the World Economy* (New York: W. W. Norton, 2010).

Stockholm International Peace Research Institute Yearbook, *Armaments, Disarmament and International Security* (Oxford University Press, 2001).

Stuntz, W., 'Self-Defeating Crimes', *Virginia Law Review*, 86 (2000), 1871–900.

Sullivan, G. R., 'Knowledge, Belief and Culpability', in S. Shute and A. Simester (eds), *Criminal Law: Doctrines of the General Part* (Oxford University Press, 2002).

'Proscribing Corruption: Some Comments on the Law Commission Report', *Criminal Law Review*, August (1998), 547–55.

'Reforming Bribery: Law Commission Consultation Paper No. 185: (2) Bribery Outside England and Wales: Corporate Liability, Defences, Consent to Prosecution', *Criminal Law Review*, 9 (2008), 687–701.

Sussman, B., *The Great Coverup: Nixon and the Scandal of Watergate* (USA: Catapulter Books, ebook Store, 2010).

Sutherland, E., *White Collar Crime* (New York: Dryden Press, 1949).

Swallow, D., 'Russia: Bribery, Corruption & the High Price of Bad Business', 24 May 2010, available at: www.deborahswallow.com/2010/05/24/russia-bribery-corruption-the-high-price-of-bad-business.

Swissinfo.ch, 'Swiss Primed to Hand Over Libyan Assets', 26 October 2010, available at: http://m.swissinfo.ch/eng/specials/the_arab_spring/Swiss_primed_to_hand_over_Libyan_assets.html?cid=30971506.

'Tunisian Request Marks a Major Step', 12 October 2011, available at: http://m.swissinfo.ch/eng/politics/Tunisian_legal_aid_request_marks_major_step.html?cid=31335162.

Szarek-Mason, P., *The European Union's Fight Against Corruption: The Evolving Policy towards Member States and Candidate Countries* (Cambridge University Press, 2010).

Tanzi, V., 'Corruption Around the World', *Staff Papers International Monetary Fund*, 45 (1998), 559–94.

Thelesklaf, D. and Pereira, P. G., *Non-State Actors in Asset Recovery* (Bern: Peter Lang, 2011).

Thomas, P. A., 'Plea Bargaining in England and Wales', *Journal of Criminal Law and Criminology*, 69 (1978), 170–8.

Tomkins, A., 'Responsibility and Resignation in the European Commission', *Modern Law Review*, 62 (1999), 744–65.

TRACE International, *The High Cost of Small Bribes* (London: TRACE, 2003).

Transparency International, *Corruption Perception Index 2011* (London: Transparency International, 2011), available at http://cpi.transparency.org.

National Integrity System Assessment: the United Kingdom (London: Transparency International, 2011).

Tricarico, A., 'Dams on Trial: The World Bank and the "Cancer of Corruption": Donor Governments, Financial Institutions and TNCs' Responsibilities in the Lesotho Case' (Rome: Reform the World Bank Campaign, 2000).

Tsang, P., 'Single-tender Contract by ICAC under Scrutiny', *South China Morning Post*, 19 March 2011, p. C1.

Tsang, P. and Fraser, N., 'Rising Star of ICAC Arrested in Graft Probe', *South China Morning Post*, 30 April 2011, p. 1.

Tsang, P. and Lo, C., 'Police Raid ICAC, Arrest Three Graft-Busters', *South China Morning Post*, 20 November 2010.

Tsang, P. and Wu, E., 'Tsang Criticized in Row over Secret Deal for ICAC Chief', *South China Morning Post*, 11 September 2009, p. 3.

Tsang, S., *A Modern History of Hong Kong* (London: I. B. Tauris, 2004).

Tu, E., *Colonial Hong Kong in the Eyes of Elsie Tu* (Hong Kong University Press, 2003).

Tyler, R., 'Lord Goldsmith Urges Plea Bargaining in Bribery Cases', *Daily Telegraph*, 13 September 2011.

Tyler, T., *Why People Obey the Law* (New Haven, CT: Yale University Press, 1990).

U4 Anti-Corruption Centre Resource Centre, *Can UNCAC Address Grand Corruption?* (November 2011), available at: www.U4.no.

United Nations, Implementation Review Group of the UN Convention Against Corruption, 2010, UN docs CAC/COSP/IRG/2010/9, available at: www.unodc.org/documents/treaties/UNCAC/WorkingGroups/ImplementationReviewGroup/29Nov–1Dec2010/V1056031e.pdf.

United States House of Representatives, House Report 95-640, 95th Congress, 1st Session, available at: http://10.173.2.10/criminal/fraud/fcpa/history/1977/houseprt.html.

United States Senate, Permanent Subcommittee on Investigations, *Keeping Foreign Corruption out of the United States*, February 2010, available at: www.financialtaskforce.org/wp-content/uploads/2010/02/Levin-report-on-US-facilitators-of-Africa-corruption-FOREIGN-CORRUPTION-REPORT-FINAL-as-of-2–210.pdf.

Vachudova, M. A., 'Corruption and Compliance in the EU's Post-Communist Members and Candidates', *Journal of Common Market Studies*, 47 (2009), 43–62 .

Vassalli, G., 'Corruzione propria e corruzione impropria', *Giust pen*, 2 (1979).

Venditti, R., 'Corruzione (delitti di)', *Enc dir*, 10 (1962), 757.

Vero, G. de, *La responsabilità penale delle persone giuridiche* (Milan: Giuffrè, 2008).

Vivarelli, M. G., 'Il fenomeno della corruzione', *Foro amm.* (2008).

Wah, N. H., 'Remedies Against Telephone Tapping by the Government', *Hong Kong Law Journal*, 33 (2003), 543–66.

Wai-man, L. and Tong, I. L. K., 'Civil Society and NGOs', in L. Wai-man, P. L-t. Lui, W. Wong and I. Holliday (eds), *Contemporary Hong Kong Politics: Governance in the Post-1997 Era* (Hong Kong University Press, 2007), pp. 135–51.

Warbrick, C. and Brookson-Morris, K., 'Conflicts of Criminal Jurisdiction', *International and Comparative Law Quarterly*, 56 (2007), 659–66.

Watson, D., 'The Attorney General's Guidelines on Plea Bargaining in Serious Fraud: Obtaining Guilty Pleas Fairly?', *Journal of Criminal Law*, 74 (2010), 77–90.

Weatherill, S. (ed.), 'The Challenge of Better Regulation', in *Better Regulation* (Oxford: Hart, 2007), pp. 1–18.

Webb, P., 'The United Nations Convention against Corruption: Global Achievement or Missed Opportunity?', *Journal of International Economic Law*, 8 (2005), 191–229.

Weber, M., *The Theory of Social and Economic Organization* (New York: Free Press, 1947).

Wei, S., 'Local Corruption and Global Capital Flows', *Brookings Papers on Economic Activity*, 2 (2000), 303–54.

Weismann, M. F., 'The Foreign Corrupt Practices Act: The Failure of the Self-Regulatory Model of Corporate Governance in the Global Business Environment', *Journal of Business Ethics*, 88 (2009), 615–61.

Wells, C., *Corporations and Criminal Liability* (Oxford: Clarendon Press, 1993).

Wheeler, D. and Mody, A., 'International Investment Location Decisions: The Case of US Firms', *Journal of International Economics*, 33 (1992), 55–76.

White, R. M., 'Civil Penalties: Oxymoron, Chimera and Stealth Sanction', *Law Quarterly Review*, 126 (2010), 593–606.

White, S., 'EU Anti-Fraud Enforcement: Overcoming Obstacles', *Journal of Financial Crime*, 17 (2010), 81–99.

Williams, S., 'The BAE/Saudi Al-Yamamah Contracts: Implications in Law and Public Procurement', *International & Comparative Law Quarterly*, 57 (2008), 200–9.

Wilsher, D., 'Inexplicable Wealth and Illicit Enrichment of Public Officials: A Model Draft that Respects Human Rights in Corruption Cases', *Crime, Law & Social Change*, 45 (2006), 27–53.

Wofensohn, J. D., 'Remarks at a Global Forum on Fighting Corruption', World Bank, 24 February 1999, available at: www.worldbank.org.

Woolf Committee, *Business Ethics, Global Companies and the Defence Industry: Ethical Business Conduct in BAE Systems Plc*, May 2008, available at: http://ir.baesystems.com/investors/storage/woolf_report_2008.pdf.

Wong, M., 'ICAC's Questionable Acts under Fire for Years', *South China Morning Post*, 20 November 2010, p. 2.

World Bank, 'Costs of Corruption', 8 April 2004, available at: http://web.worldbank.org/WBSITE/EXTERNAL/NEWS/0,contentMDK:20190187~menuPK:34457~pagePK:64003015~piPK:64003012~theSitePK:4607,00.html.

Indonesia: Fiduciary Review of the Second Sulawesi Urban Development Project Overview Report (Washington, DC: World Bank, 2002), available at: www1.worldbank.org/publicsector/anticorrupt/PoliticalEconomy/PREMCourse07/Amit%20background%20material/Fiduciary%20review%20Indonesia.pdf.

Report on Investigation and Sanctions of Staff Misconduct and Fraud and Corruption in Bank Financed Projects Fiscal Year 2004 (Washington, DC: World Bank, 2005).

Stolen Asset Recovery (StAR) Initiative: Challenges, Opportunities, and Action Plan (Washington, DC: World Bank, 2007).

World Development Report: The State in a Changing World (New York: Oxford University Press, 1997).

Wright, R., 'Why (Some) Fraud Prosecutions Fail', *Journal of Financial Crime*, 13 (2006), 177–82.

Wrong, M., *In the Footsteps of Mr Kurz* (London: Fourth Estate, 2000).

It's Our Turn to Eat: the Story of a Kenyan Whistleblower (London: Fourth Estate, 2009).

Wu, A., 'Hong Kong's Fight Against Corruption Has Lessons for Others', *Hong Kong Journal*, Spring (2006), available at: www.hkjournal.org/archive/2006_spring/wu.html.

Yenamandra, T., 'Corruption in India's Commonwealth Games, Kalmadi Arrested', 26 April 2011, available at: www.2point6billion.com/news/2011/04/26/corruption-in-indias-commonwealth-games-9163.html.

Yeoh, P., 'The Direction and Control of Corporations: Law or Strategy?' *Managerial Law*, 49 (2007), 37–47.

Yihdego, Z. and Savage, A., 'The Arms Export Regime: Progress and Challenges', *Public Law*, Autumn (2008), 546–65.

Young, S. N. M., 'The Executive Order on Covert Surveillance: Legality Undercover?', *Hong Kong Law Journal*, 35 (2005), 265–76.

Yusef, H. O., 'The Rule of Law and the Politics of Anti-Corruption Campaigns in a Post-Authoritarian State: the Case of Nigeria', *King's Law Journal*, 22 (2011), 57–83.

Zerbes, I., 'The Offence of Bribery of Foreign Public Officials', in M. Pieth, L. A. Low and P. Cullen (eds), *The OECD Convention on Bribery. A Commentary* (Cambridge University Press, 2007), pp. 45–172.

INDEX